The What, Where, When
of Landscape Gardening

OKLAHOMA
GARDENER'S
GUIDE

COOL
SPRINGS
PRESS

Dobbs, Steve, 1959—
    Oklahoma Gardener's Guide: the what, where, when, how & why of landscape gardening in Oklahoma / [Steve Dobbs]

    p.   cm.
    Includes bibliographical references (p.   ) and index.
    ISBN 1-888608-56-0   (alk. paper)
    1. Landscape plants -- Oklahoma 2. Landscape gardening -- Oklahoma
    3. Gardening -- Oklahoma I. Title
    SB407.DG3   1999
    635.9'09766 -- dc21

Cool Springs Press, Inc.
2020 Fieldstone Parkway
Suite 900210
Franklin, Tennessee 37069

First printing 1999
Printed in the United States of America
10 9 8 7 6 5 4 3

Horticultural Nomenclature Editor: Allan Storjohann, Manager,
    Myriad Botanical Gardens, Oklahoma City

On the cover: Indian Blanket

Visit the Cool Springs Press website at: www.coolspringspress.com

DEDICATION

In loving memory of my dad:

Orville Harold Dobbs
July 4, 1928 – March 5, 1992

Memories grow more precious still when loved ones have to part,
and remain forever blooming in the gardens of the heart.

—author unknown

ACKNOWLEDGMENTS

*T*O OUR CREATOR, THE ORIGINAL GARDENER, the giver of life, who grants daily miracles in our gardens and landscapes for all to enjoy. Thank you for these life-inspiring marvels where we can learn of ourselves and be closer to you!

I'm grateful too for supportive family members who encourage and allow us to tackle our dreams. Thank you to my wife Jo Alice for your love, prayers, provision, and tolerance of my sometimes-outrageous dreams and projects. Of course this whole horticultural journey would not have been possible if it weren't for my generous parents. My mother Alma taught me kindness and loyalty and continues to be a source of inspiration. My father Harold Dobbs instilled in me the values of hard work and a sense of humor.

To the many thousands of gardeners, Master Gardeners, and volunteer ambassadors who have helped shape my gardening endeavors along the way by asking questions and sharing personal encounters, I say thank you for your patience, enthusiasm, and advice.

We must not only continue to discover but always share what we learn. The Cooperative Extension Service has been an invaluable resource for doing just that both personally and professionally. My former coworkers in Oklahoma and Florida have truly made everlasting enrichments to my life for which I am so thankful.

This book is actually a compilation of my personal experiences with plants and people. Thanks especially to Greg Grant, Dennis Martin, and Steve and Sherry Bieberich for your input and time. And as Gertrude Jekyll, gardener extraordinaire, most eloquently states, "The love of gardening is a seed that once sown never dies." Thanks to all who have planted those seeds in my life!

Oklahoma
GARDENER'S GUIDE

CONTENTS

INTRODUCTION

GARDENING AND LANDSCAPING IN OKLAHOMA are alive and
well, despite the state's popular image as a flat, treeless dust bowl.
Oklahoma, the only state that has four ecoregions, has always had a diverse
natural environment. We are a land of magnificent forests, mountains, lakes,
and rivers, and four distinct growing seasons. Years ago there was some
truth in our dust bowl reputation, at least in the Panhandle and the western
part of the state, but now these regions have been stabilized with the addition of windbreaks and man-made lakes. Of course we also have heat,
humidity, drought, pests, and a range of mind-boggling temperatures! But
even with these challenging conditions, our versatile landscapes are filled
with a natural beauty that can be easily duplicated in our own backyards.

GARDENING WHERE YOU LIVE

Know your growing environment—the right plant must be matched to the
right growing site. A cold-hardiness zone is defined by the northernmost
boundary in which plants can grow when the weather is at its coldest.
Oklahoma is divided into four cold-hardiness zones: 6a, 6b, 7a, and 7b (see
map on page 240). In Zone 6 it is not uncommon for coldest temperatures to
range from 0 to 10 degrees Fahrenheit. Zone 7 cold-temperature extremes are
usually closer to 10 degrees but may be as cold as 0 degrees.

If you have spent a summer in Oklahoma, you know that heat must be
reckoned with. When choosing a planting site, keep in mind that it is not
just heat and cold that influence the way a plant will grow. Wind, humidity,
and drought also affect plants.

Our state is sometimes divided into Eastern and Western growing regions
due to great differences in soil type, wind, altitude, temperature, and moisture. I have included a chapter on Western Oklahoma plants, which are well
adapted to the Panhandle and northwestern parts of Oklahoma.

According to the USDA Forestry Service, our state is actually divided
into four ecoregions: the Great Plains (the Panhandle), the Desert Southwest
(southwestern Oklahoma), the Continental East (the northeastern counties),
and the Humid South (southeastern Oklahoma). [See map on facing page.]
No other state has four distinct growing regions. I reside in the Humid
South, and this description nails it right on the head. I must select plants
tolerant to heat and humidity as well as to cold and wind.

ECOREGIONS MAP

United States

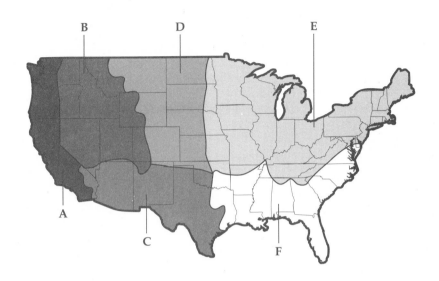

Areas with similar climate and geography

A	Pacific West
B	Mountain West
C	Desert Southwest
D	Great Plains
E	Continental East
F	Humid South

Source: USDA Forest Service. www.fs.fed

Knowing plant requirements is the key to successful plant establishment. Some plants prefer full sun, while others need part shade or full shade. Part-shade recommendations usually mean that a plant requires lightly filtered or afternoon shade. In Oklahoma, plants marked for full sun or part shade often do best in part shade. Determining whether your planting site is north, south, east, or west of structures in your yard will help you identify sun and shading patterns. Remember, too, that changing sun angles and deciduous leaf drop in winter affect the shade in your yard.

Introduction

PLANT SELECTION

In this book you will find information on a variety of plants, including plant characteristics, needs, and limitations. A few of the plants in this book may be somewhat difficult to find, but I feel it is better to provide information on additional tried-and-true plants for our state than to limit our choices. Frequent requests to retail suppliers will often bring about better plant offerings. Thanks to an active wholesale and retail nursery and garden center industry, plant selection in Oklahoma is growing. The launch of mail-order and Internet purchasing has further expanded gardeners' plant choices.

When purchasing plants, remember that common names are often interchangeable among different plants and species. This can cause unfortunate cases of mistaken identity. Confirm the genus species to ensure that you have the plant you want. When you have located the proper plant, look for healthy, pest-free specimens to take home.

WHEN TO PLANT

We are fortunate to have a growing season that lasts for seven or eight months, depending on the region. Planting times are determined by frost or freeze dates. The last frost in spring generally occurs sometime between March 31 and April 25; the first frost in fall usually takes place between October 15 and November 3 (see maps on pages 9 and 10). Milder air temperatures and natural rainfall make spring, early summer, and fall plantings the most successful. Summer plantings mean more risk as hot soil and air temperatures, as well as drought, can make establishment difficult.

SOIL TYPE

It is extremely important to know your soil type. Heavier soils have a tendency to hold water and may cause disease or plant suffocation due to a lack of oxygen in the soil. Amending the soil prior to planting, planting in raised beds, or planting above the soil grade can help, though you may sometimes find it easiest to grow plants that prefer heavy waterlogged soils.

Most soils in Oklahoma contain some percentage of our "state soil," Port Silt Loam. Port Silt Loam is a highly productive soil component that is found in thirty-four of Oklahoma's seventy-seven counties. Many areas of Oklahoma have soil that is primarily composed of heavy red clay (from red sandstone and shale) or sand. Regardless of soil type, it is always best to

FREEZE MAPS

Oklahoma

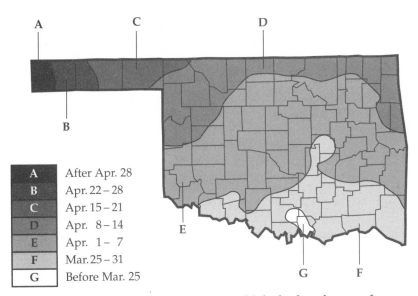

A	After Apr. 28
B	Apr. 22 – 28
C	Apr. 15 – 21
D	Apr. 8 – 14
E	Apr. 1 – 7
F	Mar. 25 – 31
G	Before Mar. 25

**Date by which the last freeze of
SPRING occurred in 50% of the years
1961–1990**

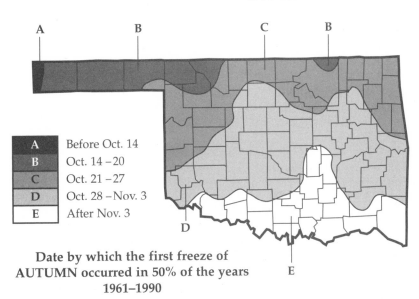

A	Before Oct. 14
B	Oct. 14 – 20
C	Oct. 21 – 27
D	Oct. 28 – Nov. 3
E	After Nov. 3

**Date by which the first freeze of
AUTUMN occurred in 50% of the years
1961–1990**

Source: Oklahoma Climatological Survey. www.ocs.ou.edu

Oklahoma

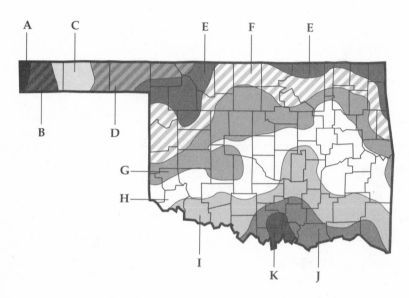

Mean length of the frost–free period in weeks

A	<24	G	29–30
B	24–25	H	30–31
C	25–26	I	31–32
D	26–27	J	32–33
E	27–28	K	>33
F	28–29		

Source: Oklahoma Climatological Survey. www.ocs.ou.edu

incorporate organic materials into the existing soil. Take the time to prepare planting beds prior to planting. Many of the major nutrients, such as phosphorus (P) and potassium (K), are best incorporated into the soil before you plant so that the slow change of soil chemistry in the root area has time to occur. Nitrogen (N), on the other hand, is more water soluble and can be applied as a topdressing on an as-needed basis; it will gradually dissolve into the root area. Water-soluble, slow-release, controlled-release, and organic (natural) types of nitrogen are great investments for the landscape. Test your soil to determine nutrient, lime, and sulfur needs. Soil testing is readily available through your county Oklahoma Cooperative Extension Service.

Introduction

Remember that great soil grows great plants! Be patient and prepare your site properly—ahead of time. It is an investment that will pay off with big dividends.

PLANTING

Leave enough room between plants so they may easily grow to their mature, fully grown size. Avoiding overcrowding will also save money, as you won't need to buy as many plants. Though they may look lonely at first, plants will quickly grow into the allotted space. When planting in singular holes (as with trees), it is not recommended that you amend the soil with peat moss, root stimulator, or other products. Trees and shrubs are better planted in holes that are as deep as and two to three times as wide as the rootball, using the existing soil as backfill. It is best to mix products into the existing soil ahead of time rather than to apply soil amendments as backfill to a small hole—this could cause the roots to grow only in the hole, creating a rootbound plant. High-nitrogen fertilizer and root stimulators may burn the roots when placed in direct contact with them, especially when used at higher-than-recommended rates. It is best to dig wide holes, and backfill with soil that is loosely dug and has plenty of moisture. Unless a soil test shows a significant need for phosphorus and potassium, wait until plants are established to fertilize. When necessary, phosphorus and potassium products can be placed in the bottom of the planting hole and covered with a layer of soil to avoid direct contact with plant roots.

I have seen numerous situations where balled-and-burlapped specimens were stunted or their root formation delayed because the burlap was left in place. Though it decomposes quickly when the plants are stored above ground, burlap buried in the soil decomposes much more slowly, and often limits root penetration. If the rootball is firm, place the plant in the hole and remove all of the burlap. If the rootball seems loose, place it in the hole and roll the burlap down to the base of the hole; cut off and remove the excess. Always remove any string from around the trunk.

MULCHING

There is probably not a better or more effective maintenance practice in the landscape than mulching. Many different kinds of mulch are available; I am particularly fond of cottonseed hulls, recycled paper Enviromulch®, pine straw, and wood chips. Cottonseed is perfect for annual plant beds, where after a couple of seasons it can be tilled into the ground for organic soil improvement. Coarse, slower-degrading products are more appropriate for trees, shrubs, and other perennials. Apply two to four inches of organic mulch, depending on the site and the plant's size. Avoid placing mulch on a plant's trunk or stems. Though mulch is an added expense, I encourage gardeners to cut back on the size of the bed or number of plants before they cut back on mulch. It can be more affordable by mulching plants in stages. Mulch minimizes weed control, holds in soil moisture, regulates soil temperature, provides slow-release nutrients, and helps stop erosion. It is true that it sometimes increases insect populations, inviting moles and armadillos; and despite mulching, weeds can still be problematic thanks to windborne or bird-scattered seed (though mulch keeps the amount of germinated seed to a minimum). Still, the benefits of mulching far outweigh the disadvantages.

The roots on some plants may grow up into the mulch itself; deep and infrequent watering will encourage deeper root growth. Because most mulch is organic and breaks down after a few years, it should be reapplied periodically (every couple of years). An inexpensive source of mulch is tree-trimming companies. Expect large quantities that are great for trees, shrubs, and walkways, even though the mulch may contain some "trash." Just be sure it has no ground-up branches or limbs from diseased trees, which can be hazardous if used around the same tree species as that in the mulch.

WATERING

Rainfall is also important for plant establishment and growth. See page 239 for a map of average rainfall for our state. The Panhandle generally receives some 20 inches of rainfall a year, while southeastern Oklahoma receives over 50 inches—as much annual rainfall as in some areas Florida. Much of our rain is seasonal, and supplemental irrigation is often needed. Once plants are established, however, many are drought tolerant.

Choose plants based on their water needs and group accordingly. Cluster water-loving plants near the home where there is greater access to supplemental irrigation. Drought-tolerant or arid plants can be located at distances farther from the home. You may ultimately find it best to invest in an irrigation system; many of the newer designs are water efficient and pay for themselves in just a few seasons of saved water and time.

The preferred method for watering plants is to water deeply and infrequently. In other words, really soak the plants down to the root system and wait a few days before the next application. This encourages roots to grow deep. Watering every day for just a few minutes at a time encourages roots to remain shallow, making plants more susceptible to drought, freeze, and stress. In general, plants thrive on one to two inches of water a week, including rainfall.

FERTILIZATION

The results of a soil test from a qualified lab will provide a starting point for figuring nutritional needs. The Oklahoma Cooperative Extension Service County Offices are accessible locations with soil-testing capabilities. Fertilizer rates are based on 1 lb. of actual nitrogen per 1000 sq. ft. To determine how much fertilizer to apply, you first have to determine how much nitrogen is in the formulation you are using. For example: 13-13-13 is a common granular landscape fertilizer that is 13 percent nitrogen. To calculate how much fertilizer you need for 1000 sq. ft., you divide 1 (for 1 lb. nitrogen) by .13 (the 13 percent nitrogen in the fertilizer). The result is 7.7, which means you should apply 7.7 lbs. of 13-13-13 fertilizer for every 1000 sq. ft. Refer to the chart on page 14 for additional information on figuring lime, sulfur, and fertilizer rates.

Plants, especially those growing in poor soil or that show signs of nutritional deficiency, may require supplemental feeding. In cases where root problems exist, do not apply additional fertilizer: this could cause even more root damage.

PRUNING

Pruning, deadheading, trimming, and pinching are often-necessary maintenance practices that help train plants, control their growth, and initiate additional growth. These methods should be performed in accordance with a plant's growth period and flowering. Pruning cuts should be made at the branch collar of the trunk limb. This is typically a swollen area where the limb emerges from the trunk. The branch collar is more noticeable on certain species and with age. Cuts made further out on branches should be made slightly above any buds or branches. Observe the direction the branch or bud is facing which determines the direction of growth. Avoid leaving stubs which eventually deteriorate further back into the plant's heartwood. Most plants don't heal from improper cuts or damage from weedeaters

FERTILIZER CHART

Fertilizer Amounts to use per 1000 sq. ft. based on
1 lb. of actual nitrogen (100%)

Fertilizer Blend Examples	Amount per 1000 sq. ft.
20-0-0	5.0 lbs.
33-0-0	3.0 lbs.
45-0-0	2.2 lbs.
10-20-10	10.0 lbs.
13-13-13	7.69 lbs.
17-17-17	5.88 lbs.
18-46-0	5.55 lbs.
11-48-0	9.09 lbs.
13-0-44	7.69 lbs.
0-0-60	6.66 lbs.*
0-20-0	20.0 lbs.*
0-45-0	8.88 lbs.*

This list is not all encompassing. The best ratio combination should coincide with up-to-date soil test results. The amounts applied can be rounded off. *Phosphorus and potassium are based on 3-4 lbs. K20 and P205 per 1000 sq. ft.

Lowering the Soil pH to 5.5 for sandy loam soils

**Existing Soil pH	Pounds of Soil Sulfur per 100 sq. ft.
9.0	7.5
8.5	6.0
8.0	5.5
7.5	5.0
7.0	3.5
6.5	1.5

Raising the Soil pH to 6.5 for sandy loam soals

***Existing Soil pH	Pounds of lime per 100 sq. ft.
6.0	2.0
5.5	4.0
5.0	6.0
4.5	8.0

** Based on an initial soil test. Some differences will occur depending on soil type. Clay soils require heavier applications. Never apply more than 5 lbs. of sulfur to a GROWING crop at one time. Wait several weeks for the remainder of the application. Total amounts can be applied to vacant new planting sites.

***Based on an initial soil test. Silt Loam and Clay soils will require heavier applications. Dolomitic, Ag, or Pelletized Lime products are best. Avoid hydrated lime for safety purposes.

or lawn mowers. They just cover up the damage and the plants may be weakened. Never remove more than one-third of a plant's canopy at a pruning time. Pruning paints or sealers are optional. See individual plant entries for the best time to prune specific plants.

Pest Control

Routine inspection of landscape plants is the best method of insect and disease management. Early detection and identification make for more effective control.

Stressed plants are more susceptible to insects and diseases. Proper site selection, soil preparation, plant selection and placement, planting method, and maintenance are all key to keeping plants healthy and resistant to pest problems. Rely on gardening friends, the Extension Service, and full-service retail garden centers for help with proper identification and control.

Book Layout

Chapters One through Nine are arranged according to the plants' size and permanence in the landscape, in an order that makes sense if you want to follow a step-by-step approach to designing your landscape:

- Chapter One is a presentation of Oklahoma **Trees,** whose location, size, and shade often set the stage for a landscape's design. Trees quickly become permanent features in the landscape, thus dictating the selection of other plants.

- Chapter Two offers **Woody Shrubs,** which are used to frame, divide, and enhance a landscape; they also begin a design's layering process.

- The plants discussed in Chapters Three through Eight are smaller plants that are used to enhance, fill, and provide color or texture: **Ground Covers, Vines, Roses, Perennials, Ornamental Grasses,** and **Annuals.**

- **Turfgrasses** in Chapter Nine put the finishing touches on a landscape;

- Chapter Ten, an exploration of **Oklahoma Natives as Ornamentals,** provides details on the best use of certain or some underused natives in our state.

Introduction

- CHAPTER ELEVEN, **Western Oklahoma Plants,** addresses Western Oklahoma landscaping interests and needs with an assortment of plant types and categories that do particularly well in this region.

Whether you are new to Oklahoma, new to gardening, or an experienced native gardener, it is my hope that this book will help make your plant selection simple and successful. Don't get so distressed over the landscaping process that you lose sight of the enjoyment and rewards plants can provide. As the late J.C. Raulston, a good friend, fellow "Okie," and renowned horticulturist, would often remind me, "You are not stretching yourself as a gardener if you aren't killing a few plants." Keep this in mind as you go about your landscaping and gardening endeavors, and most of all—have fun!

LIGHT REQUIREMENTS

Every plant entry within the chapter features a plant profile for quick reference. The following symbols indicate full sun, partial shade, and shade:

Full Sun   Partial Shade   Shade

ADDITIONAL BENEFITS

Some of the beneficial characteristics of many of the plants are indicated by symbols:

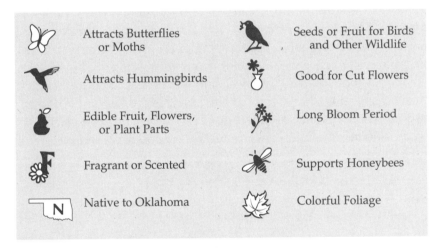

Attracts Butterflies or Moths

Seeds or Fruit for Birds and Other Wildlife

Attracts Hummingbirds

Good for Cut Flowers

Edible Fruit, Flowers, or Plant Parts

Long Bloom Period

Fragrant or Scented

Supports Honeybees

Native to Oklahoma

Colorful Foliage

 Did You Know?

Many plant entries end with a "Did You Know?" information box that offers information about the plant's uses, nomenclature, history, or other information that is little known or just plain interesting.

CHAPTER ONE

Trees

TREES ARE TRULY THE PILLARS OF OUR LANDSCAPES, homes, and communities. Think of trees as an investment for future generations, and selection as the first step in successful tree stewardship.

Unfortunately, there is no such thing as a perfect, no-maintenance, no-pest tree, but this chapter offers some of the best choices with minimal concerns. These sixteen trees are by no means an all-inclusive list for Oklahoma. Many additional choices with improved cultivars are sold in the nursery trade. But definitely think twice before considering silver maple, Lombardy poplar, tree of heaven, American elm, green ash, white poplar, and native cottonwood in your landscape. These trees are notorious for having shallow roots, weak wood, root suckers, diseases, and seed trash although some improved selections are available. Diversity is the key to planting trees in a landscape and neighborhood. A variety of tree species adds uniqueness and alleviates potential epidemic spread of pest problems.

Fall may be the best time to plant trees. The planting guidelines presented here reflect new findings of research. For example, 85 percent of a tree's roots are in the top 24 in. of soil. Roots grow wide, not deep, as we had been led to believe. Dig a planting hole two to three times the width of the rootball and the same depth. Wider, loosely prepared soil means quicker establishment for horizontal root growth. Gently backfill the hole with the original soil. Adding peat moss and other expensive organic materials is not necessary. The tree has to grow in the original soil, and in most cases the soil provides some nutrition until the tree is established. It is definitely a risk to apply high-nitrogen fertilizers and excessive amounts of root stimulator in the planting hole. These items can burn the tender, new root growth when applied at high rates.

Chapter One

Fertilizer applications can promote tree growth but are better applied after the tree is established. Building a shallow water basin with excess soil around the perimeter of the tree is imperative. The ridge holds the water and allows it to soak in around the roots. Otherwise, the water runs along the surface of the ground, never penetrating the root system.

A tall tree may be at risk of blowing over in a widely planted hole, but stake a tree if necessary and no longer than a year. The staking method should not bind the tree trunk or penetrate the bark. Soft strapping material is best. Some movement of the tree is needed to develop strength. Leaving lower branches on for the first three years encourages a bigger, stronger tree trunk. Mulch the tree to keep weeds from competing with the tree roots and to prevent lawn mower or weed-trimmer damage.

Fertilizer applications on lawns and landscapes are probably sufficient for trees in these areas. Isolated trees not receiving indirect feedings or ones showing nutritional deficiencies need supplemental applications. Split the rates between early spring and fall according to product directions. Use granular, broadcasted fertilizers.

Pruning and training the tree early on will reward you with a strong, long-lived specimen. Make small cuts anytime. But leave drastic pruning to a professional, preferably someone trained and certified as an arboriculturist. Only under very rare circumstances should a tree be topped or "coat racked." Pruning cuts should be made at the branch collar, especially on larger trees, and not flush with the trunk. Oftentimes improved selections of trees are budded onto the rootstocks of related tough species. Avoid letting suckers emerge from the lower rootstock.

Bald Cypress

Taxodium distichum

Height: 50 to 80 ft. (large tree) **Spread:** 20 to 30 ft. **Zones:** 6a, 6b, 7a, 7b *Color photograph on page 225.*	**Light Requirements:** **Beneficial Characteristic:**

At first glance this tree has the appearance of an evergreen with its needle-like foliage. Indeed, bald cypress is a conifer that forms rounded cones, but the leaves are deciduous. The fernlike growth emerges as a brilliant soft green, turning to a bright bronze-yellow in the fall before dropping. The small leaves easily break down in the fall with minimal raking. Bald cypress is also known for its distinctive reddish-brown, fibrous bark. Bald cypress requires a large space in the landscape and makes a majestic shade tree. I have seen this tough tree growing in swampy sites in eastern Oklahoma as well as in heavy clay in the western part of the state.

WHEN TO PLANT
Plant bald cypress in early spring or fall.

WHERE TO PLANT
Bald cypress grows best in moist, deep, sandy loam soils. It tolerates poor soils or grows in the edge of water, however. Use bald cypress as a specimen, shade, or lawn tree.

HOW TO PLANT
Bald cypress is available as a container-grown or balled-and-burlapped tree. Place the tree in a hole dug two to three times the width and the same depth as the rootball. Refill the hole with its original soil, and water to settle air pockets. Mulch to retain moisture, control weeds, and keep weed trimmers away.

CARE AND MAINTENANCE
Bald cypress requires minimal care. There are no prevalent pests, and the tree needs little pruning. It is a good idea to leave the lower branches on the trunk after planting to allow for thicker trunk development, especially the first couple of years. Iron chlorosis on the foliage has been known to occur in highly alkaline soils in some plantings, indicating its preference for slightly acid soils. Acidic-based mulches, such as pine needles, pecan hulls,

or pine bark, and fertilizers containing sulfur and iron correct chlorosis problems. Water during drought periods to fully establish the tree during the first two to three years. Continue to reapply mulch as needed. Supplemental applications of fertilizer can accelerate the growth of bald cypress.

ADDITIONAL INFORMATION

Trees are monocious (male and female flowers on the same plant). Scalelike cones emerge from the female flowers later in March or April. The trees are fairly fast growers with strong wood. In waterlogged conditions such as ponds, bald cypress will grow "knees" emerging from the water. Botanists believe that the knees help in translocating oxygen to the roots.

ADDITIONAL SPECIES, CULTIVARS, OR VARIETIES

'Monarch of Illinois' is a wider-spreading cultivar while 'Shawnee Brave' is more columnar than the original species. Both are somewhat hard to find in the nursery trade. Pond cypress (*Taxodium ascendens*) is a smaller-growing relative of bald cypress. Pond cypress is also a deciduous conifer but with narrower leaves. 'Nutans' pond cypress is one cultivar being sold with a more pendulous growth. 'Prairie Sentinel' is a very tall and columnar pond cypress cultivar. Bald cypress and pond cypress are known to occasionally hybridize in some native stands.

 Did You Know?

Bald cypress knees are known as pneumatophores.

Chinese Pistache

Pistacia chinensis

Height: 30 to 45 ft. (medium-sized tree)
Spread: 25 to 35 ft.
Zones: 6a, 6b, 7a, 7b

Color photograph on page 225.

Light Requirements:

Beneficial Characteristic:

My first experience with Chinese pistache was at the Oklahoma Botanical Gardens and Arboretum in Stillwater as a horticulture student in a plant identification class. The stately trees exhibited brilliant color in the fall. One distinctive identifying characteristic was the pungent odor from the compound leaves when they were bruised. I am not sure how old the trees were, but I have not seen any their size in a landscape since then. Chinese pistache will grow from one end of the state to the other and thrive in almost any soil, yet it is unknown to many gardeners. This superb tree has made the top lists of plants to use in neighboring states.

WHEN TO PLANT

Plant in spring or fall. Chinese pistache transplants well, whether in container-grown or balled-and-burlapped form.

WHERE TO PLANT

These adaptable trees tolerate poor and alkaline soils. I have seen them used as street trees in the western part of the state. Like most trees, they grow larger in moist, well-drained, fertile soils.

HOW TO PLANT

Dig the planting hole two to three times the width of the rootball and the same depth. Do not add organic backfill. Water thoroughly to settle the soil. Mulch to retain moisture and to keep a weed- and grass-free area around the tree. Chinese pistache may be sold as a staked, spindly tree. Remove the plastic attaching the tree to the stakes so that girdling does not occur. If the tree is sparse in branches, prune the central leader of the tree slightly above a group of buds to force more branching near the base.

CARE AND MAINTENANCE

Chinese pistache needs selective pruning early on to form a good, straight crown. Young trees have a tendency to grow bushy with bad angles. I have heard nursery professionals refer to these young trees as "ugly weeds" that later grow into exquisite trees. Some experts have associated this growth characteristic more with young female trees. It is a good idea to leave lower branches on the tree for a couple of years to better establish a thicker trunk early on after planting. The tree has few pest problems, with the exception of an occasional webworm in the eastern part of the state. Chinese pistache is considered a moderately fast-growing tree with exceptionally strong wood. After they are established, they are very drought tolerant. The drought of 1998 did not adversely affect them.

ADDITIONAL INFORMATION

Pistache trees are dioecious (male and female flowers on separate trees). The female produces fruit that ripens to a metallic-red or blue color in October. Blue jays and mockingbirds occasionally disperse the small, round berries. As a result, a few secluded seedlings pop up in the landscape. Nursery propagators of Chinese pistache have found the blue seed to be more viable.

ADDITIONAL SPECIES, CULTIVARS, OR VARIETIES

Many people ask, "Is Chinese pistache related to the tree producing pistachio nuts?" The answer is yes. *Pistacia vera* is a smaller tree, not cold hardy this far north.

Did You Know?

Chinese pistache is a native of China and was introduced to the United States in the 1890s.

Dawn Redwood

Metasequoia glyptostroboides

Height: 60 to 100 ft. (large shade tree)
Spread: 25 to 35 ft.
Zones: 7a, 7b

Color photograph on page 225.

Light Requirements:

Beneficial Characteristic:

Yet another deciduous conifer well adapted to the eastern part of the state is dawn redwood. It is a remarkably fast-growing tree with a soft evergreen appearance. It is a towering tree with an upright growth, often growing more than 2 ft. a year under optimum conditions. Dawn redwood and bald cypress are similar in appearance at first glance. The needlelike foliage is somewhat longer and oppositely arranged on the branches of dawn redwood but is alternately arranged on the deciduous conifer's bald cypress *distichum* species. Both trees offer an airy, soft texture to any landscape.

WHEN TO PLANT

Plant dawn redwood in late spring. Dawn redwood is not quite as cold hardy as bald cypress and pond cypress.

WHERE TO PLANT

Dawn redwood prefers somewhat acidic, moist, but well-drained soils—unlike bald cypress, which can actually grow in water. Dawn redwood requires plenty of room to mature and is a great shade or specimen lawn tree.

HOW TO PLANT

Dig the planting hole two to three times wider than and the same depth as the rootball. Organic materials are not needed as backfill. Use the original soil since the tree has to become established there. Water the tree frequently and deeply. Mulch 2 to 4 in. thick for moisture retention, but avoid direct contact with the tree trunk.

CARE AND MAINTENANCE

Dawn redwood is definitely not tough when it comes to drought tolerance. In dry conditions, supplemental water is a must. Always water for a long period of time to encourage root growth to go deep. It is considered a fast-growing tree that remains fairly strong wooded. No pruning is necessary because the tree naturally grows in a pyramidal shape with good branch angles. Leave lower branches on for a couple of years to encourage quicker and stronger trunk development. To avoid stimulating delayed growth spurts that will make the tree susceptible to winter injury, do not apply fertilizers in late summer.

ADDITIONAL INFORMATION

This historic tree was thought to be fossilized and extinct until the 1940s when seedlings were found growing in China. Seeds were collected and brought back to the United States. I have seen the tree grown fairly successfully in poor, well-drained soils, even as a street tree. The bark is a beautiful reddish brown, exfoliating for an interesting display. The fall color is typically brown with a reddish-orange tinge.

ADDITIONAL SPECIES, CULTIVARS, OR VARIETIES

'Sheridan Spire' and 'National' are two upright cultivars in the trade with little variation from the parent species.

 Did You Know?

Dawn redwood is often confused with the giant redwood (Sequoiadendron giganteum). 'Hazel Smith' is a hardier cultivar of giant redwood for gardeners with plenty of room in the landscape.

Eastern Redbud

Cercis canadensis

Other Name: Judas Tree
Height: 25 to 45 ft. (small tree)
Spread: 25 to 35 ft.
Zones: 6a, 6b, 7a, 7b

Color photograph on page 225.

Light Requirements:

Beneficial Characteristics:

Making its way across the state with a burst of early-spring color from east to as far west as Woodward is our state tree—eastern redbud. You really have to use your imagination to find red in the flower color. (The flowers have more of a purplish tinge, but you have to admit that redbud sounds much better than purplebud as a name.) The refreshing color is quite dramatic after a drab winter. This spring revival of color was emblematic in the renewal of hope to the tired pioneers seeking homes in a new land. Redbud became our state tree in 1937 as a result of its colorful role in our history and the beauty it continues to display. You cannot overlook the unique, heart-shaped foliage appearing after the enchanting blooms. Some cultivars produce prolific seedpods in the fall.

WHEN TO PLANT

Redbud transplants well in spring or fall.

WHERE TO PLANT

In its native habitat, redbud is an understory tree that prefers filtered sun. It grows best in moist, well-drained, fertile soils but tolerates a wide range of acid or alkaline soil types. In heavier clay soils the tree has a tendency to be somewhat stunted. Use redbud as a single specimen, or plant it in groups of two or more. Since redbud is a relatively small tree it can be used next to structures, especially on the east side. Plant it on the edges of woodland landscapes as it appears in its natural habitat. Some cultivars can also tolerate full sun. Redbud is a good choice of a smaller tree that will avoid growing into power lines.

HOW TO PLANT

Redbud is available as a container, bare-root, or balled-and-burlapped tree. There is no need to amend the soil. Dig the planting hole two to three times wider than and the same depth as the rootball. Backfill the hole without compacting the soil. Water thoroughly, and mulch around the tree 2 to 4 in. thick.

CARE AND MAINTENANCE

Many of the newer cultivars will grow in full sun. Too much shade can cause thinning of the tree canopy. Pruning is necessary only to train the tree. Leaving the existing lower branches for a couple of years after planting will form a stronger trunk. Redbuds respond well to regular watering, fertilizing, and mulching. Unfortunately, leaf roller, leafhopper, and scale are potential insect pests. Canker problems can arise in areas where the soil is poorly drained and compacted.

ADDITIONAL INFORMATION

Redbuds are available in multiple trunk specimens as well as single or pendulous selections, depending on the variety. Some cultivars are grown for their purplish foliage color. As trees mature, the bark has a tendency to turn an orange tinge that has nice ornamental attributes. Some selections have heavy fruit set after flowering that later form brown pods as they mature, which remain throughout the winter.

ADDITIONAL SPECIES, CULTIVARS, OR VARIETIES

'Alba' is a white-flowering cultivar with occasional tinges of pink. 'Oklahoma White' has pure-white flowers followed by bluish-green foliage that turns a golden yellow in the fall. 'Forest Pansy' is one of my favorites, with intense purple foliage emerging in the early spring and later turning a purplish green. 'Forest Pansy' will retain its purple color more in full sun. A hard-to-find cultivar with double-pink flowers and minimal fruit set is 'Flame'. Related varieties include *Cercis canadensis* ssp. *texensis* with glossy leaves and purple-pink flowers opening later than most of the eastern selections. 'Traveller' is a weeping or pendulous selection. 'Oklahoma' is a popular cultivar discovered in the Arbuckle Mountains and is known for its glossy, thick foliage. Mexican redbud (*Cercis canadensis* ssp. *mexicana*) is a smaller tree or large shrub and has unusually wavy leaf margins and large, deep-purple flowers. Because Mexican redbuds are more tolerant of heavy alkaline soils, they are suitable for southwestern Oklahoma.

 Did You Know?

The common name Judas tree was bestowed since it is believed to be the species of tree on which the apostle Judas Iscariot hung himself. But some historians debate whether the tree was of the elder or fig species.

Flowering Dogwood

Cornus florida

Other Name: Indian Arrowwood
Height: 20 to 40 ft. (small- to
  medium-sized tree)
Spread: 20 to 25 ft.
Zones: 6a, 6b, 7a, 7b

Color photograph on page 225.

Light Requirements:

Beneficial Characteristics:

Another colorful native of Oklahoma that graciously blooms in the early spring is dogwood. Dogwood is cold hardy for the entire state of Oklahoma; however, it performs best in the eastern part where the soils are less alkaline and clay. The greatest known characteristic of dogwood is the spectacular flower, which has something in common with the poinsettia. The yellow flower itself is not showy. The bracts or colored leaves catch our attention. Most selections on the market come in white, pink, or purple bracts. The flowers, which are centered in the middle of the bracts, are quite small. Dogwood is truly a plant for all seasons. It starts with colorful blooms followed by unusual foliage (some even variegated) and finishes the season with brilliant-colored seed and foliage in the fall.

WHEN TO PLANT

Spring planting of dogwood is the first choice; early fall planting is the second choice.

WHERE TO PLANT

Dogwoods definitely need to be planted in protected areas. They should be understory trees so that they can get protection from wind and hot afternoon sun, especially in central and western parts of the state. The same principle can be accomplished by planting them on the east or northeast side of a building or under existing shade trees. The soil should be fertile, moist, and well drained. Dogwoods are destined to fail in heavy, poorly drained soils.

HOW TO PLANT

Dogwoods are finicky plants to establish. There are no special tricks, though. Just dig holes two to three times wider than and the same depth as the rootballs. Do not apply root stimulators or organic amendments. Adding organic mulch to keep the soil cool, moist, and fertile is a good idea, however.

CARE AND MAINTENANCE

Dogwoods are extremely susceptible to damage by weed trimmers and lawn mowers, and they are not good selections for street trees. Locating them in full sun and in hot, windy locations contributes to the scorch around the edges of the leaf. Dogwoods need supplemental water during severe drought conditions. Potential disease problems in Oklahoma are leaf spot and powdery mildew. The eastern United States is faced with a devastating disease called dogwood anthracnose. As a result, anthracnose-tolerant selections are being introduced in many from the kousa dogwood varieties. Borer insects may attack trees that are stressed from improper site location or trunk damage.

ADDITIONAL INFORMATION

Yes, I have seen dogwoods growing in full sun. After further investigation, I found that the plants were at one time planted in protected areas, and for various reasons the environment changed to full sun. Established trees will take the heat better, but getting them to that point is a challenge. Not only are the fruit quite attractive in the fall, but they make a favorite food source for blue jays and mockingbirds. Our other native dogwood, roughleaf, is commonly found along roadsides and fencerows. The flowers are not as showy, but the fruit are favorites of quail and other Oklahoma birds.

ADDITIONAL SPECIES, CULTIVARS, OR VARIETIES

There are too many cultivars and selections of dogwood to mention, but I will note a few of my favorites. 'Ozark Spring' was released from Kansas State as a selection more tolerant of exposed locations in the prairie states; it does not take hot, full sun, though. 'Cherokee Chief' is a nice choice for a reddish-pink flower. 'Cherokee Brave'™ has a more burgundy-red flower and larger, glossy leaves. For colorful foliage and flowers consider 'Purple Glory', which has a purplish tint to the foliage as well as ruby-colored flowers. Kousa dogwood (*Cornus kousa*) selections are more cold hardy and better choices for the northern part of our state. National' is a popular kousa cultivar.

 Did You Know?

Flowering dogwood branches with buds can be cut in February and placed in water. The warm room temperatures will force early flowering indoors.

Fruitless Sweetgum

Liquidambar styraciflua

Other Name: American Sweetgum
Height: 60 to 75 ft. (large tree)
Spread: 40 to 60 ft.
Zones: 6a, 6b, 7a, 7b

Color photograph on page 225.

Light Requirements:

Beneficial Characteristic:

It is not often that I highlight a particular cultivar, but if you want to grow sweetgum in the landscape, fruitless sweetgum is the clear choice. Or maybe you like dealing with those prickly little seed balls? Granted, I have seen some unusual crafts made from them, but I have experience that overshadows the potential for art. Raking leaves is bad enough, but prickly balls—no thanks. And then there were the times when I stepped on them barefoot, when they clogged the gutters, or when they cracked windows as they ricocheted out of my lawn mower. That is why I like fruitless sweetgum 'Rotundiloba'. This cultivar has the same fragrant foliage turning a beautiful yellow to reddish purple in the fall. The only differences from the traditional sweetgum are that the leaves are more rounded instead of pointed and there are few to no fruit balls.

WHEN TO PLANT
Plant sweetgum anytime in the spring or fall.

WHERE TO PLANT
Sweetgum is native to moist, fertile, bottomland sites, so it is better adapted to the eastern half of the state. Plant it in heavy clay, alkaline soils, and you are asking for problems. Sweetgum requires plenty of space for the extensive root system and is not a good choice for a street or driveway tree. It does well as a lawn or park specimen.

HOW TO PLANT
Plant it in a hole two to three times wider than and the same depth as the rootball. No extra soil amendments are needed. Watering is critical to establish the tree and to settle the soil. Mulch helps to mimic its preferred natural conditions.

CARE AND MAINTENANCE
Sweetgum trees may appear to just sit there after they are planted. Many times the top growth does not start until the root growth is well established.

Once the growth kicks in, they are considered moderate growers. They need plenty of supplemental water during drought conditions, and they respond to minimal fertilizations. Potential pests are webworms, caterpillars, scale, and fungal leaf spot. Iron chlorosis is common when the trees are planted in alkaline soils. Pruning is seldom needed. Leaving the lower branches on for the first couple of years after planting is a good practice to encourage bigger, stronger trunks. Mulch as needed to refurbish any that has decomposed or blown away.

ADDITIONAL INFORMATION

Many people ponder how a fruitless variety is grown in the nursery trade. The trees are propagated by cuttings under special greenhouse conditions and occasionally budded or grafted.

ADDITIONAL SPECIES, CULTIVARS, OR VARIETIES

'Rotundiloba' is sometimes found in the trade as 'Obtusifolia'. Look for the distinctive rounded lobes on the leaves and a tag clarifying the selection as fruitless.

  Did You Know?

'Rotundiloba' was discovered in North Carolina in the wild in 1930.

Ginkgo

Ginkgo biloba

Other Name: Maidenhair Tree
Height: 40 to 60 ft. (large tree)
Spread: 20 to 40 ft.
Zones: 6a, 6b, 7a, 7b

Color photograph on page 225.

Light Requirements:

Beneficial Characteristic:

Talk about history. Gingko has been growing on earth for more than 150 million years. It is often referred to as a living fossil. This tree deserves respect but is still hard to find at many local garden centers. Plant named cultivars propagated from male selections. The female produces untidy and foul-smelling seed. Ginkgo is a distinctly pyramidal-shaped, picturesque tree as it matures. Unfortunately, the trees are slow growing and do not produce seed until they are several years old. Ginkgo is well worth the extra time needed to find it and grow it.

WHEN TO PLANT
Plant ginkgo in spring or fall.

WHERE TO PLANT
Ginkgo is a widely adaptable tree. Because it is heat, pollution, and salt tolerant, it makes a good street tree, although it needs plenty of space. It is very pH adaptable, drought and wind tolerant. The native preference of this tree is a sandy, deep soil with good moisture-holding capabilities and good drainage. Such conditions stimulate somewhat quicker growth. Use ginkgo as a shade or specimen lawn tree.

HOW TO PLANT
Dig a large planting hole as deep as the rootball and two to three times wider. Backfill with nonamended soil. Water to settle the soil and remove air pockets. Mulch to keep moisture in and weed trimmers away.

CARE AND MAINTENANCE
Ginkgo is a relatively slow-growing tree. It responds to fertilizer by growing somewhat more rapidly. Drastic pruning is not necessary because the tree has strong wood and grows with good branch angles. Leaving the existing lower branches on for a couple of years promotes stronger trunk development. Mulch to keep weed competition at a minimum. Ginkgo trees are typically free of pests. Occasionally, leaf scald can occur on the south-

west side of the trunk due to sparse foliage set early on in the tree's growth. The tree branches out better as it matures. Provide supplemental water during drought conditions.

ADDITIONAL INFORMATION

The foliage is a unique shape that resembles the outline of a maidenhair fern, thus the common name of the tree. The fall color is a consistent golden yellow unless there is an early freeze and the leaves quickly drop. The smaller leaf means minimal fall cleanup.

ADDITIONAL SPECIES, CULTIVARS, OR VARIETIES

'Autumn Gold' is a male selection with excellent fall color. 'Princeton Sentry' and 'Fairmount' are male cultivars more narrow in growth. These are hard to find in the trade because of their slow growth. Ginkgo trees are usually quite expensive but definitely worth the price.

 Did You Know?

Ginkgo is native to China.

Golden Raintree

Koelreuteria paniculata

Other Names: Panicled Golden Raintree; Varnish Tree

Height: 30 to 40 ft. (medium-sized tree)

Spread: 20 to 40 ft.

Zones: 6a, 6b, 7a, 7b

Color photograph on page 225.

Light Requirements:

Beneficial Characteristics:

Golden raintree has intriguing landscape features for a tree its size. It is one of the few trees in our state with elaborate, showy flowers in June. The yellow, fragrant flowers are quite impressive and grow as if they were shooting out of the tree. They later transform into a cluster of lanternlike seedpods with a golden color continuing to tower above the foliage, which remains throughout part of the winter. The tree's small, rounded canopy fits in almost any landscape, and the compound leaves provide some shade. Expect the uniquely shaped leaves to provide further orange-yellow color in the fall.

WHEN TO PLANT

Plant it in spring or fall.

WHERE TO PLANT

This tough tree is adaptable to sand, clay, or rock as long as it does not hold water. Use golden raintree as a single specimen or in groups for a bigger flower display. It is not really tall enough for a shade tree but makes a great landscape accent plant.

HOW TO PLANT

Dig the planting hole two to three times wider than and the same depth as the rootball. This extra effort encourages better root development in the loosely dug soil. Supplemental amendments and nutrients are not needed at planting time. Water to gently settle the soil and remove air pockets. Mulch after planting to keep moisture in and weeds out.

CARE AND MAINTENANCE

Golden raintree is one of the easiest trees to care for. It is considered fast growing and responds well to fertilizer. It seldom needs pruning. Leaving the existing lower branches on for the first couple of years encourages a bigger, stronger trunk. Golden raintree is fairly drought tolerant, once it is established, and pest resistant. A couple of nuisance pests attracted to golden raintrees are more frustrating to home owners than harmful to the trees. These black, gray, and red critters are called box elder or red shoulder bugs. They are more prevalent in the fall and vary in numbers from year to year. They can crawl from the tree to your home if the tree is planted nearby. These pesky bugs tend to congregate near eaves, shutters, windows, and doors searching for a place to overwinter.

ADDITIONAL INFORMATION

Some horticulturists have stated that the trees have weak wood, but I have not found that to be the case with trees I have grown. After many storms the trees seldom have limb damage. The showy flowers and compound leaves make this tree one of a kind for any landscape, especially if you like to use purple-and-yellow colors in your design.

ADDITIONAL SPECIES, CULTIVARS, OR VARIETIES

'Fastigiata', scarcely found in the trade, is more upright and narrow in growth. 'September', which is also hard to find, blooms later in the fall. Folks in southern Oklahoma can enjoy *Koelreuteria elegans* with its yellow flowers and pinkish-rose seedpods. The tree is not as cold hardy and is found more in the lower southeastern parts of the United States. The foliage is different from *K. paniculata* with twice compound leaves. 'Flamegold' is one selection released for its intense fall color.

 Did You Know?

The seedpods are frequently used in dried flower arrangements.

Japanese Maple

Acer palmatum

Height: 10 to 25 ft. (small- to medium-sized tree)
Spread: 10 to 15 ft.
Zones: 6a, 6b, 7a, 7b

Color photograph on page 225.

Light Requirements:

Beneficial Characteristics:

If *graceful* is a term that can be used to describe a tree, it applies to the Japanese maple. This small tree stands out in any situation where it is properly used. The colorful foliage is very attractive and adds both color and texture to the landscape. Fall colors can be quite intense, ranging from vibrant orange red to golden yellow, depending on the cultivar and growing season. The unique bark is a nice attribute in the winter. Japanese maples are some of the priciest trees available. Trees may range in the hundreds of dollars, depending on the species or cultivar. Most are grafted or budded to a more resilient rootstock. There are literally hundreds of cultivars from which to choose. Japanese maples are most often used as specimen plants because they offer unique upright, mounding, cascading, or textured features to a landscape design.

WHEN TO PLANT
Plant it in spring or fall.

WHERE TO PLANT
Japanese maples require protection from the wind in Oklahoma. The eastern part of the state is more suited to these beauties, although I have seen many spectacular plantings in central and western Oklahoma with protection. They prefer rich, moist soil and locations under trees or eastern or northeastern sites. The uses for Japanese maple are unlimited: as a single specimen, in a border, as an accent plant, or in groupings for a dramatic impact. They are often grown in Japanese gardens.

HOW TO PLANT
Bed preparation is recommended before planting time. Till organic matter into the bed where the plants will be located. Do not till in any material if established trees are nearby because root damage will occur and can shorten the life of the established plants. No soil amendments are necessary for a single hole, however. Japanese maples are frequently sold as balled-and-burlapped plants. Always remove the twine from the trunk and the burlap,

if possible. In situations where the rootball is loose, place the plant in the prepared hole, roll back the burlap, and cut off the excess. Personal experience and years of consulting have proven to me that leaving the burlap slows and sometimes hinders root establishment. Dig the planting hole two to three times wider than and the same depth as the rootball. Water and mulch as needed.

CARE AND MAINTENANCE

These beauties are slow growers at first, but after they are established, they grow at a moderate rate. Prune them to shape the appearance to fit your design and purpose. Do small pruning any time of year. Do drastic pruning for design (no more than one-third at a time) early in the dormant season. Overfertilizing can increase the green pigment in burgundy foliage selections. Mulching is a must with Japanese maples to protect their somewhat shallow roots by keeping them cool and moist. There are very few problems with insects or disease. Most leaf problems occur from being exposed to scorching sun and wind. Scorching also occurs from prolonged drought, so supplemental watering is necessary.

ADDITIONAL INFORMATION

Late-spring freezes can occasionally damage the foliage. Japanese maples have a tendency to leaf out early. That is another reason why site protection is important.

ADDITIONAL SPECIES, CULTIVARS, OR VARIETIES

Gardeners may choose from many cultivars. Select the appropriate ones for your particular site according to height and width. The most common varieties fall into one of two categories—dissected or nondissected, which applies to the foliage shape. Dissected, or dissectum, types have more feathery leaves with finely cut lobes. The dissectum types are often more susceptible to wind and leaf tattering. The nondissected selections are more of a typical maple leaf shape and less frilly, thus somewhat more tolerant of wind.

 Did You Know?

Japanese maple makes a great bonsai or espalier plant with intense pruning and design.

Kentucky Coffee Tree

Gymnocladus dioicus

Height: 60 to 80 ft. (large tree)
Spread: 30 to 50 ft.
Zones: 6a, 6b, 7a, 7b

Color photograph on page 225.

Light Requirements:

A nother native of Oklahoma is the Kentucky coffee tree, which is also native to Kentucky where early settlers used the seed as a substitute for coffee, thus the name. This stately tree has large, compound leaves emerging with a pinkish tint and later changing to a grayish green. The enormous compound leaves provide more-than-adequate shade. After the leaves drop in the winter, the trees reveal sparse branches for better sunlight penetration. As a result this tree is often promoted as an energy-efficient planting for the landscape because it will heavily shade homes in the summer and more readily allow sun in the winter. The compound leaves are not considered a litter problem in the fall. Unfortunately, that is not the case with the female Kentucky coffee tree, which produces numerous large seedpods not as inconspicuous as the foliage when they drop to the ground.

WHEN TO PLANT
Plant Kentucky coffee tree in the spring or fall.

WHERE TO PLANT
Kentucky coffee tree is found in rich, bottomland soils or deep ravines with moist slopes. A moist, well-drained soil provides the best growth and display. It tolerates poor soils, however. To fully reach its potential, this tree needs a large space. Plant it as a shade tree in a lawn or park setting.

HOW TO PLANT
Plant the tree in a hole two to three times wider than and the same depth as the rootball. Soil amendments, such as compost, peat moss, or root stimulators, are not needed. Add mulch after planting to simulate the moist, fertile conditions in which the tree thrives.

CARE AND MAINTENANCE
Young nursery seedlings are often tall and lanky with few branches; tip pruning the main trunk slightly above a group of buds forces lower branches. Leave existing lower branches for the first couple of years to

encourage a bigger, stronger trunk. Kentucky coffee tree wood is fairly strong, even though the tree grows rather quickly. These potentially enormous trees respond to supplemental feedings. There are no major pest problems. Water them during drought conditions, and reapply mulch as needed.

ADDITIONAL INFORMATION

The trees are dioecious (separate male and female plants). The female plant has fairly fragrant flowers. Soon after flowering, a beanlike seedpod develops, which is 5 to 10 in. long. As you can imagine, these pods could become a litter nuisance in the landscape. Once again, the male tree is a better choice for the landscape. Even though used for coffee in pioneer times, the seedpod has been reported to be potentially toxic to cattle.

ADDITIONAL SPECIES, CULTIVARS, OR VARIETIES

Unfortunately, improved male cultivars are hard to find in the trade. There are three named male selections to date. 'Espresso' is a seedless male with upright branching growing about 70 ft. by 40 ft. wide in an elm-like form. This cultivar will probably be the most likely to find but not without effort. J. Frank Schmidt and Son in Boring, Oregon is producing 'Espresso' for introduction into the nursery trade. 'Prairie Titan'® (J.C. McDaniel), and 'Stately Manor' are other name male selections but with limited production and availability.

 Did You Know?

There is a rare variegated selection of Kentucky coffee tree called 'Variegata'.

Lacebark Elm

Ulmus parvifolia

Other Name: Chinese Elm
Height: 40 to 60 ft. (large tree)
Spread: 30 to 40 ft.
Zones: 6a, 6b, 7a, 7b

Color photograph on page 225.

Light Requirements:

Beneficial Characteristic:

As you travel across our great state, you will see that elms like it here, too. Unfortunately, many of the American elms that dotted our highways and byways have succumbed to the infamous Dutch elm disease. To date, Chinese elm seems to be somewhat resistant to this epidemic disease. The tree is quite elegant with its oval growth habit. As it matures, the bark begins to exfoliate, leaving behind a most unusual mottled combination of colors, thus the name lacebark elm. The decorative bark pattern is truly a landscape attribute. One of the most spectacular specimens in Oklahoma is located at the Oklahoma Botanical Gardens and Arboretum in Stillwater where visitors can get a first-hand look at the landscape potential of this elegant tree.

When to Plant

Plant lacebark elm in spring or fall.

Where to Plant

Lacebark elm is a very tough and durable tree that is generally litter free in the fall. It will grow in a wide range of conditions and is suited for the entire state. Lacebark elm and Chinese pistache are two trees with the distinction and toughness to thrive in statewide conditions.

How to Plant

This fast-growing shade tree prefers a hole that is dug at least two to three times wider than and the same depth as the rootball so that its roots can quickly establish in the loosely worked soil. Water deeply to settle the soil and soak the roots. Mulch for added environmental benefits such as weed control, moisture retention, and protection from weed trimmers.

Care and Maintenance

Elms respond well to supplemental fertilizations and mulch. These trees are fairly drought and wind tolerant. Chinese elm shows significant tolerance of the elm leaf beetle and Japanese beetle that spread Dutch elm disease. In far eastern Oklahoma a critter known as the elm flea beetle is starting to cause problems. About the time the leaves unfurl, the black, hopping beetle skeletonizes the leaves, making them unsightly. In severe outbreaks they will defoliate. The beetles are around only in early spring; generally, the trees put out another set of leaves. One way to look at it is that this natural pest encourages additional growth each season. But as you can imagine, it takes a lot of the tree's energy to put on two flushes of growth in a year. Supplemental fertilization is important after the beetles have finished their cycle. Water during drought conditions.

ADDITIONAL INFORMATION

Lacebark elm is sometimes confused with Siberian elm (*Ulmus pumila*). They are two completely different species. The true Chinese or lacebark elm is a great choice for our state. One of Oklahoma's great plantsmen, Steve Bieberich of Sunshine Nursery in Clinton, is doing quite a bit of work and propagation to make sure we have a good selection at our nurseries.

ADDITIONAL SPECIES, CULTIVARS, OR VARIETIES

'Athena', previously known as 'Emerald Isle', is a rounded-growing cultivar with thick leaves and consistent exfoliating bark. 'Allee', formerly known as 'Emerald Vase', is more upright in growth habit with good fall color. 'Drake' lacebark elm is fairly easily found in the nursery industry; it has a more upright growth habit and is better suited to the warmer zones of the state. 'Golden Ray' (sometimes found as 'Rey's Golden') offers unique light-green to yellow foliage during the summer with a combination of gray, orange, and brown exfoliating bark. 'Red' is another colorful selection with dark-green summer foliage turning a reddish fall color. Many hybrid crosses using lacebark elm are filtering into the landscape trade with potential Dutch elm disease tolerance. Now if we could just find one to withstand the flea beetle.

 Did You Know?

Lacebark elm blooms in late summer with seed ripening in the fall.

Pine

Pinus species

Height: 5 to 100 ft. (depending on species)
Spread: 5 to 60 ft.
Zones: 6a, 6b, 7a, 7b

Color photograph on page 225.

Light Requirements:

Beneficial Characteristics:

There are numerous pine species growing in our state, many of which are native. Pines offer ever-so-important green color during a drab winter. They provide height and unique texture to our landscapes. The narrow height and airy appearance of pines are landscape attributes provided by few plants. Another benefit is the pine needle mulch for other shrubs and trees. Gardeners in the southeastern United States pay good money for bales of pine straw to use as landscape mulch.

WHEN TO PLANT

Pines can be planted in the fall or spring in most locations in the state, but spring planting is preferable in the Panhandle. They are most readily available in containers or as bare-root seedlings.

WHERE TO PLANT

Pines prefer a slightly acidic soil and absolutely cannot withstand wet feet or waterlogged soils; drainage is of utmost importance. Many pine species should be planted in groups of three or five to simulate a naturalized stand. It is also easier to gather needles below such groups.

HOW TO PLANT

Towering pines need widely dug holes two to three times the width and the same depth as the container rootballs. In heavy soils they can be planted slightly above soil grade to keep the roots from being smothered. Always mulch to protect the roots when pines are planted above grade. Pine seedlings can be quickly planted in a slit in the ground at the same depth that they were grown. Look for a dark ring on the stem where the soil line was previously located. Mulching newly planted seedlings is a necessity, or weeds and grass will overtake them.

CARE AND MAINTENANCE

A frequent killer of pine is a high rate of nitrogen fertilizer. These plants respond to slow-release organic mulches and/or fertilizers. They cannot withstand compacted soils after being planted. In other words, parking cars and permitting heavy foot traffic over the shallow roots can shorten the lives of trees. Most pine disease and insect problems occur as a result of stress in landscape settings like drought, winter injury, compaction, poor soils, and weed-trimmer blight. Pinewood nematode is a common pest in eastern Oklahoma and spreads by vector insects feeding on the trees. Pine tip moth can wreak havoc by feeding on the growing points of the branches. Pines are susceptible to needle fungal diseases, called needle cast or needle or tip blight. Leaving the needles on the ground under the pine tree promotes reinfection, so needle removal is a good sanitation practice for pines in Oklahoma. In critical cases using a labeled fungicide may be needed to prevent the spread of the disease and decline of the tree. Severely infected needles will likely shed prematurely.

ADDITIONAL INFORMATION

Pines, even though they are evergreen, drop older needles from the center of the crown in late summer or fall. New growth occurs each spring with the emerging candles or buds. Pine needles make a great mulch for ornamental trees and shrubs, especially acid-loving plants such as blueberries, azaleas, and fringe flowers. Freeze damage is sometimes seen on younger trees or new growth. As a result the needles quickly turn brown on the ends of the branches. The discolored needles will either drop prematurely or remain until their normal shedding in the fall. Prune pines in the spring before the candles start to elongate and needles form.

ADDITIONAL SPECIES, CULTIVARS, OR VARIETIES

Scotch and Japanese black pine are favorite hosts for the pine-wood nematode. Pine tip borer frequently disturbs loblolly and mugo pines. Most of the commonly grown species in Oklahoma are susceptible to the needle diseases. Other pines tolerant of Oklahoma conditions are pinyon, shortleaf, Austrian, limber, Japanese red, digger, and slash.

 Did You Know?

Pines are identified and categorized by the primary number of needles per bundle.

Red Maple

Acer rubrum

Other Names: Swamp Maple;
  Scarlet Maple
Height: 40 to 80 ft. (large tree)
Spread: 40 to 60 ft.
Zones: 6a, 6b, 7a, 7b

Color photograph on page 226.

Light Requirements:

Beneficial Characteristics:

Maple is another large category of trees with hundreds of selections. Red maple in particular has a lot to offer gardeners since it is native to our state, especially the central and eastern parts. They take our cold as well as our heat. Red maples grow moderately fast and provide beautiful fall color. They are fairly tolerant of many soil types, depending on the cultivar. They make excellent specimen trees and have stronger wood than other fast-growing maples.

WHEN TO PLANT

Red maples are successfully planted in spring or fall. Selecting cultivars in the fall with coloration ensures color in the future when weather conditions cooperate.

WHERE TO PLANT

Maples are indigenous to moist, slightly acid, deep soils. They adapt to poor soils, rocky sites, and heavy clay with supplemental moisture during dry times but need good drainage.

HOW TO PLANT

Prepare the planting site two to three times the diameter of the rootball and the same depth. No organic backfill is recommended; just use native soil. Water thoroughly until the tree is well established. Mulch is very beneficial for a newly planted tree.

CARE AND MAINTENANCE

Occasional pruning will promote a straight central leader and better branch angle. Pruning to train and direct growth of the tree should be started at planting time and each year after that until the desired framework has been started. Intermittent nutrition through synthetic or organic fertilizer applications is beneficial. Manganese deficiency may be a problem in highly alkaline soils. Symptoms are similar to those of iron chlorosis, which is typical in such circumstances. Water during drought conditions, and reapply mulch as needed.

ADDITIONAL INFORMATION

Do severe pruning of maples in early winter, preferably December. Do small directional pruning at any time necessary throughout the growing season. Pruning paint is not necessary. Most of the research concludes that it only helps the gardener feel better. Making proper pruning cuts is more important. Prune at the branch collar, not flush with the trunk, especially on mature branches.

ADDITIONAL SPECIES, CULTIVARS, OR VARIETIES

'Red Sunset'®, which is known for holding its fall color longer, and 'Autumn Flame'™, which is recognized for early fall color, are two of the most commonly sold in Oklahoma. 'Drummond', an old-time favorite, has colorful seeds in addition to leaves. 'October Glory'® has a more rounded growth habit. 'Karpick' is a unique selection with reddish twigs in addition to its fall color. 'Autumn Blaze'™, often sold as a red maple, is actually a cross between red maple (*Acer rubrum*) and silver maple (*A. saccharinum*). It is also sold as *A.* × *freemani* (freeman maple). It has brilliant fall color and is very fast growing but with somewhat weaker wood. It is thought to be more tolerant of alkaline soils. Shantung maple (*A. truncatum*), trident maple (*A. buergeranum*), tatarian maple (*A. tatarocim*), and hedge maple (*A. campestre*) are all underused trees and make great choices for small- to medium-sized trees in all parts of the state. These, in addition to amur maple (*A. ginnala*), are often sold as small clump or multi-trunk specimens. 'Flame' is a commonly sold amur cultivar with spectacular fall color.

 Did You Know?

Leaves and stems are oppositely arranged on all maples.

Shumard Oak

Quercus shumardii

Height: 80 to 100 ft. (large tree)
Spread: 50 to 60 ft.
Zones: 6a, 6b, 7a, 7b

Color photograph on page 226.

Light Requirements:

Beneficial Characteristics:

Oh, the mighty oak, which truly lives up to its name in our growing region. Just visit any part of the state and enormous oaks prevail, many of which are native. Oaks are quite drought tolerant after they are established. They also willingly take the notorious Oklahoma temperature variations. Not only do oaks make strong shade trees, but they provide an important food source for our native wildlife with their plentiful acorn supply. Many childhood memories center on oak tree swings or tree houses, and one of the most suitable oak trees for the entire state is shumard. Shumard closely resembles another popular oak—pin oak. The biggest difference in the two is the lower branches. The lower branches of shumard oak grow more upright and those of pin oak grow down.

When to Plant

Spring or fall planting is routinely done with either container-grown or balled-and-burlapped trees.

Where to Plant

These large, towering trees need plenty of room in a lawn or park setting. Shumard oak is naturally found in rich, moist bottomlands. Fortunately, this tree adapts well to poor soils in dry conditions once it is established. It is occasionally used in urban street settings.

How to Plant

The planting hole should be 2 ft. wider than the plant root system and no deeper. It is no longer recommended to add organic backfill. Organic materials make great mulch, however. Water deeply to adequately soak the roots. Mulch as needed.

Care and Maintenance

Oak trees respond well to commercial fertilizers. The strong-wooded trees are moderately fast growers and make excellent choices for shade trees. Pruning may be necessary to assist in proper structural growth of the tree.

Leave existing lower branches for a couple of years to encourage a bigger, stronger trunk. Oak trees are fairly resilient to pests, yet a few critters persist in our state. Insect galls are frequent ornaments on oak trees. These knotty, round, or hairy appearances are found on twigs or leaves as part of the insect reproduction cycle. They are generally superficial or cosmetic and are basically harmless to the tree. Oak decline, on the other hand, is not as forgiving and is the slow death of trees. Little can be done to infected trees that are generally suffering as a result of stress from environmental situations. Hypoxylon canker is another disease that affects weakened, stressed or damaged trees. The earliest symptoms are yellowing and wilting of the foliage. Once the disease is well established, the bark begins to slough, revealing a grayish-white lining, which is the fruiting structure of the fungus. There is no effective control other than removing and burning infected trees. Oak leaf blister occurs as a small, dark lesion sporadically located on the leaves. The fungus-causing pathogen usually occurs as a result of wet, warm weather as the leaves unfurl. Typically, no control is needed.

ADDITIONAL INFORMATION

The size of acorns can range from 1/4 to 2 in. in diameter, depending on the variety. Consider potential litter problems from the acorns when planting trees near driveways and sidewalks. If it becomes too much of a concern, you can always try your hand at acorn pancakes.

ADDITIONAL SPECIES, CULTIVARS, OR VARIETIES

Shumard oak is a better choice for a landscape tree in alkaline soils—unlike the popular pin oak. Pin oak (*Q. palustris*) is notorious for developing iron chlorosis in alkaline soils in central and western Oklahoma. Shumard is more tolerant of these conditions and heavy clay soils. Consider bur oak (*Q. macrocarpa*), English oak (*Q. robur*), sawtooth oak (*Q. acutissima*), chinkapin (*Q. muehlenbergii*), and northern red oak (*Q. rubra*). Oklahoma also has a native live oak (*Q. fusiformis*), found occasionally in the Quartz Mountains in southwestern counties of the state, which is more cold hardy and is an evergreen alternative for a specimen landscape tree.

 Did You Know?

Shumard is in the red oak group because of its pointed, needlelike leaf lobes. The white oak group has rounded lobes with no points.

Southern Magnolia

Magnolia grandiflora

Other Names: Evergreen Magnolia;
  Bull Bay
Height: 60 to 80 ft. (medium to large tree)
Spread: 30 to 50 ft.
Zones: 6b, 7a, 7b

Color photograph on page 226.

Light Requirements:

Beneficial Characteristics:

This Southern charmer is best known for its fragrant, showy flowers. Magnolias are native to the Southeast and Texas, but grow quite well in the eastern parts of Oklahoma. A few established trees are performing nicely in central portions of Oklahoma, so they will tolerate clay soils; cold hardiness is more of a concern in establishing these beauties in the landscape. The large leaves are an attractive component of this aristocratic tree, but also an occasional nuisance. The leaves may have a dark-cinnamon-brown or gray underside, depending on the cultivar, which makes for an interesting color combination.

WHEN TO PLANT
Plant them in early spring to establish magnolias before harsh winters.

WHERE TO PLANT
Plant these large trees in protected areas because cold winds can occasionally burn the foliage. Plant these trees as if they were full grown to give them plenty of room for the lower branches to develop and cascade down naturally. There is nothing worse than seeing branches pruned up the trunk on a magnolia tree. The best display of these unique trees is to allow the branches to grow naturally all the way to the ground. Magnolias prefer well-drained, acidic soils.

HOW TO PLANT
Choose a healthy container-grown or balled-and-burlapped tree. Plant it in a hole two to three times wider than and the same depth as the rootball. Amend the soil slightly with soil sulfur according to directions where acidic soils are not obtainable. Water to establish the tree and to offset drought stress. Organic mulches are necessities for these evergreen beauties.

CARE AND MAINTENANCE
Pruning is generally not necessary; however, tall, lanky trees may need to be tip pruned to encourage lower branching. Older leaves drop in the

spring and can be messy in certain landscape settings. Flowers occur in early summer, followed by red, showy fruit on conelike structures. Do not be alarmed if the leaves appear to wilt during the bloom time. It is Mother Nature's way of bowing to the elegant flowers to bring more attention to their beauty. There are essentially no serious pest problems, other than an occasional disease leaf spot.

ADDITIONAL INFORMATION

Supplemental applications of acid fertilizers can pay big dividends in foliage and flower set. Winter organic mulches provide slow-release nutrients. Another common practice is to apply Epsom salts at a rate of 1 lb. per 10-ft. width of branch spread to provide magnesium to the plant.

ADDITIONAL SPECIES, CULTIVARS, OR VARIETIES

Cold-hardy selections for Oklahoma include 'Bracken's Brown Beauty', 'Edith Bogue', 'D. D. Blanchard', and 'Glen St. Mary'. 'Little Gem' is also cold hardy and a compact tree selected especially for the small landscape. Deciduous magnolias are adapted to Oklahoma conditions. Saucer magnolia (*M. × soulangiana*) and other hybrids offer a wider range of flower colors from yellow to red. These beauties bloom before the leaves come out. Late frosts can damage the blooms, however. Another relative, *M. stellata* or star magnolia, is a small tree suitable for our landscapes. It is deciduous and with earlier blooms than saucer magnolia.

 Did You Know?

Magnolia flowers make great cut flowers for indoors and are also used in dried arrangements.

Sugar Maple

Acer saccharum

Other Names: Hard Maple; Rock Maple
Height: 60 to 80 ft. (medium to large tree)
Spread: 40 to 60 ft.
Zones: 6a, 6b, 7a, 7b

Color photograph on page 226.

Light Requirements:

Beneficial Characteristics:

As the name implies, sugar maple or hard maple is one of the strongest-wooded maples available. It is adapted to northern climates; however, some varieties tolerate Oklahoma heat. Gardeners visit the New England states in the fall, see the breathtaking colors of sugar maple, and want to duplicate them at home. I hate to break the bad news to you, but if you want that particular tree and color, you will have to move there instead of bringing the tree to Oklahoma. The true sugar maple is generally short-lived in our climate. Never fear, though, Oklahoma has a native sugar maple, 'Caddo', found in the southwestern part of the state. As you can imagine, it is drought and heat tolerant after it is established. The fall color is a vibrant orange red.

WHEN TO PLANT
Plant maples in fall or spring.

WHERE TO PLANT
'Caddo' sugar maple prefers well-drained, moderately moist soil. It requires somewhat better soil than other trees discussed in this chapter. Grow it in full sun for the best color, and allow plenty of space for it to reach its optimum size as a shade tree.

HOW TO PLANT
Dig a planting hole at least two to three times the width and the same depth as the rootball. Then the roots can grow horizontally for quicker establishment. Water deeply to settle the soil and thoroughly soak the roots. Mulch for moisture retention, weed control, and prevention of damage by weed trimmers or lawn mowers.

CARE AND MAINTENANCE
Pruning to encourage a well-trained tree is occasionally needed. Make small directional pruning cuts at any time throughout the year. Make larger cuts when the trees are dormant in December or January. Leave the existing

lower branches on the tree for the first couple of years to encourage a bigger, stronger trunk. Mulch and fertilize to push the growth since sugar maples are somewhat slow-growing trees. Leaf scorch from heat and wind is a typical problem with maples. Anthracnose fungal disease may affect the foliage in early spring. Repeated heavy infections may need preventative sprays early in the spring as leaf buds break dormancy. Damaged leaves will remain on the tree until fall drop unless they are severely infected. During dry summers, leaf drop as a result of drought may occur. The leaves on the interior of the tree canopy drop first. Mulch for moisture retention, cooler soil temperatures, and weed control. Water during drought conditions to prevent stress and premature leaf drop.

ADDITIONAL INFORMATION
Moisture, temperature, and short days determine fall color, which can vary from year to year with each tree. A cousin of the sugar maple is the silver maple, which is a fast-growing, weak-wooded tree typically with shallow roots. I am not a big fan of silver maple and can remember recommending it to someone only once—a woman in her nineties wanted a fast-growing shade tree. The seeds from silver maple are more apt to germinate in your flower bed than are those of sugar maple.

ADDITIONAL SPECIES, CULTIVARS, OR VARIETIES
'Commemoration', 'Legacy', 'Green Mountain', and 'Summer Proof' are other sugar maple cultivars considered more heat tolerant and resistant to wind tattering. Southeastern Oklahoma is home to a native southern sugar maple known as *A. barbatum*. It is a somewhat smaller tree with smaller leaves found growing near stream beds. It is hard to find in the trade and sometimes is thought to be a subspecies of northern sugar maple (*A. saccharum*). It is also sold as *A. floridanum*, or Florida maple.

 Did You Know?

Shantung, trident, tatarian, hedge, and amur maples are great choices for small- to medium-sized Oklahoma trees.

Woody Shrubs

IF TREES ARE THE PILLARS OF THE LANDSCAPE, then shrubs are the framework. Shrubs provide filler, height variation, texture, color, and just about any presentation needed for a personalized design. Like all plants, shrubs have their specific growing preferences of sun or shade and soil type. Shrubs are categorized primarily as woody plants, either evergreen or deciduous, ranging in height from inches to several feet. Some could even be considered small trees.

Home owners frequently make the mistake of improperly spacing shrubs. Plant shrubs as if they were fully grown. Give them plenty of room, especially when planting them near the foundation of your home. Allow widths of 5 to 8 ft. for a bed design. In a couple of years shrubs will fill in all the open space. Cluster shrubs in groups to make a bigger impact. Use shrubs to form curves and divide areas of the landscape.

Planting shrubs is a little different from planting trees since they are more likely to be planted together in landscape beds rather than as single specimens. Group like-growing plantings together, such as azaleas, loropetulam, and other acid-loving plants. If possible, prepare the bed before planting time by incorporating organic matter, complete fertilizers, and other amendments. Such preparation is especially important if lime, sulfur, potassium, or phosphorous is required; soil test results and the preferences of particular plants dictate this need. Mix the materials by tilling them into the soil. If the beds are in association with existing trees, skip the tilling process, or damage can occur to the shallow roots and shorten the lives of the trees. Never add more than 6 to 8 in. of soil on top of tree roots, or the planting depth will change and create future problems. Plant a single shrub the same way you plant a tree, without adding organic backfill. Refill with the original soil.

Chapter Two

Mulch landscape beds around shrubs. Mulch will occasionally wash, blow, and decay, so reapply it every two or three years. Grass allowed to grow around and in shrubs is a problem in the making. Routine spot applications of glyphosate or glyphosinate herbicides are well worth the investment to keep weeds out, especially pesky Bermuda. Supplemental feedings are beneficial. Simply broadcast fertilizers on the surface of the ground around the shrubs according to product directions. Split the application in early spring and summer. Fall applications can potentially stimulate new growth that is more susceptible to freezing conditions.

Shrubs frequently need pruning and training to keep from overpowering other plants in the landscape. As a general rule, flowering shrubs should be pruned as soon as they have finished flowering. Small tip prunings can be done at any time throughout the growing season.

Frequently scout for pests to shortcut epidemics. Shrubs such as arborvitae and Japanese euonymus are magnets for bugs, no matter what conditions are provided. Avoid these plants unless you have time to pamper them.

I have included twenty-five selections of shrubs in this chapter and their latest cultivars that are generally considered low maintenance in the appropriate planting sites. There is something for sun or shade or just about any landscape situation.

Abelia

Abelia grandiflora

Other Name: Glossy Abelia
Height: Up to 6 ft.
Spread: Almost as wide as tall
Flowers: Showy white or pink,
   tubular flowers
Bloom Period: Summer, primarily
   May and June
Zones: 6a, 6b, 7a, 7b

Color photograph on page 226.

Light Requirements:

Beneficial Characteristics:

Abelia can offer texture, size, and color to a landscape—all with minimal care. I have included a dwarf abelia in my garden as a specimen plant because of its mounding form. It fills a corner as a background plant with lovely cascading texture and provides delightful flowers in late summer. The only attention it requires is an occasional pruning of shoots emerging from the crown. The plant is about 3 ft. tall and nearly 6 ft. wide. I have seen the taller, upright form used as a hedge. The flowers are the most prominent during early summer; however, sporadic blooms continue until frost. The charming bell-shaped blossoms are white, pink, or lavender, depending on the cultivar.

WHEN TO PLANT

Plant abelia in the spring in western Oklahoma; plant it in spring or fall in eastern parts of the state.

WHERE TO PLANT

Use abelia as a background or specimen plant. Plant it on slopes or as a hedge. Abelia prefers rich, moist, well-drained, slightly acidic soil. Although it is hardy for most of the state, abelia is probably better suited for central and eastern Oklahoma.

HOW TO PLANT

Abelia is most readily available as a container plant. Plant it in a hole two to three times wider than and the same depth as the rootball. Water and mulch as needed. No amended backfill is necessary in a single planting hole unless materials are incorporated into the complete bed ahead of time.

CARE AND MAINTENANCE

Abelia readily responds to supplemental fertilization, but too much can cause an overabundance of growth with minimal flowering. Flowers occur on new growth of the season, so prune for shape in the fall. Occasional pruning of suckers or shoots can be done at any time throughout the growing season. There seem to be no serious pests; however, powdery mildew can occur in too much shade.

ADDITIONAL INFORMATION
Occasionally in dwarf cultivars, woody shoots appear above the more typical mounding growth. Avoid overfertilization, and prune shoots back to the base of the plant. The flowers are showy and somewhat scattered, nothing like a forsythia display, but still a nice attribute—and hummingbirds love them. In southeastern Oklahoma, abelia is often evergreen, and farther north it is semievergreen.

ADDITIONAL SPECIES, CULTIVARS, OR VARIETIES
The standard white-flowering glossy abelia easily grows to 6 ft. 'Compacta' and 'Sherwoodii' are dwarf-mounding cultivars, maturing to nearly 3 ft. Selections of variegated foliage types include 'Frances Mason' and 'Sunrise'. Hybrid crosses are also available with more choices in flower color. 'Edward Goucher' is 3 to 5 ft. in height with pink flowers. 'Purple Rain' is dwarf with a pale-purple flower.

Did You Know?

Another relative is Chinese abelia (A. chinensis*), which blooms more in the fall with fragrant flowers and is not quite as cold hardy—only through Zone 7.*

Azalea

Rhododendron hybrids

Other Name: Rhododendron
Height: Up to 8 ft.
Spread: 3 to 6 ft.
Flowers: Many colors and sizes available, typically pink, red, white, and yellow
Bloom Period: April, early May
Zones: 6a, 6b, 7a, 7b

Color photograph on page 226.

Light Requirements:

Beneficial Characteristics:

A zaleas are plants that just scream color for a couple of weeks in the spring, thus enticing gardeners to want several in their landscape. Unfortunately, the Oklahoma climate is not always kind to these spring beauties. I have often proclaimed in garden lectures that the most popular plants, such as roses, azaleas, and fruit trees, are also the most challenging to grow. Azaleas are very specific in their soil requirements. To make things more overwhelming, there are close to one thousand species of rhododendrons and many more cultivars. Azaleas are generally categorized as having smaller, evergreen or deciduous leaves, and rhododendrons have large, evergreen leaves. Both are rhododendrons. Cold-hardy selections need to be considered for northern and western areas of the state.

WHEN TO PLANT
Spring planting of rhododendrons is preferred, although fall planting is feasible in the milder portions of the state.

WHERE TO PLANT
Azaleas make great foundation or understory plants in sites where they can receive filtered afternoon shade. Full shade thins the plants, and hot, direct sun can scorch them. Rhododendrons of all types are suited for the eastern and southeastern counties; however, I have seen successful plantings farther west if specific soil and fertilization guidelines are implemented.

HOW TO PLANT
Acidic soil is a must! Design azalea planting beds slightly above soil grade for better drainage and for easier bed preparation. Use soil amendments such as soil sulfur and peat moss, pecan hulls, coconut coir, or other acid-based organic products. Follow directions on the bag for sulfur rates. Mix organic materials into the existing soil for close to a fifty-fifty mixture, 12 to 24 in. deep. When planting under trees, do not till organic mixes into the

existing soil, and apply only 6 to 8 in. deep. Mulch azaleas with
pine bark, pecan hulls, pine needles, or other acidic mulches.

CARE AND MAINTENANCE

A common sight on azaleas is yellow foliage with green veins
known as iron chlorosis, caused by high pH or alkaline soils. The
preferred pH for azaleas is 4.5 to 5.5. Routine feedings after bloom
should include iron, sulfur, and other acid-changing nutrients.
Stop fertilizing in June to avoid late-growth spurts susceptible to
freeze. Lacebugs generally attack weak plants by sucking plant
juices from the underside of the foliage. Severe infestations cause
a speckled or mottled appearance on the foliage. When left
untreated, these critters can stunt and potentially kill the plants.
Disease problems are occasional leaf spots and galls. A grayish-
green, almost rubberlike fungal gall is formed on the new leaves
during wet, mild spring conditions. Controls may be needed
under severe cases, but generally the galls can be picked before
they turn white and discarded off the property. Prune azaleas as
soon as they finish blooming. Buds for next season's bloom are
typically in place by late summer.

ADDITIONAL INFORMATION

If these soil preparation requirements seem like too much effort,
consider weigela, flowering quince, and spirea as alternatives.
These colorful beauties are less picky about soil conditions.

ADDITIONAL SPECIES, CULTIVARS, OR VARIETIES

Azalea selections and hybrids are often categorized in groups
with several cultivars within the category. Kurume azaleas (*Rhododendron obtusun*) and *Gable* hybrids are semidwarf and often
touted as the most cold-hardy. *Glenn Dale* hybrids are a semidwarf
with good hardiness and considerably larger flowers. Taller
selections, reaching 6 to 8 ft., are generally found in the *Northern
Lights* hybrid group. *Girard* hybrids are adapted to most of the
state. Southern indicas are best for the southeastern counties, and
Belgian types are the most dwarf. Satsuki azaleas are small in
size and bloom later, extending the season. Underused azaleas
include deciduous or Exbury types. They come in many colors,
even yellow, which is hard to find in the evergreen groups.

 Did You Know?

*Loropetalum (fringe flower) and Epimedium (barrenwort) are
great companion plants for rhododendrons.*

Burning Bush

Euonymus alatus

Other Name: Winged Euonymus
Height: 5 to 20 ft.
Spread: 5 to 10 ft.
Flowers: Not showy
Bloom Period: May or early June
Zones: 6a, 6b, 7a, 7b

Color photograph on page 226.

Light Requirements:

Beneficial Characteristics:

I am not a big fan of euonymus because of past experiences with euonymus scale. Burning bush is definitely the exception to the rule. Not only does this deciduous plant offer unique foliage that turns a glowing-red fall color, but it has interesting winged, corky twigs just as appealing later in the winter. On mature plants you will find capsulelike red berries in the fall. Euonymus scale does not seem to be too interested in this particular species. Burning bush lives up to its name in late fall with red foliage unmatched by any landscape plant.

WHEN TO PLANT

Burning bush is a tough plant adaptable to spring or fall planting.

WHERE TO PLANT

Use *Euonymus alatus* for a hedge or as a single specimen. I have seen it successfully used as a background landscape plant and as a foundation plant in conjunction with two-story homes. The flaming-red fall color complements evergreen companion plants. The greenish-gray, dormant twigs have an evergreen appearance. Consider planting it in deciduous perennial beds. Burning bush will tolerate just about any soil type as long as it is not waterlogged.

HOW TO PLANT

Burning bush is commonly sold as a container-grown or balled-and-burlapped plant. Dig the hole at least two times wider than and the same depth as the rootball. Refill the hole with the original soil, but do not compact the soil during planting. Mulching is very beneficial when growing this plant. Water to settle the soil and as needed.

CARE AND MAINTENANCE

Burning bush develops a shallow, fibrous root system similar to that of azaleas. Mulch as often as the organic products decompose or wash away.

Allowing the roots to be exposed to heat and cold adds stress that makes the plants more susceptible to pests. Water during drought conditions. The plants are considered slow growing, but the species plant can reach 20 ft. tall under optimum growing conditions in fifteen to twenty years. They respond to pruning to keep the height more manageable as a hedge. Pruning can be done anytime as needed. Pest problems are minimal, other than an occasional leaf spot and sunburn on foliage in full sun during a drought.

ADDITIONAL INFORMATION

The initial growth habit of burning bush is upright with a flat top, which again is especially nice for hedges or background borders. The plants lose their colorful leaves in the late fall, but with their thick, greenish-brown branches they have an ever-green look in the winter. The growth becomes spreading as the plants mature. The twiggy growth attracts nesting birds.

ADDITIONAL SPECIES, CULTIVARS, OR VARIETIES

Dwarf cultivars are often requested but hard to find. 'October Glory' matures at 6 to 8 ft., making it somewhat more compact than the species. 'Compactus' and 'Rudy Haag' are the most compact cultivars available. Both are more mounding in growth, reaching 4 to 5 ft. in height. The wings and corky twigs are not as prominent, but the color is a vibrant pinkish red.

 Did You Know?

A tree form relative is Euonymus bungeanea *(winterberry euonymus). This small tree has minimal pest problems, the same nice fall color, and showier, more colorful fruit in the fall, shaped like a bishop's hat.*

Butterfly Bush

Buddleia davidii

Other Name: Summer Lilac
Height: 5 to 15 ft.
Spread: 5 to 10 ft.
Flowers: Showy color variations of white, pink, purple, and yellow
Bloom Period: June through frost
Zones: 6a, 6b, 7a, 7b

Color photograph on page 226.

Light Requirements:

Beneficial Characteristics:

Since the stems are not as woody on this plant, it is sometimes categorized as a perennial instead of a shrub. In the colder areas of the state butterfly bush can freeze to the ground, but it comes back from the roots. Whether you call it a shrub or a perennial, you should include it in your landscape. Although it needs plenty of room, it will reward you with fragrant flowers all summer. It is a favorite of butterflies, thus the name butterfly bush. Due to its long blooming period late in the summer, it has also had the name summer lilac bestowed upon it.

WHEN TO PLANT
Plant butterfly bush in spring.

WHERE TO PLANT
Butterfly bush thrives in fertile, well-drained soil. Even in years that it dies back to the ground, it does not take long for new growth to explode into a ball of color. Most cultivars grow in an arching form, which adds texture to the landscape. It is often used as a specimen in the back of perennial or shrub beds; however, designs implementing groups of butterfly bush offer a more colorful display. Avoid placing butterfly bush too close to sidewalks or front doors because it can attract bees.

HOW TO PLANT
These are typically container-grown plants. Dig planting holes at least 2 ft. wider than and the same depth as the rootballs. No soil amendments are needed in a single hole; however, preparing a complete bed with organic materials before planting time is recommended. Water deeply to soak the roots and settle the soil. Mulch to hold soil moisture and keep weeds in check.

CARE AND MAINTENANCE

Flowers are borne on current-season growth, starting in early summer and continuing through frost. There are occasional lulls between flower spurts. Deadheading "spent" or old flowers encourages quicker flower rejuvenation. The foliage is typically a gray or blue-green color. Spider mites are the biggest nuisance for butterfly bush, especially in areas with poor aeration. Watch for yellowing or speckling of the foliage. Spider mites typically suck the plant juices from the undersides of the foliage, which causes this mottling appearance on the tops of the foliage. Tap the foliage on a white sheet of paper; if any of the specks start crawling, the plants have been invaded by these aggressive critters.

ADDITIONAL INFORMATION

Butterfly bush can be severely pruned during the summer in years when the foliage looks ragged from stress or spider mites. Regrowth occurs quickly and will produce a flush of flowers later in the season.

ADDITIONAL SPECIES, CULTIVARS, OR VARIETIES

Most of the *B. davidii* selections reach 6 to 10 ft. in a season. For smaller landscapes consider the *B. nanhoensis* Nanho or Petit Series for a more compact growth. Just about any color is available in either case. For a most unusual-shaped flower, look for *B. globosa* (orange butterfly bush). This shrub produces rounded flowers from previous-season growth. Unfortunately, it is not very cold hardy. It is better suited for the southernmost counties in the state. Others have successfully grown this interesting beauty as an annual for the unusual flower display.

 Did You Know?

Butterfly bush makes a good cut flower. The flowers do not last very long, but the elongated shape adds texture to most flower arrangements.

Chaste Tree

Vitex agnus-castus

Other Names: Lilac Chaste Tree; Sage Tree; Hemp Tree; Indian Spice
Height: 12 to 20 ft.
Spread: 10 to 20 ft.
Flowers: Lavender, pink, or white
Bloom Period: Summer through fall
Zones: 6a, 6b, 7a, 7b

Color photograph on page 226.

Light Requirements:

Beneficial Characteristics:

Chaste tree is a shrub that can become quite tall, forming what is often thought of as a small tree. I have included it as a shrub because of its multiple trunk appearance and overall smaller, woody growth. It can occasionally be nipped back by a severe winter but grows back readily, like many perennial plants. Both flowers and foliage are unique on this species. The somewhat fragrant flowers emerge on the ends of current-season growth and are very showy. The species plant has flower color almost more blue than lavender. The foliage is often compared to an illegal crop in Oklahoma (cannabis) with five to seven palmately arranged leaflets. Chaste tree leaves are typically a dull gray green with a slightly pungent aroma when bruised.

WHEN TO PLANT

Plant chaste tree in the spring in northern and western Oklahoma. Plant it in spring or fall in the milder locations of the state.

WHERE TO PLANT

Chaste tree requires plenty of room and is often found in lawns as a specimen plant. Although it tolerates poor soils, it performs better in well-drained, fertile soils. The unique arrangement and shape of the foliage make it a great choice for offering texture features to the landscape.

HOW TO PLANT

It is sold as a container-grown or balled-and-burlapped plant. Plant it similarly to a tree in a hole two to three times wider than and the same depth as the rootball. No organic backfill is required. Water deeply to settle the soil, soak the roots, and water as needed, especially during a drought, while establishing the plants. Mulch to keep grass and weeds from competing during the establishment period.

CARE AND MAINTENANCE

Other than occasional winter injury to branches, very few pest problems have been reported. Spider mites are a potential pest in stressed situations. The attractive blooms are formed on the current season's growth, so any severe pruning should be done while the plant is dormant. Flowers can be trimmed after the initial bloom to encourage more blossoms in the fall. I like to remove the lower branches on multiple trunk specimens to better expose the elegant base. Chaste tree responds well to fertilizer during the growing season. Mulch it as needed.

ADDITIONAL INFORMATION

Chaste tree was once a widely popular plant and is often found near older home sites. It is not nearly as common today but should be used more because of its tolerance of drought and poor soils after it is established. It is a good alternative for gardeners who have not had success with growing lilac. "Old-timers" frequently refer to *Vitex* as lilac chaste tree. The growth habit is somewhat similar, but the well-known, fragrant lilac flower is missing.

ADDITIONAL SPECIES, CULTIVARS, OR VARIETIES

'Silver Spire' and 'Alba' are cultivars with white flowers. 'Rosea' has pink blooms. *V. latifolia* is sometimes found in the trade as a more cold-hardy variety with more oblong leaves. *V. negundo* is a larger selection of chaste tree but with more pronounced, serrated leaf margins.

 Did You Know?

In Brazil the flowers are used to make perfume, and foods are seasoned with the aromatic leaves. The seed is even thought to have calming qualities.

Crapemyrtle

Lagerstromia indica

Other Name: Crepemyrtle
Height: 18 in. to 25 ft.
Spread: 2 to 20 ft.
Flowers: Red, pink, purple, and white
Bloom Period: Summer to frost
Zones: 6a, 6b, 7a, 7b

Color photograph on page 226.

Light Requirements:

Beneficial Characteristics:

This delightfully engaging shrub gets my vote for the "Summer Flowering Queen" of the state. Crapemyrtle is easy to grow and provides us with breathtaking color all summer and fall. To top it off, it is one of the many deciduous shrubs with an added bonus of dazzling golden-rose leaf color in the fall. Crapemyrtle offers quite an array of various shapes in the landscape, depending on the cultivar. Some grow into small trees; others are more upright. Several are considered dwarf, ranging in height from 3 to 6 ft. The true dwarf types are the weeping or cascading Dixie and Pixie Series, maturing at 15 to 24 in. If that is not enough to encourage you to use crapemyrtle in your landscape, there is added character from the unique exfoliating bark as the plants mature.

WHEN TO PLANT
Plant crapemyrtle in spring in colder locations of the state. Plant it in spring or early fall in the southeastern regions.

WHERE TO PLANT
Most often crapemyrtle is found as a specimen plant in lawns or landscapes. Potential mature height dictates its location in these areas. Usually, taller plants are placed in the back or off center. Crapemyrtles also work well as a screen or a hedge, especially in the summer months. Space them properly to avoid crowding. Plant them in groups of three when using the miniature selections for a bigger show of flower color. They prefer moist and well-drained soil.

HOW TO PLANT
Dig the planting hole at least 2 ft. wider than and the same depth as the rootball. No organic amendments are needed as backfill. Deeply water to settle the soil and adequately soak the roots. Mulching on a regular, as-needed basis is rewarded with brilliant summer flower color.

CARE AND MAINTENANCE

Crapemyrtles are likely to succumb to powdery mildew on the foliage in shaded locations. Good air circulation is essential between adjoining plants. Powdery mildew is less prone to occur in Oklahoma than in even more humid locations. Selecting mildew-resistant cultivars is always a good idea, however. Aphids are a potential insect pest on stressed plants. Large populations of aphids will secrete honeydew on the foliage, forming a secondary grayish-black mold. The mold is not harmful, but the large numbers of aphids need to be controlled. Prune during the winter or early spring. Flowers are set on current-season growth. Sometimes Mother Nature does the pruning for us with a sudden drop in winter temperatures. The plants almost always grow back from the crown in a bushy appearance. Some home owners prefer to prune the plants back each year to 6 to 8 in. from the ground to always encourage a bushy appearance. Single- or multiple-trunk tree specimens are best achieved in milder locations of the state. Fertilize crapemyrtles early in the season to stimulate growth. Avoid feeding them after July so that the plants will be more winter hardy.

ADDITIONAL INFORMATION

Crapemyrtles are one of the latest shrubs to break dormancy in the spring, sometimes in May. Do not give up on the plants after a freeze. Wait to see where the growth emerges before pruning. Trimming spent flowers before they set fruit will promote a longer bloom period.

ADDITIONAL SPECIES, CULTIVARS, OR VARIETIES

There are definitely too many cultivars of crapemyrtle to list. Choose varieties based on color, disease resistance, and height for your location.

 Did You Know?

The usually harmless grayish-black mold occasionally found on crapemyrtles is called "sooty mold." It grows on the sap secreted by the aphid.

 WOODY SHRUBS

Dwarf Fothergilla

Fothergilla gardenii

Height: 2 to 6 ft.
Spread: 3 to 5 ft.
Flowers: White and fragrant
Bloom Period: Spring (April or May)
Zones: 6a, 6b, 7a, 7b

Color photograph on page 226.

Light Requirements:

Beneficial Characteristics:

If you are looking for a companion plant for azaleas with brilliant fall leaf color, then look no more. Fothergilla is not a well-known plant in Oklahoma, but should definitely be used more often, especially in the eastern and southeastern parts of the state. The foliage and flowers add uniqueness to any shade garden. The foliage has a soothing blue tint and the white, bottlebrushlike flower invigorates the air with a sweet fragrance. The foliage and flower color combinations of fothergilla added to the assorted colors of azaleas are a goofproof landscape match. These plants thrive in appropriate planting locations with adequate soil preparation.

WHEN TO PLANT
Plant fothergilla in spring or fall.

WHERE TO PLANT
Fothergilla works well as a foundation plant or background plant in shade gardens. The plant's distinctiveness also affords it the opportunity to move front and center as a feature plant. It must be planted in filtered or afternoon shade, for example, under a shade tree or on the east-northeast side of a structure. When used as a companion plant for azaleas, loropetalum, and epimedium, fothergilla must be in moist, but well-drained, acidic soil.

HOW TO PLANT
Before planting time, work peat moss or other organic material into the soil. Then dig the hole at least two times wider than the rootball and slightly above soil grade for each individual plant. Constructing the entire bed for acid-loving plants slightly above soil grade also allows for better drainage. Mulching with acidic materials is recommended.

CARE AND MAINTENANCE
These eye-catching plants are often touted as trouble free—but only after the right environmental conditions have been met. Prune after flowering

since blooms are formed on the previous season's growth. Minimal fertilization is needed. Any applications should be done soon after flowering with an acid-formulated product including iron and sulfur.

ADDITIONAL INFORMATION

In soils that are too basic or alkaline, iron chlorosis of the foliage can occur. Iron chlorosis is an overall yellowing of the leaf with green veins. Soil sulfur should be applied according to directions for a long-term fix. Foliar applications of iron chelates will correct the problem for the short term. Routinely apply acid fertilizers as needed.

ADDITIONAL SPECIES, CULTIVARS, OR VARIETIES

'Mt. Airy' and 'Blue Mist' are the two most common dwarf cultivars sold in our state. *F. major* (large fothergilla) is a taller species, reaching 10 to 15 ft. tall in optimum sites.

WOODY SHRUBS

Did You Know?

The brilliant fall leaf color for which this plant is known occurs in late November, extending the fall foliage season.

English Boxwood

Buxus sempervirens

Other Name: Common Boxwood
Height: 2 to 15 ft.
Spread: 3 to 6 ft.
Flowers: Not showy and somewhat fragrant
Bloom Period: Early spring
Zones: 6a, 6b, 7a, 7b

Color photograph on page 226.

Light Requirements:

Beneficial Characteristics:

I recommend English boxwood over Japanese or littleleaf boxwood. I cannot count the number of foliage disease problems I have encountered on consulting jobs with *Buxus microphylla* (Japanese or littleleaf boxwood). These experiences have been enough to discourage me from recommending it. English boxwood, on the other hand, seems more resistant to blights and leaf spots. These evergreen plants with their perfect, deep-green color help any landscape make it through the most drab winter. The compact, tight growth is perfect for shearing and is best used as a foundation plant. There is an assortment of sizes, depending on the cultivar. English boxwood is a basic, green foundation plant with minimal problems.

WHEN TO PLANT

Plant English boxwood in the spring or early fall. It is available as a container-grown or balled-and-burlapped plant.

WHERE TO PLANT

Use English boxwood as a foundation shrub, a companion to neighboring deciduous plants, a hedge for screening purposes, or topiary plants in formal gardens. I have occasionally seen plants in full sun but with protection from harsh summer winds. Afternoon shade is definitely the preferred site in Oklahoma's hot summers. English boxwood likes a good soil with some moisture retention and good drainage. Slightly acidic soil is an added bonus. Heavy, waterlogged soils will shorten the lives of these shrubs.

HOW TO PLANT

These plants are somewhat shallow rooted. Dig the holes wider than and at the same depth as the initial rootballs. Mulching and supplemental watering are necessities, especially during hot, dry conditions.

CARE AND MAINTENANCE

English boxwood responds well to shearing. The plants are considerably slow growing but have the potential to become quite large in optimum conditions over time. Supplemental fertilizers speed up the growth somewhat, but the shallow roots are easy to burn with frequent and high-nitrogen applications, especially during drought conditions. Do not apply fertilizer after June or plants will become more susceptible to winter injury. Mulch them to keep the roots cool and moist on an as-needed basis.

ADDITIONAL INFORMATION

During the harshest winters, the lustrous, green foliage may turn a brownish tint. Even though English boxwood is evergreen, do not be alarmed to see the plants shed older foliage at certain times throughout the year. Male dogs consistently visiting the plants have been known to burn the foliage. The flowers are imperfect and inconspicuous. Both male and female are on the same plant. The female flowers occasionally set a green, capsule-like fruit.

ADDITIONAL SPECIES, CULTIVARS, OR VARIETIES

There are several cultivars of English boxwood. Probably the most dwarf and rounded selection is 'Suffruticosa'.

 Did You Know?

The individual leaves of English boxwood are typically pointed whereas the leaves of Japanese boxwood are more rounded with an indention at the tip.

Flowering Quince

Chaenomeles speciosa

Height: 4 to 10 ft.
Spread: 4 to 6 ft.
Flowers: Pink, red, salmon, or white
Bloom Period: Early spring (April)
Zones: 6a, 6b, 7a, 7b

Color photograph on page 227.

Light Requirements:

Beneficial Characteristics:

This deciduous shrub has much to offer at times when there is little going on in the landscape. It is one of the earliest to flower from the previous season's growth in the spring. The flowers are quite showy and appear generally before the leaves emerge. As the leaves unfurl, there is a hint of burgundy color before turning a glossy green. Do not be surprised to see large, pearlike fruit develop. The shrubs are likely to attempt to flower again later in the season. Flowering quince has made a name for itself in landscaping by discouraging prowlers near homes, thanks to the spines on the stems. Flowering quince is a perfect no-fuss plant often used as a substitute for the picky rhododendron. Both bloom in early spring.

WHEN TO PLANT

Plant flowering quince in spring or fall.

WHERE TO PLANT

Flowering quince prefers full-sun sites with good air circulation, but it accepts some morning-shade locations. This tough plant is not nearly as picky as azaleas about soil preference. Flowering quince tolerates almost any soil site as long as it drains well. Groupings of these plants offer the best color display. They are often used as back border plants in conjunction with evergreens.

HOW TO PLANT

Dig the planting hole at least two times wider than and at the same depth as the rootball. Water to settle the soil and soak the root system. Mulch with pine bark, cottonseed hulls, compost, or any type of water-holding organic material.

CARE AND MAINTENANCE

Potential pests include scale, aphids, and spider mites. These critters can attack almost any plant in stressed situations. Late freezes can damage flower buds in some years. Prune the plants after flowering, just as you would azaleas. Flowering quince is considered a tough plant when it comes to drought tolerance and overall care. It responds to minimal feedings but requires no special formulations. As mulch decomposes or blows away, reapply it as needed.

ADDITIONAL INFORMATION

Branches can be cut a few weeks earlier in February and forced indoors. The blooms inside and out are fairly short-lived but quite colorful.

ADDITIONAL SPECIES, CULTIVARS, OR VARIETIES

There are several cultivars from which to choose, based on height and color. Some cultivars offer a double flower.

  Did You Know?

Although the fruit is bitter when eaten raw, it makes a great jelly or preserve when cooked.

Heavenly Bamboo

Nandina domestica

Other Name: Nandina
Height: 2 to 10 ft.
Spread: 2 to 6 ft.
Flowers: Formed in white clusters
Bloom Period: May or June
Zones: 6a, 6b, 7a, 7b

Color photograph on page 227.

Light Requirements:

Beneficial Characteristics:

Nandina is without a doubt one of my favorite landscape plants. It is kind of like the famous pink bunny of the battery advertisements—it keeps going and going, no matter what the environment. Nandina provides gardeners with attractive foliage, flowers, and fruit. The enormous, compound, semievergreen leaves are almost feathery in appearance. Depending on the selection and cultivar, the foliage changes color as it grows throughout the year. The flowers are fairly showy, but in my opinion they are just the tip of the iceberg before the real show of bright-red fruit emerges in the late summer and fall.

WHEN TO PLANT
Plant nandina in the spring or early fall.

WHERE TO PLANT
Use nandina as a background border plant, a hedge, or a foundation plant near buildings. It can be a single specimen plant that can be placed just about anywhere, depending on the size of the cultivar. Compact varieties definitely make a better show as groups than as singles. They tolerate rocky sites, heavy clay, sand, and most soil conditions as long as they do not stand in water.

HOW TO PLANT
Most nursery plants are containerized and should be planted in holes the same depth as but two to three times wider than the rootballs. Water deeply to thoroughly soak the roots on a regular basis until the plants are well established.

CARE AND MAINTENANCE
Do not overfertilize, or too much foliage and little berry set will be encouraged. The most frustrating trait of the species or standard nandina is the tendency to grow tall and get woody at the base. When that happens, prune the top back each spring to force additional growth from the base. Selected,

older woody stems can be completely removed to thin plants and encourage more growth. Other than occasional foliage diseases in heavily shaded sites with poor air circulation, pest problems are very rare.

ADDITIONAL INFORMATION

Nandina almost has an exotic look, thus the name bamboo. In some selections the attractive foliage turns a purplish-maroon color in the fall. The foliage will remain evergreen in milder winters but can also defoliate in severe cold spells. The berries, although showy, are not favored by birds. They are generally too big for most birds to eat; however, I have seen blue jays and mockingbirds try them. Birds enjoy the bushy stems for nest building.

ADDITIONAL SPECIES, CULTIVARS, OR VARIETIES

The old-time favorite plant is often sold as species or standard nandina. There are now more than twenty cultivars now on the market, and some are easier to find than others. 'Royal Princess' grows about 5 ft. tall but has a spreading growth habit to a width of nearly 6 ft. 'Atropurpurea Nana' is a dwarf selection with consistent yellow-green and reddish-purple, twisted foliage. Many horticulturists sense this appearance is a result of a virus. 'Fire Power', another dwarf selection with the same brilliant color, has somewhat smoother foliage, which is thought to be virus free. My favorite dwarf selection, 'Harbour Dwarf', looks more like the traditional species foliage with berry set but is only 2 to 3 ft. tall and performs best in afternoon shade. 'Gulf Stream' and 'Moon Bay' are great selections that are very similar with compact foliage. 'San Gabriel' is a dwarf selection with thin, almost feathery foliage, but it is not as cold hardy and is better used in protected areas. The new kid on the block is 'Plum Passion'. This eye-catching cultivar has foliage that emerges as a purplish color throughout the growing season.

 Did You Know?

There is a yellow-fruited selection like the standard type with showy, yellow berries. It is more difficult to find in the trade but well worth the search.

Japanese Kerria

Kerria japonica

Other Name: Japanese Rose
Height: 3 to 6 ft.
Spread: 6 to 9 ft.
Flowers: Bright yellow
Bloom Period: Spring, early summer
Zones: 6a, 6b, 7a, 7b

Color photograph on page 227.

Light Requirements:

Beneficial Characteristics:

Shade gardeners, rejoice! Kerria is a great flowering shrub for such sites. The yellow flowers brighten up shady locations for several weeks in the early spring. The upright-growing, deciduous shrub loses its foliage in the winter, but the remaining plant has an evergreen appearance, thanks to the green stems. The leaves are simple with serrated margins and provide a unique textured feature to the landscape. I have used kerria in several of my landscapes through the years. The plants were perfect background plants in perennial shade gardens, especially in locations with adequate soil moisture. The showy flowers are a real treat when used in color combinations of purple, yellow, and white.

WHEN TO PLANT

Plant kerria in spring, early summer, or early fall.

WHERE TO PLANT

This plant likes shady sites—afternoon shade or dappled shade—with humus-rich, moist soil. Deep, heavy shade with poor air circulation can promote foliar diseases. Because of its loosely upright and arching growth, use this plant for background borders. The plant has a tendency to spread with age (not aggressively). Plant it in masses.

HOW TO PLANT

Kerria is usually available as a container-grown plant and occasionally found as a balled-and-burlapped plant. Dig a hole at least two times wider than and the same depth as the rootball. There is no need for soil amendments in the hole unless the entire bed was prepared before planting time. Water at planting and as needed to establish plants. Mulching is a beneficial practice with this shade-loving plant to hold in soil moisture. After they are established, the plants are somewhat drought tolerant, but supplemental watering may prevent leaf scorch.

CARE AND MAINTENANCE

Flowers originate from the previous year's growth, so prune them after flowering. The foliage has a tendency to scorch and the flowers fade prematurely when planted in full sun in Oklahoma. Minimal fertility is required, or the shallow-rooted plants will burn. Overfertilizing encourages weedy stem growth and less flowering. Occasional leaf blights and spots are possible but not severely enough to discourage more use of this unusual plant.

ADDITIONAL INFORMATION

The narrow, elongated leaves are loosely arranged on the attractive stems, making for a great texture plant. Sparse flowering can occur later in the season.

ADDITIONAL SPECIES, CULTIVARS, OR VARIETIES

In addition to the bright-yellow flowers there are cultivars with variegated or chartreuse foliage. One of the most interesting cultivars is 'Pleniflora', with double, golden-yellow flowers. 'Albaflora' is a new white flowering cultivar.

 Did You Know?

Kerria is a native of China and was introduced to the United States in the 1830s.

Loropetalum

Loropetalum chinensis

Other Name: Fringe Flower
Height: 4 to 10 ft.
Spread: 3 to 6 ft.
Flowers: Pink
Bloom Period: Early spring
Zones: 7a, 7b

Color photograph on page 227.

Light Requirements:

Beneficial Characteristics:

Fringe flower, or loropetalum, is another great choice for acidic shade gardens. This evergreen plant is gaining in popularity in the landscape trade. Because it is not very cold hardy, it does better in southeastern portions of the state. The more northern counties should plant fringe flower in areas protected from cold winter winds. The weeping growth habit and the burgundy foliage of loropetalum are very appealing. The glowing, deep-burgundy leaves usually catch gardeners' attention first. In warmer climates the foliage is evergreen. In my landscape the leaves are semievergreen; if the winter is really cold, the foliage can drop. As the new growth emerges in the spring, it is almost purple, changing to a reddish purple and remaining this glorious color throughout the season. The flowers—except for the pink color—remind me of a witch hazel flower. The frilly flowers are often described as fringe shaped, thus the name fringe flower.

WHEN TO PLANT
Plant fringe flower in early to late spring.

WHERE TO PLANT
This plant prefers afternoon shade or dappled shade. Soils must be acidic with a pH of 5.5 to 6.5. I have seen some plants tolerating afternoon sun in well-prepared, acidic, moisture-retentive soils. Location of the plants should be determined by the cultivar size. Some may become quite large and could easily hide smaller plants. Fringe flower is impressive when planted in groups but also works well as a single planting.

HOW TO PLANT
Till peat moss (or other acidic organic materials) and soil sulfur into the landscape bed before planting time. Do not damage existing tree roots nearby. Dig the hole at least two times wider than and the same depth as the rootball. If good drainage is not available, place the rootball slightly

above soil grade. Mulching with pecan hulls, pine straw, or pine bark is imperative with acidic-loving plants to protect the shallow roots.

CARE AND MAINTENANCE

Supplemental watering is needed during drought periods, but pay attention to good drainage. The fragrant flowers are produced on the previous season's growth, so prune the plant after flowering if needed. The flowers last two to three weeks if a late frost does not get them first. Mulch every couple of years to replace wind-blown, washed, or decomposed mulch. Side-dress after flowering with acid-formulated fertilizers that contain sulfur and iron. Pest problems are minimal.

ADDITIONAL INFORMATION

Planting fringe flower in Zone 6 is not advised because it is more likely to receive winter injury. This beautiful plant may be worth the gamble, however. Besides, that is what gardening is all about—trying new things!

ADDITIONAL SPECIES, CULTIVARS, OR VARIETIES

'Rubrum', sometimes sold as 'Roseum', is probably the original selection that can easily reach 10 ft. under optimum growing conditions. 'Zhuzhou' is a tall, more upright-growing variety often trained as a multitrunk small tree in warmer regions of the country. 'Blush' is a new cultivar that matures at 6 ft. with initial rose-colored leaves turning olive green. 'Burgundy' can reach 6 to 8 ft. with new red leaves turning a yellow green and with repeat blooms. A more compact, rounded-growing cultivar is 'Ruby'. 'Monraz Razzleberri'™ and 'Pizzaz'™ are the more compact, weeping cultivars available to date.

 Did You Know?

Fringe flower, fothergilla, and perennial Epimedium *are great companion plants for azalea beds.*

Korean Lilac

Syringa meyeri

Other Name: Meyer's Lilac
Height: 4 to 8 ft.
Spread: 4 to 7 ft.
Flowers: Predominantly lavender, also pinkish red
Bloom Period: Late April, May
Zones: 6a, 6b, 7a, 7b

Color photograph on page 227.

Light Requirements:

Beneficial Characteristics:

I remember as a kid the fragrant blooms of lilac at neighboring homes. I also recall that most of the plants were not attractive and always seemed to be overgrown. Yet the distinct fragrance seemed to overshadow the appearance of the plant. As I began to develop my gardening interests, I learned that the common lilac (*Syringa vulgaris*) is more adapted to northern climates. Common lilac is also notorious for powdery mildew in the humid South and does not have nearly the number of flowers as plants grown in colder climates. But after much searching, I have discovered another species of lilac that will take our heat and humidity. Korean lilac is a smaller-growing plant that provides fragrant flowers and healthy foliage.

WHEN TO PLANT

Lilacs respond to spring planting or to planting in the fall when they are dormant.

WHERE TO PLANT

Korean lilac prefers full sun but accepts a half-day of shade. It likes good garden soil but tolerates poor soils as long as they have good drainage. Use these prized beauties as single specimen plants, or show them off in groups of three. Using evergreen shrubs as a background promotes the beauty of these plants in the spring and winter. Some cultivars are successfully grown in containers.

HOW TO PLANT

Dig a hole at least two times wider than and the same depth as the rootball. Backfill with the original soil. Mulch the plant, and water it as needed.

CARE AND MAINTENANCE

Flowers emerge from buds set on the previous year's growth. Late cold spells can occasionally damage flower buds. Prune after flowering, although it is seldom needed with Korean lilacs because of their overall compact growth. Lilac responds well to rich soil and occasional fertilizer sidedressings. Too much shade can cause sparse growth and flowers. Korean lilacs seem to be fairly resistant to mildew but can be found with an occasional aphid early in the spring.

ADDITIONAL INFORMATION

Korean lilacs flower at an early age; common lilacs flower later as they mature. The flowers also emerge before the new leaves are fully developed.

ADDITIONAL SPECIES, CULTIVARS, OR VARIETIES

The species parent plant has a lavender flower with a pinkish tint. It typically grows as a small, bushy plant. 'Palibin' is probably the most readily available cultivar with a mature height reaching 4 to 5 ft. and with fragrant, reddish-purple buds opening to a pinkish white. Some nurseries sell 'Palibin' as dwarf Korean lilac. 'Miss Kim' (*S. patula*) is another species from Korea that is considered trouble free. Blooming occurs a little later than other lilacs to extend the season, and the growth is quite compact.

Did You Know?

Cutleaf lilac (S. laciniata) is another great selection for southern climates, but it is hard to find in Oklahoma.

Oakleaf Hydrangea

Hydrangea quercifolia

Height: 4 to 6 ft.
Spread: 4 to 8 ft.
Flowers: White clustering
Bloom Period: Early summer
Zones: 6a, 6b, 7a, 7b

Color photograph on page 227.

Light Requirements:

Beneficial Characteristics:

You must make room for oakleaf hydrangea in your landscape. This deciduous beauty is nothing like the old-time snowball types (*Hydrangea macrophylla*). This unique landscape plant offers truly eye-catching features throughout the growing season. The new leaf growth starts with a grayish-purple tint at emergence, changing to a deep green during the summer and to a brilliant display of orange-red fall color. And just as the name implies, the leaf is shaped like an oak leaf. Sometime around May, the white flower spikes proudly emerge as if they were a cluster of grapes dangling from the foliage. The perfect flowers later change to a pinkish-purple tint before turning a coppery brown. Both foliage and flower spikes remain on the plant well into the middle of winter.

WHEN TO PLANT

Plant them in spring since younger plants are somewhat tender until established.

WHERE TO PLANT

Oakleaf hydrangea prefers afternoon or filtered shade and performs better in moist, fertile soil. Taller selections need plenty of room and do well as a background.

HOW TO PLANT

A hole dug two to three times the width and the same depth as the rootball is recommended for most trees and shrubs. Oakleaf hydrangea establishes better with such planting conditions. Space plants 6 ft. apart when planting in rows. Water deeply to settle the soil and on a frequent basis until plants are established. Mulching is beneficial.

CARE AND MAINTENANCE

Hydrangeas bloom at an early age and usually from terminal growth that occurred last season. Prune them after flowering. The plants send out root suckers and spread as they mature, although the growth is not considered invasive. The stems turn a reddish-gray color with exfoliating bark as they mature. During drought conditions, supplemental watering and mulching are of utmost importance. Leaf spot and an occasional powdery mildew occur in heavy shade.

ADDITIONAL INFORMATION

Oakleaf hydrangeas prefer a somewhat acid soil, but do not expect to change the flower color, as with the French types. Yes, *H. macrophylla* flower colors can be changed from pink to blue or vice versa depending on the soil pH. Aluminum sulfate is applied to obtain blue flowers, and lime is used to encourage pink. Not all cultivars and species respond to this pH variation.

ADDITIONAL SPECIES, CULTIVARS, OR VARIETIES

'Snow Queen' is probably the most popular tall cultivar, and 'Pee Wee' is the compact version, reaching 2 to 3 ft. 'Lynn Lowrey' is said to be more tolerant of sun. Similar in flowers but different in foliage is *H. paniculata* (panicle hydrangea). This species has the same pyramidal flower spikes but blooms in the late summer and early fall. The flowers often weigh down the foliage and give it a weeping appearance. The leaves are a coarser, elliptical shape. Cultivars include 'Pee Gee' (sometimes sold as 'Grandiflora'), a rather large plant, and 'Bush Pee Gee', not to be confused with the dwarf 'Pee Wee' (*H. quercifolia*). 'Tardiva', 'Unique', and 'Kyushu' are popular white cultivars. The latest introduction is a pink-flowering cultivar called 'Pink Diamond'.

 Did You Know?

Hydrangea flowers make great fresh cut as well as dried flowers.

Oregon Grape Holly

Mahonia aquifolium

Other Name: Holly Grape
Height: 3 to 6 ft.
Spread: 3 to 5 ft.
Flowers: Yellow
Bloom Period: March or April
Zones: 6a, 6b, 7a, 7b

Color photograph on page 227.

Light Requirements:

Beneficial Characteristics:

*M*ahonia is another great selection for shade gardens. I often hear gardeners complain that there are not enough choices for shade-garden plants. I hope to show that there are several selections available, and *Mahonia* is one of the best. It is known more for its lustrous, evergreen foliage; the yellow flowers and blue-black berries are added bonuses. As the new foliage emerges, expect tinges of red and purple to brighten the display. The prickly foliage is best used in the background of landscape beds and not close to sidewalks. The compound, thick, evergreen leaves add texture and provide consistent color to deciduous companion shade plants.

WHEN TO PLANT
Plant it in spring or fall.

WHERE TO PLANT
This foundation or shrub border plant requires partial shade. I have not been impressed with this one as a specimen plant unless it is *Mahonia bealei* (leatherleaf mahonia), with its robust foliage. Otherwise, most other species work best in groups to provide massive evergreen color during the winter. As a companion plant, the coarse foliage complements finer-textured plants. This plant prefers a somewhat acidic, moist soil. Dry soils and hot locations easily scorch most of the *Mahonia* selections. They tolerate sandy and clay soils as long as they drain well.

HOW TO PLANT
Plant container-grown selections in holes two times wider than but the same depth as the rootballs. No amended backfill is needed. Water and mulch the plants.

CARE AND MAINTENANCE
M. aquifolium is somewhat sparse on foliage set. The upright stems are more pronounced and can be easily trimmed in early spring. This species is

typically stoloniferous in growth; that is, it spreads readily in moist, fertile landscape sites. The fruit form late in the season and resemble a true berry, thus the name grape holly. Iron chlorosis can develop in alkaline soils, and disease leaf spots may occur in damp conditions with poor air circulation.

ADDITIONAL INFORMATION

All mahonias are known for their prickly foliage, so do not plant these varieties in high-traffic areas. The leathery leaves may turn a purplish color during the fall and winter.

ADDITIONAL SPECIES, CULTIVARS, OR VARIETIES

There is not much difference between the species and some of the introduced cultivars, other than various shades of leaf color in the spring and early fall. Leatherleaf mahonia (*M. bealei*) has bigger, more prominent foliage, making it a nice specimen plant. The foliage at times has a bluer tint than that of *M. aquifolium*. Leatherleaf is not as cold hardy as Oregon grape. Chinese mahonia (*M. fortunei*) probably has the more delicate foliage, although it is still slightly prickly, and is a good choice for the southern areas of the state.

 Did You Know?

Even with the prickly foliage, birds will make their way in for the fruit in the fall.

Possumhaw

Ilex decidua

Other Names: Deciduous Holly;
  Prairie Holly
Height: 10 to 20 ft.
Spread: 6 to 15 ft.
Flowers: Not showy
Bloom Period: Spring
Zones: 6a, 6b, 7a, 7b

Color photograph on page 227.

Light Requirements:

Beneficial Characteristics:

Possumhaw is native to the southeastern part of the state. This large shrub or small tree is gaining in popularity because of the brilliant berry set in the fall, catching the attention of both gardeners and birds. The small, glossy, gray-green foliage drops late in the fall, giving rise to the colored berries. The stems are usually a light-gray color. Both single- and multiple-trunk selections are available in the nursery trade. These natives frequently pop up in my pasture fencerows where birds have distributed the seeds. It is almost as if Mother Nature is decorating for the holidays since the glowing, red berries reach their peak from Thanksgiving until Christmas.

WHEN TO PLANT
Deciduous holly is available in container-grown or balled-and-burlapped choices that are easily planted in the spring or fall.

WHERE TO PLANT
Deciduous holly tolerates alkaline soils quite well and will grow in central and western Oklahoma, even though it is native to the slightly acidic soils of the eastern part of the state. The plants need plenty of room and work as a single specimen or in conjunction with evergreen backgrounds.

HOW TO PLANT
Plant deciduous holly in a hole two to three times the width of the container and the same depth. No backfill with organic amendments is required. Water and mulch after planting and as needed.

CARE AND MAINTENANCE
Deciduous holly generally has both male and female flowers on the same plant; therefore, additional pollinators are not required but can enhance berry set. Fruit set typically increases with age and is most often found on

short spurs on the branches. The colorful red, orange, or yellow fruit persist on the branches most of the winter until possums or birds finish them off. Many of the deciduous hollies are found in moist sites. Once it is established in the landscape, possumhaw is more drought tolerant than one would expect. Do not overfertilize, or excess growth can occur with minimal berry set.

ADDITIONAL INFORMATION

Winterberry (*Ilex verticillata*) is a similar deciduous holly in acceptance as a landscape plant. Winterberry has less-prominent, spur-type growth and generally needs a pollinator companion to achieve the best berry set, even though both female and male flowers are generally present. The foliage of winterberry is typically more elliptical where possumhaw is more rounded on the ends.

ADDITIONAL SPECIES, CULTIVARS, OR VARIETIES

'Byers Golden' is a yellow-fruited cultivar, 'Council Fire' and 'Sundance' are orange-red selections, and 'Warren Red' is a popular red-berried cultivar of possumhaw. Favorite winterberry cultivars include 'Winter Red', 'Scarlet O'Hara', and 'Afterglow'. 'Red Sprite' (sometimes sold as nana or compacta) is a dwarf cultivar. Male selections include 'Jim Dandy', 'Red Escort' and 'Raritan Chief' (hybrid). The newest release to the United States is 'Ostervik', which is promoted to hold its berries a month longer.

 Did You Know?

Possumhaw- and winterberry-ripened fruit are favorites of more than twenty species of birds, including many prairie ground birds such as quail and pheasant.

Soft Touch Holly

Ilex crenata

Other Name: Japanese Holly
Height: 4 to 6 ft.
Spread: 3 to 5 ft.
Flowers: Inconspicuous
Bloom Period: Early summer
Zones: 6a, 6b, 7a, 7b

Color photograph on page 227.

Light Requirements:

Beneficial Characteristics:

Japanese holly is a commonly used plant in Oklahoma, and with its lustrous green foliage it can be quite impressive all year long. Japanese holly is a great substitute for Japanese boxwood. Most Japanese hollies are somewhat brittle and stiff, however. 'Soft Touch' Japanese holly, on the other hand, is a softer-feeling, more eye-appealing cultivar. The foliage is a soothing deep green, which makes it a wonderful contrast plant in any landscape. 'Soft Touch' is the focal shrub in my front landscape. The curving row of plants creates separate levels of the landscape and provides important winter color. The soft, dark-green foliage is a perfect complement for my pink-, red-, or white-flowering annuals dotting the landscape bed each summer.

WHEN TO PLANT

Early-spring plantings of 'Soft Touch' holly are best. Most hollies can be planted in late spring, early summer, or early fall, however.

WHERE TO PLANT

Japanese hollies as a whole can take full sun or partial shade. I have found over the years that they perform better when they get morning sun and afternoon shade. The same holds true for 'Soft Touch'. The plants are better suited for eastern Oklahoma but adapt as far west as Oklahoma City and at an angle down to Altus. Preferred sites are fertile, slightly acidic, well-drained soils, but they adapt to clay soils. Japanese hollies are used most often as foundation plants and borders and in mass groupings.

HOW TO PLANT

Dig the holes at least two times wider than and the same depth as the rootballs. Water gently and deeply to settle the soil and soak the entire root system. Mulch with pine straw, pine bark, pecan hulls, or other acidic products.

CARE AND MAINTENANCE

Japanese hollies respond to shearing and selective pruning. Pruning is typically done in early spring as new growth emerges; however, occasional maintenance pruning can be done throughout the season. Japanese hollies are inclined when stressed to succumb to spider mites, twig blight, and leaf spot. During the driest and hottest times, they sunburn when they are grown in full sun. Monitoring plants for these problems will ensure quicker response to controls. Fertilizing a couple of times throughout the growing season, preferably in late April and again in June, will ensure vigorous plants. Later applications are not advised, for they increase the chance of winter damage. Supplemental watering and mulching are good practices.

ADDITIONAL INFORMATION

I. glabra (inkberry) is another nice choice for a tough evergreen plant. Inkberry is carefree and has a deep, lustrous-green foliage that reminds me of a small cleyera shrub leaf. Inkberry tolerates wet sites somewhat more than most hollies.

ADDITIONAL SPECIES, CULTIVARS, OR VARIETIES

The cultivar 'Soft Touch' is primarily distributed by Flowerwood Wholesale Nursery out of Mobile, Alabama, to various nurseries in Oklahoma. The most commonly available cultivars of Japanese holly are 'Helleri', 'Hetzi', and 'Compacta'.

 Did You Know?

Female Japanese hollies occasionally produce black berries late in the fall that may remain until spring.

Southern Waxmyrtle

Myrica cerifera

Height: 5 to 20 ft. **Spread:** 5 to 20 ft. **Flowers:** Not showy **Bloom Period:** Early summer **Zones:** 6b, 7a, 7b *Color photograph on page 227.*	**Light Requirements:** ☀ ☀ **Beneficial Characteristics:** 

I have been a fan of southern waxmyrtle ever since I lived in northern Florida. It was native to moist, acid soils and often found growing under pine trees. Once it was established, you could grow this charming evergreen in full sun, even in poor, dry soils. Wow, what a diverse plant! The unique yellowish-green foliage is quite appealing to use for a different kind of color scheme. It was mostly grown as a multitrunk small tree and became the focal point of many landscape designs. Strangely enough, it is native to southeastern areas of our state, but will survive in the heavy soils of west-central Oklahoma.

WHEN TO PLANT
Plant southern waxmyrtle in early spring, early summer, or fall.

WHERE TO PLANT
The standard waxmyrtle is often too big for foundation plantings unless it is used in large beds in association with two-story homes. Use it as a feature plant in island bed designs, as a hedge screen, or as a specimen in lawns. A dwarf species does well as a foundation plant or small hedge. It is probably risky to plant southern waxmyrtle in the Panhandle because of its potential for severe cold injury. The yellowish-green, contrasting foliage is a nice color to complement shades of purple-yellow companion plants. This plant is not picky about its soil type.

HOW TO PLANT
Dig the hole two to three times wider than and the same depth as the rootball. Deeply water immediately after planting to settle the soil and adequately soak the root system. Waxmyrtle responds favorably to mulch.

CARE AND MAINTENANCE
These trees can be pruned as a hedge or "limbed up" for a multitrunk display. The bark is an attractive gray-green color. Continued mulching as needed and occasional fertilizing will turn this plant into quite a display. There are no serious reports of insect problems. In humid, poorly circulated

sites an occasional fungal leaf spot may be detected. I have been told by gardeners that waxmyrtle is resistant to deer feedings. Occasionally, root suckers may be a problem in beds where the roots are disturbed.

ADDITIONAL INFORMATION

Southern waxmyrtle comes as a male or female plant (dioecious). The female plants produce a grayish berry late in the season that occurs on previous-season growth, usually along stems below the foliage. Both have pungent-smelling foliage reminiscent of the northern bayberry (*M. pensylvanica*) frequently used in aromatic products.

ADDITIONAL SPECIES, CULTIVARS, OR VARIETIES

There are few improved cultivars of southern waxmyrtle other than the species plant, which is the most common selection in the nursery trade. 'Emperor' is a new release of the species and has prominent, more serrated foliage. A related species is compact—*M. pussilla* (dwarf waxmyrtle). This species is not quite as cold hardy and does well in the sandy, piney woods of eastern and southern counties of the state or Zones 7a and 7b. It matures to an average of 5 ft. Cultivars of dwarf waxmyrtle are 'Fairfax' and 'Georgia Gem'. 'Georgia Gem' has a more mounded growth form, reaching 18 to 24 in. by 3 ft. wide. Both are difficult to find in our state.

 Did You Know?

The dense, shrubby growth of waxmyrtle is a favorite for vegetative nesting birds, and the fruit is favored by many species of birds, including quail and turkey.

Spirea

Spiraea species

Height: 2 to 6 ft.
Spread: 2 to 5 ft.
Flowers: Primarily shades of white, pink, and red
Bloom Period: May and June
Zones: 6a, 6b, 7a, 7b

Color photograph on page 227.

Light Requirements:

Beneficial Characteristics:

Spirea is tolerant of many conditions and comes in a wide range of white to reddish-pink shades. Several cultivars are known for their attractive summer and fall foliage. The soft, delicate, deciduous foliage provides unique texture combinations. Fall brings even more color as the leaves turn a yellow-bronzy-red tint. The branches have a dense, twiggy growth habit, requiring minimal care. Spirea is a good substitute for the more picky rhododendron, even though spirea blooms a few weeks later.

WHEN TO PLANT
Plant container-grown spirea selections in spring or fall.

WHERE TO PLANT
Spireas make great foundation plants, especially when used in combination with evergreen varieties. The dwarf cultivars can be placed in front borders of landscape beds without blocking nearby companions. Spirea prefers full-sun locations or partial sun, preferably in the afternoon. Too much shade increases the chances of powdery mildew and other foliage diseases. Good, rich, garden soil provides the best growth, but spireas adapt to poor and heavy soils if they drain well.

HOW TO PLANT
Digging a wide hole the same depth of the container root system is the most successful way to plant. Water to establish plants, and then they are somewhat drought tolerant. Mulching is a good idea for most plants.

CARE AND MAINTENANCE
Spirea generally flowers on new growth, so pruning during the dormant season or immediately after flowering is acceptable. Trimming spent blooms encourages regrowth and additional blooms in the fall. Thinning of overgrown canes may be needed with age to stimulate new growth. In

addition to sunny locations, proper spacing with a little extra room between plants allows for more air circulation. This planting method will minimize the chance of foliar disease. Aphids can occasionally appear in early spring, but ladybugs generally take care of the threat. Spirea responds well to supplemental feedings. Reapply mulch as needed.

ADDITIONAL INFORMATION

Many horticultural experts claim that spirea is overused in the landscape. My good friend and Mississippi gardener Felder Rushing says it best: "Spireas are easy." I agree; they are downright easy to grow. Find an abandoned home site and you will most likely find a thriving spirea.

ADDITIONAL SPECIES, CULTIVARS, OR VARIETIES

Numerous species and hybrids of spirea are available on the market. The majority of the cultivars come from the hybrid cross *Spiraea* × *bumalda*. Japanese spirea (*S. japonica*) is a very popular species with several colorful selections. Double reeves spirea (*S. cantoniensis*) is a graceful selection that is especially nice for southern areas of the state. Bridalwreath (*S. prunifolia*) and thunberg spirea (*S. thunbergii*) offer interesting features for most landscapes. 'Magic Carpet', 'Alpina', and 'Norman' are very compact spireas. 'Goldmound', 'Goldflame', and 'Magic Carpet' are known for their chartreuse foliage. For a unique crinkled foliage, consider 'Crispa'. 'Shirobana' is known for red, pink, and white flowers all on the same plant. The newest arrivals to the nursery trade are 'Neon Flash', a compact plant with bright-pink flowers, and 'Dakota Goldcharm', a dwarf chartreuse-foliage selection.

 Did You Know?

If you want blue flowers, consider blue mist spirea—which is not really a spirea but Caryopteris clandonensis.

Sweet Box

Sarcococca hookerana

Other Name: Himalayan Sweet Box
Height: 12 in. to 3 ft.
Spread: 12 in. to 3 ft.
Flowers: Inconspicuous, but fragrant
Bloom Period: Late winter, early spring
Zones: 7a, 7b

Color photograph on page 227.

Light Requirements:

Beneficial Characteristics:

Seldom heard of in Oklahoma and just as hard to find at garden centers is sweet box. This shade-loving, drought-tolerant plant needs to find a home in our state. Its glossy, evergreen foliage is consistent all year long. There is no spectacular fall color. Sweet box does not have showy flowers, but when they bloom sometime between February and April, you will know it! The name sweet is bestowed because of the sweet-smelling, fragrant flowers. Occasionally, small, black berries develop as the season progresses, but they are hardly visible because they are hidden in the foliage. Again, the most notable feature of this plant is the consistent, green, lustrous foliage, a trait important in landscape design, especially in winter settings.

WHEN TO PLANT
Spring planting of sweet box is better for establishment before winter.

WHERE TO PLANT
Use dwarf sweet box as a border plant near sidewalks or for the front of landscape beds. Because of its spreading nature, it is a great filler plant, reaching only 12 to 18 in. Plants prefer sites with afternoon shade and somewhat acidic soil. They tolerate alkaline soils but are not as prolific. Sweet box has been found to grow in protected areas of Zone 6, but the risk of winter injury is great.

HOW TO PLANT
Loosely dig holes two to three times wider than the rootballs and the same depth. Water is essential during the establishment period. Once it is established, sweet box is quite drought tolerant and prefers somewhat drier shade. Mulch is vital in any landscape bed, especially with this tough shrub.

CARE AND MAINTENANCE
Some selections spread as a result of stoloniferous growth but are not aggressive. The spreading growth easily emerges through any mulch.

Pruning is seldom needed, other than to keep the plant in specified areas. Supplemental fertilization is usually not needed unless the foliage shows nutrient deficiencies. Mulch should be reapplied to keep weeds at bay until plants are well established. Pests are not serious concerns. Supplemental water is needed during drought periods until plants are established.

ADDITIONAL INFORMATION

Sweet box has been getting more attention lately in the nursery trade as a "praiseworthy plant" and "one to grow for the future." Sweet box is rarely seen in the Oklahoma nursery trade. It is definitely one to encourage retailers to carry since it thrives in dry shade, which is typical of many Oklahoma landscapes.

ADDITIONAL SPECIES, CULTIVARS, OR VARIETIES

S. hookerana var. *humilis* is known for its low-growing ground cover traits. Slightly taller is *S. hookerana* var. *digyna*, which has lighter-green foliage with purplish stems. The leaves are also somewhat narrower. *S. confusa* and *S. ruscifolia* are other popular species, but they are less cold hardy and are primarily recommended for Zone 8 or in protected areas of Zone 7.

Did You Know?

Sweet box is an excellent plant for cut, fresh, green holiday foliage.

Viburnum

Viburnum species

Other Name: Cranberry Bush
Height: 3 to 15 ft.
Spread: 6 to 12 ft.
Flowers: Traditionally white and fragrant
Bloom Period: April, May, or June
Zones: 6a, 6b, 7a, 7b

Color photograph on page 228.

Light Requirements:

Beneficial Characteristics:

Showy, berry-producing plants are gaining in popularity in home land-scapes. Viburnums are plants known for such flamboyant qualities. There are many species, hybrids, and cultivars of viburnum with an assortment of characteristics. The good news is that viburnums are fairly easy to grow and make attractive landscape plants for both home owners and wildlife garden friends. Some are known for their fragrant flowers while others are known for their showy fruit. In all cases the plants give height and glory to any site.

WHEN TO PLANT
Plant viburnums in spring, early summer, or early fall.

WHERE TO PLANT
Species and cultivar selection determine sun preference and landscape use. Viburnums prefer slightly acidic, well-drained soils. Most are utilized as specimen plants in background areas because of their space requirements. In large turf areas the plants can be clustered in groups of three to form island beds for a most attractive display, especially in combination with assorted perennials.

HOW TO PLANT
Definitely dig the hole two to three times wider than and the same depth as the rootball. Organic backfill is not needed in the planting hole. Instead, complete bed preparation with such materials before planting time is sug-gested when possible. Mulch is essential to keep the soil moist and acidic. Water at planting and as needed to establish the plants.

CARE AND MAINTENANCE
Pruning is generally done to thin branches or shape for specimen design. Prune it after flowering, depending on the cultivar, although some berry

loss will occur. Most viburnums respond to minimal fertilizations. Watering is necessary during drought periods. Mulch should be reapplied as needed.

ADDITIONAL INFORMATION

Viburnums are often associated with cranberries because of the fruit. To make things more confusing, some selections have cranberry in the name. The true holiday cranberry is a northern crop in the *Vaccinium* genus.

ADDITIONAL SPECIES, CULTIVARS, OR VARIETIES

There are more than two hundred cultivars and hybrids of viburnum. Some are evergreen while others are deciduous. I have tried to provide some of the more common selections that offer a variety of uses for the landscape. 'Mohawk' is considered one of the most fragrant selections, with orange-red berries. 'Korean Spice' is another well-known fragrant selection, with red fruit that turns black in the late summer. *V. opulus* 'Zanthocarpum' is a yellow-fruited selection often called yellow-fruited European cranberry bush, and it needs afternoon shade. 'Summer Snowflake', 'Shasta', and 'Mariessii' are double-file viburnums with attractive white flowers, later producing red fruit. 'Eskimo' is a compact specimen. 'Snowball' viburnum is best known for its showy, white snowball flowers but is sterile and does not produce fruit. Leatherleaf viburnum is a semievergreen selection best used for its dark-green, coarse foliage; its flowers and fruit are not particularly showy.

Did You Know?

Viburnum is in the honeysuckle family.

Weigela

Weigela florida

Other Name: Cardinal Flower
Height: 3 to 9 ft.
Spread: 3 to 12 ft.
Flowers: Pink, red, white
Bloom Period: Spring, early summer
Zones: 6a, 6b, 7a, 7b

Color photograph on page 228.

Light Requirements:

Beneficial Characteristics:

Weigela is known for its distinctly dazzling early flowers. I enjoy the flowers and use them as a gauge to detect when the hummingbirds have arrived. Hummingbirds definitely seem to prefer this plant to the feeders—at least while the flowers last. The medium-green foliage is fairly coarse and located on upright, gray-brown stems with notable lenticels often mistaken for scale insects. The spring display is well worth the use of this plant in the landscape. The remainder of the season leaves much to be desired, however. Using weigela in combination with evergreen shrubs and ornamental grasses distracts from its unimpressive summer growth. But you cannot beat the long-lasting display of showy spring blooms with this easy-to-grow spring beauty.

WHEN TO PLANT
Plant weigela in the spring.

WHERE TO PLANT
Weigela is seldom used as a foundation plant. The dormant appearance is quite boring, so planting it in association with winter-attractive plants is preferred. The best display I have seen was weigela planted in an irregular row in the background of a landscape bed and dwarf yaupon planted in front of the weigela to add winter color and hide the barren stems.

HOW TO PLANT
Plant it in a hole two to three times wider than and the same depth as the rootball. Water after planting to settle the soil and thoroughly soak the roots. Mulch to keep moisture in and weed competition down.

CARE AND MAINTENANCE
Weigela blooms on the previous season's growth. Prune it after flowering. Expect some blooms again in late fall but nothing like the spring display.

The foliage typically takes on a bronzy-purple, almost stressed appearance during the summer. Heat stress seems to be the cause. Some experts claim it is characteristic of the species. Planting weigela more in shade to compensate for the scorched look seems to reduce the flower display. I just live with the appearance. Weigela flowers are worth any annoying idiosyncrasies of the plant. There are no serious pest problems worth mentioning.

ADDITIONAL INFORMATION

Weigela is often used for early color by gardeners who do not want to pamper azaleas. The most common flower color is red or pink. Occasionally, stems are damaged from severe winter spells but will usually come back from the root system.

ADDITIONAL SPECIES, CULTIVARS, OR VARIETIES

There are many more cultivars than ever seen at garden centers in Oklahoma. At last count there were some 160 selections. Most are similar to the species. 'Minuet' is a dwarf, compact selection remaining about 3 ft. 'White Knight' is a white-flowering introduction, and 'Variegata' is a variegated foliage selection with soft-pink flowers. 'Polka' is the most cold-hardy selection. 'Carnival' has pink, red, and white flowers, all at the same time. The newest rave is a brilliant selection called 'Wine & Roses'™, sometimes also sold as 'Alexandra'. The uniqueness of this cultivar is the burgundy-purple, satin foliage. The leaf color does not fade much as the season progresses and seems to intensify in the fall. The rosy-pink foliage is spectacular. This selection does not have a problem with the "scorched foliage" appearance noted among other cultivars.

 Did You Know?

The unique name weigela is pronounced "vie-ge-la." The plant was named after a German botanist.

Winter Jasmine

Jasminum nudiflorum

Height: 3 to 4 ft.
Spread: 4 to 6 ft.
Flowers: Yellow
Bloom Period: February, early March
Zones: 6a, 6b, 7a, 7b

Color photograph on page 228.

Light Requirements:

Beneficial Characteristics:

My first experience with this dependable plant was as a horticulture student at OSU. Winter jasmine dotted the campus in full-sun and partial-shade locations. I was amazed by how many times it displayed bright-yellow flowers in February, even as snow blanketed the ground. The deciduous plant masquerades as an evergreen, thanks to its dark-green, slender, arching stems. The mounded growth habit has a unique arching habit, offering an uncommon presentation for landscape texture. Once a widely sold plant in the trade, winter jasmine is making a comeback for many landscape uses.

WHEN TO PLANT

Plant container-grown selections in either spring or fall.

WHERE TO PLANT

Use winter jasmine as a foundation plant in areas at least 5 ft. wide. Plant it for background borders and in combination with deciduous shrubs such as spirea. The texture tones down many coarse companion plants. Jasmine is a great choice for sites where the stems are allowed to cascade over a wall, slope, or berm. In full sun, the plants grow and flower better, but they accept partial shade. Winter jasmine tolerates a wide range of soils.

HOW TO PLANT

Plant it in a hole at least two times the width and the same depth as the rootball. Water after planting and as needed until plants are readily established. Mulch is very beneficial for all shrubs, but especially winter jasmine.

CARE AND MAINTENANCE

Initial plantings of winter jasmine have a tendency to send stems crawling along the surface of the ground where they root along the way. Tip these stems to force growth more upright in the center of the crown. As the plants mature, they will grow in a mounding, arching appearance. Winter jasmine is considered a fast-growing plant. Fertilizer applications are recommended in poor soils but seldom needed in rich, garden soils. Prune the plants after flowering, usually in late March. Many gardeners rate the flowers secondary to the remarkable green plant form. There are seldom reports of pest problems.

ADDITIONAL INFORMATION

Any rooted stems can be cut and easily transplanted. Occasional pruning may be needed to keep plants intact. The flowers are some of the earliest to bloom in late winter/early spring. Although the flowers may succumb to freezing temperatures, the hardy plant is rarely harmed.

ADDITIONAL SPECIES, CULTIVARS, OR VARIETIES

This plant was once a common sight in garden centers and for reasons unknown to me fell out of production. It is starting to make a comeback, thanks to its resilience in the landscape. The dark-green species is the primary selection available; however, 'Aureum' is a lightly variegated form that is even more difficult to locate. Other jasmine species are available, but most are not as cold hardy as *J. nudiflorum*.

 Did You Know?

The stems can be cut in early February, placed in water, and forced to bloom indoors.

Yaupon Holly

Ilex vomitoria

Height: 3 to 20 ft.
Spread: 4 to 15 ft.
Flowers: Inconspicuous
Bloom Period: Early spring
Zones: 6b, 7a, 7b

Color photograph on page 228.

Light Requirements:

Beneficial Characteristics:

Yaupon holly is one of my favorite landscape shrubs. It is one tough cookie, taking all kinds of environmental abuse. The evergreen foliage offers year-round enjoyment. Some selections are known for their colorful berry set in the fall. The dwarf selections are typically very dense in growth. The new growth on many forms emerges with a purplish tint, later turning a lustrous gray green. The selections are phenomenal in height, texture, and berry set, and they can truly fit any landscape design need. Throw in the toughness and tolerance of many environmental situations, and yaupon holly belongs at the top of your plant list.

WHEN TO PLANT

Plants are available as container or balled-and-burlapped specimens. Plant yaupon holly in spring, early summer, or early fall.

WHERE TO PLANT

Dwarf selections are great foundation or grouping plants because they naturally grow in a mounding form. Upright varieties make excellent single specimens or informal screens. Yaupon holly is commonly used as a topiary plant. It favors full sun but tolerates partial shade. These tough plants will grow in a multitude of soil conditions—dry or swampy. Even soil pH does not seem to matter too much. Winter damage is likely in the Panhandle.

HOW TO PLANT

Widely dug holes at the same depth as the roots are the favored way to plant yaupons. Water them to settle the soil and then on a regular basis. Their fibrous roots make them a prime candidate for mulching. Once established, they are somewhat drought tolerant.

CARE AND MAINTENANCE

Since yaupons are used frequently as topiaries, they obviously respond well to shearing and pruning. Berry-producing varieties should be pruned in early spring. Others can be trimmed anytime throughout the growing season. Supplemental feedings are optional. Reapplication of mulch every couple of years is beneficial. Other than an occasional leaf miner, pest problems are generally of no concern. In the far eastern part of the state, leaf-chewing caterpillars are common in early spring but are easily controlled. Yaupons are sensitive to frequent visits by male dogs and are likely to burn as a result.

ADDITIONAL INFORMATION

Most yaupon hollies are considered dioecious (separate male and female plants). Pollination can occur from almost any nearby holly species; however, planting dwarf male types, such as 'Stokes' or 'Schillings', in close proximity will increase fruit production. Select berry-producing forms in the late summer or fall from your local garden center. This ensures a female with the potential for berries in the future.

ADDITIONAL SPECIES, CULTIVARS, OR VARIETIES

Dwarf types include 'Stokes' or 'Schillings' (said to be one and the same), 'Nana', and a relative newcomer, 'Bordeaux'. 'Bordeaux' tends to have a more prominent purple hue on the new growth. 'Pride of Houston' is a popular, upright, multitrunk selection. One of my favorite multitrunk cultivars is 'Grey's Little Leaf', which is seldom found in Oklahoma garden centers but does exceptionally well here. The leaves are a deep green and are more tightly clustered with short internodes. The red berry set is phenomenal. 'Pendula' and 'Folsom's' are two excellent, tall, weeping forms that are not quite as cold hardy and are suited more for southeastern areas of the state. There are some yellow-berried cultivars, but they are quite rare in the nursery industry.

 Did You Know?

The species name vomitoria *was given by botanists who learned of the common practice of Native Americans to use the berries in a drink until it made them vomit. It was thought to cleanse the body of impurities and ready them for war.*

Yew

Taxus species

Height: 3 to 15 ft.	**Light Requirements:**
Spread: 5 to 10 ft.	
Flowers: Nonshowy	
Bloom Period: March, April	
Zones: 6a, 6b, 7a, 7b	
Color photograph on page 228.	

Yew is another superior choice for shade gardens. There is nothing comparable in Oklahoma to the dark evergreen foliage display that yew provides
in the winter landscape. And the lustrous needle foliage is soothing during the
hot summers. There is quite a range in widths and textures available in this
prominent landscape favorite. Although tough plants, yews did not hold up
well in the drought of 1998. Despite that, consider yews for your landscape.

WHEN TO PLANT
Yews are typically planted in spring or fall.

WHERE TO PLANT
Yews are almost always field grown in sandy-type soils and sold as balled-
and-burlapped plants. They are most often used as foundation plants or as
background plants in partially shaded landscapes. Group plantings make
better shows and are frequently used in association with deciduous plants
requiring the same soil conditions. Taller cultivars make effective hedges
and screens. *Taxus* are very specific to their soil types. Rich, fertile, moist,
and well-drained soils are a must for the best plant health. Yews tolerate
sun, especially morning sun, as long as they are not planted in the direct
paths of sweeping winds.

HOW TO PLANT
Dig a planting hole two to three times wider than and the same depth as
the rootball. In poorly drained soils, plant them slightly above the soil
grade. Water to settle soil and frequently during establishment. Mulching is
of utmost importance. Remove the burlap from intact or firm rootballs.
Otherwise set the plant in the hole and cut off burlap near the soil surface.

CARE AND MAINTENANCE
Yews respond well to shearing to keep plant forms intact. Do not overfertilize the tender roots. Reapply mulch occasionally to keep the roots

cool and moist. Yews are not drought tolerant; just ask any gardener how they held up in the drought of 1998. Foliar diseases, such as needle and twig blight, are the most common diseases. Root rot occurs in poorly drained soils. Needles are likely to burn in winters with severe temperature changes. Although yew is evergreen, older needles located in the center of the plants normally drop as the plants mature.

ADDITIONAL INFORMATION

Plants are male and female with seeds occasionally appearing on female plants.

ADDITIONAL SPECIES, CULTIVARS, OR VARIETIES

Most yew cultivars' growing conditions are similar. More so, consider height, width, and plant form when choosing the cultivar. Some not-so-common selections to consider are: 'Emerald Spreader' (also sold as 'Monloo') is a great low-growing cultivar that matures around 18 to 24 in. by a width of 8 ft. 'Tautonii' shows more resistance to winter burn. The hybrid cross Anglojap Yew *T.* × *media* is more tolerant of wind and sun but also even more difficult to find in the trade. 'Runyan' and 'Thayerae' are two Anglojap cultivars. Japanese Plum Yew (*Cephalotaxus harringtonia*) is an unusual species with wider and longer needles resembling Podocarpus, a popular southern evergreen.

  Did You Know?

Yews are reported to be toxic when ingested. Reactions depend on the person's size, age, health, and quantity consumed.

CHAPTER THREE

Ground Covers

A S THE NAME IMPLIES, ground covers are plants growing and spreading along the ground. I have been using more ground covers lately since they do not require a large initial investment. With only a few plants and a little time ground covers can easily fill large, vacant landscape spaces. Another nice thing about ground covers is that they work as living mulch. Organic mulches need to be replaced every couple of years, but ground covers are permanent once they are established.

Ground covers can be described as herbaceous (soft stemmed) or woody. Some spread by underground stolons, others root along their stems, and a few vine up nearby objects. Ground covers are evergreen (retaining most leaves year-round) or deciduous (losing leaves in the winter).

Turfgrass is also a ground cover. Most gardeners have finally come to the realization that grass, although very important to the landscape, is not well adapted to shade. Many ground covers, on the other hand, serve the same purposes as turf and tolerate various levels of shade. As result, they are perfect understory companions for trees. Ground covers help in erosion control and are often planted on sloping sites or allowed to cascade over walls. Many of these prostrate growers are gaining in recognition as container or windowbox companion plants.

Incorporating organic materials and slow-release nutrients into planting beds ahead of time is always a good idea, except when planting ground covers around trees. The products can be applied on top of the ground but no thicker than 4 to 6 in. Do not till or mix the materials with the existing soil or the fibrous roots can be readily damaged, shortening the life of the tree. Instead plant the ground cover plants singly at the proper recommended spacing where they can later spread. Following this method does minimal damage to tree roots.

Chapter Three

Spacing is determined by the spread of the particular plant. Measure from the center of one plant to the center of the next for proper placement. Arrange plants diagonally to get a quicker fill. Avoid planting too close to borders. The chart "Calculating Plant Quantities" will help you determine the number of plants needed for a bed. Do not overcrowd ground covers because they will spread and mature as the season progresses.

Calculating Plant Quantities

1. Determine planting bed area: _____ (width × length = sq. ft.)

2. Recommended Spacing   Number of Plants Per Sq. Ft.

Recommended Spacing	Number of Plants Per Sq. Ft.
6 in.	4.0
8 in.	2.25
10 in.	1.44
12 in.	1.0
18 in.	0.44
24 in.	0.25

3. Multiply the number of plants for the recommended spacing by the sq. ft.

4. Example: 125 sq. ft. with 10-in. spacing = 180 plants needed (1.44 × 125 sq. ft. = 180)

Mulch between plants 2 to 4 in. thick to minimize weed growth until the plants spread and thickly fill the bed. Pine bark, cottonseed hulls, shredded leaves, compost, and pine straw mulches are best for ground covers. It usually takes two to three years for ground covers to completely fill in a landscape space. Weeding, mulching, fertilizing, and watering speed up the establishment process. Pinching or tipping the vines or branches throughout the first couple of growing seasons will promote a thicker-spreading growth.

Archangel

Lamium maculatum

Other Name: Spotted Deadnettle
Height: 8 to 12 in.
Spread: 12 to 24 in.
Flowers: White, pink, yellow
Bloom Period: Late spring, early summer
Zones: 6a, 6b, 7a, 7b

Color photograph on page 228.

Light Requirements:

Beneficial Characteristics:

A rchangel is an attractive plant with colorful flowers and glistening foliage. The flowers are borne in whorls on small, upright stems emerging from the foliage. They remind me somewhat of a snapdragon flower and are available in white, pink, or yellow. The foliage is shaped like a spade and covered with a fine hairlike pubescence. The foliage colors range from gray to yellow to light green, depending on the cultivar. The plant is deciduous in most parts of Oklahoma, although occasionally semievergreen in mild winters. Archangel is not likely to survive severe heat and drought. Planting it in afternoon shade, mulching it, and providing supplemental irrigation are practices to keep it thriving.

WHEN TO PLANT

Plant archangel in spring, early summer, or early fall.

WHERE TO PLANT

This plant definitely needs afternoon shade or dappled sun. Plant it in hot, scorching sun, and *Lamium* will live up to its other name of deadnettle. It prefers fertile, moist, well-drained soils. Use it as a border or foreground plant in perennial shade gardens, or use it as a companion plant with shade-tolerant perennials, especially ones with white, purple, or yellow flowers.

HOW TO PLANT

Plant archangel in groups 15 to 18 in. apart. Be careful not to set them too deep when planting. Divide these plants in the spring or early fall when they become overcrowded.

CARE AND MAINTENANCE

Pruning is seldom needed because of their low-growing habit. Taller selections can be trimmed back after flowering to keep them more orderly. Mulching is almost a necessity to keep the soil moist. Supplemental water will be needed during dry conditions. Even though the plants prefer moist sites, they need good drainage. Spider mites and heat scorch are occasional problems in sunnier locations. Fungal leaf spots and powdery mildew are not common but can occur.

ADDITIONAL INFORMATION

Lamium has square stems like mint and is in the mint family (*Labiatae*). It is not nearly as invasive as mint, although the species selection can be fairly aggressive. Most often our dry Oklahoma soils restrict the plant's aggressiveness.

ADDITIONAL SPECIES, CULTIVARS, OR VARIETIES

A cultivar known for its silver leaves with narrow, green edges and pink flowers is 'Beacon Silver'. 'White Nancy' looks like 'Beacon Silver', but it has white flowers. 'Pink Pewter' and 'Shell Pink' are other cultivars with pink flowers. 'Chequers' has uniquely marbled foliage with rose-pink flowers. 'Aureum' has golden foliage with pink flowers and is not quite as aggressive. One of my favorites is 'Beedham's White' with wonderful chartreuse foliage and white flowers. *Lamium galeobdolon*, sometimes listed as *Lamiastrum galeobdolon*, is known as yellow archangel. 'Herman's Pride' is a noninvasive cultivar with attractive yellow flowers featured on silver-flecked foliage.

 Did You Know?

Lamium can be used as a colorful filler in container displays for shade or in hanging baskets.

Blue Plumbago

Ceratostigma plumbaginoides

Other Name: Leadwort
Height: 8 to 12 in.
Spread: 12 to 18 in.
Flowers: Blue
Bloom Period: June, July
Zones: 6a, 6b, 7a, 7b

Color photograph on page 228.

Light Requirements:

Beneficial Characteristics:

Gardeners really get their money's worth with this plant. Blue plumbago offers unique landscape appeal from May until November. This outstanding deciduous ground cover emerges late in the spring with lush foliage. The shiny, ovate foliage forms along small, woody stems later supporting some of the bluest flowers I have ever seen. The flowers mature into an attractive coppery seedhead persisting most of the summer into late fall. As the days get shorter and temperatures cooler, the foliage turns a bronzy-red fall color. Leadwort is an effective companion plant with yellow-flowering Asiatic lilies and other yellow-flowering, partial-shade perennials. It is often used in combination with chartreuse or variegated shade plants. The yellow-and-blue colors make nice contrasting landscape colors. Pink-flowering plants are a good combination with leadwort.

WHEN TO PLANT

Plumbago is typically sold in 4¹/₂-in., 1-qt., or 1-gal. containers and can be planted in April, May, or June. You probably will not see too many available at garden centers any earlier in the season since they are late to break dormancy—unless they have been forced inside a greenhouse.

WHERE TO PLANT

Use blue plumbago as a filler in front portions of landscape beds or as a border along sidewalks. It prefers afternoon shade or sites with dappled sun. It can occasionally take sun in moist, well-drained sites. Moist, fertile soils provide the best growth for this blue-flowering beauty, although leadwort will take drier conditions once it is established. Soggy, compacted soils put a quick end to this plant. Leadwort does not always compete well in beds with shallow-rooted trees such as silver maples.

How to Plant

Set the plants at the same depth that the rootballs were in the containers. Space plants 12 to 18 in. apart. Mulch them to prevent competition from weeds until they are established.

Care and Maintenance

Flowers are formed on new growth. Once in a while blue plumbago thins in the center of the initial planting. Shearing the plant to the ground in early spring forces more uniform growth. Other than that, pruning is seldom needed. Fertilize once the new growth has started to emerge in the spring and possibly again in late June/early July. Do not fertilize any later, especially with high-nitrogen fertilizers, so that the plants will appropriately harden off before the onset of winter. Always water after granular fertilizer applications to keep from burning the foliage. Water is essential during drought conditions and as needed. There are no reports of significant pests.

Additional Information

Plumbago's low-growing habit makes it a suitable plant for companion bulb plantings. Bulbs easily emerge through the foliage. Leadwort can be divided and moved to other locations in the landscape in the spring. Dig small plugs at least 4 in. in diameter and 4 to 6 in. deep near the end of the existing plant clump. Plant these small plugs in their new location at the same depth that they were grown. Fill the original hole with excess soil. The plants will soon fill in and cover the bare spot.

Additional Species, Cultivars, or Varieties

Be careful not to select Chinese plumbago (*C. willmottianum*) for a perennial in Oklahoma. This similar-looking species will not tolerate our winters and is hardy only through Zone 8.

Did You Know?

Plumbago comes from the Latin name plumbum, *which means "lead," thus the common name leadwort.*

Bugleweed

Ajuga reptans

Other Names: Ajuga; Carpetbugle
Height: 6 to 9 in.
Spread: 5 to 10 in.
Flowers: Shades of purple, pink, and white
Bloom Period: Early to late spring
Zones: 6a, 6b, 7a, 7b

Color photograph on page 228.

Light Requirements:

Beneficial Characteristics:

A longtime favorite ground cover with creeping stems is ajuga. Certain culti-vars can be vigorous in growth and cover large areas fairly rapidly. Most selections send up spikes of whorled flowers in late spring, and purple is the most predominant color. Many cultivars are being introduced with unique foliage that adds continuous appeal to landscape borders. In some cultivars the colorful foliage is showier and longer lasting than the actual flower. One of the unique ways I have seen ajuga used was on a nonfunctional wooden bridge, which was a landscape feature at the gardens of Dr. Leonard Miller in Grove, Oklahoma. The arching bridge was topped with soil and compost, then the ajuga was planted in the shallow soil and mulched to hold it in place. The planting was well established and had completely carpeted the bridge. The flower display in the spring was one of a kind.

WHEN TO PLANT

Plant ajuga in spring or early summer.

WHERE TO PLANT

In optimum growing conditions, some cultivars are quite aggressive and have been known to grow into lawns. This invasive nature is a benefit in areas where a thick ground cover is needed. Use bugleweed in beds adjoining sidewalks to keep the plants in check. Plant ajuga in borders and containers. Make it a companion plant for low-traffic areas between shrub beds in moist, partially shaded sites. Adequate moisture seems to be the biggest factor in the plant's success. In drier sites the plant is less aggressive. Drainage is important, though, or the plant can succumb to crown rot. It prefers dappled or afternoon shade. In full-sun sites the plant needs good, moist soil and wind protection.

How to Plant

Plant on 12- to 24-in. centers at the same depth as the rootballs. Mulching until the plants are established minimizes weed growth. The ajuga runners easily emerge through the mulch as it spreads.

Care and Maintenance

Many cultivars are deciduous in severe winters. In milder winters the plants can retain their foliage. Fertilizing in the spring promotes quicker regrowth and spread. Wash granular fertilizer off the foliage to prevent burning. Ajuga is not very drought and heat tolerant, so supplemental water is needed to avoid leaf scorching.

Additional Information

Ajuga is easy to propagate by dividing the plant clumps, but the division should be done before temperatures become too hot. The plants spread naturally by sending out stems that root, similar to the way that strawberries spread. These newly formed stems can be rooted in moist soil or sand. Ajuga is not very tolerant of foot traffic. Variegated forms of ajuga occasionally revert to the solid colors of the parent plant and can be removed.

Additional Species, Cultivars, or Varieties

More unusual colors include 'Alba', a white-flowering selection, and 'Pink Beauty', with pink flowers. 'Burgundy Glow', 'Burgundy Lace', 'Jungle Beauty', and 'Silver Beauty' are all cultivars with various foliage variegation. 'Bronze Beauty', 'Gaiety', and 'Braunherz' have diversified shades of purple foliage. 'Cristata' probably has the smallest foliage that is strongly crinkled, and 'Catlin's Giant' has the largest foliage. For less-aggressive species, consider *A. pyramidalis* and *A. genevensis*, which are more clumping forms. 'Metallica Crispa' is a popular cultivar of the pyramidal type.

Did You Know?

Ajuga is related to mint but is not nearly as invasive. They are in the same family, Labiatae.

Creeping Euonymus

Euonymus fortunei

Other Name: Wintercreeper Euonymus
Height: 4 to 12 in.
Spread: 2 to 4 ft.
Flowers: Not showy
Bloom Period: June, July
Zones: 6a, 6b, 7a, 7b

Color photograph on page 228.

Light Requirements:

Beneficial Characteristics:

I rarely recommend many of the *Euonymus* species, but *E. fortunei* and the shrub form (*E. alatus*) are exceptions to the rule. Wintercreeper euonymus is a great evergreen plant for a ground cover with a deep forest-green color during the growing season, topped off with a violet-purple fall color. This plant is more woody than herbaceous but makes a thick cover fairly quickly. Some of the shrubbier cultivars of this species have clinging characteristics and can potentially grow up walls and other structures with time. Creeping euonymus is probably the ground cover to plant when tying a group of trees together to form one landscape bed. As it matures, its vines mat together and form a thick, 6- to 8-in. living mulch to keep weeds in check. Creeping euonymus needs plenty of space for its greatest impact.

WHEN TO PLANT
Plant creeping euonymus in spring, early summer, or fall.

WHERE TO PLANT
Size depends on the cultivar and determines placement in the landscape. Most are considered foreground plants or mid-level shrubs. They are often used for erosion sites and even for cascading wall plants. The plants prefer afternoon shade, although some can adapt to full sun. These plants are very adaptable to soil types and pH. They cannot tolerate waterlogged soils, however.

HOW TO PLANT
Planting holes should be at least two times wider than and the same depth as the roots. No organic amended backfill is required. Space wintercreeper euonymus at least 2 to 3 ft. apart in new plantings. Add mulch to keep weeds at bay until the plants have spread into unplanted areas.

CARE AND MAINTENANCE

These tough plants respond well to pruning just about any time of the year. On newly planted sites, tipping the ends of the elongated runners may be needed to encourage spreading and bushy, uniform growth. Mature or well-established sites of creeping euonymus can be sheared or edged to keep a uniform straight edge on the sides of the beds. Supplemental fertilizer applications can speed growth of the plants. Euonymus scale can be a problem on some cultivars of the *E. fortunei* species, especially in stressed situations. When euonymus is planted in heavy shade, powdery mildew and other leaf diseases are potential threats.

ADDITIONAL INFORMATION

The foliage can burn and partially defoliate in severe winters, but new growth quickly emerges in the spring. The beautiful fall color is one of the attributes of this ground cover.

ADDITIONAL SPECIES, CULTIVARS, OR VARIETIES

My favorite cultivar is 'Coloratus', which is more low growing with superb fall color. It is a good choice for large areas. 'Coloratus' is often substituted in Oklahoma for Asian (Asiatic) jasmine (*Trachelospermum asiaticum*), which is a popular ground cover in Texas. Asian jasmine offers a finer texture but is not as cold hardy for most of our state and does best in Zones 7b and lower. The "emerald" selections of wintercreeper euonymus are more upright in growth and come in a wealth of foliage colors.

  Did You Know?

Flowers and berries are more likely to occur as wintercreeper euonymus matures. Juvenile plants seldom exhibit flowers or fruit.

Creeping Phlox

Phlox subulata

Other Names: Flowering Moss; Moss Pink; Moss Phlox

Height: 3 to 6 in.

Spread: 2 ft.

Flowers: Pink, purple, and white

Bloom Period: Early spring

Zones: 6a, 6b, 7a, 7b

Color photograph on page 228.

Light Requirements:

Beneficial Characteristics:

Creeping phlox brings a breath of freshness each spring, thanks to its massive color impact. Few plants start off the season with such a bang. There is something rejuvenating about a landscape filled with the magical colors of phlox, daffodils, dogwoods, and redbuds after a winter's rest. I wish their flowers lasted longer, but at least the foliage remains somewhat evergreen, providing filler for the remainder of the year. Creeping phlox with its evergreen foliage is a great plant to use in the foreground of deciduous, sun-loving perennials.

WHEN TO PLANT

Plant in spring to ensure that you are getting the correct colors.

WHERE TO PLANT

Full-sun locations are best for border or edging plants. Plant them on slopes or near walls where they are allowed to cascade. Planting in too much shade causes the plants to become tall, leggy, and sparse with few flowers. Creeping phlox prefers well-drained, fertile soil, but the plant is adaptable.

HOW TO PLANT

Diagonally space plants 12 to 18 in. apart to get the best fill. Plant them in groups of at least five to make a more dramatic impact with color.

CARE AND MAINTENANCE

Pruning is generally not needed since the growth habit is compact and mounding. Shearing plants after blooming can promote more mounding growth in leggy plants, however. Be sure the plants receive at least four to five hours of sun for the best growth and bloom. Fertilizing stimulates healthy growth. During drought conditions, supplemental water is recommended. Flower blooms are formed later in the season, and drought can affect the flower set. Spider mites are a potential threat in drought-stressed, full-sun locations.

ADDITIONAL INFORMATION

Digging portions of the mounded plants after flowering is a good way to divide plants. Division is recommended in early spring. Many times the plants will have sporadic blooms again in late summer or early fall.

ADDITIONAL SPECIES, CULTIVARS, OR VARIETIES

Many cultivars come with a solid flower and an alternately colored center, or eye. White, pink, and blue (purple) are the most popular cultivars; however, 'Crimson Beauty' is closer to red than most. 'Candy Stripe' is a pink-and-white-striped cultivar actually blooming later than the solid colors. Planting 'Candy Stripe' with the solids will extend the bloom period. 'Nettleton's Variation' is a highly variegated foliage selection with pink flowers.

 Did You Know?

Another early, lavender, blooming prostrate plant often referred to as wild phlox is actually Verbena bipinnatifida, *or our native prairie verbena. Wild phlox is more upright in growth habit.*

English Ivy

Hedera helix

Height: 6 to 10 in. as a ground cover
Spread: Several ft.
Flowers: Nonshowy on mature vines
Bloom Period: Fall
Zones: 6a, 6b, 7a, 7b

Color photograph on page 228.

Light Requirements:

Beneficial Characteristic:

Most gardeners are familiar with this lustrous evergreen ground cover or vine. The stems easily form roots along leaf nodes, transforming the plant into a true clinging vine that attaches itself to anything getting in its way. I have seen English ivy climbing up trees, brick walls, and utility posts. The deep-green color is consistent year-round. Ivy rapidly covers a lot of space, such as a large landscape bed, when allowed to grow as a ground cover. English ivy is a great companion ground cover around tree beds because of the spreading and rooting growth habit. Just a few plants can be placed without damaging too many tree roots and can fill in an entire bed within a couple of growing seasons.

WHEN TO PLANT
Plant English ivy in spring, early summer, or fall.

WHERE TO PLANT
This plant favors partial shade in moist, fairly organic sites. It tolerates acid or alkaline soils. Plant it as a ground cover to tie trees together in island bed designs, or use it as a green barrier, adding texture and color to fences and two-story walls.

HOW TO PLANT
English ivy transplants easily and roots fairly quickly. Space plants 12 to 24 in. apart in holes that are slightly wider than and as deep as the rootballs. Mulching keeps soil moist and weeds in check until the ivy forms its own mulch barrier. Supplemental moisture is necessary until plants are well established.

CARE AND MAINTENANCE
Pruning long, extending vines early on promotes more uniform, bushy coverage. Supplemental feedings encourage quick growth and cover. Granular fertilizers left on the foliage can burn the leaves in moist situations, so

water the plants as soon as fertilizer is applied. Once the plants are established, they require minimal care. Leaf diseases are possible in environments with poor air circulation. Spider mites are potential pests.

ADDITIONAL INFORMATION

As the vines are allowed to mature, leaf shape changes. The leaves are typically lobed on juvenile growth and become more elliptical without pronounced lobes as they emerge from old vines. Flowers and fruit are more prominent on older growth.

ADDITIONAL SPECIES, CULTIVARS, OR VARIETIES

Many cultivars of English ivy are often used as indoor plants for topiaries. Many of them are not cold hardy as outdoor ground covers. 'Bulgaria' is a tough, cold-hardy variety more tolerant of heat and drought, however. 'Baltica' with its unique, smaller leaves is fairly hardy through Zone 6. Quite cold hardy is '238th Street', which has more heart-shaped leaves. 'Gold Heart' has dark-green foliage with a gold splash down the center of the leaf, and 'Thorndale' is a small, variegated leaf selection—both significantly cold hardy. 'Pixie' is a distinctive white-veined selection with crinkled leaves, hardy for most of the state, and 'Buttercup' is a lime-green cultivar tolerating a little more light, but not full sun.

 Did You Know?

A close cousin of H. helix *is colchis ivy (*H. colchica*) with larger, more heart-shaped leaves. The cultivar 'Dentata' is cold hardy and more tolerant of sun and dry soils after it is established. There is also a variegated form, 'Dentata Variegata'.*

Hardy Ice Plant

Delosperma cooperi

Height: 2 to 12 in.
Spread: 8 to 24 in.
Flowers: Purple
Bloom Period: June through fall
Zones: 6a, 6b, 7a, 7b

Color photograph on page 228.

Light Requirements:

Beneficial Characteristics:

If you are looking for an extremely low ground cover that loves the heat and full sun, look no farther. This succulent plant thrives on harsh conditions and rewards gardeners with bright, daisylike, eye-catching flowers most of the summer. Few ground covers provide the length of bloom displayed by hardy ice plant. Hardy ice plant makes many Xeriscape (drought-tolerant landscaping) lists touting its minimal care. This native of South Africa loves our Oklahoma summers. Most *Delospermas* are hardy through Zone 6, and *cooperi* is the most common. Even though this plant has a succulent appearance, it offers truly glistening blooms. The plant slowly spreads by underground runners and occasionally reseeds, making it a manageable ground cover.

WHEN TO PLANT

Plant hardy ice plant in early spring or summer.

WHERE TO PLANT

Plant *Delosperma* in full sun in a rock garden, or use it as a border plant near sidewalks. Hardy ice plant spreads but is noninvasive. It is easy to pull up if it grows out of its designated area. Bulbs and other perennials can readily grow through hardy ice plant. Match yellow-and-purple-flowering perennials with the violet-magenta color of this brilliant-flowering ground cover. This plant does well in sandy, well-drained soils; waterlogged sites can cause quick death.

HOW TO PLANT

Plant it at the same depth as the rootball in a hole two times the width. Space plants 12 to 18 in. apart.

CARE AND MAINTENANCE

Hardy ice plant is semievergreen and can die back to the ground in cold, wet winters. It will usually emerge the following spring as soil temperatures begin to warm. Cool, damp conditions in early spring tend to delay the emergence of this plant, but do not give up on it. As soon as the temperatures rise, so does the succulent foliage of hardy ice plant. This trouble-free plant seldom needs additional care. There are no serious insect or disease problems. Occasional watering is needed while the plants are getting established; otherwise they are very drought tolerant. Hardy ice plant is easy to divide in early spring and summer. Dig clumps 3 to 4 in. in diameter in the outer edges of the existing plant mass. Fill the hole with soil, and ice plant will quickly grow back. Supplemental feedings should be minimal at most.

ADDITIONAL INFORMATION

Hardy ice plant is a popular West Coast plant where conditions are somewhat arid and dry. It is one of the first plants you will see exiting the San Diego airport, and the ravishing color is one you will not soon forget.

ADDITIONAL SPECIES, CULTIVARS, OR VARIETIES

D. cooperi (hardy ice plant) blooms are typically a magenta-rose pink. There are other hybrids and species with white, pink, or yellow flowers. There are also some differences in the coarseness of the succulent foliage. Not all ice plant varieties are hardy in Oklahoma.

 Did You Know?

D. floribundum *'Starburst' was recognized as a Plant Select® winner for the Rocky Mountain and plains states. It is a good selection for the Panhandle counties of the state with its hardy, clumping foliage and shimmering, pink flowers.*

Juniper

Juniperus species

Height: 1 to 3 ft.	**Light Requirements:**
Spread: 3 to 8 ft.	
Flowers: Inconspicuous	
Bloom Period: March or April	**Beneficial Characteristic:**
Zones: 6a, 6b, 7a, 7b	
Color photograph on page 229.	

This bristly conifer is one of the most widely adapted and commonly used evergreen plants in the United States. I have included juniper in the ground cover section primarily because of the many compact forms used for that purpose. The standard upright species are used frequently as foundation plants, hedges, screen plants, windbreaks, and individual specimens, and in massed plantings. Ground cover junipers offer distinct color and texture for landscape in harsh conditions. Depending on the cultivar, some junipers change colors in the fall and winter. Junipers are available in various shades of green, gray, and yellow.

WHEN TO PLANT
Plant in spring, early summer, and fall.

WHERE TO PLANT
These plants must have full-sun sites. With too much shade, juniper foliage becomes spindly and thin. Junipers are adapted to many conditions and soil types as long as the site is not waterlogged. Use juniper ground covers as medium-sized filler plants, especially in combination with deciduous plants, or use them in rock gardens and on slopes. Good air circulation between plants minimizes disease and insect problems.

HOW TO PLANT
Junipers are available in container-grown and balled-and-burlapped forms. Plant them in holes at least two times the width of the rootballs and the same depth. Planting slightly above grade is acceptable with junipers in heavy, poorly drained soils. Mulching is needed in such cases. Plant them in groups for a more significant display.

CARE AND MAINTENANCE
Junipers may need to be pruned in early spring but only with tip cuts or shearing. Severe pruning to woody growth of junipers is not recommended since they typically do not form secondary buds. They respond to supple-

mental feedings in early spring and summer. Mulch the plants every couple of years to replace decomposed or weathered mulch. Twig blight and phomopsis blight are probably the most frustrating disease problems affecting junipers. The damage can look like that caused by spider mites, another common pest. Twig blight may be caused by poor air circulation, an overly shady site, or stress. Phomopsis results from cool, wet conditions in late spring and early summer. Root rot may occur in heavy, poorly drained soils. Bagworms are another insect attracted to junipers.

ADDITIONAL INFORMATION

Plants are typically dioecious (male and female flowers are on separate plants). The male blooms are generally loaded with pollen early in the spring. The pollen of some species can frequently be seen blowing from plants on windy days, settling on cars, lawn furniture, and other outdoor items.

ADDITIONAL SPECIES, CULTIVARS, OR VARIETIES

J. horizontalis, *J. procumbens*, and *J. sabina* have the largest selections of ground cover cultivars. Try to choose ones that are tolerant of blight diseases, such as 'Blue Forest', 'Arcadia', 'Broadmoor', and 'Skandia'. 'Blue Carpet' is a species of *J. squamata* and has a blue-gray color that makes it an interesting ground cover. Be sure to check whether the cultivar you are choosing retains its rich, green color during the winter. Some are known to turn a purple, almost bronzy brown.

Did You Know?

*Russian cypress (*Microbiota decussata*) is an evergreen conifer with a juniperlike appearance that tolerates shade.*

Moneywort

Lysimachia nummularia

Other Names: Creeping Jenny; Creeping Charlie
Height: 2 to 4 in.
Spread: 12 to 24 in.
Flowers: Yellow
Bloom Period: Spring
Zones: 6a, 6b, 7a, 7b

Color photograph on page 229.

Light Requirements:

Beneficial Characteristic:

Moneywort is one of my favorite truly low-growing ground covers. It is evergreen in most seasons and produces a thick, lush green growth, seldom growing taller than 4 in. The carpetlike growth is a perfect living mulch that rarely allows weeds through it. Easily grown, it is used to cascade over walls, banks, or slopes. It is a perfect border plant, too. Moneywort is gaining in popularity as a combination plant for container gardens, patio bowls, and windowboxes. This beauty is grown primarily for its ruffled, lush foliage, but it can exhibit occasional yellow flowers. Moneywort is adapted to and thrives in full shade.

WHEN TO PLANT
Plant it in spring, summer, or fall.

WHERE TO PLANT
Moneywort will not tolerate dry soils. It must have consistent moisture. The soil quality is not as important as the moisture. It prefers afternoon shade but tolerates full shade as long as there is good drainage. The low-growing nature of moneywort makes it a perfect choice for sidewalk and landscape borders. Many gardeners plant it to cascade over walls and out of containers.

HOW TO PLANT
Moneywort is sold most often in 2-, 4-, or 6-in. containers. It readily establishes when it is planted in loosely dug holes the same depth as the roots. Space plants 12 to 18 in. apart. Water is a necessity to establish moneywort. Mulch after planting to hold in soil moisture until the plant spreads and acts as mulch itself.

CARE AND MAINTENANCE
This plant requires little maintenance other than an occasional trimming when it grows beyond its borders. Supplemental feedings will help to

establish the plants, but be careful not to burn the foliage with granular fertilizers. Always water after granular feedings to wash the fertilizer from the foliage. In severe winters the foliage may be scorched but will return the next season. There are no serious pest threats.

ADDITIONAL INFORMATION
Moneywort is easy to divide and share with gardening friends. It is the perfect plant for moist, shaded sites where nothing else seems to grow. It propagates easily by division or cuttings.

ADDITIONAL SPECIES, CULTIVARS, OR VARIETIES
In addition to the solid-green species, a cultivar with light-green, almost yellow foliage is sold as 'Aurea' and sometimes as 'Goldilocks'. Occasionally, it will revert to solid green.

 Did You Know?

In addition to being used in container displays, moneywort can be successfully grown in a hanging basket.

Pachysandra

Pachysandra terminalis

Other Names: Japanese Pachysandra; Japanese Spurge
Height: 6 to 8 in.
Spread: 12 to 18 in.
Flowers: White
Bloom Period: Early spring
Zones: 6a, 6b, 7a,7b

Color photograph on page 229.

Light Requirements:

Beneficial Characteristic:

Pachysandra is another evergreen ground cover that prefers shade. The wedge-shaped foliage is arranged in whorls along the stem. My first experience with pachysandra was in college in a plant identification class. It was easy to identify with its uniquely shaped foliage. Pachysandra spreads by stolons and is a great filler plant in shade gardens. It also offers a coarser texture for design. Pachysandra is useful in combination with shade-loving deciduous perennials. When pachysandra is planted in and around deciduous plants, the evergreen foliage commands attention, especially in dormant winter landscapes. 'Green Sheen' pachysandra is one of the glossiest green-leafed plants I have ever seen. It almost looks as if someone has sprayed and cleaned the foliage.

WHEN TO PLANT
Plant container-grown pachysandra in spring or early summer.

WHERE TO PLANT
Overall growth is more upright than spreading but still appears very compact. Use pachysandra as a border or foreground filler plant. It is not a good cascading plant as are some of the other ground covers in this chapter. Gardeners like to plant it in shaded courtyard areas, around trees, and in shade rock gardens. It should not be planted in high-traffic areas since it does not withstand heavy foot traffic. Pachysandra must grow in moist, fertile soils with a slightly acidic pH. It will not tolerate dry, sunny locations.

HOW TO PLANT
Space plants about 15 in. apart.

CARE AND MAINTENANCE
Pachysandra generally does not need pruning. The almost succulent-looking stems are low growing and spread with underground stolons.

Pachysandra is not generally considered invasive and will stay fairly well within its boundaries, especially in drier soils. Plants are typically evergreen in the southern counties of the state and semievergreen in the northern locations.

ADDITIONAL INFORMATION

Pachysandra is often overplanted in other regions of the United States, but it is seldom used in Oklahoma. It has its place in our landscapes where the appropriate sites are provided, and some of the new cultivars should be considered more often in areas that need a ground cover.

ADDITIONAL SPECIES, CULTIVARS, OR VARIETIES

'Green Sheen', a lustrous, shiny-leafed selection, is probably the best choice for our hot and humid conditions. It is also disease tolerant and hardy through Zone 5. 'Green Carpet' is the old standard, and 'Silver Edge' has a variegated, creamy-white leaf margin.

 Did You Know?

Pachysandra is in the boxwood family (Buxaceae).

Peacock Moss

Selaginella uncinata

One of the most unusual ground covers I have ever grown is peacock moss. The delicate foliage actually has an iridescent look, and it resembles a low-growing fern more than anything else. *Selaginella* is not a moss or a fern, however. The growth is probably the flattest of any ground cover, almost mat forming. The various shades of blue and green glisten in dappled light. The colors resemble those of a peacock feather, and the plant is almost as soft, thus the name peacock fern. I have used peacock moss next to a rock sidewalk leading into a shaded area by a water hydrant. The moist, shady site seems to be perfect for this one-of-a-kind ground cover. Planting the lower-growing peacock moss in front of the taller *Selaginella pallescens* (arborvitae fern) makes for a refreshing, almost tropical look in the summer.

WHEN TO PLANT

Plant it in late spring or early summer.

WHERE TO PLANT

This low-growing ground cover is definitely a border plant in partial shade. It works well in shaded rock gardens and as a lower foreground plant in combination with ferns, hostas, and other shade-loving plants. It tolerates full shade, but the various displays of colors are sometimes lost. Peacock moss suffers in a site with heavy foot traffic. It prefers fertile, moist, and well-drained soils. Where possible, amend the soils before planting time.

HOW TO PLANT

Place the rootball in a widely dug hole the same depth that it was grown. Plant on 15- to 18-in. centers. Mulch the plants to preserve moisture. They can grow in Zone 6 if protected and mulched in the winter.

CARE AND MAINTENANCE

Peacock moss requires minimal maintenance. Fertilizer is seldom needed if an organically rich soil is prepared before planting time. Ordinarily, the foliage will die back in severely cold winters. The dead foliage should be removed in late spring as the new growth emerges. In milder winters, the plant acts as an evergreen, retaining its unique foliage. Mulching conserves moisture and minimizes weed growth until the plants are well established. To avoid smothering this delicate plate, be careful not to get the mulch more than 2 to 3 in. thick.

ADDITIONAL INFORMATION

Peacock moss is late to emerge in the spring, sometimes not growing until late April or early May. Do not give up on it and forget where it is planted. Reapply mulch as the new growth emerges.

ADDITIONAL SPECIES, CULTIVARS, OR VARIETIES

Another species, *Selaginella pallescens*, is commonly called arborvitae fern because the foliage resembles arborvitae (only without the bagworms). The flat foliage is a deep green and softer to the touch than arborvitae. It gets a little taller, maturing at 15 to 18 in. Arborvitae fern is primarily deciduous in the winter but cold hardy in Zone 6.

Did You Know?

The fine foliage makes a nice green filler companion with cutflower arrangements.

Stonecrop

Sedum species

Other Name: Sedum
Height: 4 to 24 in.
Spread: 12 to 24 in.
Flowers: Red, pink, or yellow, depending on the cultivar
Bloom Period: Spring, summer, or fall
Zones: 6a, 6b, 7a, 7b

Color photograph on page 229.

Light Requirements:

Beneficial Characteristics:

Sedum is one of the best choices for hot-sun landscape beds. It thrives on heat and is frequently used as an accent plant in rock gardens. Some cultivars take partial shade, but sedums present their best display in the sun. Many offer both flower and foliage characteristics. Height variation and foliage texture vary, depending on the species. The very showy blooms occur in spring, summer, or fall, again depending on the cultivar. Many times the best display comes from using combinations of sedum textures and colors. Sedum is frequently combined with hardy ice plant, which produces blooms longer in the summer.

WHEN TO PLANT

Plant sedum in spring, summer, or fall.

WHERE TO PLANT

Consider the height of the cultivar to determine its placement in the landscape. Plant dwarf types in the front and taller ones in the middle or back of the site. Plant sedum in full-sun sites for erosion control. Arrange taller clumping types in groups of three or five. Use the more spreading, prostrate forms for cascading over rock walls. Well-drained soils are key in growing sedum. They accept heavy soils, rocky soils, sandy soils, and just about anything in between as long as they are not waterlogged.

HOW TO PLANT

Plant sedum at the same depth as the rootball in loosely dug soil. No amended backfill is needed. Space plants 15 to 18 in. apart.

CARE AND MAINTENANCE

The primary effort involved with sedum is planting it. Sedum generally takes care of itself. Some cultivars need to have the dead flower stalks removed once a year. There are seldom disease problems. Aphids, particularly black aphids, favor some sedums early in the spring, but they are easily controlled. Fertilize only if the plants demonstrate deficiency symptoms.

ADDITIONAL INFORMATION

Sedums are easy to divide. Ground cover or spreading sedums can be propagated just about anytime during the growing season. Clump-forming sedums should be divided and replanted in very early spring before the shoots emerge from the winter mound. 'Autumn Joy' sedum is an example of a mounding form often compared to cabbage in its early stages of growth. Sedums are primarily deciduous, going dormant in the winter. Some cultivars retain their green foliage, however.

ADDITIONAL SPECIES, CULTIVARS, OR VARIETIES

Because there are more than six hundred species, I am going to mention only a few favorites. 'Autumn Joy' has a wonderful mounding appearance in early spring. It later grows into a beautiful upright plant with burgundy-pink flowers, turning even more bronze in the fall. 'Autumn Joy' complements ornamental fountain grass. 'Rosy Glow' grows to 6 to 8 in. but does not spread well, so I have planted a prostrate, more spreading cultivar, 'John Creech', to fill in around the 'Rosy Glow'. It makes a pleasing combination of textures and colors. 'Vera James', 'Elizabeth' ('Red Carpet'), 'Dragon's Blood', and 'Purple Form' are colorful types with reddish-purple foliage in addition to their flowers.

 Did You Know?

Sedum is a great companion plant for bulbs planted in the fall. Both prefer full sun. The bulbs can easily emerge through the low-growing sedum foliage in early spring.

Vinca

Vinca minor

Other Names: Common Periwinkle;
  Trailing Myrtle
Height: 3 to 10 in.
Spread: 12 to 24 in.
Flowers: Pink, purple, and white
Bloom Period: April, March
Zones: 6a, 6b, 7a, 7b

Color photograph on page 229.

Light Requirements:

Beneficial Characteristic:

This ground-hugging plant is widely grown and commonly used in landscapes. Vinca tolerates partial shade and offers uniquely shiny opposite leaves on cascading stems. Most cultivars are evergreen; however, there are a few deciduous selections. Many perennial periwinkles have attractive flowers early in the spring with sporadic blooms through the summer and fall. The flowers are pleasant enough, but the plant is probably better known for its tough growth and attractive foliage texture display. Flower colors are typically purplish blue, although violets and whites are gaining in popularity and availability.

WHEN TO PLANT
Plant vinca in spring, early summer, or fall.

WHERE TO PLANT
Vincas like partial dappled or afternoon shade. Full sun has a tendency to scorch the leaves. Use the plants as fillers for borders and landscape beds or as a quick-growing ground cover under trees. Plant vinca so that it can cascade over walls. The plants are considered fairly quick growers, especially when planted in moist, fertile soils.

HOW TO PLANT
Space plants on 12-in. centers to get the quickest fill. Spacing them wider apart takes them longer to grow together. Dig holes wider than and the same depth as the rootballs of the plants.

CARE AND MAINTENANCE
Pruning is seldom needed other than to trim back growth escaping from the border. Fertilizing speeds up the growth habit for a quicker fill. Be careful not to overdo it and burn the foliage, especially with granular fertilizers.

Mulch keeps weeds in check and retains moisture during the establishment period. The vines easily grow through the mulch as they mature. Occasional leaf and stem diseases occur as well as powdery mildew in heavy shade with poor air circulation. Supplemental water is needed during drought conditions.

ADDITIONAL INFORMATION

The perennial ground cover periwinkle should not be confused with the annual flowering periwinkle or vinca (*Catharanthus roseus*). The flowers are somewhat comparable, but that is the primary similarity. Annual vinca is upright in growth, and perennial ground cover vinca has a cascading form.

ADDITIONAL SPECIES, CULTIVARS, OR VARIETIES

Vinca minor typically has smaller leaves than *Vinca major*. The flowers are very similar. The foliage can be various shades of green or even variegated, depending on the cultivar. In addition to the standard species, popular *V. minor* cultivars include 'Ralph Shugert', an elegant, white-variegated leaf form with colorful blue-purple flowers; 'Alba', 'Emily Joy', and 'Jekyll's White', with white flowers and green foliage; 'Bowles' ('La Grave') and 'Shademaster', with lavender flowers; and 'Rosea', with a more violet-pink color. Double-flowering types are somewhat harder to find; they include 'Mutliplex' and 'Rosea Plena'. *V. major* cultivars include 'Variegata' (yellow deciduous leaf variegation and more aggressive growth), 'Aureomaculata' (variegated with a yellow blotch down the center), and 'Jason Hill' (violet-blue flowers).

Did You Know?

Vinca is a great cascading plant to use in color bowls or container displays as well as in windowboxes.

Vines

VINES ARE PERFECT PLANTS for offering height and individuality to the landscape. They create suspense by subdividing gardens into different rooms. Vines quickly become part of the welcoming ambiance when they are allowed to grow over entrance gate archways. Sun-loving vines grown on large arbors can create shade gardens below and create outdoor areas for relaxation. They hide eyesores or add character to ordinary fences. If space is a concern, try growing vines in containers where they can grow up a trellis or an adjoining wall. The colors and textures of vines are numerous, with something for any gardener's particular interest.

Some of the vines discussed in this chapter are quite common. Others are unfamiliar to Oklahoma gardens. Some prefer shade, and others prefer sun—but all have minimal maintenance requirements. Although many of the vines are somewhat woody, the majority are deciduous (they lose their leaves in the winter).

Vines typically have the ability to grow or trellis up nearby objects. Some are more aggressive than others. A few form aerial roots along the way, others are equipped with gripping tendrils, and some need a little help getting started by weaving them in and out of their support system. Trellises and support systems must be strong and well built since many vines can become quite heavy as they mature. It may be frightening to read about the potential size of some vines, but height is often dictated by the size of the structure upon which they are grown.

Prepare the soil in landscape beds by tilling or adding organic materials and slow-release nutrients before planting time. Dig a hole two to three times the width of the rootball and the same depth as

Chapter Four

with all planting procedures. Routine watering, mulching, and fertilizing are beneficial practices in growing vines. Pruning is most often done for controlling height and width of aggressive vines. Prune at the appropriate time of year to avoid reducing flower set.

Many of the vine selections described in this chapter are readily available through garden centers. Others may be ordered through specialty nurseries.

Akebia

Akebia quinata

Other Names: Five-Leaf Akebia;
Chocolate Vine
Height: Up to 30 ft., or as tall as its support
Spread: 8 to 10 ft.
Flowers: Showy chocolate purple
Bloom Period: March or April
Zones: 6a, 6b, 7a, 7b

Color photograph on page 229.

Light Requirements:

Beneficial Characteristics:

If you have not introduced yourself or your garden to this vine, put it first on your list. I grow this vine for its unique foliage, but the unusual flower color is an added bonus. The twining vine sends out palmately compound foliage (that is, with five leaflets) each spring that is truly a delight. The new growth has a purplish tint maturing to a glossy blue green. The chocolate-purple blooms occur as the new growth emerges. Very seldom is there fall foliage color as the leaves drop in early winter. In mild winters the plants retain their leaves most of the season. Occasionally, the flower stems set fruit later, developing into a small, violet-colored pod in the fall. I once used akebia in a landscape where it grew up a cattle panel fence among perennial coreopsis and daylilies. The purple flowers along with the dark, unusual leaves of akebia made a perfect background for the yellow flowers of the perennials.

WHEN TO PLANT

Plant akebia in early spring, early summer, or early fall.

WHERE TO PLANT

Use this fast-growing, twining vine on trellises, arbors, pergolas, or fences. It also grows along the ground as a matted cover if no support is provided, but it can choke out adjoining plants. Akebia can be used singularly as a specimen or massed as a hedge. The plants tolerate full sun or partial shade, and they are not picky about soil type or pH.

HOW TO PLANT

Most often akebia is available in staked 1-, 2-, or 3-gal. containers. Set the plant in a hole dug at least two times wider than the rootball and the same depth as the container. Place the plants 4 ft. apart to become a hedge. No soil amendments are needed. Mulch after planting. If possible, remove the stake from the plant, and gently weave the vine in the support system to start it in the right direction.

CARE AND MAINTENANCE

Because the growth rate is quite fast, pruning will be needed to keep the plant within the boundaries of its support system. Tip pruning can be done anytime through the year. The flowers are generally produced on previous season's growth. The vining stems increase in size as they mature and turn from green to brown. Overfertilizing this vine can cause too much growth and thus require higher maintenance. Reapply mulch as the initial applications weather or wash away. There are no serious pest problems.

ADDITIONAL INFORMATION

Five-leaf akebia is not common, but three-leaf akebia (*A. trifoliata*) is even rarer in the nursery trade. A hybrid cross, *A × pentaphylla*, contains both three and five leaflets on compound foliage.

ADDITIONAL SPECIES, CULTIVARS, OR VARIETIES

'Alba' is a uniquely white-flowering and fruiting cultivar. 'Rosea' has a lighter-violet-colored flower than the traditional species, and 'Shiro Bana' from Monrovia Nursery in California has white flowers with purple fruit.

 Did You Know?

Akebia is a native of Asian countries and was introduced to the United States in the 1800s.

Boston Ivy

Parthenocissus tricuspidata

Other Name: Japanese Creeper
Height: Up to 30 ft., or as tall as its support
Spread: 10 to 15 ft.
Flowers: Yellowish green, nonshowy
Bloom Period: June, July
Zones: 6a, 6b, 7a, 7b

Color photograph on page 229.

Light Requirements:

Beneficial Characteristics:

This deciduous vine has spectacular fall colors. In the spring the green, lustrous foliage unfurls, providing a thick cover to produce shade for walls, fences, and arbors. The vining growth spreads by attaching small tendrils to its support system. The coarse foliage has three distinctive, dark, glossy-green lobes. There are several cultivars of this intriguing vine—some with purplish leaves throughout the growing season. Boston ivy and its relatives (Virginia creeper) are some of the earliest plants to turn a vibrant color in the fall. This tough plant attaches to almost anything. I have seen it grow up concrete walls. Boston ivy is a perfect camouflage for structures that are eyesores.

WHEN TO PLANT
Plant this vine in early spring, summer, or fall.

WHERE TO PLANT
Boston ivy can grow up support systems, trees, or concrete walls. It also grows as a ground cover. It tolerates many soil types and environmental conditions, but it prefers moist, fertile soils. Boston ivy can grow in full sun but performs best in afternoon shade in Oklahoma.

HOW TO PLANT
Space plants 12 to 18 in. apart. Place the plant at the same depth that it was grown, in a hole two times the width of the rootball. Water to settle the soil. Mulch to keep moisture in and weeds out during the establishment period. If the planting site is near a wall, leave stakes in the planting hole until the vine attaches to its support system. Guiding the vine in the right direction may be a routine chore.

CARE AND MAINTENANCE
If there is a downside to Boston ivy, it is the lack of color in the winter months. The deciduous foliage drops fairly early in the fall and emerges in the spring. The stems are a light-brown color and not showy when the plant

is dormant. Pruning is seldom needed, other than to keep the vine within its allotted growing space. Occasional leaf spot diseases may occur in locations with too much shade. Watch for leafhoppers, spider mites, and scale (an infrequent problem). The plants respond to supplemental feedings to get better established. After they are established, too much fertilizer causes excess growth.

ADDITIONAL INFORMATION

Boston ivy is fairly easy to start from rooted vines near the ground. These cuttings can be planted in a container or in moist, sandy soils. A colorful cousin of Boston ivy is Virginia creeper (*P. quinquefolia*), with five leaflets per compound leaf. 'Engelmannii' is an improved, smaller-leafed selection of Virginia creeper, which is less vigorous than the species and attaches better to concrete. Virginia creeper 'Star Showers' ('Monham') has smaller foliage with a splattering of white and pink. Both are tough vines or ground covers grown and used like Boston ivy. The two species of *Parthenocissus* produce berries more visible in the fall after the leaves drop. Birds enjoy the fruit and easily spread them throughout the landscape and garden.

ADDITIONAL SPECIES, CULTIVARS, OR VARIETIES

'Beverly Brooks' and 'Green Showers' are two cultivars of Boston ivy with larger leaves and brilliant fall color. A smaller-leafed version is 'Lowii'. 'Purpurea' has predominantly purple-tinged foliage all summer, especially when grown in more sun, and 'Veitchii' has new growth emerging as purple and turning more green at maturity. A waxier, thick, green-leafed selection is 'Robusta', with an orange-red fall color.

 Did You Know?

*Virginia creeper with its five compound leaflets is often incorrectly mistaken for poison ivy (*Toxicodendron radicans*), which has only three leaflets.*

Carolina Jasmine

Gelsemium sempervirens

Other Name: Carolina Yellow Jessamine
Height: Up to 20 ft., or as tall as its support
Spread: 5 to 6 ft.
Flowers: Yellow and showy
Bloom Period: Early spring, March or April
Zones: 6a, 6b, 7a, 7b

Color photograph on page 229.

Light Requirements:

Beneficial Characteristics:

This vine commands all the attention in the landscape with its impressive burst of yellow blooms. This early-flowering vine has fragrant, funnel-shaped flowers that make quite a show in March or April. The growth habit is best described as a tangled mingling of wiry stems, which sounds worse than it appears. The foliage is evergreen, providing year-round lustrous, dark-green color. During the winter months, the foliage may turn a yellowish green with a hint of purple for a nice display during drab times. Carolina jasmine will grow as tall as its support or make a mound if left alone.

WHEN TO PLANT

Plant it in early spring or summer.

WHERE TO PLANT

The best show of flowers occurs in full or partial sun, although the plant tolerates shade. It prefers moist, well-drained, slightly acidic soils, especially when planted in full sun. In scorching hot environments afternoon shade is recommended. Carolina jasmine tolerates some alkalinity. I have seen these beauties frequently growing up mailboxes and light poles. They are perfect for fences and trellises. Carolina jasmine is occasionally allowed to cascade as a ground cover, but it would need a site where it would not hide other plants. Jasmine is also planted in large containers where it is allowed to fall over the sides.

HOW TO PLANT

Dig a hole two to three times wider than and the same depth as the root-ball. No organic backfill is necessary unless incorporated ahead of time into the entire planting bed. Mulch and water the plants as needed.

CARE AND MAINTENANCE

The better the soil, the better the growth, which is the case with most plants. I have seen jasmine growing quite well in alkaline soils, even though it is naturally found in slightly acidic soils. Carolina jasmine seldom has pest problems. Pruning should be done after flowering since it typically blooms on the previous season's growth. Occasional sporadic flowering occurs again in the fall. Reapply mulch as it weathers or washes away.

ADDITIONAL INFORMATION

Carolina jasmine is considered a moderate- to fast-growing vine. The flowers are quite fragrant, especially in the stillness of the night, and they are favorites in southern gardens. In the coldest winters the plants may lose foliage. They grow better in Zone 7 but will grow in Zone 6 when planted in protected areas and mulched during the winter.

ADDITIONAL SPECIES, CULTIVARS, OR VARIETIES

In addition to the species there are several cultivars. 'Compacta' is a more dwarf, mounding form that does not need staking. 'Pride of Augusta' ('Plena') is a spectacular double-flowering selection. A related species, swamp jasmine (*G. rankinii*), is not as cold hardy and typically flowers in the fall. As the name implies, it tolerates somewhat wet conditions. Hybrid crosses are being introduced between the two species.

 Did You Know?

Carolina jasmine is the state flower of South Carolina and is native to the southeastern United States.

Chinese Wisteria

Wisteria sinensis

Height: 30 ft. or more
Spread: 15 to 20 ft., depending on
the structure
Flowers: Violet-blue or white clusters
Bloom Period: April, May
Zones: 6a, 6b, 7a, 7b

Color photograph on page 229.

Light Requirements:

Beneficial Characteristics:

There is probably not a vine better known for its large, brilliant flower clusters. The violet-blue or white flowers are absolutely spectacular with their long clusters dangling from the vines. The deciduous, compound foliage is perfect for providing shade in the summer when wisteria is used on arbors. I have seen wisteria growing up telephone poles, trees, and houses and along fences. Fall color is virtually nonexistent, and after the leaves drop, brown, velvety pods persist into early winter. Chinese wisteria is not quite as cold hardy or as fragrant as its cousin, Japanese wisteria, but is generally more widely available in the nursery trade. Chinese blooms prior to foliage set while Japanese blooms as the leaves emerge. Just as roses are associated with love, wisteria is a symbol of "I cling to thee." And when it is grown in the landscape, there is probably not a stronger clinging vine available.

WHEN TO PLANT
Plant wisteria in spring or early summer.

WHERE TO PLANT
These aggressive plants need plenty of room to grow, preferably in full sun. They tolerate partial shade; however, dense shade creates potential blooming and disease problems. Wisteria demands well-drained soil, but it is not too picky about soil type. Common garden wisdom is that the plants favor a slightly alkaline pH. Yet in soils with very high pH, they can become chlorotic. In very fertile soils the plants have a tendency to put on excess vegetative growth and are often slow to flower. Support structures need to be very strong and sturdy.

HOW TO PLANT
The planting hole should be at least two times wider than and the same depth as the rootball. The only soil amendment required is phosphorus in the bottom of the planting hole covered with a little soil. Mulch after planting, and water.

CARE AND MAINTENANCE

Flowering—or the lack thereof—seems to be the most frustrating challenge for some gardeners when growing wisteria. Buy named cultivars propagated from mature flowering vines. Such cultivars can flower in the first couple of years after establishment. Seedlings and other unknown origin selections are slow to bloom, taking six to ten years to initiate flowering. Fertilizer with excess nitrogen promotes vegetative growth and little flowering. In plants slow to flower, root and stem pruning is suggested. Use a sharp shovel, and cut into the roots sporadically around the plant. Heavy pruning of the vines to two or three buds may initiate more productive wood. Pests are seldom a concern.

ADDITIONAL INFORMATION

The flowers are typically produced on year-old growth or older. Occasionally, flowers will be seen on new growth of the season. Once the plants begin to bloom, pruning should be done after flowering. Tip pruning to keep plants under control can be done throughout the growing season. Dormant pruning should primarily remove dead, diseased, or damaged wood.

ADDITIONAL SPECIES, CULTIVARS, OR VARIETIES

Chinese wisteria has shorter flower clusters that are not as fragrant but often more prolific. The leaves are somewhat smaller with fewer leaflets. In some cases Chinese wisteria reblooms in the fall. 'Alba' (white) and 'Caroline' (blue) are two of the most common Chinese types. Double-flowering cultivars such as 'Black Dragon' and 'Plena' are generally more erratic blooming but still unique. Japanese wisteria (*W. floribunda*) is known for its fragrant, long flower clusters. 'Macrobotrys' is an old selection known to have the longest, cascading, violet-flower clusters of any cultivar. 'Alba', 'Issai Perfect', and 'Ivory Tower' are popular white-flowering types. 'Lawrence' has paler-blue flowers and is exceptionally cold hardy. 'Royal Purple' and 'Texas Purple' are two violet-colored forms, and 'Rosea' is slightly pink.

 Did You Know?

Tree forms of wisteria are vining types heavily pruned for several years to force a stronger-standing, upright trunk.

Clematis

Clematis species

Height: 5 to 8 ft.
Spread: 4 to 6 ft.
Flowers: Assorted colors (single and doubles)
Bloom Period: Spring, summer, or fall (cultivar dependent)
Zones: 6a, 6b, 7a, 7b

Color photograph on page 229.

Light Requirements:

Beneficial Characteristics:

Clematis has a spectacular range of flower colors. The deep, almost-velvety shades of pinks, purples, reds, yellows, and whites will brighten up anyone's day. Most gardeners are familiar with clematis and probably have tried growing them. In Oklahoma, growing them is not as simple as one would hope. Clematis will grow in our hot, humid summers as long as mulch and shade are provided to the roots. There are hundreds of cultivars from which to choose, with single or double blossoms generally grouped by flowering times. The flowering period is the key to pruning clematis to initiate continued growth and flowering. Remember this rule—warm top, cool bottom—and you can enjoy clematis in your Oklahoma landscape.

WHEN TO PLANT
Plant clematis in the spring.

WHERE TO PLANT
Plant clematis in loamy, fertile, moderately moist, well-drained soils. Soil pH is not critical as long as there is good drainage. Clematis prefers lightly dappled sun or afternoon shade. But equally important are mulching and shading of the roots (preferably by another plant). Full sun can scorch the foliage, although these plants can tolerate more sun if they are protected from the wind. These vines grow on walls, rock walls, trellises, fences, mailboxes, and almost any structure where the tendrils and vines can attach.

HOW TO PLANT
Plant clematis in a hole that is wider than and the same depth as the rootball. Mulching is essential to keep the roots cool and damp. Planting clematis between shrubs and other perennials provides further protection to the root system. The vines are then allowed to tower above these companion plants where the top foliage can enjoy warm temperatures and partial

sun. One of the most interesting plantings I have observed was clematis growing between and on dwarf yaupon holly.

CARE AND MAINTENANCE

Leaf spot and stem rot are problems in heavily shaded sites with poor drainage. Other pests are of minimal concern. Pruning is probably the next issue demanding attention. Knowing the group or blooming time of your particular clematis is imperative. For example, the 'Jackman' group flowers on new growth in June, July, and August. Therefore, pruning can occur in early spring when the plants are dormant. Early-spring-flowering types should be pruned after flowering. Some flower in June from the previous season's growth and should be pruned after flowering. And to make things more confusing, some bloom in spring and in fall on both old and new wood. Prune them only by removing dead and weak stems when needed. If you are not sure about a clematis's group, observe when it flowers and on which type of wood—old or new.

ADDITIONAL INFORMATION

Most pruning of clematis is done for shaping purposes. Severe pruning is seldom needed unless plants become woody and non-productive. Most clematis take at least a couple of years to be fully established before they start their spectacular flower show. Soil moisture is critical; these plants want consistent moisture—never very dry or very wet.

ADDITIONAL SPECIES, CULTIVARS, OR VARIETIES

There are truly too many to cover. Before making a choice, consider flower type (double or single), size, color, and bloom time. A close and quite aggressive relative is sweet autumn clematis (*C. terniflora*, *C. paniculata*, or *C. maximowicziana*), which blooms in late summer, usually August, with a knock-your-socks-off fragrance. The creamy-white flowers later develop attractive seedheads that provide long-lasting fascination.

Did You Know?

Most clematis are deciduous, but C. armandii *is an evergreen species that is cold hardy only in Zone 7 of Oklahoma. Another unusual, hard-to-find plant is bush clematis (*C. integrifolia*).*

Crossvine

Bignonia capreolata

Height: Up to 30 ft., or depends on support **Spread:** 4 to 6 ft. **Flowers:** Orange-red and showy **Bloom Period:** April **Zones:** 6a, 6b, 7a, 7b *Color photograph on page 229.*	**Light Requirements:** **Beneficial Characteristics:** 

This tough vine definitely needs to be used more often in our Oklahoma landscapes. Crossvine has unique semievergreen leaves assembled on the stems somewhat like a cross. The showy flowers emerge in early spring with an orange-red display that is described as chocolate scented. Tendrils easily attach crossvine to its trellis system, and like that of most vines, the height is determined by where it is allowed to grow. I have a crossvine growing up a telephone pole, which is also home to a bird nest box. The nesting box peeks through the lush foliage, making the birds feel right at home.

WHEN TO PLANT
Plant crossvine in spring or early summer.

WHERE TO PLANT
Use crossvine for fences, concrete walls, arbors, pergolas, and trellises. It prefers full or partial sun. Too much shade reduces flowering. Crossvine tolerates poor soils but is most aggressive in moist, humus-rich soils.

HOW TO PLANT
Dig the hole two times wider than and the same depth as the rootball. Soil amendments are not needed unless they have been incorporated into the bed before planting time. Mulching and providing supplemental moisture quickly establish this underused vine. Because crossvine needs initial help in getting attached to its support structure, weave the vines through the support.

CARE AND MAINTENANCE
Bignonia readily responds to occasional feedings. Reapply mulch as needed. Crossvine seldom has pest problems. This tough plant is drought tolerant when it is established, although the foliage can scorch in hot sun with windy, dry conditions. Crossvine is considered a fast-growing vine, which

blooms on the previous season's growth in early spring. The bell-shaped flowers are quite attractive. They may sporadically rebloom on new growth later in the summer or early fall. Severe pruning should be done after flowering; however, tip pruning to keep plants in shape can be done throughout the growing season.

ADDITIONAL INFORMATION

The foliage turns a bronzy color in the fall and will remain on the vines during milder winters. Later in the season a long, green, capsulated seedpod turns a brownish color but is not showy. Crossvine flowers are similar in appearance to those of trumpet vine and are often classified in the same genus.

ADDITIONAL SPECIES, CULTIVARS, OR VARIETIES

'Atrosanguinea' is a selection with tinged reddish-purple, narrower foliage and reddish-purple flowers. 'Tangerine Beauty' is a yellowish-tangerine color, and 'Jekyll' is reddish; both have showier flowers than the native species. 'Helen Friedel' is thought to have the largest flowers to date.

Did You Know?

Crossvine is native to moist sites in the southeastern United States and in Oklahoma.

Honeysuckle

Lonicera species

Height: 6 to 30 ft., depending on selection and trellis
Spread: 4 to 10 ft.
Flowers: Fragrant, creamy white to shades of pink
Bloom Period: Early spring or summer
Zones: 6a, 6b, 7a, 7b

Color photograph on page 230.

Light Requirements:

Beneficial Characteristics:

Honeysuckle gives most vines a run for their money as far as fragrance goes. As the name implies, the flowers are very sweet smelling. The strong fragrance is so aromatic that it can be sensed in the garden for days at a time. The "wild" honeysuckle often found remaining at homesteads or escaped in pastures is Japanese honeysuckle. It is one of the most fragrant and a childhood favorite of many people, although it is almost too invasive in the landscape unless a home owner has plenty of space. Fortunately, there are more manageable species and hybrids of honeysuckle with fragrant, showy flowers perfect for landscape use. Honeysuckle is often associated with "bonds of love" in symbolic writings.

WHEN TO PLANT
Plant honeysuckle in early spring, early summer, and early fall.

WHERE TO PLANT
There is a species of honeysuckle to match almost any landscape situation, from mounding to vining. It is also a great plant to use for erosion control. Honeysuckle is typically used to grow up trellises or allowed to cascade over retaining walls. The bushy growth is a favorite for many birds, so honeysuckle is frequently planted in wildlife habitat landscapes for protection and nesting. Most selections prefer full-sun locations; however, a few like afternoon shade. As with most plants, honeysuckle performs best in fertile, moist, well-drained soils. It is durable and tolerates most soil types.

HOW TO PLANT
Dig the planting hole two times wider than and the same depth as the rootball. No amended backfill is required. Water and mulch as needed to establish the plants.

CARE AND MAINTENANCE

Honeysuckle is fairly carefree, other than an occasional pruning to keep plants in control. Many of the early-spring-flowering types can be pruned after flowering. Plants that bloom in late summer or fall should be pruned when dormant or in early spring before new growth begins. Overgrown plants can be cut back to the ground where they will develop new growth. Fertility should be minimal, or excess growth can occur. Pests include an occasional aphid and foliage leaf spot or powdery mildew in heavily shaded sites.

ADDITIONAL INFORMATION

There are literally hundreds of species and hybrid crosses of honeysuckle. Many are evergreen in southern parts of the state but are more semievergreen in northern Oklahoma, depending on the severity of the winter. Some are typically deciduous, losing their foliage each winter. Decide whether fragrance or flower color is more important in your landscape, and choose cultivars accordingly. Occasionally, foliage may turn a bronze fall color.

ADDITIONAL SPECIES, CULTIVARS, OR VARIETIES

Trumpet (same as coral or crimson) honeysuckle (*L. sempervirens*) and tatarian honeysuckle (*L. tatarica*) and their hybrid crosses are probably the most suitable species for landscape use. In addition to their showy flowers with color shades of yellow, red, and orange, they produce colorful berries in the fall. They are not known for their fragrant blooms. 'John Clayton', (yellow flowers), 'Alabama Crimson', (vivid scarlet flowers), 'Arnold Red', and 'Magnifica' (red) are probably the most colorful cultivars of these species. 'Dropmore Scarlet' is a multicolored hybrid cross and Goldflame has pinkish-rose blooms with a yellow center. Both have bluish-green foliage throughout the year. Japanese honeysuckle is very twining in growth with either green or purple foliage and very fragrant blooms. 'Purpurea' is probably the best adapted to landscape sites. 'Aureoreticulata' is a variegated foliage selection with yellow blooms. Deciduous winter honeysuckle (*L. fragrantissima*) is very fragrant and one of the earliest blooming species. Woodbine honeysuckle (*L. periclymenum*) has the best fruit set of any selection, which is an asset in wildlife landscapes.

 Did You Know?

Spring-blooming honeysuckle vines can be cut in late February, placed in a vase of water, and forced to bloom inside.

Porcelain Vine

Ampelopsis brevipedunculata

Height: 10 to 20 ft.
Spread: 6 to 10 ft.
Flowers: Creamy white, nonshowy
Bloom Period: Spring, early summer
Zones: 6a, 6b, 7a, 7b

Color photograph on page 230.

Light Requirements:

Beneficial Characteristics:

New to the nursery trade is porcelain vine, which resembles a grapevine. As a matter of fact, both are in the same family *Vitaceae*, and the genus *Ampelopsis* means "vinelike." The deciduous leaves are grapelike in appearance but somewhat variegated with shades of green and white. The flowers are not showy, but mildly fragrant. The true selling point for this vine—in addition to the unique foliage—is the berry fruit following the flowers. The small, marblelike berries emerge green and later turn a glossy, almost metallic blue green to purple, thus the name porcelain vine. The small berries last into the fall before being quickly consumed by birds.

WHEN TO PLANT

Plant this vine similar to the way that grapes are planted as a dormant plant in early spring or as a containerized plant in late spring or early summer.

WHERE TO PLANT

Porcelain vine is not quite as woody as its grape cousin, but it spreads with gnarling tendrils attaching to its support system. Use it for arbors, fences, pergolas, and trellises. Locate the plants in full sun or partial shade. This native plant prefers rich, humus, moist, well-drained soil; however, it adapts to poor soils.

HOW TO PLANT

Prepare the soil before planting time to a pH of 6.5 to 7. Plant porcelain vine in a widely dug hole the same depth that it was grown in the nursery. Mulch and water the plant as needed.

CARE AND MAINTENANCE

Few maintenance chores are associated with this plant. Stick it in the ground, and let it do its thing. Summer pruning to keep the vine within the confines of its support system is the only routine task. As is the case with grapes, pests are typically not a serious concern. Feeding should be minimal so that excessive growth is not encouraged. Just like the fruit of grapes, fruit are produced on current-season growth from last year's wood. Dormant pruning should not include too much one-year-old wood or stems.

ADDITIONAL INFORMATION

The berries are a favorite of cardinals, brown thrashers, wood thrush, and quail. The fragrant flowers are known to attract many insects and bees. Grow this vine on a fence in the garden to attract birds and pollinators.

ADDITIONAL SPECIES, CULTIVARS, OR VARIETIES

Porcelain vine is often sold by the cultivar name 'Elegans'. It is well adapted to Oklahoma conditions with many related species native to our state. These include heartleaf ampelopsis (*A. cordata*) and pepper vine (*A. arborea*). Another species occasionally found in the nursery trade is monk's hood vine (*A. aconitifolia*). This species has finely cut foliage and makes a great covering for walls, fences, and arbors.

 Did You Know?

*Pepper vine (*A. arborea*) has compound leaves often mistaken for poison ivy.*

Trumpet Vine

Campsis radicans

Other Names: Trumpet Creeper;
  Trumpet Flower
Height: Up to 40 ft., or as tall as
  its support
Spread: 6 to 10 ft.
Flowers: Showy orange, red, and yellow
Bloom Period: June through September
Zones: 6a, 6b, 7a, 7b

Color photograph on page 230.

Light Requirements:

Beneficial Characteristics:

Sound the horns! This trumpet-shaped flower is delightfully showy. It is native in our state and is a good choice for larger support systems with plenty of space. Many horticulturists describe this vine as rampant. I have even seen it climb up a telephone pole, bushing out at the top as if it was waiting for the pole to catch up with the vine. I have also seen it used in landscapes where routine pruning made the summer show of blooms worth the effort. The lustrous, green foliage is compound, changing to a yellow green in the fall accompanied by a long seedpod. The large flowers are a perfect trumpet shape, ranging from 3 to 4 in. long. The hummingbirds love them, and so do I.

WHEN TO PLANT
Plant trumpet creeper in the spring, early summer, or fall.

WHERE TO PLANT
Use this fast-growing plant as a screen on fences or stout trellises. I have seen it used to cover a dead tree kept in place for woodpeckers. It requires plenty of space and a strong support. Trumpet creeper can grow horizontally as a bushy ground cover when no support is available. This tough beauty requires no special soil. Trumpet creeper is very adaptable. In rich soils, the plant can become aggressive.

HOW TO PLANT
Dig the hole two times wider than and the same depth as the rootball. Mulch for weed control, and water as needed. After it is established, trumpet vine is drought tolerant.

CARE AND MAINTENANCE

The flamboyant flowers appear late in the summer on new season's growth. Pruning can be done anytime throughout the growing season to keep vines under control. Severe pruning should be done when the plant is dormant. Insect pest problems are usually not serious enough for control action. Foliar disease may occur in sites with too much shade. Supplemental feedings are needed only when nutritional foliar symptoms are present.

ADDITIONAL INFORMATION

Trumpet vine is very late to leaf out in the spring, sometimes not emerging until May. It is like hardy hibiscus; once the buds emerge, the growth quickly takes off and provides summer-long intrigue and color. Occasionally, the species or native vine will sucker from its roots in disturbed soils.

ADDITIONAL SPECIES, CULTIVARS, OR VARIETIES

The species has showy, smaller flowers with predominantly orange-red color. 'Crimson Trumpet' has larger, red flowers with no orange. 'Flava' has showy, solid-yellow blooms, and 'Flamenco' has large, scarlet flowers with a more prominent golden fall color. 'Madam Galen' is a hybrid cross with huge, showy, coral-red flowers. A northern introduction from Canada is 'Indian Summer' with distinctly yellow flowers and orange-red centers. Chinese trumpet vine (*C. grandiflora*) has even wider and longer blooms but is not as cold hardy in the state; it performs better in the southern Zones 7a and 7b.

 Did You Know?

Trumpet vine is in the Bignoniaceae *family and is sometimes listed as* Bignonia *genus, which is the same as crossvine— another native vine suitable for Oklahoma landscapes. The flowers are very similar in appearance as well.*

Roses

*E*VERYBODY LOVES ROSES, but not everybody loves to grow them! I really admire the rosarians who spend countless hours spraying, feeding, and pruning their prized beauties. Rose growing is a passion with beautiful rewards, but I personally refuse to put that much time into any plant. Luckily, some rose selections perform acceptably with minimal care.

PESTS

Foliar diseases include primarily black spot and powdery mildew. Insect pests are likely to include spider mites, aphids, and thrips. The best management practice in controlling these critters is to grow healthy plants; that means having healthy soil and spraying when needed. There are numerous control products on the market, and there are home remedies that use household products. One popular disease control is made from 1 Tbsp. baking soda mixed with 2 1/2 Tbsp. Sunspray Ultra-Fine Horticultural Oil per gallon of water. Mix 2 to 4 Tbsp. dishwashing detergent with 5 Tbsp. vegetable oil per gallon of water for insect control. These products should be inter-changed with other over-the-counter sprays and natural controls to avoid pest resistance to the chemicals.

SOIL PREPARATION

Properly prepare rose beds before planting time. Till rich, organic humus and fertilizer with phosphorus and potassium—and lime, depending on soil test reports—into the existing soil. I will never for-get visiting the late rose expert C. W. Sturdivant in Muskogee, who literally had hundreds of dollars invested in his planting beds, and the end result was astonishing. He was notorious for his soil mix concoctions of alfalfa pellets, compost, fish emulsion, and who knows what all. The saying about "a $10 plant in a $50 hole" literally applied to his rose growing techniques.

FERTILIZATION

Successful rose growing comes down to healthy green foliage,
which produces vibrant flowers. Just about any routine fertilizer
combination will work as long as fertilizer salt deposits in the soil
are visually monitored. The white, chalky fertilizer salt buildup
along the rims of container plants can occur in overfertilized soils.
Irrigating for long periods can flush salt residues below the root
system. I know gardeners who prefer slow-release products; others
like to pour on water-soluble fertilizers. Many swear by natural or
organic products. Whatever the choice, I can assure you that the
prevailing growers have properly prepared the soil ahead of time
and practice routine feedings.

PLANTING

Location of the rose bed is important. It should be in full sun for
a minimum of four hours, and more sunlight is better. Few roses
are known to be shade tolerant. More shade generally means less
foliage, a smaller number of blooms, and more disease. Proper spacing between plants creates better air circulation, which reduces pest
problems. Soil preparation and site location are only preludes to
proper planting, however.

Modern hybrid roses are usually packaged as bare-root plants,
which should be planted in early spring while they are dormant.
Dormant roses are packaged in assorted materials—most often
sawdust to hold moisture in the roots—until they can be planted.
Container-grown roses, like many of the ones discussed in this
chapter, can be planted in early spring or summer.

After the soil beds have been properly prepared, dig a hole two to
three times wider than the root mass of the rose. Mound excess soil
in the bottom of the hole in the shape of a pyramid to spread out the

roots and support the plant at the appropriate height. Roses are typically planted a couple of ways, depending on the growing climate.
In milder-growing zones, gardeners position roses so that the bud
union (swollen area on the stem) is just above the soil level. In colder
climates farther north, gardeners plant roses so that the union is
about 1 in. below the soil surface. In Oklahoma, most gardeners
place the union above the ground but mulch around cold-sensitive
cultivars for winter protection. The insulator mulch should be
removed in late spring as new growth emerges. Many of the container-grown selections should be planted at the same depth as the
rootballs. Since most are not budded, they do not need winter
mulching. Refill the hole without compacting the soil. Water deeply
to settle the soil and soak the roots. Mulch to keep out weeds and
hold in soil moisture. Compost, shredded leaves, cottonseed hulls,
pine bark, and Enviroguard® recycled paper are good mulch choices
for roses.

Pruning

Pruning keeps roses more manageable and promotes new growth.
As a general rule, roses blooming on new growth—like many of
the modern roses—can be pruned in late Spring while they are still
dormant. Pruning too early may force new growth susceptible to
later spring freezes. Pruning cuts should be made at an angle above
rose buds and covered with a pruning sealer formulated for roses.
Pruning sealers discourage cane borers. Note which direction the
bud is facing. Selecting buds pointing out will encourage more
open growth and air circulation. Prune modern roses after each
flowering period to keep the plants bushy. A new flush of growth
will soon appear, followed by more blooms. The process should be
continued until early fall. Fertilize after each pruning but no later

than September. Fall feedings, especially ones high in nitrogen, can potentially stimulate late-season growth, which will be more susceptible to winter injury. Roses blooming on previous season's growth should be pruned after flowering.

Good soil, proper planting, frequent pruning, supplemental feeding, and routine irrigation are the keys to successfully growing roses. Modern roses are breathtaking, but if you do not have time for the added chores required to grow them, consider some of the minimal-care and disease-tolerant selections from the climbing, heirloom, rugosa, shrub, and species varieties.

Climbing Rose

Rosa species

Height: 6 to 20 ft.
Spread: 4 to 6 ft.
Flowers: White, red, pink, and yellow
Bloom Period: Early summer around June
(some rebloom late in the season)
Zones: 6a, 6b, 7a, 7b

Color photograph on page 230.

Light Requirements:

Climbing roses are basically roses with long canes needing support. They can be trained to cascade over a wall, crawl along a fence, or climb up a trellis, pergola, or any type of support system. Climbers are most often used on arbors for specimen displays, but can enclose spaces or hide structural features. Some are considered more shade tolerant. The shade amount should be minimal, however, or the results may be less bloom and more disease. Do not expect large, florist-type flowers; they are smaller, showier, vibrant flowers formed in brilliant mass. Many are fragrant and later form colorful fruit.

Climbing roses require fertile, well-drained soil but are not as demanding about routine feedings unless nutrient deficiencies are observed. Mulching is always a good idea with any plant. They are generally cold hardy and sold on their own rootstock, not grafted or budded. Winter mulching is usually not necessary.

The brilliant flowers on climbing roses are best displayed in early summer around late May or June. Some cultivars typically rebloom later in the season but not with quite the same show. To successfully prune climbing roses, identify where the blooms are formed. Most climbing roses bloom on old canes from previous-season growth, so do not prune climbing roses in the spring. Do severe pruning after the primary summer flowering. Occasional summer tip pruning to encourage more canes is helpful. Dormant pruning should consist of removing dead or old, nonproductive canes.

There are several categories of the climbing rose group, such as ramblers, everbloomers, and trailing and climbing moderns. Some of the most disease-tolerant cultivars include 'New Dawn', which has pale-pink double flowers for a great spring display and readily reblooms; 'America', which is a coral-pink color, is fragrant, and reblooms; and 'Lady Banks' (sometimes sold as 'Lutea'), which has butter-yellow, fragrant flowers blooming in early spring on vigorous canes. 'Red Cascade' is a vibrant red with good disease tolerance, and 'Zephrine Drouhin' has fragrant, pink flowers and is more shade tolerant, thornless, and resistant to powdery mildew. 'Joseph's Coat', also somewhat disease tolerant, blooms in clusters opening yellow-orange and turning to scarlet and red. 'Climbing Old Blush' (*Rosa chinensis*), a southern favorite with shades of pink, is a rebloomer with good disease tolerance and does better in Zone 7. Recently released is 'Fourth of July', one of the few climbing roses to receive All America Rose Selection honors. This vibrant red-and-white-striped bloomer had minimal disease problems in many of its test gardens.

Heirloom Rose

Rosa species

Height: 3 to 6 ft.
Spread: 3 to 6 ft.
Flowers: White, pink, and red
Bloom Period: Late May, June
Zones: 6a, 6b, 7a, 7b

Color photograph on page 230.

Light Requirements:

Gardeners are rediscovering a love for "old" roses. Old garden roses have stood the test of time and include all selections developed before 1867, which is the year the first hybrid tea rose was introduced. Other names used to describe these beauties are "heirloom," "antique," and "old-fashioned." Overall, these groups tend to be more disease tolerant, tremendously fragrant, and quite cold hardy. Typically, they are shrubby and thorny; some are categorized as climbers, however.

Old roses are somewhat limited in their color offerings and bloom intervals, but their fragrance and no-fuss attitude easily compensate for their shortcomings. Flowers are available, depending on the selection, in single, semidouble, or double blooms. 'Damasks', 'Gallica', 'Moss', 'China', 'Alba', 'Old Europeans', and 'Bourbons' are a few of the categories of old-fashioned roses.

Good soil preparation, proper planting, and mulching as discussed in detail in the introduction to this chapter are good gardening practices with these reliable selections. Supplemental feeding is generally not needed unless the foliage shows chlorotic nutrient symptoms. These roses are fairly drought tolerant after they are well established. Mulch them as needed. Black spot and powdery mildew do not affect them as much as other roses, but the problems can occur in shaded sites or stressed conditions. Spider mites are not common in locations with good air circulation, but watch for them anyway.

Pruning old-fashioned roses depends on where the flowers are produced. Many set flowers on the previous season's growth. Limit spring or dormant pruning to old, weak, or dead wood. Do severe pruning to control growth after the primary bloom period. If you are not sure when to prune, observe where the blooms are formed—whether on new growth or previous season's growth. Plants that flower on previous season's growth should be pruned after flowering. Plants that bloom on new growth should be pruned in early spring just as the plants begin to break dormancy.

'Mrs. Dudley Cross' is pale yellow with pink blush; it is thornless and fragrant, and it reblooms. 'Old Blush' is also available in a shrub form with soft-pink blossoms. 'Rosa Mundi' is a semidouble with pink-and-white stripes. Intensely fragrant is 'Louise Odier' with double, medium-pink blooms.

If you want true antique roses, be careful not to confuse the 'New English' or 'Romantica' types with them. These new selections are modern hybrids patterned after the characteristics of heirlooms. If you seek disease tolerance, many of these new "old roses" have been bred for such resistance.

Rugosa Rose

Rosa rugosa

Height: 4 to 6 ft.
Spread: 4 to 6 ft.
Flowers: Rose, white, and yellow
Bloom Period: June through August
Zones: 6a, 6b, 7a, 7b

Color photograph on page 230.

Light Requirements:

*R*osa rugosa is often proclaimed as one of the most trouble-free roses available. Its shrubby habit is covered with thick, almost-velvety foliage during the growing season. Fragrant flowers are brilliantly displayed against the lustrous foliage in the summer. But the most well-known and eye-catching attribute of rugosa roses as a whole is the colorful fruit. Rose hips, as they are commonly called, arise from the ovary of the flower. The vivid red or orange fruit can be 1 in. in diameter and make quite a display as they mature. Ripened rose hips are frequently used in jams and tea recipes. Rugosa foliage on some cultivars also exhibits a charming golden-yellow fall color.

As with most roses, rugosas perform best in fertile, well-drained soils. This tough rose is more tolerant of poor soils, however. The soil pH should be slightly acidic because in soils that are too alkaline, iron chlorosis has been a problem. Rugosas make great single-plant specimens, flowering hedges, or windbreaks for gardens. They are very cold hardy and grown on their own roots instead of budded to a separate rootstock. Oklahoma is just about the southernmost border for growing rugosas. These unusual shrubs will grow in full sun or afternoon shade. They are somewhat drought tolerant after they are established; nevertheless, supplemental water is recommended during extremely dry conditions. Mulch to keep weeds in check and soil moist.

Although rugosa flowers generally on new growth, some selections flower from the previous season's growth. Rugosa roses seldom need pruning the first few years. Observe on which growth the flowers are formed to determine the best pruning method. When flowers are formed on current-season growth, prune plants while they are dormant in early spring. When flowers are produced on the previous year's growth, prune plants after they flower. Remove only old, nonproductive, diseased, or dead canes.

There are many old-fashioned rugosas as well as new hybrid crosses. Always select cultivars with disease resistance to black spot and powdery mildew for minimal maintenance. The species has fragrant, single blooms, usually pink to red with bright-red hips. 'Alba' and 'Alba Plena' are white-flowering cultivars with orange hips and fall foliage color. 'Souvenir de Philemon Cochet' is a fragrant, double, white, which is disease tolerant and has minimal fruit. 'Therese Bugnet' has lilac-pink blossoms with a spicy fragrance on blue-green leaves, which are fairly disease tolerant. 'Purple Pavement' ('Rotes Meer') has fragrant, double, lavender flowers on bright, glistening, disease-tough foliage, which also turns a golden fall color, as well as scarlet hips. The Pavement Series overall is a tough group of rugosas with assorted colors. 'Agnes' is a fragrant, double, pale yellow that is cold hardy in Oklahoma and has minimal fruit. 'Linda Campbell' and 'Mrs. Anthony Waterer' have crimson-red flowers. 'Hansa' is a disease-tolerant introduction with fragrant, double, crimson-violet flowers and red fruit in the fall.

Shrub Rose

Rosa species

Height: 4 to 6 ft.
Spread: 4 to 8 ft.
Flowers: Pink, red, white, and yellow
Bloom Period: Summer
Zones: 6a, 6b, 7a, 7b

Color photograph on page 230.

Light Requirements:

Shrub, landscape, or ground cover roses are fairly new introductions—often hybrids not fitting into any other specific category. They are generally trouble free and require minimal care, other than occasional pruning to keep them within their boundaries. The flowers are not large but are developed in masses for a brilliantly colorful display over the entire plant. Most rebloom throughout the season. The flowers are available in single, semidouble, and double in an assortment of colors, typically pink, red, white, or yellow.

As the name implies, these tough roses make great shrub border displays. They need plenty of room, for example, in the center or back of landscape beds. They can provide massive color in fencerows and create hedges. Many are perfect for cascading over walls and berms. A few can be trained onto support systems for a climbing effect. Spacing should be 5 to 6 ft. between plants. The roses prefer fertile, well-drained soils, but they tolerate poor soils. Mulch them as needed.

Pruning is seldom needed if plants are allowed to reach maturity. Tip pruning throughout the season gives a more mounding appearance. Observe where the flowers are produced if further pruning is needed. Plants producing flowers on new, current-season growth can be pruned when they are dormant. Plants producing flowers on the previous season's growth should be pruned after they flower. Shrub roses are very cold hardy and grow on their own roots instead of being budded to a rootstock.

'Bonica' (double, soft pink), 'Carefree Wonder' (semidouble, medium pink), 'All That Jazz' (semidouble, salmon), and 'Topaz Jewell' (yellow) are some of the most trouble-free shrub selections. Also popular, very rugged, and disease tolerant are the Meidiland™ Series, which now has more than fifteen cultivars and assorted colors. Also new to the nursery trade is the ground cover shrub rose, or Flower Carpet™ Series. These compact plants are renowned for their pink pots and touted as the some of the most disease-resistant roses ever bred.

Species Rose

Rosa species

Height: 6 to 20 ft.
Spread: 4 to 8 ft.
Flowers: White, yellow, pink, and red
Bloom Period: Spring or summer
Zones: 6a, 6b, 7a, 7b

Color photograph on page 230.

Light Requirements:

Species roses are typically those true to seed, which are found in the wild. Generally, they grow quite large and require minimal care. Many are the parents of today's modern hybrids. Species roses are also thought to be some of the cold hardiest available, with refreshing fragrance, bright fruit, and colorful fall foliage. Species roses are probably the least picky about their soil type. Like all roses, they perform best in well-drained, humus-rich soils. Mulching benefits species roses. Give them too much tender loving care, however, and they are likely to take over. These roses can be stuck in the ground and left alone.

Pruning practices should be matched with the flowering time of the particular species selection. Plants flowering on the previous season's growth, like climbers, should be pruned after flowering. Plants that bloom on new growth can be pruned in early spring, as the plants begin to break dormancy. In most cases prune only to remove old, diseased, or dead canes. Occasionally, tip pruning may be required to keep the plants more vigorous and bushy.

Species types can be climbers or shrubs. A few were introduced before 1867 and are also considered heirloom. The colors vary, depending on the cultivar or selection. 'Butterfly Rose' (*Rosa chinensis*)—sometimes found as 'Mutabilis'—is a pleasingly fragrant plant, reaching almost 6 ft. at maturity. The orange buds open to yellow flowers and change to pink, then crimson. They are long blooming and thrive in Oklahoma summers. *Rosa laevigata* ('Cherokee Rose') is naturalized in the Southeast and has beautiful, fragrant, white or pink flowers in early spring and summer. *Rosa banksiae* ('Lady Banks Rose') is a vigorous climbing rose with cultivars available in white or yellow and in either single or double blooms. *R. roxburghii* (chestnut rose) and *R. palustris* (swamp rose) are good choices for tough, disease-tolerant, species landscape roses.

Perennials

Soft-stemmed, herbaceous plants known as perennials are the hottest-selling plants in the nursery trade. Plant them, and enjoy their beauty for years to come. That does not mean they are no-maintenance plants, which is often implied. They frequently need deadheading to encourage more bloom. The dormant foliage should be trimmed each year. Many need dividing every few years. And there are fertilizing, mulching, and pest patrol duties.

The flowers of some long-blooming perennials last six to fifteen weeks. But the majority bloom only a couple of weeks throughout the growing season. To use perennials to advantage, plant several different kinds with various blooming times so that something will be in bloom from spring to frost. Perennial beds need to be big enough to accommodate numerous plants. Island beds are nothing more than large beds in the middle of a lawn. Flower beds adjacent to fencerows or corners of lots are conducive to a perennial garden. Near the home, perennials should be grouped among shrubs or made focal plants in clusters of three or more, again with assorted bloom periods. Design the landscape with at least half the plants composed of evergreen shrubs or specimens to offset the dormant periods of perennials and other deciduous plants. The ideal design includes assorted blooming perennials, deciduous and evergreen shrubs, and designated locations for annuals of various colors.

Identify before planting time the sun and shade patterns to match the plant to its preferred growing site. Soil preparation is beneficial. Invest in a soil test from your County Extension service to find out which nutrients and pH adjustments need to be made. Then incorporate nutrients and organic material weeks, even months, before you plant, and kill weeds and grass. The time, money, and patience will pay off in the long run with vigorous plants and eye-catching color.

Chapter Six

Perennials may seem to just sit there the first year after planting. But the second and third years they get bigger and better. Follow recommended plant spacing to allow for future growth. Some perennials can be downright invasive. At the nursery or garden center ask questions about their growth habits to avoid these problems. *Houttuynia cordata* (chameleon plant) and *Oenothera berlandieri* or *speciosa* (evening primrose) are two overpowering plants.

Once the plants are in the ground, mulch, mulch, and mulch some more to retain moisture, keep weeds at a minimum, and provide slow-release nutrients. Cut back on the size of the bed or the number of plants, but never cut corners on your mulch. Mulching properly will mean less work over time, and the plants will reward you for the extra effort. Weed management will be a continual task until the plants have grown together and filled open areas. Bermuda grass is notorious for creeping in from the edges, and birds and wind distribute weed seeds in the beds. Provide supplemental irrigation at a rate of 1 to 2 in. per week, especially the first year of establishment.

Gardeners often debate the issue of when to remove dormant foliage. I have found the following recommendations to be effective. Leave the foliage to better insulate the plants throughout the cold months, especially the first winter after planting. Trim the foliage as soon as new growth emerges in the spring. The dead growth withers down eventually and traps leaves to further insulate the plants. Every spring, around early March, pull the leaves in between the plants for mulch, remove the dead tops, and wait for the perennial process to start again. Once the plants are growing, provide supplemental fertilizer to those appearing less vigorous. The only work left is occasional trimming or deadheading of the spent flowers to further extend the blooming season.

Asiatic Lily

Lilium species

Other Name: Garden Lily
Height: 2 to 3 ft.
Spread: 1 to 2 ft.
Flowers: Assorted shades of pink, red, white, and yellow
Bloom Period: Early to midsummer
Zones: 6a, 6b, 7a, 7b

Color photograph on page 230.

Light Requirements:

Beneficial Characteristics:

Lilies are majestic flowering perennials. The large, colorful, trumpet-shaped flowers are elegant and artistic. Lilies are often associated with English cottage gardens or Easter. They make great indoor potted plants and cut flowers but are also excellent choices for the perennial garden. Most hardy lilies bloom in late May or June, depending on the species, but Asiatic lilies bloom earlier in May. Asiatic lilies are primarily hybrids bred for vigor, pest resistance, hardiness, and strong stems. These lilies flourish in almost any growing zone but prefer afternoon shade in Oklahoma. They seldom reach 3 ft. tall and rarely need staking or extra support. The range of breathtaking colors is hard to describe as they open to a truly glorious display. They multiply rapidly and flourish in the right garden conditions.

WHEN TO PLANT

Most bulbs are planted in the fall; however, lily bulbs should be planted in early spring. Some lily selections are started by seed or small bulblets. Seed-grown plants can take a couple of years to flower.

WHERE TO PLANT

The plants are similar to clematis in their site preferences. Give them cool roots and warm tops. In other words, plant the bulbs among shorter ground covers so that they are allowed to emerge above the foliage into a partially shaded site. The ground cover and mulch will keep the roots cool and moist in the summer. A fertile garden site with rich soil humus is perfect for these beauties. It should be well drained or the bulbs will easily rot. Afternoon sun or dappled shade is best for these plants in the hot Oklahoma summers.

HOW TO PLANT

Place the bulb in a hole at least twice as deep as the bulb is tall (6 to 8 in. deep). Single specimens are showy, but groups of five or more are even better. Space bulbs 2¹/₂ to 3 ft. apart for good air circulation and future growth

and spreading. Water thoroughly, and mulch 2 in. thick with shredded leaf mold, fine pine bark, or cottonseed hulls.

CARE AND MAINTENANCE

Lilies need good soil fertility, and they respond well to supplemental feedings if fertile soil was not provided before planting time. Fertilizers with a high nitrogen content should not be applied after August or early September to allow the plants to go dormant before winter. Always permit the foliage to remain until it goes completely dormant because the foliage feeds the bulbs for next year's flowers. After the flowers have faded, pinch off the blossoms to prevent seedpods from forming and to direct more energy into the bulbs for bigger and better future flowers.

ADDITIONAL INFORMATION

The flowers of Asiatic lily make great fresh cut flowers. Remove the pollen tubes to keep pollen from getting all over the house. Typically, several buds per flower stalk open at different times with the first usually being the largest. Be careful not to remove excessive amounts of the plant's stems and flowers when using it for cut flowers. Removing too much growth may weaken the bulb and affect next year's flowering. The overall flower bloom lasts seven to ten days, with individual flowers lasting two to three days.

ADDITIONAL SPECIES, CULTIVARS, OR VARIETIES

The Emperor Series with a wide range of colors is one of the most popular Asiatic hybrid sellers. The most dwarf cultivar to date, maturing around 18 in., is the Pixie Series with various shades of yellow, white, pink, red, and orange. 'Sorbet' is one of my favorites, offering white blooms brushed with a violet pink on the petal tips. The color combinations of Asiatic lilies go on and on and are often sold in blends or mixes with assorted colors.

 Did You Know?

Formosa lily (Lilium formosanum) is a selection of lily that thrives in the southern heat. It flowers later in the season—around August—with flower stalks potentially reaching 6 ft. as the plant matures. This unusual plant will flower the first year from seed.

Barrenwort

Epimedium species

Other Name: Bishop's Hat
Height: 8 to 18 in.
Spread: 2 to 3 ft.
Flowers: Showy yellow, white, pink, and red
Bloom Period: Early to mid-spring
Zones: 6a, 6b, 7a, 7b

Color photograph on page 230.

Light Requirements:

Beneficial Characteristics:

B arrenwort is not an attractive name, but the plant is anything but boring! The semievergreen, perennial ground cover emerges in the spring with ruby-colored, heart-shaped foliage. In just a short time loads of attractive flowers peek above the dainty foliage. Flower colors are typically crimson, pink, or yellow. The foliage on many cultivars remains a ruby tint most of the growing season while others mature to a lime or dark green. The noninvasive plant seldom reaches 18 in. tall and spreads slowly. There are not many compatible acidic-soil-requiring plants smaller than azaleas, but *Epimedium* is the perfect low-growing border plant for azalea beds. The wonderful blooms and foliage of barrenwort are added displays during the early azalea show of flowers.

WHEN TO PLANT

Spring planting is best for *Epimedium*. Planting it in early summer is second best, with fall planting as a last resort.

WHERE TO PLANT

Use *Epimedium* as a border plant for shade gardens, rock gardens, or perennial beds. It is also compatible as a container plant.

HOW TO PLANT

These perennial beauties prefer moist, yet well-drained, humus-rich soils. Most established woodland sites are somewhat acidic in nature. Proper soil preparation must be accomplished ahead of planting time if natural woodland conditions are not available. Peat moss, soil sulfur, and other acid-changing products should be incorporated, according to package directions, into the existing soil. Do not damage shallow tree roots during bed preparation. Plant the dormant bare-root plants or container plants at the same depth that they were previously grown. The hole should be at least two times wider than the rootball to establish the fibrous roots. Since the plants are slow growing and spreading, the initial plant spacing should be about 12 in. apart to get a quicker fill. Mulch 2 in. thick around plants with acidic organic products, such as pine straw, pine bark, or pecan hulls.

CARE AND MAINTENANCE

Avoid dry conditions for this perennial ground cover. Providing supplemental moisture is essential during drought conditions. There are no major pests to consider. Pruning is seldom needed. Occasionally, in milder winters the foliage does not go dormant. You may prune the foliage and stems in early spring just above the ground to remove ragged or discolored leaves from the previous winter and summer. The new growth will soon reemerge, followed by flowers. Fertilizer applications should consist of products including iron and sulfur to keep soils acidic. Additional feedings should occur after flowering and once again during the growing season. *Epimedium* can defoliate in cold winters but readily emerges in early spring.

ADDITIONAL INFORMATION

Epimedium is an excellent ground cover at maturity, but gardeners must be patient with it. Gardeners trying *Epimedium* typically fall in love with it and want more in the landscape. The plants can be easily divided in spring or fall to transplant in other areas of the garden or share with neighbors. Barrenwort is not readily found in Oklahoma garden centers, but it is available through mail-order or on-line garden catalogs.

ADDITIONAL SPECIES, CULTIVARS, OR VARIETIES

There are more than twenty-five species of *Epimedium* and many improved hybrids. 'Rubrum' is probably the most commonly found; it has red-tinged foliage in the spring and fall. The flowers are primarily yellow with crimson tones. 'Versicolor' has spectacular early-spring, ruby foliage with chartreuse veins and is probably more tolerant of dry, shade conditions. The flowers of 'Versicolor' are yellowish pink. 'Niveum' has white flowers, and 'Roseum' has pink ones.

 Did You Know?

Plant breeders gave it the common name of barrenwort early on because they thought the plant was barren with sterile flowers. The belief was false, and today we have beautiful hybrids.

Beebalm

Monarda didyma

Other Names: Horsemint; Monarda; Bergamot; Oswego Tea
Height: 15 to 36 in.
Spread: 2 to 4 ft.
Flowers: Pink, purple, and white
Bloom Period: Summer
Zones: 6a, 6b, 7a, 7b

Photograph on page 230.

Light Requirements:

Beneficial Characteristics:

This native Oklahoma plant with its balmy fragrance and aromatic foliage is a favorite of bees and hummingbirds. The native species are found to thrive in dry conditions; however, the new garden species and hybrids prefer moist sites. The showy and colorful blooms have clusters of tubular flowers perfect for nectar-feeding wildlife. In addition to beebalm's wildlife benefits the showy flowers are engaging in the perennial garden, blooming on and off through most of the summer. Monarda is related to mint; it has square stems and, like mint, is somewhat invasive.

WHEN TO PLANT
Plant it in spring or early summer.

WHERE TO PLANT
Many *Monarda* cultivars, especially the species selection, can become somewhat aggressive but controllable. Plants seem to be even more aggressive and more susceptible to disease in heavier shade. Some of the newer cultivars are less aggressive. Allow plenty of room for these plants. The appropriate location and space will reward you will eye-catching summer color. Dry, nonproductive soil restricts the growth of beebalm and limits the amount of summer color display. Beebalm prefers moist, fertile soils.

HOW TO PLANT
Dig the planting hole two times wider than and the same depth as the rootball. Space plants 3 to 4 ft. apart. Space dwarf selections 18 to 24 in. apart. Mulch plants to conserve moisture, and water them as needed.

CARE AND MAINTENANCE
The blooms are produced on new growth, so deadheading the spent flowers ensures additional color throughout the season. Pruning is needed only to remove the dormant foliage in the fall or early spring. Keep a careful eye

on the foliage for yellow discoloration followed by a whitish-gray color, which is symptomatic of powdery mildew. Left untreated, the disease can prematurely drop the foliage, weakening and eventually killing the plants in worst-case scenarios. Spraying with a fungicide for powdery mildew, according to directions, will prevent the spread of this pathogen. Where powdery mildew poses a problem, move the plants to sunnier locations with better air circulation and good soil moisture. Definitely remove and dispose of infected dormant foliage to reduce the source of infection for next year's growing season. Planting disease-resistant cultivars is one way to avoid the problem.

ADDITIONAL INFORMATION

Do not overfertilize *Monardas* or plants can be even more aggressive. Let the plants be the gauge for the need for supplemental feedings. Replace decomposed mulch as needed.

ADDITIONAL SPECIES, CULTIVARS, OR VARIETIES

'Cambridge Scarlet' is one of the most readily available and taller cultivars but with poor resistance to disease. 'Snow White' and 'Alba' are popular white-flowering selections. 'Marshall's Delight' (medium pink), 'Gardenview Scarlet' (red), 'Jacob Kline' (dark red), 'Blaustrumpf' (purple), 'Scorpion' (red), and 'Aquarius' (light pink) are cultivars with various levels of disease resistance. Probably my favorite is the new release 'Petite Delight' with uniquely crinkled, dark-green foliage. It has great mildew resistance and attractive lavender-pink flowers on top of compact, noninvasive plants.

 Did You Know?

Oklahoma is home to several native **Monardas.** *Horsemint or prairie monarda (*M. punctata*) has pale-yellow flowers with purple spots later in the summer, and it is found growing in dry, sandy, western locales of the state. Russell's horsemint and wild bergamot (*M. Russeliana *and* M. fistulosa, *respectively) are commonly found in the eastern half of the state with pale-lavender blooms from May to September. Lemon monarda (*M. citriodora*) thrives on dry plains with blooms of pink and lavender fading to white from June through September.*

Black-Eyed Susan

Rudbeckia fulgida

Other Name: Orange Coneflower
Height: 2 to 6 ft.
Spread: Average 2 ft.
Flowers: Yellow
Bloom Period: Late May, June, July, and again in fall
Zones: 6a, 6b, 7a, 7b

Color photograph on page 230.

Light Requirements:

Beneficial Characteristics:

This native prairie plant in well-established sites is like a sea of yellow in the peak of its magnificent bloom. Black-eyed Susan is a no-fuss plant that brightens any perennial garden. The golden-yellow flower petals surround a dark-brown or black center, or eye, and can range in size from 2 to 5 in. wide, depending on the species. The daisylike flowers are long-lived and make nice cut flowers. The grayish-green foliage is known for its coarse texture due to small, hairlike petioles. Many selections bloom again in late summer or early fall, especially if the initial spent blooms are removed. *Rudbeckia* is a low-maintenance, enduring perennial plant, providing a wealth of showy color for years to come.

WHEN TO PLANT

Black-eyed Susan is sold in many ways. The seed can be planted in the fall or early spring. Bare-root plants should be planted in the spring. Container plants can be set out in spring or summer.

WHERE TO PLANT

The plants are not too picky about their soil as long as it drains well. They prefer full sun but accept partial shade. The most magnificent display of color results from planting these perennials in drifts or uneven groups. In perennial beds *Rudbeckia* is typically placed as a middle or background plant because of its height. Black-eyed Susan is also used in wildflower gardens and sold in wildflower seed mixes.

HOW TO PLANT

Dig the planting hole slightly wider than and the same depth as the root-ball. Well-worked soil permits better root development. Space plants 15 to 36 in. apart, depending on the cultivar. The plants fill in the space as they age and should be divided every three to five years. Water the plants as needed, especially during the establishment period. Mulch to keep weeds under control.

CARE AND MAINTENANCE

Rudbeckia plants go dormant in the winter, and the old foliage can be removed in the winter or early spring. Trimming spent flowers encourages more blooms later in the season. Potential insect pests include aphids and nasty larvae of the sawfly, which can skeletonize the foliage quickly if not controlled early on. A foliage disease is the typical powdery mildew, which is more persistent in shade. Minimal feedings are needed only in poor sites with nonproductive plants.

ADDITIONAL INFORMATION

There are three primary native species of black-eyed Susan in Oklahoma. *Rudbeckia grandiflora* is the largest flowering, *R. hirta* var. *pulcherrima* is the most widely distributed, and *R. amplexicaulis* (clasping-leafed coneflower) is more likely to be found in moisture-retentive soils in the state. Another prairie native is often confused with *Rudbeckia*. *Ratibida columnifera* (Mexican hat, also called prairie coneflower) has more upright centers with yellow or yellow-purple flower petals.

ADDITIONAL SPECIES, CULTIVARS, OR VARIETIES

'Indian Summer', 'Sputnik', and 'Gloriosa' are cultivars that are common yellow with black centers. 'Rustic Dwarf' and 'Becky' are the most compact selections. 'Marmalade' and 'Triloba' are solid golden yellow. Double-flowering, solid-yellow cultivars include 'Gold Drop', 'Goldquelle', and 'Goldilocks'. 'Irish Eyes' and 'Double Golden Glow' are yellow flowering with green centers. The largest-flowering and tallest plant is *R. maxima* (giant coneflower or black-eyed Susan).

 Did You Know?

R. fulgida *'Goldsturm' is the 1999 Perennial Plant of the Year as selected by the Perennial Plant Association. It is sometimes sold as 'Goldstrum'.*

Blue Mist Spirea

Caryopteris clandonensis

Other Names: Blue Spirea; Bluebeard
Height: 3 to 4 ft.
Spread: 3 to 4 ft.
Flowers: Blue-lavender
Bloom Period: August, September, and
   October
Zones: 6a, 6b, 7a, 7b

Color photograph on page 231.

Light Requirements:

Beneficial Characteristics:

Spirea is generally thought of as a shrub, and even blue mist spirea is occasionally grouped as a shrub. But in my garden *Caryopteris* tends to be a more herbaceous perennial with tender, twiggy shoots, often succumbing to the winter's cold and reemerging from the crown in the spring. It can be sold either way, so do not give up when you look for this truly spectacular beauty. It is without a doubt one of the few plants with nearly blue flowers. The flowers emerge along the stem and are a welcome sight later in the season until frost. The lovely, bright flowers are very fragrant and attract birds, bees, and butterflies. The plant's flowers are arranged among grayish foliage for a perfect color combination. Use this plant among pink and other pastel colors for an eye-catching display. An added bonus to the long fall bloom is the use as a cut flower.

WHEN TO PLANT
Plant blue mist spirea in spring, summer, or fall.

WHERE TO PLANT
With its medium-sized, uniform foliage, blue mist spirea makes a great background in a perennial garden, especially when it is used in association with evergreen companions. You may want to plant it as a border near fencerows. This interesting plant can stand alone as a specimen or catch your attention in groups of three or more. Whatever you do, include this plant in your garden to attract bees later in the season for late-summer or fall-blooming crops. Do not locate this plant next to a frequently used sidewalk or the entrance to a home unless you are willing to dodge the numerous bees attracted to this beauty. Blue mist spirea prefers well-drained, fertile soils, but it tolerates almost any soil type or condition.

How to Plant

Dig a planting hole 2 to 3 ft. wider than and the same depth as the container root system. Space plants on 2-ft. centers. No amended organic backfill is needed. Water to settle the soil, and mulch for added benefits.

Care and Maintenance

Flowers are produced on new season's growth. Pruning should be done in late winter or early spring to remove winter-damaged or dead twigs. Occasionally, the plants will be killed to the ground by severe winters, but they readily rebound in the spring. In some years the plants will decline in bloom by the end of August or early September. In such cases, shear the plants for new growth and later blooms in the fall. The plants prosper with a yearly feeding in spring or early summer. There are no serious pests. I have found spider mites on new plants, but they were probably brought in from the nursery.

Additional Information

Most blue mist spireas are hybrid crosses. The characteristic colors, pleasantly scented blooms, and benefits to garden wildlife friends are enough reasons to make room for this enchanting plant in any landscape or garden setting.

Additional Species, Cultivars, or Varieties

'Blue Mist', 'Dark Knight', and 'Longwood Blue' are typically the most easily found in Oklahoma nurseries. Other cultivar hybrids that are well worth the hunt include 'Kew Blue', 'Azure', and 'Heavenly Blue'. 'Worcester Gold' has golden-yellow foliage during the summer with blue flowers in the fall.

 Did You Know?

Blue mist spirea is a perfect companion plant for pink-flowering hardy hibiscus in the perennial flower garden.

Canna

Canna hybrids

Other Name: Canna Lily
Height: 2 to 7 ft.
Spread: 2 to 3 ft.
Flowers: Assorted colors
Bloom Period: Summer
Zones: 6a, 6b, 7a, 7b

Color photograph on page 231.

Light Requirements:

Beneficial Characteristics:

Cannas were longtime favorite perennial plants before perennial gardening became so popular. These tough plants have lush, tropical-like foliage supporting vivid flowers all summer. Well, if you think cannas are boring, you have not seen some of the new selections boasting incredible foliage as well as a kaleidoscope of blooms. Some cannas are not cold hardy in Oklahoma winters, but many will make it through the winters without special care. These beauties thrive in our hot summer heat and provide spectacular bold foliage and flower combinations.

WHEN TO PLANT
Spring or summer plantings are most common with these sun-loving charmers.

WHERE TO PLANT
Cannas are perfect background plants in the perennial garden, but they make a statement in a bed all by themselves. The more compact cultivars can be moved to the middle or off center in the landscape. Cannas are popular as container plants—obviously requiring good-sized pots. Plant cannas in a garden soil high in organic material and you will not be disappointed.

HOW TO PLANT
Cannas spread quickly over the years, so allow room for growth. Space plants 2 to 3 ft. apart. Plant rhizomes 6 to 8 in. deep. Place a container-grown plant in a hole wider than and the same depth as the container. Mulch to conserve moisture and keep the weeds in check. Water as needed, especially during drought conditions. Once they are established, the plants are fairly drought tolerant.

CARE AND MAINTENANCE
Cannas are heavy feeders and respond to supplemental feedings, especially in poor soils. Light, chlorotic foliage is a sure sign of a need for fertilizer,

whether organic or synthetic. Cannas are prone to caterpillar damage. The critters like to get in the new growth before the leaves unfurl and chew holes that look as if someone shot BBs in the foliage. Most insecticides control these critters and prevent further damage. Actively growing plants with healthy foliage are less prone to such problems. Japanese beetles and cucumber beetles occasionally favor the flowers when cannas are planted in the vegetable garden. Root rot occurs on the rhizomes in poorly drained soils. Potential, but infrequent, problems are rust and mosaic or aster yellows virus. Cannas are tough plants. If the foliage becomes too ratty, the plants can literally be cut to the ground during the growing season to force new, healthy foliage.

Additional Information

Cannas are readily sold as dormant rhizomes or containerized plants. Some selections are available as seed, however. These resilient plants should be divided, thinned, and separated after three or four years when the beds become crowded. Divide perennials in early spring as new growth begins to emerge. Cannas sometimes will not emerge in the spring until late April if the soil temperatures are too cold. The rhizomes of nonhardy types should be dug after the first light frost and stored in peat moss or sawdust in a cool, dry location. Do not let the rhizomes dry out during storage. Check routinely for rotting rhizomes, and discard them immediately.

Additional Species, Cultivars, or Varieties

'Tropicanna (Phaison)', 'Bengal Tiger', 'Minerva', 'Pink Sunburst', 'Stuttgart', 'Durban', and 'Kansas City' are some of the popular variegated foliage cultivars. 'Miss Oklahoma', 'President', 'Black Knight', and 'Wyoming' are some of the "oldie goldie" favorites. I especially like two fairly new dwarf cultivars available by seed or rhizomes called 'Tropical Rose' and 'Tropical Red'. The Liberty™ Series are relatively new dwarf hybrids bred for tolerance to heat and resistance to leaf roller worms, and for quick, self-cleaning flowers.

 Did You Know?

Oklahoma has the largest wholesale grower of cannas in the United States—Horn Canna Farm in Carnegie.

Catmint

Nepeta gigantea

Other Name: Catnip
Height: 12 to 36 in.
Spread: 24 to 36 in.
Flowers: Violet-blue, pink
Bloom Period: Summer and fall
Zones: 6a, 6b, 7a, 7b

Color photograph on page 231.

Light Requirements:

Beneficial Characteristics:

Many gardeners know catmint as a popular herb plant. Pet lovers recognize *Nepeta cataria* as a plant that drives cats crazy. Yet many gardeners have not caught on to its use as a herbaceous perennial providing summer-long color in the landscape. Even more impressive is the fact that catmint thrives in poor soils, heat, and drought. It is a wonderfully bright and colorful blooming plant with grayish foliage compatible with a wealth of colors. It is also a great landscape substitute for lavender and can be used as a border plant offering a well-maintained, unwavering appearance. Lavender-flowering plants are tighter whereas catmint is somewhat more open and airy. Catmint has the well-known square stem characteristic of the *Labiatae* family. Unlike its cousin *mentha*, which is so invasive, catmint grows in a mound or spreading clump, seldom reaching more than 3 ft. wide at maturity. The violet-lavender blooms complement other plants with soft-pink, yellow, or other pastel colors in the garden.

WHEN TO PLANT
Plant catmint in spring or summer.

WHERE TO PLANT
Use catmint as a border plant framing other, taller perennials. The showy plants do well as filler plants grouped in clusters of three or more. Do not hesitate to use the plant singularly as a specimen in combination with other broadleaf plants such as roses, hibiscus, or cannas. It prefers full-sun sites in northern counties but likes afternoon shade in hot, humid locations. There is no need to make a fuss over the soil. The most important requirement is a well-drained site.

HOW TO PLANT
Catmint is available as seed or as a container-grown plant. Plant seeds 1/3 in. deep. I recommend starting them in containers and later transplant-

ing them. Place a container-grown plant in a hole dug wider than and the same depth as the rootball. Space grouped plants 24 to 30 in. apart. Water to settle the soil, to soak the roots, and as needed to establish the plants. Mulch is worth the investment in keeping weeds at bay and moisture in the soil.

CARE AND MAINTENANCE

The tough plants are quite tolerant of most environmental stresses after they are well established, usually within a couple of years. Severe drought can decrease the amount and show of blooms, so providing supplemental moisture is always a good idea. Pruning is seldom needed, other than to initiate new growth and blooms during lull flowering periods. Fertility needs are minimal. Mulch as needed. The only pest problems are occasional spider mites. Catmint can be divided in the spring.

ADDITIONAL INFORMATION

Since catmint is related to catnip, care must be taken during the establishment period to keep cats from chewing the plants. The plants can die if too much top growth is removed before they are well rooted with plenty of foliage (again, about the second season after planting). Afterward, cats can graze at will. Most of the *Nepeta* species are favorites of cats; the exception is *N. nervosa*.

ADDITIONAL SPECIES, CULTIVARS, OR VARIETIES

They are probably four species and a few hybrids of *Nepeta* suited for the landscape as flowering perennials. 'Blue Wonder' seems to be the best cultivar for compact, upright growth, especially in borders. 'Blue Wonder' seldom reaches more than 15 in. tall or 24 in. wide. 'Walker's Low' is more spreading, almost like a ground cover, maturing at 10 in. by 24 in. 'Six Hills Giant' is more upright in growth, reaching 3 to 4 ft. 'Alba' and 'Snowflake' are white-flowering forms, and 'Dawn to Dusk' is pink.

Did You Know?

Catmint is a great plant to use in the garden to attract bee populations and beneficial insects.

Coneflower

Echinacea purpurea

Height: 2 to 4 ft.	**Light Requirements:**
Spread: 2 to 3 ft.	
Flowers: Purple or white	
Bloom Period: Summer	**Beneficial Characteristics:**
Zones: 6a, 6b, 7a, 7b	
Color photograph on page 231.	

This native prairie plant is a real showstopper in the perennial garden. The bold flowers perched on top of stately stems and foliage provide some of the most spectacular summer displays. The name coneflower is descriptive of the cone-shaped center of the flower, encircled by either purple or white rays of petals. The daisylike flowers can be 2 to 4 in. in diameter and are produced in several clusters per plant, making for an even more brilliant fanfare. Coneflower is considered a long-blooming perennial with flowers emerging for five to eight weeks in the middle of the summer. The long, dark-green, straplike leaves have a rough, bold presentation and add coarse texture in the garden. As a result coneflower is suited to be used near softer-textured plants such as fountain grass, coreopsis, and catmint.

WHEN TO PLANT

Coneflower can be planted in spring or summer. Coneflowers are available as seed, dormant-root cuttings, and container-grown plants.

WHERE TO PLANT

These long-flowering beauties are perfect for sunny borders, prairie gardens, or wildflower meadows. I have seen the plant used as a single specimen near mailboxes or in groups for filler in a perennial bed. In plantings associated with other perennials, coneflower is typically placed in the back or on the sides because of its taller height. Planting white and purple together presents a nice display. Coneflower accepts full sun or afternoon shade. *Echinacea* is native to dry, prairie conditions, but it performs better in the garden in well-drained, fertile soils.

HOW TO PLANT

The clump-forming plants improve with age. Plant them in loosely prepared soil in holes that are slightly wider than and the same depth as the rootballs. Space plants 18 to 24 in. apart. Mulch after planting, and water on a regular basis to establish the plants.

CARE AND MAINTENANCE

Coneflowers typically bloom in late June, July, or August. The flowers are produced on current season's growth. Removing faded flowers ensures longer bloom. Supplemental feedings should occur early in the season as the dormant plants begin to emerge from their winter's rest. Dead, dormant foliage can be removed anytime during the winter months or when the new growth begins to emerge in the spring. I like to leave the flower seedheads on the plants in the fall for winter bird feeding and then remove the foliage in early spring. Continue mulching as needed to replace decomposed or weathered materials to keep the soil moist and weed free. Plants can be divided in early spring every three to five years to thin overgrown clumps. Coneflower is fairly disease tolerant. It can succumb to sawfly larvae feeding on the foliage, however.

ADDITIONAL INFORMATION

Occasionally, some of the taller cultivars may need extra support in the garden to keep them from falling over. Before bringing cut flowers of this plant indoors, check for ants or other insects attracted to the pollen. The flowers also dry well.

ADDITIONAL SPECIES, CULTIVARS, OR VARIETIES

'Purpurea', 'Leuchtstern', 'Bright Star', and 'Bravado' are the most common purple cultivars. Coneflower is also available in white with cultivars such as 'White Swan', 'Alba', and 'White Lustre'. 'Crimson Star' is known for its more crimson-violet flower petals.

 Did You Know?

The 1998 Perennial Plant of the Year was Echinacea *'Magnus', known for its large, violet flowers on compact plants. Other cultivar petals point down, but the petals of 'Magnus' are held more horizontally and even somewhat upright.*

Coral Bells

Huechera species

Other Names: Huechera; Crimson Bells; Alumroot

Height: 10 to 24 in.

Spread: 15 to 24 in.

Flowers: Spikes of white, pink, or coral

Bloom Period: May, late spring, or early summer

Zones: 6a, 6b, 7a, 7b

Color photograph on page 231.

Light Requirements:

Beneficial Characteristics:

Coral bells are my answer for alternatives to hostas. The scalloped foliage may not be as bold, but the color variations are equally appealing. As shade-garden plants, coral bells are more forgiving of drought, wind, and heat. These mounding perennials are best grown for their foliage; however, many produce colorful flower spikes that are dazzling above the leaves in colors of white, pink, or coral. The plants get better with age and are long lasting with minimal care. The smaller growth makes them a nice choice for border plants in the front of the flower bed or next to sidewalks. Heuchera is basically a no-quirk choice for the perennial garden.

WHEN TO PLANT
Set out containerized plants in spring or early summer.

WHERE TO PLANT
Use coral bells as a border in afternoon or dappled shade, as a contrast when planted in groups of three to be fillers in the perennial garden, or as a display in a container. Coral bells need good drainage. They are very showy in any soil type, but in highly organic, fertile sites, the foliage becomes even more engaging.

HOW TO PLANT
Space plants 24 in. apart. Mulch the plants to retain moisture and minimize weed growth. Water especially during the early stages of establishment and during severe drought.

CARE AND MAINTENANCE
Coral bells are often touted as no-fuss plants. The routine chores consist of trimming the dormant foliage in early spring and removing the flower

spikes after the bloom. In established gardens the plants can send up twenty or more flower spikes starting in May and June. Supplemental feedings a couple of times throughout the growing season are recommended, especially during the first couple of years. Plants are fairly shallow rooted. Reapply mulch as needed, and water during severe droughts to keep the plants from scorching. Plants can be divided when their centers become woody, every four to five years. In mild winters the plants may retain their foliage, but typically, they are deciduous. The foliage should be removed in the spring if it is scorched or tattered.

ADDITIONAL INFORMATION

Coral bells are notably pleasing if you are looking for a season-long, showy perennial. Deadhead the flowers for prolonged flowering. The flower may last only a couple of weeks, but the foliage remains eye appealing until frost. Some varieties manifest elegant multicolored canopies of bronze, purple, variegated, or marbled foliage.

ADDITIONAL SPECIES, CULTIVARS, OR VARIETIES

There are numerous species, hybrids, and cultivars of *Heuchera*. Some of my favorite foliage types include 'Ruby Veil', 'Chocolate Ruffles', 'Mint Frost', 'Plum Pudding', 'Pewter Moon', 'Persian Carpet', 'Bressingham Bronze', and 'Purple Petticoats'. Colorful flowering selections include 'Mt. St. Helens' (red), 'Raspberry Regal' (raspberry red), 'Chatterbox' (rose pink), 'Coral Cloud' (coral pink), 'June Bride' (white), 'Northern Fire' (dark red), 'Jack Frost' (rose), and 'Firefly' (red). A close relative of *Heuchera* is *Tiarella* species (foamflower). The foliage and flowers are very similar and have been crossed with *Huechera*. Such crosses are sold as *Heucheralla*, or foamy bells.

Did You Know?

Heuchera 'Palace Purple', with its brilliant purple foliage, was the 1991 Perennial Plant of the Year.

Coreopsis

Coreopsis species

Other Name: Tickseed
Height: 12 to 32 in.
Spread: 15 to 24 in.
Flowers: Yellow, pink
Bloom Period: May through frost
Zones: 6a, 6b, 7a, 7b

Color photograph on page 231.

Light Requirements:

Beneficial Characteristics:

If you are looking for a low-maintenance, high-performance plant, look no farther than coreopsis or tickseed. It received the name tickseed because of the tiny, dark seeds somewhat resembling—you guessed it—ticks. The flowers are elegant, offering a burst of bright color for most of the growing season. Coreopsis is a long-blooming perennial that thrives in the sun. Coreopsis is another native of the prairie states, and it withstands poor soils, heat, wind, drought, humidity, and cold. If that is not enough to cheer you up, keep in mind that coreopsis represents cheerfulness in literary folklore. Add a little cheer to your landscape with the bright, sunny coreopsis.

WHEN TO PLANT

Some species are planted as seed in the fall, but most landscape perennials are container grown and can be planted in spring or summer.

WHERE TO PLANT

Depending on the size of the cultivar, coreopsis can be used as a border, background, or filler plant. It is a favorite in wildflower meadows. The delicate foliage of some cultivars softens harsh textures in landscape design. With its long-blooming display, it should be placed front and center for everyone to enjoy. Massed plantings are best. This plant is not picky about soil type, but it requires good drainage. It demands full sun and grows more robust in moist, fertile soils.

HOW TO PLANT

Space the plants 15 to 24 in. apart, depending on the cultivar. Water the plants as needed, and mulch them for weed control.

CARE AND MAINTENANCE

Coreopsis is late to emerge in the spring. The new growth is somewhat delicate in appearance at first but later takes off to support its wonderful color throughout the season. Trim dormant foliage in late winter or early spring as the new growth emerges. Supplemental feedings are generally not needed in good soil sites unless the plant foliage appears nutrient deficient. Mulch as needed to replace decomposed or weathered mulch. The plants are considered drought tolerant, but in severe drought conditions, providing supplemental moisture is a good idea or the plants may dwindle in bloom. Pests are unlikely, but occasionally, caterpillars may chew on the foliage and form silklike webbing. These chewing critters are very easy to control upon early detection.

ADDITIONAL INFORMATION

Spreading forms of coreopsis may need to be divided every four to five years. Some cultivars reseed themselves each fall. In such cases the plants should not be trimmed so that seeds may mature and drop. Some cultivars need deadheading in the summer to force continued bloom. Large-flowering coreopsis varieties make great cut flowers. Birds favor these tough natives.

ADDITIONAL SPECIES, CULTIVARS, OR VARIETIES

There are a multitude of species of coreopsis, so the number of cultivars is impressive. 'Goldfink', 'Sunray', 'Baby Sun', 'Nana', 'Flying Saucer', and 'Robin' are some of the larger-flowering selections that need deadheading. 'Early Sunrise', 'Double Sunburst', and 'Sundancer' are semidouble, flowering types. 'Moonbeam' (1993 Perennial Plant of the Year), 'Zagreb', and 'Golden Gain' are my favorites with more dainty, thread-leaf foliage and yellow, self-cleaning flowers. 'Rosea' and 'American Dream' are pink-flowering, thread-leaf types and self-cleaning. 'Rosea Alba' is a dainty white but very invasive. The newest introduction is 'Tequila Sunrise' with variegated foliage and yellow flowers.

 Did You Know?

The native Oklahoma golden coreopsis (C. tinctoria) or wild flax (sometimes referred to as garden tickseed) has yellow petals with a reddish-brown base. It is a common sight in moist pastures most of the summer, throughout much of the state.

Cupflower

Nierembergia hippomanica

Other Name: Nierembergia
Height: 4 to 15 in.
Spread: 8 to 15 in.
Flowers: Purple or white
Bloom Period: Summer
Zones: 6a, 6b, 7a, 7b

Color photograph on page 231.

Light Requirements:

Beneficial Characteristic:

Cupflower is an elegant, fine-textured, perennial- or annual-bedding plant, depending on where it is grown in the state. Cupflower is a semievergreen perennial in the southern and east-central regions of the state. In milder winters the plant can remain evergreen, but in extremely cold conditions the plant may go dormant, emerging again the following spring. In the colder, northwest locales the plant is best used as an annual bedding plant. Nierembergia is known for its cupped, star-shaped flowers averaging 1/2 in. in diameter. Although the plants can bloom until frost, the peak bloom time is June. The foliage has a soft, delicate, threadlike appearance. Cupflower has the ability to thrive in heat, drought, and humidity, which makes it an impeccable selection for Oklahoma gardens.

WHEN TO PLANT

Nierembergia is most often found as a containerized plant, which can be planted in spring or summer. Seed should be started indoors in late January.

WHERE TO PLANT

Use the purple selections that are more upright in growth as fillers in the front of a perennial garden in full sun or afternoon shade. Or plant the purple-flowering form as a border or in windowboxes, rock gardens, or patio containers. Use the dwarf, white-flowering cultivar as an edging plant in the front of perennial or annual beds and near sidewalks. I have seen 'Mont Blanc' successfully grown in containers, windowboxes, mailbox planters, and hanging baskets. All cupflowers make impressive displays in clusters of three or more or in double rows when used as edging plants. Cupflower is not picky about its soil preference as long as the soil drains well. Rich, fertile soils reward gardeners with more vigorous plants.

HOW TO PLANT

The planting hole should be two times wider than and the same depth as the rootball. Space the purple cultivars 15 in. apart. The truly dwarf, white-flowering cultivar grows in a mound, reaching 4 to 6 in. in height and width. Space these plants 6 to 8 in. apart. Mulch for moisture retention and weed control. Water at planting and as needed.

CARE AND MAINTENANCE

This free-flowering plant usually requires pruning only in early spring to remove winter-damaged foliage. Once the plants start flowering, pruning is not needed unless the plants stall out later in the season. Lightly shearing the spent blooms and then applying fertilizer will send out new growth and more flowers. Supplemental feedings throughout the season benefit this plant. Although pests are unlikely, watch out for spider mites. The narrow foliage will appear speckled and nonproductive. In severe outbreaks apply a miticide or horticultural oil to control the pests.

ADDITIONAL INFORMATION

The purple-and-white-flowering cultivars of cupflower complement yellow or pink companion bloomers. The soft texture of nierembergia is compatible with coarser-foliage perennials, such as daylilies, coneflowers, and cannas.

ADDITIONAL SPECIES, CULTIVARS, OR VARIETIES

'Mont Blanc' is the dwarf, mounding, white-flowering cultivar with yellow eyes. It is without a doubt one of the most compact-blooming plants I have ever used, and it takes full sun. 'Purple Robe' and 'Regal Robe' are taller, upright growers with violet-blue flowers. Both hold their color well in full sun.

Did You Know?

In 1993 'Mont Blanc' was selected as an All-America Selection award winner and a Fleuroselect Gold Medal winner. It has also been selected by many states as a top performer in plant promotion programs.

Daylily

Hemerocallis species

Other Names: Hemerocallis;
   Poor Man's Orchid
Height: 10 to 36 in. and more
Spread: 12 to 24 in.
Flowers: Assorted
Bloom Period: Early and late summer
Zones: 6a, 6b, 7a, 7b

Color photograph on page 231.

Light Requirements:

Beneficial Characteristics:

One of the top-selling perennial plants year in and year out is the daylily. It is no wonder, either, because there are literally hundreds of hybrid cultivars when you consider the numerous professional as well as backyard plant breeders. They are beautiful, drought-tolerant, pest-tolerant, and all-around-tough plants. If there is a shortcoming, it is that the blooms last only one day. But the successive blooms stretch the season out to four to six weeks, thanks to the numerous buds per scape or stem. Even more exciting is the trend in daylily production to release "repeat" bloomers, providing more abundant color throughout the season.

WHEN TO PLANT

Daylilies sold as containerized plants are usually planted in spring or summer. Bare-root daylilies can be planted in early spring, late summer, or early fall.

WHERE TO PLANT

The clump-forming plant is a great filler in perennial gardens, and the restricted growth makes daylily a natural choice for a border plant. The cascading foliage is a nice contrast for placement near rocks, garden art, and other hardscape features. The most dramatic display occurs when daylilies are planted in groups, but some cultivars are so unique that they can stand alone as a specimen. Daylilies can be used as container plants for a patio display. Daylilies respond to well-drained, fertile soils; however, they easily adapt to a wide range of soil types. The plants prefer full sun but tolerate a half day of shade.

HOW TO PLANT

Incorporating a balanced fertilizer with phosphorus and potassium into the perennial landscape bed before planting time is always a good idea. Place containerized plants in holes two to three times wider than and the same depth as the rootballs. Set bare-root plants in wider holes but the same depth that they were previously grown. Place the crown where the leaves and roots join at the soil line. Space plants 15 to 24 in. apart, depending on the plant maturity size. Mulch to retain soil moisture and keep weeds under control. Water them as soon as planted and as needed.

CARE AND MAINTENANCE

Daylilies are considered drought tolerant, but only in the sense that they can survive such conditions. Provide supplemental water to keep plants flourishing. Some daylilies are evergreen or semievergreen, but most are deciduous in Oklahoma. The dead foliage can be removed anytime during the dormant period. Many daylily experts suggest leaving the foliage until early spring and cutting it back as soon as new growth emerges. Hemerocallis responds well to supplemental feedings in early spring and at least once again during the growing season. Insect pests that may affect daylilies are spider mites, aphids, thrips, and slugs. Potential diseases are fungal leaf streak and bacterial soft rot of the roots.

ADDITIONAL INFORMATION

Divide overgrown daylily clumps every three to five years in early spring, late summer, or early fall. Trim the foliage back to 6 to 8 in. to minimize dehydration of the plant. Trimming the roots in a neatly fanned shape is a good idea for easy planting. Remove the spent flower stalks to encourage more growth and repeat blooms.

ADDITIONAL SPECIES, CULTIVARS, OR VARIETIES

Decide what you want—color, flower shape, height, and added benefits of fragrance or repeat bloom—before you go shopping for daylilies or you will be overwhelmed. 'Stella de' Oro' (yellow) and 'Black-Eyed Stella' (yellow with dark eye) are two of the most widely sold repeat-blooming cultivars. 'Eanie Weanie' (yellow), 'Pardon Me' (red), and 'Happy Returns' (yellow) are also some of my favorite repeat bloomers. 'Miss Mary Mary' (yellow gold), 'Raspberry Pixie' (pink), 'Lemon Lily' (yellow), and 'Luxury Lace' (purple) are fragrant. Other than that, you are on your own. Good luck!

Did You Know?

The botanical name Hemorocallis *is derived from two Greek words meaning "beauty for a day."*

Dianthus

Dianthus species

Other Names: Cottage Pink; Miniature Carnation; Border Pink; Cheddar Pink
Height: 10 to 15 in.
Spread: 8 to 24 in.
Flowers: Rose, pink, white, or bicolored
Bloom Period: Late spring, early summer
Zones: 6a, 6b, 7a, 7b

Color photograph on page 231.

Light Requirements:

Beneficial Characteristics:

Perennial dianthus is similar to annual dianthus in that it prefers cooler temperatures and is planted in partial or dappled shade. Dianthus flowers are fringed, single or semidouble, and are produced in mass for a brilliant early-spring display. The most popular colors are rose and pink, which truly add to the early flower show along with redbuds, dogwoods, daffodils, and other spring bloomers.

WHEN TO PLANT
Plant dianthus in early spring or early fall.

WHERE TO PLANT
These cool-season lovers prefer dappled sun or afternoon shade but on occasion can tolerate full sun with plenty of mulch and moisture. The small clumping and dainty height are perfect for borders, rock gardens, edging plants, or container patio displays. Soils should be fertile, moist, but definitely well drained. Waterlogged soils may cause crown or root rot. Many of the plants prefer somewhat alkaline soils instead of acidic soils; they are suitable for northwestern Oklahoma.

HOW TO PLANT
Dig the hole slightly wider than and the same depth as the rootball. Place dianthus slightly above soil grade in poorer soils. The spacing for dianthus is determined by the mature size of the species, from 8 to 24 in. Do not overcrowd plants, or disease can be more prevalent, especially in heavy shade. Mulch with a light leaf mold or compost. Heavy, thick mulches can smother the plants if they are placed too close to the plant crown.

CARE AND MAINTENANCE

In most cases, dianthus is evergreen or semievergreen in the winter; that is, it will retain green foliage all season long. Some deciduous species go dormant in the winter. The severity of the winter temperatures dictates this plant's hardiness. For evergreen species, prune to remove flowers and stalks after they bloom. The peak blooming time is late March and April but can recur in the fall on some selections. Foliage damaged by the winter can be sheared back in very early spring, usually February or early March. Supplemental fertilizations should be minimal, usually in early spring as new growth emerges, with a complete fertilizer containing phosphorus, potassium, and low amounts of nitrogen. Provide supplemental irrigation during drought times. Other than occasional aphid insects and powdery mildew foliage disease, pests are not a concern.

ADDITIONAL INFORMATION

The bloom period usually lasts a couple of weeks. Shearing the flower stalks after bloom ensures more vigor to the plants and possible rebloom again in the fall. Some of the flowers are very fragrant. A few of the taller species make nice cut flowers.

ADDITIONAL SPECIES, CULTIVARS, OR VARIETIES

There are more than 350 species, cultivars, and hybrids of dianthus. Some of the more heat-tolerant selections referred to as cheddar pinks include 'Bath's Pink', 'Firewitch' (magenta), 'Mountain Mist' (pink and taller), 'Spotty' (speckled red), and 'Tiny Rubies' (double red, dwarf). 'Old Spice' is one of the most fragrant. Popular white-flowering cultivars include 'Aqua' (double) and 'It Saul White' (frilly single and takes heat). The old-fashioned *Dianthus barbatus* (sweet William) is a favorite of cottage gardens but is typically a biennial-blooming plant (every other year).

Did You Know?

Dianthus *was also given as the botanical name, which means "divine flowers." Plant a few in your garden and you will see why!*

Foamflower

Tiarella cordifolia

Other Names: False Mitrewort; Allegheny
Foamflower
Height: 6 to 15 in.
Spread: 12 to 24 in.
Flowers: White and pink
Bloom Period: Mid-spring
Zones: 6a, 6b, 7a, 7b

Color photograph on page 231.

Light Requirements:

Beneficial Characteristics:

This low-growing and clumping plant rewards gardeners with dainty, white flowers elevated above the lime-green foliage in mid-spring. The Latin name actually means "little tiara," which relates to the almost crownlike flowers and fruit formed in a cluster for an exquisite fanfare. The foliage itself is attractive and unique with its lobed, heart-shaped arrangement. Most species go dormant in the winter, with the foliage dying back to the ground and reemerging the following spring. A few, especially in the *T. cordifolia* species, retain a semievergreen appearance, depending on the severity of the winter. Some of the more promoted selections have attractive mottled or variegated foliage, and a few have pink blooms. Foamflower is a unique plant to consider for moist, woodland gardens.

WHEN TO PLANT

Foamflower can be planted in early spring as a bare-root plant or in late spring and early summer as a container-grown plant.

WHERE TO PLANT

This broadleaf, clumping plant is a good filler or border plant in shade gardens with moist soil. Plant foamflowers in groups of three or five for the best arrangement and display. Use them in association with hardscape items such as rocks, yard art, birdbaths, and fountains. They like woodland soil that is high in organic matter and moisture retentive. Partial or dappled shade cools the plants in harsh summers.

HOW TO PLANT

Dig the planting holes two times wider than and the same depth as the rootballs. Space the plants 18 to 24 in. apart. Mulch with an organic material such as compost, shredded leaves, or composted manure. Water routinely during the establishment period and on a regular basis.

CARE AND MAINTENANCE

In good soil this unusual plant can spread by underground stems without being invasive, and it almost forms a clumping ground cover. Flowers typically appear in late April or May and look almost like a white carpet in groups of established plants. Trim the spent flowers after blooming, which usually lasts two to six weeks. Another flush of blooms may occur later in the season. The maplelike foliage can turn a reddish cast in the fall. Pests are of no concern. Overgrown clumps can be divided every four to five years.

ADDITIONAL INFORMATION

Tiarella is very similar in shape to *Huechera*, another clumping perennial favorite. Both are comparable in appearance and growing conditions, but *Huechera* is somewhat more tolerant of dry soils. The two have been crossed to form hybrids with more improved characteristics of environment and color. Such crosses are called foamy bells (*Huecherella*). Foamflower is a good companion plant with astilbe, hosta, ferns, and other woodland plants.

ADDITIONAL SPECIES, CULTIVARS, OR VARIETIES

'Dark Star', 'Mint Chocolate', and 'Dark Eyes' are colored foliage selections, each with characteristic dark, blotchy markings on green foliage. Collections grown more for their unusual-shaped leaf include 'Ninja', 'Skeleton Key', and 'Filigree Lace'. 'Eco Running Tapestry' and 'Winterglow' are better choices for actual ground covers. 'Wherryi' is the best nonspreading form. Pink-flowering cultivars include 'Ink Blot', 'Purpurea', 'Cygnet', and 'Pink Bouquet'.

 Did You Know?

The common name is given because the white flowers resemble foam coming from the stems.

Hardy Hibiscus

Hibiscus moscheutos

Other Names: Rose Mallow; Mallow Rose; Swamp Rose; Wild Cotton

Height: 3 to 8 ft.

Spread: 3 to 6 ft.

Flowers: Red, pink, white, and bicolored

Bloom Period: Summer and fall

Zones: 6a, 6b, 7a, 7b

Color photograph on page 231.

Light Requirements:

Beneficial Characteristics:

If you want big—and I mean really big—perennial flowers, there is not a better choice than hardy hibiscus. Years ago I was fortunate enough to get a beautiful start from Professor Raymond Kays (former *Oklahoma Gardening* host), who liked to hybridize hardy hibiscus as a hobby. *H. moscheutos* flowers are often compared to dinner plates in size analogies. Hibiscus is native to southeastern Oklahoma roadside wetlands, riverbeds, marshes, and shallow swamps. One of the most popular white introductions was discovered near the Blue River in Oklahoma and is given the trade name 'Blue River'.

WHEN TO PLANT
Hardy hibiscus can be planted as dormant bare-root plants in early spring or as container-grown plants in spring, summer, or fall.

WHERE TO PLANT
These tall-growing beauties can be used as single-plant specimens or as groups for even more breathtaking displays. The height makes them conducive to background border plants in island perennial beds. I have seen them used as a hedge with phenomenal summer exhibition. The plants prefer moisture-retentive soils, but they tolerate dry sites once they are established. Rich, fertile soils accelerate growth and promote better blooms.

HOW TO PLANT
Dormant bare-root plants should be planted in containers and later planted outside. The bare-root plants can be directly planted into well-worked soil in late spring at the same depth that they were grown. Container-grown plants should be placed in holes dug two times wider than and the same depth as the rootballs. Mulch to conserve moisture, and water as needed.

CARE AND MAINTENANCE
Hardy hibiscus is one of the latest perennials to break dormancy, sometimes

not until May. These cold-hardy plants go dormant after the first killing frost and emerge from the root crown with long, tendril-like growth when soil temperatures begin to warm. In just a few weeks, the foliage sets forth the spectacular display of flowers for the rest of the summer. The blooms last only a day, but the stalks form continuous buds and bloom until the first frost. In the colder climates of the state such as the Panhandle, they may need mulch over the roots for protection during the winter months. Other than an occasional aphid, spider mite, or chewing beetle on the flowers, pests are not a serious problem. Larvae may feed through the flower bud before it opens, causing the bud to abort prematurely. Most labeled insecticides will control this pest with thorough spraying on additional, newly formed buds. Foliar diseases are usually more of a problem in heavy shade with poor air circulation.

ADDITIONAL INFORMATION

The tall plants seldom need staking. Summer pruning may be needed to control growth. Do not crowd the plants unless they are to form a hedge. *H. moscheutos* is not as prone to litter the ground with old flowers as is its cousin *H. syriacus* (rose of Sharon).

ADDITIONAL SPECIES, CULTIVARS, OR VARIETIES

'Lord Baltimore' (solid red) and 'Lady Baltimore' (pink with red center) are very popular cultivars. The Disco Series, with a more compact growth habit, is readily available and in colors of pink, red, and white. 'Blue River II' is an improved version of the original solid white. If you want a mix of different flower colors all on one plant, consider 'Southern Belle'. 'Turn of the Century' is a bicolored combination of white, pink, and red shades on the same flower arranged like a pinwheel. One of the largest flowering selections is 'Moi Grande', with rose-pink flowers potentially reaching a 12 in. diameter, and the plants are quite vigorous, maturing at 5 1/2 by 6 ft. in good soils. The Mammoth Series touts large flowers. *H. rosa-sinensis* (Chinese hibiscus) is the tropical species, not cold hardy as a perennial in Oklahoma but often used as a container plant.

 Did You Know?

The hardy hibiscus flowers can be cut early in the morning as soon as they open and placed bottomside down in a bowl of water for an enjoyable display indoors all day.

Japanese Painted Fern

Athyrium niponicum

Other Names: Lady Fern; Glade Fern
Height: 8 to 20 in.
Spread: 15 to 36 in.
Flowers: Flowerless
Zones: 6a, 6b, 7a, 7b

Color photograph on page 231.

Light Requirements:

Beneficial Characteristics:

*A*thyrium is a large genus of shade-loving ferns with assorted foliage colors known for their tropical presentation. There is something appealing about ferns and their cooling effect in a shady landscape. Although most of them are basic green, they provide texture, filler, and background for any woodland design. Ferns need protection from the tough Oklahoma summers and require moist, shaded sites. In these conditions, the ferns thrive for years. Japanese painted fern is one of the few ferns offering a variation in foliage color—a combination of gray green, silver, and maroon. These natural color combinations are perfect for brightening and soothing the shade garden at the same time. They work well with other plants, highlighting the same color combinations.

WHEN TO PLANT

Ferns are often sold as bare-root plants, which should be planted in the spring. Container-grown plants can be set out in spring or early summer. Some ferns are started in tissue culture and later transferred to containers.

WHERE TO PLANT

The airy fern appearance softens harsher textures of coarse, broadleaf plants such as mahonia, hosta, and bergenia. Some of the taller selections are great background border plants. More compact versions can be used in the front perimeter. Ferns can be clumped in groups as filler. In certain situations the entire shade garden can be filled only with ferns for a bold, uniform appearance. Ferns work well in association with garden sculptures, rocks, and other hardscape items.

HOW TO PLANT

Apply organic materials before planting time, and work them into the planting bed—unless shallow tree roots exist. In that case the amendments should be left on the surface and no thicker than 6 in. Most ferns prefer slightly acidic soils with a pH of 5.5 to 6.5. Set bare-root plants slightly

below the ground with the dormant foliage buds facing up. Place container-grown plants in holes wider than and the same depth as the rootballs. Space plants 12 to 24 in. apart.

CARE AND MAINTENANCE
Most ferns in Oklahoma are deciduous, going dormant in the winter. Mulching around ferns with organic leaf mold and other products holds in moisture and provides slow-release nutrients. Ferns are light feeders, and in most cases organic or natural fertilizers are recommended because of their slow-release nature. If ferns are healthy and growing, there is probably no need to feed. Most ferns are relatively pest free, with occasional spider mites.

ADDITIONAL INFORMATION
Ferns produce spores, known as sori, clustered on the underside of the foliage (fronds). This is a natural reproduction feature, which may be mistakenly identified as insect scales. The fern clumps can be divided in early spring as needed, every three to five years.

ADDITIONAL SPECIES, CULTIVARS, OR VARIETIES
Japanese ferns are relatively slow growing. 'Pictum' and 'Ursula's Red' are two of the most popularly sold with distinct tricolors. Another popular, primarily green fern is lady fern (*Athyrium*), which is somewhat more tolerant of dry soils but not severe drought. *Athyrium* 'Cristatum' has delicate, crested fronds. The other reliable Oklahoma performer in moist soils is *Dryopteris* species, such as autumn fern, shaggy shield fern, or remote wood fern.

  Did You Know?

Athyrium otophorum *(Asian lady fern) is also hardy in Oklahoma with larger and taller foliage. The new growth emerges as a reddish tint, turning almost plasticlike green. Asian lady fern is more difficult to find but well worth the pursuit.*

Lavender

Lavendula angustifolia

Other Names: English Lavender;
Lavandin
Height: 10 to 36 in.
Spread: 12 to 36 in.
Flowers: Purple or violet-blue
Bloom Period: Summer
Zones: 6a, 6b, 7a, 7b

Color photograph on page 232.

Light Requirements:

Beneficial Characteristics:

Some herb plants also make wonderful landscape perennials. Take lavender, for example, with its compact growth, brilliant flower display, and pleasant aroma. Who would not want to include such a plant front and center in the perennial landscape? The International Herb Association has deemed this plant the 1999 Herb of the Year. Lavender is a southern plant that thrives in heat and dry conditions. Waterlogged, heavy soils, high humidity, or extreme cold, however, can spell doom for lavender. Cultivar selection alleviates some of these problems.

WHEN TO PLANT
Plant lavender in late spring or summer.

WHERE TO PLANT
These tough plants prefer full sun; they tolerate a half day of shade as long as the site has good drainage. The soils do not have to be overly fertile, but the plants like a sandy loam. Heavy, waterlogged soils will kill this species fast. The plants make a perfect border in the back or front of perennial beds. They can be used as filler, and some gardeners use them in rows as a small hedge. I have seen them in windowboxes and patio pots, and they are frequently grown in the vegetable or herb garden.

HOW TO PLANT
Most plants are container grown and planted the same depth as the rootballs. Planting slightly above soil grade is warranted in heavier soils. Starting plants from seed should be done in containers instead of directly in the ground. Space plants 12 to 36 in. apart, depending on the cultivar. Mulch after planting to keep weeds at bay; however, the mulch should not be too thick, especially near the plant stems. Water after planting to establish plants, but allow time to dry between waterings.

CARE AND MAINTENANCE

Pruning typically consists of shearing off the old blooms to promote additional blooms later in the season. Winter-damaged foliage can be sheared in early spring. If the plants are healthy and actively growing, feeding is not necessary. Be careful not to apply fertilizer if the plants are declining or rotting. After a couple of seasons the plants are fairly drought tolerant.

ADDITIONAL INFORMATION

Lavender is used for cut flowers, potpourri, sachets, aromatherapy, dried arrangements, and a flowering landscape plant. Harvest fresh flowers and foliage in the morning. Some cultivars of lavender need to be well established and will not bloom until the second growing season. Pests are not a problem; an occasional caterpillar or leaf spot may affect plants in heavily shaded, humid, or damp sites. Root rot is the biggest concern in poorly drained soils.

ADDITIONAL SPECIES, CULTIVARS, OR VARIETIES

English lavenders are more likely to produce seed, whereas vegetatively propagated hybrids are not. The new hybrids are more consistent in growth, which is especially important when using them as a hedge. 'Twickle Purple' is a compact, semievergreen plant with purple flowers and gray-green foliage turning a purple tint in the winter. 'Hidcote' and 'Munstead' are probably the most popular and readily available. 'Lady' was a 1994 All-America Selection chosen for its tough dwarf growth and flowering ability the first year of planting. Cultivars known more for their feathery foliage are 'French Lace', 'Goodwin Creek', and 'Pinnata'. 'Fred Boutin' is a good choice for cut flowers with lighter-colored foliage. 'Nana Alba' is white flowering, and 'Melissa' has almost pinkish-white flowers. 'Rosea', 'Jean Davis', and 'Hidcote Pink' are even more pink in flower color. 'Provence' is known as a more rot-resistant selection that tolerates more humidity and moister soils.

Did You Know?

Greeks and Romans used lavender as an additive to bath water. The actual Latin name lavare *means "wash."*

Mexican Petunia

Ruellia brittoniana

Other Names: Ruellia; Wild Petunia;
 Dwarf Ruellia
Height: 6 to 36 in.
Spread: 10 to 36 in.
Flowers: Purple, pink, or white
Bloom Period: Summer
Zones: 6b, 7a, 7b

Color photograph on page 232.

Light Requirements:

Beneficial Characteristics:

Greg Grant, Texas horticulturist and plant guru, first introduced me to *Ruellia*. Most experts tout this beauty as cold hardy to Zone 8, so I was expecting to grow it as an annual. Imagine my surprise when I was scoping out the plant material around the Oklahoma County Extension office in Oklahoma City one spring when I came upon *Ruellia* growing at the south entrance—yes, as a perennial. I had to go home and try it, and sure enough, to this day *Ruellia* has worked as a perennial for me in Stillwater and in Vian. Even if it was not hardy, I would grow it because of its large, colorful, petunialike flowers. And the shiny-green, straplike foliage makes for a splendid texture choice in the landscape. The plant thrives in soggy or dry soils, and I have used it as a water garden bog or container plant as well.

When to Plant
Plant *Ruellia* in spring or summer.

Where to Plant
Although seeds are available, most plants are sold as container grown. The taller-growing species make great background border plants when they are allowed to spread. The compact cultivars mature at 10 to 12 in. for a border or edging plant. They work well in clusters where height needs to be dropped in the perennial landscape. The low-spreading types can be a ground cover. There is literally a species or cultivar for almost any landscape situation, whether in sun or partial shade. This plant likes humus-rich soils; it tolerates soggy or dry soil types, but prefers moist soils.

How to Plant
Dig a hole wider than and the same depth as the rootball. Space plants 12 to 36 in. apart, depending on the species. Mulch to keep weeds at bay and to retain moisture.

CARE AND MAINTENANCE

Blooms occur starting in late May or June and continue until frost. The plants go dormant in the winter and come back in late spring from the crown or root. Some reseed. Pests are minimal, other than an occasional aphid in early spring.

ADDITIONAL INFORMATION

Prune only to keep plants in check. The flowers are self-cleaning on the taller selections and much the same on the compact versions. Occasionally, they may need help to remove some of the flowers on the dwarf types, especially after a rain. Many *Ruellia* species that are not cold hardy in the state make wonderful annual bedding plants for the summer.

ADDITIONAL SPECIES, CULTIVARS, OR VARIETIES

Ruellia brittoniana comes in dwarf or upright selections with narrower leaves. 'Katie' (also sold as dwarf, compact, or 'Nolan's Dwarf' ruellia) is the smallest clumping form, maturing at 8 to 12 in. with a heavy set of purple flowers most of the summer. 'Bonita'™ (colobe pink) is a pink-flowering, dwarf form, like 'Katie'. 'Strawberries and Cream' is a compact variety with speckled cream, pink, white, and green variegation. The upright selections grow to 30 to 36 in., and purple is the most readily found color. 'ChiChi' is an upright, pink-flowering cultivar that is not quite as common. *R. malacosperma* is an upright version with slightly wider foliage. It is available in purple or in a named white, most often sold as 'Alba'. *R. caroliniensis* ('Blue Shade') is a spreading, ground cover type with purple flowers and velvety leaves.

 Did You Know?

Ruellia *is not a petunia at all. The common name is related to the petunialike flowers.* Ruellia *is in the* Acanthaceae *family, and petunia is in the* Solanaceae *family.*

Oregano

Origanum laevigatum

Other Names: Marjoram; Ornamental Oregano

Height: 15 to 30 in.

Spread: 15 to 36 in.

Flowers: Purple, pink, or white

Bloom Period: July through September

Zones: 6a, 6b, 7a, 7b

Color photograph on page 232.

Light Requirements:

Beneficial Characteristics:

Oregano is an aromatic plant most widely known for its culinary use as a herb. But did you know that this fragrant herb is available as an exquisite blooming perennial? *O. vulgare, O. heraclitum,* and *O. majorana* are the popular, annual, seasoning herbs whereas *O. laevigatum* is more cold hardy with showier flowers, making it an excellent landscape plant. The late-summer bloomer is loaded with dazzling fragrant flowers, which attract bees and beneficial insects to the garden. Because of its popularity with bees, ornamental oregano should be planted away from sidewalks and high-traffic areas. The truly stunning, hardy plant will thrive in full sun or afternoon shade and should definitely be included in any perennial flower or vegetable garden.

WHEN TO PLANT

Ornamental oregano can be started from seed in a container around mid-winter. But it is easier to purchase container-grown plants in the spring and plant anytime throughout the summer.

WHERE TO PLANT

Set out this lovely, free-flowing plant in a rock garden, or allow it to cascade from a rock wall. Many cultivars do well in the perennial flower garden as mid-level or border plants. Planting ornamental oregano in groups offers more of an impact in flowering. This aromatic perennial prefers full-sun or afternoon-shaded sites. In colder regions of the state, plant oregano in sheltered sites to provide winter protection. Well-drained soil is the most important factor to consider when growing oregano. Oregano tolerates more alkaline soils, typical of the western portions of the state.

HOW TO PLANT

Space plants 18 to 24 in. apart. Planting them diagonally instead of in a straight line helps cluster plants.

CARE AND MAINTENANCE

Fertile soils offer better conditions for vigorous growth and spreading; however, ornamental oregano tolerates poor soils where it attains a more compact growth habit. Flowering occurs on new growth of the season and starts in late summer, either in June or July, continuing into the fall. Any lag in flowering later in the season can be rejuvenated by shearing the plants slightly below the flower stalks. Plants do not tolerate wet sites. Be careful not to mulch too heavily close to the plants, or rotting can occur near the base. Winter-damaged foliage should be trimmed in early spring as soon as new growth starts to emerge.

ADDITIONAL INFORMATION

Ornamental oregano is a member of the mint family, and certain  species spread like ground covers in the landscape, especially in partial shade. The plants are not nearly as invasive as their true mint counterparts. The tubular flowers are borne on short spikes above the aromatic foliage and are favorites of hummingbirds, bees, and butterflies.

ADDITIONAL SPECIES, CULTIVARS, OR VARIETIES

The cold hardiest and probably the most popular floriferous ornamental cultivar is 'Herrenhausen' with pinkish- purple flowers on dense growth, maturing near 24 in. in height. 'Hopley's Purple', with its mauve-purple flowers, also has a bluish tint to the foliage but is best for Zones 7a and 7b of the state. 'Album' is a whiter-flowering cultivar of *laevigatum*. *O. acutidens* (Turkish oregano) has spicy, aromatic, mounding foliage that sends up arching flower stalks of pink flowers. *O. rotundifolium* and its hybrids are clump-forming plants with almost wiry stems, heart-shaped leaves, and whorls of flowers resembling hops. 'Kent Beauty', with pink flowers, and the hybrid 'Barbara Tingley', with lavender blooms, are two tender perennial selections performing best in Zone 7 or in protected areas of Zone 6.

 Did You Know?

The culinary species, O. vulgare, *has a few nice selections grown as ornamental annuals including* 'Compactum', 'Thumbles Variety', 'Aureum,' *and* 'Silver Anniversary'.

Oxblood Lily

Rodophiala bifida

Other Name: Schoolhouse Lily

Height: 12 to 15 in

Spread: 15 to 24 in.

Flowers: Red, pink, coral

Bloom Period: Fall

Zones: 7a, 7b

Color photograph on page 232.

Light Requirements:

Beneficial Characteristics:

If you are looking for a naturalizing bulb that thrives in the Oklahoma heat better than tulips, consider oxblood lily. Oxblood lily is more common in neighboring Texas, although it does quite well in the southern zones of our state. It does not need chilling hours to prosper and bloom. The other difference is that *Rodophiala* species bloom in late summer/early fall. The primary color available is intense red, but others are said to be in the works. The straplike foliage emerges in late fall after it blooms and grows throughout the winter as a semievergreen perennial where the foliage dies in the early to midsummer. The flower stalks later burst through the ground after our first good rain in August, producing vivid, eye-catching perennial color. The best comparison for oxblood lily is the familiar *Lycoris* (surprise lily). After a two- to three-week bloom period, the flower stalks wither away, starting the process all over again.

WHEN TO PLANT

Plant the bulbs in the middle of summer when foliage goes dormant.

WHERE TO PLANT

Oxblood lilies are so tough that they will easily naturalize in perennial beds, through ground covers, in lawns, and in roadside rights-of-way. Planting them in rows or drifts where they are allowed to fill in with time makes for the most spectacular display. The bulbs will grow in full sun or partial shade. These tough perennials will thrive under deciduous trees where the bulb foliage will get winter sunlight. Do not forget to put a few in permanent patio containers for an added late-summer surprise. The plants adapt to almost any type of soil—clay, rocky, or sandy loam—as long as it drains well. Like most plants, they are more vigorous in better soils.

HOW TO PLANT

Plant the bulbs 3 to 4 in. deep and 8 to 12 in. apart. Oxblood lilies are no different from any other perennial; they get better with age. Adding a light organic mulch consisting of shredded leaves, pine bark, or compost rewards you with beautiful color.

CARE AND MAINTENANCE

Pruning is not necessary. The foliage in particular should be allowed to turn yellow and die on its own to feed the bulb for its grand finale of color. The withered flower stalks can be removed, although they fade out of sight quickly on their own. The lilies respond to early-spring and summer feedings, but these are not necessary in rich, humus soils. Pests are of no concern. In heavy, water-soaked soils the bulbs can rot. Oxblood lily is quite drought tolerant once established.

ADDITIONAL INFORMATION

Other southern, heat-tolerant, fall-blooming bulbs to include in the landscape are spider lily (*Lycoris* species), rain lily (*Zepheranthes candida*), and spider lily (*Hymenocallis* species). Autumn crocus (*Sternberia lutea*) is another fall-blooming bulb, also called autumn daffodil. Hardy crinum lily (*Crinum bulbispernum*) is an earlier-flowering bulb, blooming in accordance with its foliage. Daffodils and narcissus are great choices for spring-blooming bulbs, with numerous selections from which to choose. Crocus and hyacinth are adapted to Oklahoma conditions. Tulips are pickier for year-after-year growth and flowering. They do best in Zone 6 of the state and require winter chilling for successful blooming. Choose "naturalizing" varieties unless you like to replant every two to three years. Always allow the foliage to die on its own with all spring- and summer-blooming bulbs. For a season-long bloom, plant daffodils for spring flowers, crinums for summer, and oxbloods for fall.

ADDITIONAL SPECIES, CULTIVARS, OR VARIETIES

Oxblood lily is available to date only in red.

 Did You Know?

The common name of schoolhouse lily refers to the time that the plant blooms—about the time that school starts in the fall.

Phlox

Phlox paniculata

Other Names: Garden Phlox;
  Large Leaf Phlox
Height: 3 to 4 ft.
Spread: 2 to 3 ft.
Flowers: Assorted shades of red and white
Bloom Period: Summer
Zones: 6a, 6b, 7a, 7b

Color photograph on page 232.

Light Requirements:

Beneficial Characteristics:

My first experience with herbaceous perennial plants was a "good news, bad news" scenario. A neighbor gave me starts of iris and phlox from his bed after he cleaned it out. There were so many iris that I pitched the extras out in the pasture. I knew I had a winner when the discarded plants started to grow on top of the ground. The bad news was the garden phlox. The plants lasted two years and finally bit the dust, thanks to a foliage disease called powdery mildew. Thankfully garden phlox has been greatly improved with many cultivars resistant to this dreaded pathogen. It is a good thing, too, because I do not know what a perennial garden would be without the towering stalks of the refreshing summer blooms. If you are going to grow this old-time favorite in the Oklahoma heat and humidity, you almost have to start with disease-tolerant strains.

WHEN TO PLANT
Phlox can successfully be planted as a bare-root start in early spring or as a container-grown plant in spring or summer.

WHERE TO PLANT
Use garden phlox in the back of perennial beds or as a border plant. Group the plants in clusters of three or more, or plant them in diagonal rows for the best color effect. Garden phlox likes full sun or a half day of shade. The plant prefers moist, but well-drained, fertile soils.

HOW TO PLANT
Taking the time to prepare humus-rich soil will nurture vigorous green plants, rewarding you with tremendous color. Dig holes in loosely worked soil that are wider than and the same depth as the rootballs. Mulch between and around plants to hold in moisture and keep weeds out. Water after planting and on a regular basis to keep the soil moist, but well drained.

CARE AND MAINTENANCE

These tall, dynamic plants are heavy feeders. Give them supplemental feedings a couple of times a year after the new growth emerges in the spring. The foliage typically goes dormant with the first freeze in the fall and emerges again next spring.

ADDITIONAL INFORMATION

Garden phlox blooms on new growth starting sometime in May or June. Trimming the spent blooms just below the flower head will encourage more color later in the summer. Many of the phlox selections are fragrant, attracting butterflies and "hummers." The height of phlox offers depth to the perennial landscape. If plants have a history of falling over, pinch the new growth a couple of times as it emerges in the spring. Doing this will cause the plants to become more compact and bushy. It can also mean somewhat smaller blooms and a little later flowering, but I prefer both to using plant stakes or support hoops.

ADDITIONAL SPECIES, CULTIVARS, OR VARIETIES

'David' is a disease-resistant white. 'Eva Cullum' (bright pink) is more tolerant but not always mildew proof. 'Red Magic', 'Flamingo', 'Miss Kelly', 'Elie', and 'Laura' are new, highly resistant cultivars. 'Norah Leigh' is not as resistant as some others but deserves a place in the garden, especially with afternoon shade. This beauty is better grown for its unusual variegated foliage but has light-pink blooms with dark centers. Another attractive variegated selection is 'Harlequin' with somewhat narrower foliage and more lavender flowers. Very similar in appearance is *P. maculata* 'Alpha' with pink flowers and disease-resistant foliage.

Did You Know?

P. pilosa *(native prairie phlox) is more tolerant of dry soils and blooms earlier than garden phlox, extending the flowering season even more. Gardeners in eastern counties may also observe smaller-growing* P. divaricata *(wild blue phlox) in early bloom.*

Rosemary

Rosmarinus officinalis

Other Name: Hardy Rosemary
Height: 24 to 36 in.
Spread: 24 to 36 in.
Flowers: White or blue
Bloom Period: Early to midsummer
Zones: 7a, 7b (6b with winter protection)

Color photograph on page 232.

Light Requirements:

Beneficial Characteristics:

This perennial does not offer beautiful flowers but should be included in the perennial border for no other reason than its prominent, pinelike fragrance. On windy days (there are plenty of those in Oklahoma) the foliage brushes together, filling the garden with a distinctive aroma. When it is planted near the sidewalk, people brushing against it release its wonderful scent. Fragrance alone is reason enough to grow rosemary but add the finely textured, colorful foliage and somewhat showy flowers, and you have a great package for any landscape. In Zone 7 the almost-velvety, dark-green foliage typically remains evergreen all winter. This plant provides gardeners with other benefits in using the leaves for culinary or decorative functions.

WHEN TO PLANT

Spring planting allows this sometimes tender perennial plenty of time to get established before the onset of winter.

WHERE TO PLANT

The evergreen presence of hardy rosemary is especially nice as a background plant in the perennial garden. Many perennials go dormant, leaving the bed empty in the winter, but rosemary adds refreshing color to an otherwise mundane site. Even during the growing season, the solid background of rosemary accentuates the colors in bloom. The stately growth habit works well as a hedge or border plant. Trailing forms can freely cascade in rock gardens or perimeters. Do not forget to include a few in containers for the patio. Rosemary tolerates full sun or partial shade. There should be at least four or five hours of sun. The most important factor to consider is well-drained soil since these plants easily rot in waterlogged or heavy soils.

HOW TO PLANT

Fertile, garden soils are perfect. If such sites do not exist, blend a complete fertilizer, peat moss, and other organic materials before planting time.

Mulch to keep weeds out and grass from competing. Soak the soils for a long period of time to encourage deeper roots, and water on a regular basis to establish the plants.

CARE AND MAINTENANCE

Frequent shearing of the leaves and stems for culinary or aromatic uses keeps the plants more compact and is a good idea throughout the growing season. Otherwise, prune winter-damaged growth, or prune to prevent branches from getting too woody. In colder climates the plants need protective mulch around the roots at least 4 to 6 in. angled down to the stem. Do not cover the foliage or place the mulch thick on the stem, or it can cause the plant tissue to rot, killing the entire plant. The top will come back from the soil crown as long as the roots do not completely freeze.

ADDITIONAL INFORMATION

Supplemental feedings are typically not needed in good, fertile soils. Provide supplemental irrigation during dry spells. Reapply mulch as needed. Pests are highly unlikely in proper planting sites with good air circulation and soils. In stressed situations insects, such as aphids and spider mites, and diseases, such as powdery mildew and botrytis, may affect plants.

ADDITIONAL SPECIES, CULTIVARS, OR VARIETIES

The most cold-hardy selection that is best suited for Oklahoma is 'Arp', sometimes sold as 'Madeline Hill', with dark-green foliage and light-blue flowers. Most other cultivars to date are not as winter hardy and are somewhat riskier but well worth the try. 'Golden Rain' is not as winter hardy but has variegated new growth. 'Huntington Carpet' and 'Irene' do well in southeastern Oklahoma and are more prostrate spreading with frequent blue blooms. 'Majorica' is not quite as cold hardy but has showier, blue flowers. Not all of the selections have showy flowers.

 Did You Know?

Container-grown rosemary can be sheared throughout the summer into a pyramidal shape perfect for patio Christmas decorations.

Russian Sage

Perovskia atriplicifolia

Other Name: Azure Sage
Height: 3 to 4 ft.
Spread: 3 to 4 ft.
Flowers: Lavender-blue
Bloom Period: Summer
Zones: 6a, 6b, 7a, 7b

Color photograph on page 232.

Light Requirements:

Beneficial Characteristics:

I was not too impressed by my first encounter with Russian sage. A gardener had placed the tall plant near the entrance of the home where it looked rather weedy and out of place. I always try to be open minded, and if that was where he wanted the plant, so be it. But I never wanted to include this plant in my perennial bed because I had never seen it used suitably for my interest. A few years later I needed a large plant with silvery foliage to fill in a large, sunny, perennial bed. I knew of the many rave reviews of this popular plant and decided to give it a try. Anytime you are going to try a new perennial, you need to give it at least two years before deciding its fate because it gets better with age. The 1-gal. plant turned into a phenomenal specimen, blooming from July through September the first year. The blue flowers and silver-gray, airy foliage are a perfect combination with pink- or yellow-blooming perennials. The best news, though, is its resilience in poor soils, heat, and drought. Now I think it is one plant that everyone should find a place for in the landscape.

WHEN TO PLANT
Perovskia can be planted in spring, summer, or fall.

WHERE TO PLANT
The almost-shrublike growth of this plant requires plenty of space. Russian sage is definitely a background plant and appears best in large, perennial beds. The size seems out of place in smaller beds. The cool colors are nice for contrasting displays and seem to soften more dramatic, harsh textures. To get the most out of this plant, set it in full sun. These plants perform adequately in poor soils. Rich, humus soils tend to cause quite vigorous growth. Good drainage is important.

HOW TO PLANT
Dig the planting hole at least two times wider than and the same depth as the rootball. Allow plenty of space between plants for good air circulation

and growth. Space plants 3 to 4 ft. apart. Mulch them to keep weed competition down. Water after planting and as needed during the first few weeks to establish plants if rainfall is not adequate.

CARE AND MAINTENANCE

Once established, Russian sage is quite drought tolerant. The blooms form in late June or July and continue through September and sometimes until the first frost. The flower production varies throughout the season and occasionally needs trimming back to promote more growth. The plants receive various degrees of winter kill, depending on the severity of the temperatures. Shear dead growth in early spring. If no winter kill occurred, trim the foliage back to several inches from the ground to keep the plants more manageable. Doing this also forces new growth, which later produces the summer flower color. Fertilize only if the plants appear to be lagging in growth. Reapply mulch as needed. Pests are not a serious problem, although spider mites may appear.

ADDITIONAL INFORMATION

The foliage of Russian sage has a very pungent smell; consequently, the plant is sometimes sold as a herb. The silvery-gray foliage is finely cut with velvety, lavender flowers emerging from the upright, loosely grouped stems. I have found this plant to be a great companion for hardy hibiscus, daylily, garden phlox, *Rudbeckia*, and canna. The long sprays of flowers are good additions to cutflower arrangements.

ADDITIONAL SPECIES, CULTIVARS, OR VARIETIES

Most of the cultivars to date are hybrid crosses. They include 'Filigran', an improved selection with finer-cut foliage and lavender blooms; 'Longin', with narrow foliage, lavender-blue flowers, and distinctly upright growth; and 'Blue Haze', known for its pale-blue flowers. For darker, more-violet blooms, look for 'Blue Spire'. Another species found in the trade is *P. scrophularaefolia*, with coarser foliage.

 Did You Know?

Russian sage (P. atriplicifolia) was named the 1995 Perennial Plant Association's Perennial Plant of the Year.

Sage

Salvia species

Other Names: Perennial Salvia;
Hardy Salvia; Meadow Sage
Height: 2 to 3 ft.
Spread: 24 to 30 in.
Flowers: Purple, pink, or white
Bloom Period: Summer
Zones: 6a, 6b, 7a, 7b

Color photograph on page 232.

Light Requirements:

Beneficial Characteristics:

If there is one plant that I always use in my personal gardens and landscape designs, it would have to be hardy salvia. I guess the biggest reason is that it tends to ignore the summer heat and go about its business of providing towering blooms of color throughout the summer. It is always dependable and the perfect height for most perennial beds. Hardy salvia can quickly become an integral part of any colorful border. It can be used in large island beds or next to the house. There are so many species, cultivars, and hybrids from which to choose, I can almost always find one to match any landscape need. An added benefit is the attraction for another popular garden visitor—hummingbirds. If you only know salvia as the red annual, boy, are you missing out!

WHEN TO PLANT
Salvias can be planted from container-grown stock in late spring or summer.

WHERE TO PLANT
Grow these beauties in masses along borders and as fillers in the perennial garden. Plant them to complement mailboxes, rock walls, and other hardscape items. They prefer full sun or partial shade with at least four to five hours of sun. Rich, humus soils that drain well are ideal for these plants.

HOW TO PLANT
Incorporating organic materials into the soil before planting time is well worth the effort and investment. In loosely dug soil, set the plants in holes wider than and the same depth as the rootballs. Mulch to provide added organic nutrients, moisture retention, and weed control. Water regularly.

CARE AND MAINTENANCE
The flowers are produced on new growth, usually in late May and June. Cut the flower stalks back after the first flush of blooms to induce more compact growth and later flowering. Salvias usually go dormant in the

winter. Cut the dead foliage off in early spring just as new growth begins to emerge from the ground. Some experts proclaim that cutting back the foliage on sage in early winter allows moisture to get down in the hollow, square stems and freeze the root crown. Supplemental feedings are needed only when soils are nonfertile, plant foliage shows nutrient deficiency, or growth is nonproductive.

ADDITIONAL INFORMATION

There are more than seven hundred species of *Salvia*. *S. leucantha* is a tender perennial in Oklahoma, which means that it may or may not overwinter. I grow it every year anyway because it is the only late-summer-, fall-blooming plant with majestic height and velvety, purple-and-white flower spikes lasting for weeks. 'Midnight' is a solid-purple selection. Also not dependably cold hardy is *S. elegans* (pineapple sage), with pineapple-scented foliage and bright fuschia-red flowers in the fall. *S. azurea* v. *grandiflora* is our native purple 'Pitcher's Sage', found in the eastern two-thirds of the state.

ADDITIONAL SPECIES, CULTIVARS, OR VARIETIES

Most of the hardy selections in Oklahoma are hybrid crosses. Lavender-blue selections include 'Blue Hill', 'East Friesland', 'Blue Queen', 'Purple Rain' (*S. verticillata*), and 'May Night'. 'Rose Wine', 'Rose Queen', and 'Plumosa' are more rose-violet-colored flowers. 'Snow Hill' is white. *S. officinalis* cold-hardy selections include 'Albiflora' (white), 'Purpurescens' (lavender), and 'Tricolor' (multicolored foliage with mauve flowers). There are many *S. greggii* cultivars, but they do better in far southeastern portions of the state. Some of the most unique salvias are yellow flowering, which include *S. koyamae* and *S. glutinosa*—they require afternoon or full shade. If you are interested in variegated foliage, consider *S. nipponica* 'Fugi Snow' with pale-yellow flowers, also a woodland-shade plant.

 Did You Know?

'May Night' salvia was named the 1997 Perennial Plant of the Year. It has deep, dark-violet-purple flower spikes on a fairly low-growing herbaceous plant. It also blooms earlier, starting in May.

Solomon's Seal

Polygonatum odoratum

Height: 6 in. to 6 ft.
Spread: 2 to 3 ft.
Flowers: White
Bloom Period: Late spring
Zones: 6a, 6b, 7a, 7b

Color photograph on page 232.

Light Requirements:

Beneficial Characteristics:

Solomon's seal is a delightful woodland plant for perennial shade gardens. This elegant, upright, and arching plant has glossy leaves with spreading growth, offering a coarse-textured, almost fernlike presentation. Once the stems and foliage emerge in the spring from their winter's rest, they quickly develop white, tubular flowers gently dangling from the arching stems almost as if they were bells. Even though the flowers are showy, the graceful foliage seems to steal the show during the bloom period. If you need height with this type of landscape effect, some species mature at 6 ft. tall while others are more compact at 6 in. Solomon's seal is available in solid-green foliage or variegated white, with fragrant flowers. In a couple of seasons this hardy plant quickly becomes the backbone of the shade garden with its wonderful foliage display.

WHEN TO PLANT

Solomon's seal spreads with underground rhizomes and is available as dormant bare-root plants or container-grown herbaceous perennials. The dormant bare-root selections can be planted in early spring, and container plants can go in the ground in spring or summer.

WHERE TO PLANT

Depending on the height, *Polygonatum* can be a background or foreground border plant. It is also a graceful filler plant with its spreading, but generally noninvasive habit. The soil should be fertile, moisture retentive, and well drained.

HOW TO PLANT

Plant rhizomes slightly below the soil level, and plant container-grown selections in holes wider than and the same depth as the rootballs. Mulch with leaf mold or other highly organic materials to provide slow-release nutrients, hold in moisture, and minimize weed growth.

CARE AND MAINTENANCE

The plants go dormant in the winter and emerge each spring from the rhizomes. Remove old, winter-damaged foliage as new growth begins to emerge. No other pruning should be needed. Flowers form along the base of the arching stems from the leaf axis. Some of the species are somewhat aggressive as a ground cover, which is a nice feature in large, shaded gardens where a lot of filler is needed. The spreading is usually more prominent in moist, fertile soils. Many of the shade gardens in Oklahoma are drier and hotter in nature, and the spread is somewhat limited under stress. Supplemental feeding is needed only to push the growth for a quicker fill. Remulch as needed, and water during drought conditions.

ADDITIONAL INFORMATION

In good soils the plants may need to be divided every three or four years. Division should occur in early spring or fall.

ADDITIONAL SPECIES, CULTIVARS, OR VARIETIES

There are quite a few species of Solomon's seal with various degrees of height, spread, foliage, and fragrance distinctions. There are not too many improved cultivars, however. Most are the true species' parent. There are a few hybrids, such as 'Variegatum', with white variegated foliage, and 'Flore Pleno' (hard to find), with double flowers. *P. odoratum* selections are the most fragrant. Dwarf Solomon's seal (*P. humile*) is the most compact, maturing at 6 in. *P. multiflorum* typically has more blooms. *P. biflorum* develops black berries after it flowers, which are favorites of birds. The tallest species, giant Solomon's seal (*P. canaliculatum* or *P. commutatum*), reaches nearly 6 ft. in height in optimum soil conditions.

 Did You Know?

There is another woodland plant known as false Solomon's seal (Smilacina racemosa), which is actually in the lily family. It has solid-green foliage resembling Polygonatum but feathery-white, fragrant flowers borne on the stems followed by red berries.

Speedwell

Veronica spicata

Other Names: Spike Speedwell; Veronica
Height: 12 to 36 in.
Spread: 18 to 24 in.
Flowers: Pink, white, purple
Bloom Period: Late spring and
    midsummer
Zones: 6a, 6b, 7a, 7b

Color photograph on page 232.

Light Requirements:

Beneficial Characteristics:

*V*eronica is often confused with perennial *Salvia* because of the similarities in growth and flowering habits. Both require similar soil conditions and sites. The flowering times are overlapped, although some *Veronicas* may flower a couple of weeks earlier. After bloom, they need to be deadheaded to stimulate more flowering later in the season, just like *Salvia*. So what are the big differences? The biggest difference is probably the variation in growing prominence, with *Veronicas* offering a few more growing habits and heights. Some of the more prostrate species have very different flower shapes. Overall, *Veronica* offers additional color and growth distinctions for the perennial sun garden.

WHEN TO PLANT

Plant container-grown speedwell in late spring or summer.

WHERE TO PLANT

These tough-growing herbaceous perennials are often used as border plants at mid-level or in the back of the bed, depending on the height. The more prostrate growers are used for ground covers or front border plants. They easily cascade over walls, over berms, and in rock gardens. Cluster them in groups for a more significant display of color when planting them for filler. Fertile, moist, well-drained soils are necessary for the success of this plant species. This plant prefers full-sun locations but tolerates shade for three or four hours.

HOW TO PLANT

Plant them in holes wider than and the same depth as the container root-balls. Space plants 24 in. apart. Mulch and water plants as needed.

CARE AND MAINTENANCE

The foliage of *Veronica* goes dormant in the winter and reemerges in the spring. Leave the dormant foliage until new growth begins to emerge. Also prune after the first flush of flowers. Trim below the flower spikes to encourage compact growth and more flowering later in the summer or fall. Fertilize if the plants are stunted or show signs of chlorosis, which is a yellowing of the foliage. Reapply mulch as it weathers or decomposes. Supplemental irrigation will be needed during drought conditions. On average the plants need 1 to 2 in. of water per week, including rainfall, depending on the time of the year. There are few pest problems, but keep an eye out for aphids and powdery mildew.

ADDITIONAL INFORMATION

Speedwell typically grows in a clump or mound, but there are spreading forms. As plants mature, division may be needed to thin and rejuvenate the parent plants. Any division or relocation of the plants should be done in early spring.

ADDITIONAL SPECIES, CULTIVARS, OR VARIETIES

Upright-growing, blue- or purple-flowering cultivars or hybrids include 'Royal Blue', 'Blue Giant', 'Midnight', 'Blue Charm', 'Goodness Grows', and 'Crater Lake Blue'. Pinkish-violet flowers are popular, and some of the cultivars are 'Rosenrot', 'Heidekind', 'Spikata Fox' (more shade tolerant), and 'Minuet'. White-flowering selections are represented by 'Icicle', 'Snow White', and 'Alpina Alba'. Ground cover or prostrate forms are 'Georgia Blue', 'Blue Carpet', 'Waterperry Blue', and 'Mann's'. 'Variegata' and 'Noah Williams' are white, variegated forms while 'Trehane' and 'Sunshine' have yellowish-golden foliage with occasional purple spikes.

Did You Know?

The Perennial Plant Association has recognized Veronica *as an award winner. 'Sunny Border Blue' was the 1992 recipient.*

Verbena

Verbena canadensis

Other Names: Hardy Verbena; Vervain
Height: 4 to 6 in.
Spread: 24 to 30 in.
Flowers: Purple, pink, red, white
Bloom Period: All summer
Zones: 6b, 7a, 7b

Color photograph on page 232.

Light Requirements:

Beneficial Characteristics:

Perennial is where it's at when it comes to verbena. I have been a longtime fan of fragrant perennial or hardy verbenas. They are not picky about soil type. They thrive in the summer heat and are virtually pest free. They are low growing and spreading but not invasive. Annual-seed types, on the other hand, are notorious for powdery mildew disease in Oklahoma. And keeping aphids away from them is a challenge. The biggest frustration with the perennial types is trying to get the cultivar names straight. Because many are renamed, it is easy to plant the same selection with different names.

WHEN TO PLANT

Container-grown plants can be set out late spring or summer. Fall planting is discouraged because there will not be time to establish before winter hits. Remember, you want these beauties to come back year after year.

WHERE TO PLANT

With their low-growing habit, verbenas can go front and center in the flower bed. Planted as borders next to sidewalks or in front of the landscape bed, they can show off their color. Their free-flowing form cascades over rock walls or from landscape slopes. They also make perfect windowbox or container plants. These plants prefer full sun but accept two to three hours of shade. With too much shade, they may have problems. I have seen these plants thriving in sandy, clay, rocky, or loamy soils. Good drainage and fertile soils are the important elements.

HOW TO PLANT

Plant verbenas at the same depth that they were grown. Mulch them to keep weeds from creeping through the spreading foliage. Water on a regular basis to establish the plants.

CARE AND MAINTENANCE

These sun lovers tolerate drought after they are established, but they spread more quickly and bloom more profusely with consistent irrigation in well-drained sites. Provide supplemental feeding when new growth begins to emerge in the spring and maybe again after the first flush of heavy bloom. Fertilizing past July may promote new growth that would be more susceptible to winter injury. Mulch around plant clumps as they spread to insulate roots and keep moisture in and weeds out. Pruning is needed to contain plants within their boundaries. When flowers stall out from stress, shear the plants just below the spent blooms to encourage more growth and later flowering.

ADDITIONAL INFORMATION

In addition to the spreading verbena selections, another one of my favorites has upright growth. It is commonly referred to as verbena-on-a-stick (*V. bonariensis*). The upright, 30-in., green-foliage-laid stalks reward gardeners with pinkish-lavender blooms most of the summer. This verbena is suited for Zone 7 in Oklahoma or in protected and winter-mulched areas of Zone 6b. Occasionally, this extraordinary verbena will reseed itself.

ADDITIONAL SPECIES, CULTIVARS, OR VARIETIES

Some of my favorite named hardy selections include 'Homestead Purple', 'Blue Princess', 'Kemerton', and 'Taylortown Red'. The 'Temari™' series also overwinters in milder winters. I have also found success with what I call the lacy- or cutleaf-foliage types, including *V. tenuisecta* and a few other species and hybrids. These lacy types seem to be more pest resistant with wonderful flower color. They bloom their hearts out in early summer with a little rest in between, followed by two or three more repeat flowerings, which typically last two to three weeks at a time. 'Imagination' (purple), 'Tapien™' (assorted colors) and 'Edith' (pink) are such named cultivars. Cutleaf types are also available in white, lavender, and red.

 Did You Know?

Good friend and Texas horticulturist Greg Grant has named selections that are starting to find their way into the nursery trade. Look for 'Texas Appleblossom', 'Fiesta', and 'Batesville Rose'.

Wormwood

Artemesia species

Other Names: Artemesia; Sagebrush;
  Southernwood; Mugwort
Height: 24 to 48 in.
Spread: 24 to 36 in.
Flowers: Inconspicuous
Bloom Period: Nonshowy
Zones: 6a, 6b, 7a, 7b

Color photograph on page 232.

Light Requirements:

Beneficial Characteristics:

Perennials do not need wonderful flowers to make an impact in the landscape. Artemesia is a good example of what foliage can do for texture, color, and design. The gray-green foliage is eye-catching but also tends to soften or tie other colors together. It can be used to divide or separate beds without using physical structures. The consistent, solid foliage can accentuate other flowering colors. The feathery foliage creates an atmosphere of tranquillity. Artemesia is distinctly known for its pungent odor when the foliage is crushed or bruised. Gray or silver colors are very trendy in many landscape designs. Artemesia can offer all this and more, with dependability year after year and little to no care.

WHEN TO PLANT
Artemesia can be planted in spring or summer.

WHERE TO PLANT
Wormwood is generally used as a border or "blender" plant. Its uniform growth makes it suitable for borders or hedges. The soothing colors tie in or emphasize other colors in the perennial bed. It likes full-sun locations; however, some prefer afternoon shade when faced with hot, windy sites. Artemesia is not picky about soil type as long as good drainage is provided. Waterlogged soils will put a quick end to this plant.

HOW TO PLANT
Place a container-grown plant in a hole two to three times the width of the rootball and the same depth. Mulch to keep weeds out. Water to settle the soil and as needed during the establishment year.

CARE AND MAINTENANCE
Since artemesia is grown for its foliage and not flowers, pruning can occur at any time to keep plants bushy. Severe pruning may be needed in early

spring to remove winter-damaged branches and to promote new, vigorous growth. Minimal fertilizing is required. The biggest harm to artemesia comes from high humidity, which routinely occurs in Oklahoma. Planting with open spacing and air circulation somewhat alleviates this problem. Plants tending to "melt down" during the summer can be moved the following spring to afternoon-shaded sites. Too much shade will cause the foliage to lose its unique color.

ADDITIONAL INFORMATION

The lovely foliage of wormwood and other species makes nice filler in fresh cutflower arrangements. It is also successfully used in dried arrangements. There is a wide range of foliage textures, from coarse to more fine-leafed, almost airy growth habits. Artemesia is an effective companion plant with coreopsis, salvia, veronica, Russian sage, and coneflower.

ADDITIONAL SPECIES, CULTIVARS, OR VARIETIES

'Silver King' and 'Powis Castle' are cultivars with lacy-type foliage. 'Huntington' and 'Valerie Finnis' have bolder, coarser foliage. For a more mounding growth habit, consider 'Silver Mound'. 'Silver Brocade' is often compared to a hardy dusty miller. *A. lactiflora* (white mugwort) is probably the most dramatic, and 'Guizhou' is a selection with purple-stemmed plants displaying white-flowering spires in late summer. *A. versicolor* 'Seafoam' probably has the airiest appearance and uniquely shaped, silver leaves.

 Did You Know?

Artemesia is often called sagebrush, a common native of our state. It is not the same as our indigenous, now cosmopolitan "tumbleweed," which is Artemesia albus—a relative of pigweed.

"The love of gardening is a seed that

once sown never dies."

—Gertrude Jekyll

Bald Cypress
Taxodium distichum

Chinese Pistache
Pistacia chinensis

Dawn Redwood
Metasequoia glyptostroboides

Eastern Redbud
Cercis canadensis

Flowering Dogwood
Cornus florida

Fruitless Sweetgum
Liquidambar styraciflua

Ginkgo
Ginkgo biloba

Golden Raintree
Koelreuteria paniculata

Japanese Maple
Acer palmatum

Kentucky Coffee Tree
Gymnocladus dioicus

Lacebark Elm
Ulmus parvifolia

Pine
Pinus species

Red Maple
Acer rubrum

Shumard Oak
Quercus shumardii

Southern Magnolia
Magnolia grandiflora

Sugar Maple
Acer saccharum

Abelia
Abelia grandiflora

Azalea
Rhododendron hybrids

Burning Bush
Euonymus alatus

Butterfly Bush
Buddleia davidii

Chaste Tree
Vitex agnus-castus

Crapemyrtle
Lagerstromia indica

Dwarf Fothergilla
Fothergilla gardenii

English Boxwood
Buxus sempervirens

Flowering Quince
Chaenomeles speciosa

Heavenly Bamboo
Nandina domestica

Japanese Kerria
Kerria japonica

Loropetulam
Loropetulam chinensis

Korean Lilac
Syringa meyeri

Oakleaf Hydrangea
Hydrangea quercifolia

Oregon Grape Holly
Mahonia aquifolium

Possumhaw
Ilex decidua

Soft Touch Holly
Ilex crenata

Southern Waxmyrtle
Myrica cerifera

Spirea
Spiraea species

Sweet Box
Sarcococca hookerana

Viburnum
Viburnum species

Weigela
Weigela florida

Winter Jasmine
Jasminum nudiflorum

Yaupon Holly
Ilex vomitoria

Yew
Taxus species

Archangel
Lamium maculatum

Blue Plumbago
Ceratostigma plumbaginoides

Bugleweed
Ajuga reptans

Creeping Euonymus
Euonymus fortunei

Creeping Phlox
Phlox subulata

English Ivy
Hedera helix

Hardy Ice Plant
Delosperma cooperi

Juniper
Juniperus species

Moneywort
Lysimachia nummularia

Pachysandra
Pachysandra terminalis

Peacock Moss
Selaginella uncinata

Stonecrop
Sedum species

Vinca
Vinca minor

Akebia
Akebia quinata

Boston Ivy
Parthenocissus tricuspidata

Carolina Jasmine
Gelsemium sempervirens

Chinese Wisteria
Wisteria sinensis

Clematis
Clematis species

Crossvine
Bignonia capreolata

Honeysuckle
Lonicera species

Porcelain Vine
Ampelopsis brevipedunculata

Trumpet Vine
Campsis radicans

Climbing Rose
Rosa species

Heirloom Rose
Rosa species

Rugosa Rose
Rosa rugosa

Shrub Rose
Rosa species

Species Rose
Rosa species

Asiatic Lily
Lilium species

Barrenwort
Epimedium species

Beebalm
Monarda didyma

Black-Eyed Susan
Rudbeckia fulgida

Blue Mist Spirea
Caryopteris clandonensis

Canna
Canna hybrids

Catmint
Nepeta gigantea

Coneflower
Echinacea purpurea

Coral Bells
Huechera species

Coreopsis
Coreopsis species

Cupflower
Nierembergia hippomanica

Daylily
Hemerocallis species

Dianthus
Dianthus species

Foamflower
Tiarella cordifolia

Hardy Hibiscus
Hibiscus moscheutos

Japanese Painted Fern
Athyrium niponicum

Lavender
Lavendula angustifolia

Mexican Petunia
Ruellia brittoniana

Oregano
Origanum laevigatum

Oxblood Lily
Rodophiala bifida

Phlox
Phlox paniculata

Rosemary
Rosmarinus officinalis

Russian Sage
Perovskia atriplicifolia

Salvia
Salvia species

Solomon's Seal
Polygonatum odoratum

Speedwell
Veronica spicata

Verbena
Verbena canadensis

Wormwood
Artemesia species

Fountain Grass
Pennisetum alopecuroides

Inland Wild Oats
Chasmanthium latifolium

Japanese Blood Grass
Imperata cylindrica

Lily Turf
Liriope muscari

Maiden Grass
Miscanthus sinensis

Mondo Grass
Ophiopogan japonicus

Plume Grass
Erianthus ravennae

Reed Grass
Calamagrostis species

Sedge
Carex species

Sweet Flag
Acorus gramineus

Switch Grass
Panicum virgatum

Tufted Hair Grass
Deschampsia caespitosa

Begonia
Begonia semperflorens-cultorum

Bidens
Bidens ferulifolia

Copper Plant
Acalypha wilkesiana

Esperanza
Tecoma species

Firebush
Hamelia patens

Globe Amaranth
Gomphrena globosa

Impatiens
Impatiens walleriana

Joseph's Coat
Alternathera species

Lantana
Lantana camara

Licorice Plant
Helichrysum petiolare

Melampodium
Melampodium paludosum

Mexican Bush Sage
Salvia leucantha

Mexican Heather
Cuphea hyssopifolia

Million Bells®
Calibrachoa hybrid

Ornamental Sweet Potato
Ipomoea batatas

Persian Shield
Strobilanthus dyerianus

Pinwheel Zinnia
Zinnia angustifolia

Princess Flower
Tibouchina grandiflora

Purple Heart
Setcresea pallida

Scaevola
Scaevola aemula

Shrimp Plant
Justicia brandegeana

Starflower
Pentas lanceolata

Summer Snapdragon
Angelonia angustifolia

Sun Coleus
Solenostemon scatellariodes

Swedish Ivy
Plectranthus species

Swiss Chard
Beta vulgaris

Twinspur
Diascia hybrids

Vinca
Catharanthus roseus

Waffle plant
Hemigraphis alternata

American Beautyberry
Callicarpa americana

Blazing Star
Liatrus spicata

Bushy Bluestem
Andropogon glomeratus

Butterfly Weed
Asclepias tuberosa

Cardinal Flower
Lobelia cardinalis

Carolina Buckthorn
Rhamnus carolina

Carolina Snail Seed
Cocculus carolinus

Elderberry
Sambucus canadensis

False Indigo
Baptisia australis

Gaura
Gaura lindhermeri

Goldenrod
Solidago canadensis

Indian Blanket
Gaillardia pulchella

Indian Grass
Sorghastrum nutans

Indian Paintbrush
Castilleja indivisa

Joe-Pye Weed
Eupatorium fistulosum

Passion Flower
Passiflora incarnata

PawPaw
Asimina triloba

Sassafrass
Sassafras albidum

Sunflower
Helianthus species

237

Sumac
Rhus glabra

Winged Elm
Ulmus alata

Alaska Cypress
Chamaecyparis nootkatensis

Arizona Cypress
Cypressus arizonica

Cockspur Hawthorn
Crataegus crusgalli

Colorado Spruce
Picea pungens

European Mountain Ash
Sorbus aucuparia

Korean Evodia
Evodia daniellii

Osage Orange
Maclura pomifera

Pinyon Pine
Pinus cembroides

Rocky Mountain Juniper
Juniperus scopulorum

Western Soapberry
Sapindus drummondii

Oklahoma

PRECIPITATION MAP

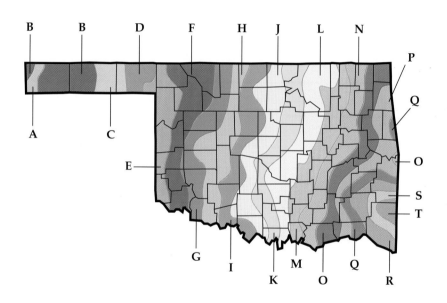

Normal precipitation (1961–1990)

A	≤16″	F	24–26″	K	34–36″	P	44–46″
B	16–18″	G	26–28″	L	36–38″	Q	46–48″
C	18–20″	H	28–30″	M	38–40″	R	48–50″
D	20–22″	I	30–32″	N	40–42″	S	50–52″
E	22–24″	J	32–34″	O	42–44″	T	≥52″

Source: Oklahoma Climatological Survey. www.ocs.ou.edu

Oklahoma

USDA
COLD-HARDINESS
ZONE MAP

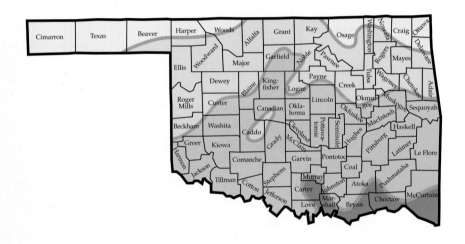

Temperature (F°)

6A	-5 to -10
6B	0 to -5
7A	5 to 0
7B	10 to 5

Our versatile landscapes are filled
with a natural beauty that can be
easily duplicated in our own
backyards.

CHAPTER SEVEN

Ornamental Grasses

ORNAMENTAL GRASSES are also considered perennial herbaceous plants, but because of their sheer uniqueness and popularity, I have included them in a separate chapter. Although pampas and monkey grass are the most well-known landscape grasses, other grasses have caught the attention of gardeners. You probably will not find ornamental grasses in the garden centers until late spring or early summer because of their slow nature to break dormancy in the spring. They lack eye appeal in the spring, but as the season progresses, their landscape brilliance and grandeur progress as well.

Ornamental grasses offer many unique characteristics to the landscape. Most are clump forming and noninvasive. They provide height, texture, softness, color, and sound. They send up flower plumes, known as inflorescences, which later change to seed spikes. Some provide bird seed, others are great additions to cut or dried arrangements, and many are sources of alternative color in the winter months. Ornamental grasses often become the center of attention in late summer and fall. And like most perennials, they get better with age, almost doubling in size the year after planting.

Most ornamental grasses go dormant in the winter. That is when some selections take on their most spectacular appearance with golden foliage color, elegant, feathery seed plumes, and dried foliage rustling in the winter winds. Definitely leave the foliage in place all winter on most selections. The main maintenance chore is cutting back the dormant foliage in early spring to 4 to 8 in. from the soil just as the new, green grassy growth begins to peek through. Ornamental grasses are truly the mow-once-a-year grass. Too bad they don't work as a lawn grass.

During the first few weeks of emergence, ornamental grass looks much like a typical grass. But as it grows taller, the foliage starts to cascade, mound, or stand at attention, depending upon the species. The airy foliage softens harsh corners, provides drastic contrasting texture, and offers alternative color choices for any landscape. As the summer progresses, the seed stalks emerge, further changing the appearance with assorted colors and shapes. When the flowers are pollinated and start to dry, they glisten with the sunlight, becoming almost translucent. Fall assures that plants will be at their peak for all to enjoy.

Warm-season ornamental grasses are typically the ones to go dormant during the winter, emerge in the spring, and actively grow when the temperatures warm up. They traditionally bloom later in the summer or fall and thrive in full sun. Cool-season grasses, on the other hand, put on their best growth when temperatures are cooler in the fall or spring. They ordinarily just sit there in the summer heat and perform better in Oklahoma with partial or afternoon shade. Most of the time they bloom earlier in the year. Some cool-season grasses are more likely to overwinter as semievergreen or evergreen, depending on the severity of the cold temperatures.

Planting ornamental grasses with evergreen shrubs often intensifies the winter colors. The loosely textured grasses also are very compatible with coarser broadleaf plants and hardscape items such as rocks, birdbaths, and other garden art.

Ornamental grasses are moderate feeders and respond to supplemental fertilizer applications. Always wash off the foliage after applying granular fertilizer to avoid discoloration. Ornamental grasses put on quite a show and perform best in fertile, moist soils. Mulching is always beneficial, and supplemental irrigation will be needed during severe dry spells. Pests are usually no threat. With all of their attributes it is no wonder that ornamental grasses are fast becoming a common sight in the garden center and landscape.

Fountain Grass

Pennisetum alopecuroides

Other Names: Perennial or Hardy Fountain Grass; Chinese Pennisetum

Height: 2 to 5 ft.

Spread: 2 to 5 ft.

Flowers: White, pink, reddish brown to black

Bloom Period: Midsummer (warm-season grass)

Zones: 6a, 6b, 7a, 7b

Color photograph on page 233.

Light Requirements:

Beneficial Characteristics:

Fountain grass is one of my favorites because of the uniform cascading foliage appearing as a fountain rising from the earth. In late May, June, or July the flower plumes resembling a bottle brush emerge. Some are elongated and narrow while others are quite showy and wide. The flower plume colors are typically reddish brown to black, depending on the cultivar. *Pennisetum* seed spikes do not hold up in the winter as well as *Miscanthus* spikes. But the foliage retains an attractive color and shape throughout the winter months. The soft foliage can easily hide unsightly objects and soften landscape corners.

WHEN TO PLANT

Fountain grass is sold generally as a container-grown plant that can be placed in the ground in late spring or early summer. .

WHERE TO PLANT

Use the 2- to 4-ft. plants on landscape corners, near hardscape items, or as a background or border. Plant in groups for a better display. Fountain grass prefers full sun. It accepts a minimum of four or five hours of shade. Too much shade will result in fewer flower spikes. Rich, humus soils are perfect but not necessary. A moisture-retentive soil with good drainage is probably more critical. The plants tolerate most soil types with a pH of 5.5 to 7.5.

HOW TO PLANT

Most often the container plants are rootbound; that is, the roots grow compacted in a circle near the base of the pot. Trim the roots by cutting off the thick 2 or 3 in. near the very bottom and severing the sides three or four times to promote more horizontal growth. Planting a compacted rootball seldom allows water penetration, which invites more stress and even death of the plant. The roots tend to grow the same way, making them even more rootbound. Space the plants 3 to 4 ft. apart.

CARE AND MAINTENANCE

Trim the dormant growth in early spring 4 to 6 in. from the ground before new, green growth emerges. If you wait too long, the new growth grows up into the old, making it hard to cut without damaging the new, lush foliage. Provide supplemental feedings as the new growth reaches 8 to 10 in. tall and again in midsummer before the flower plumes emerge. The plants are somewhat drought tolerant once they are established. But it is a good idea to water during severe droughts, or the foliage tips will scorch and the blooms will not fully emerge.

ADDITIONAL INFORMATION

Spider mites are the primary pest problem but are of minimal concern. An indication of spider mite attack is a speckling of the foliage.

ADDITIONAL SPECIES, CULTIVARS, OR VARIETIES

P. alopecuroides is the standard species, maturing around 4 ft. 'Japonicum' is the tallest selection, reaching nearly 5 ft. I especially like the more compact cultivars 'Hameln', 'Cassian', 'Autumn Magic', and 'Little Bunny'. They range in size from 1 to 3 ft. in height with about the same width. 'Moudry' has broader foliage and sends up later-blooming, distinctively black seed plumes. The plant matures around 4 by 4 ft. in rich soils and is quickly becoming one of my favorites. 'Little Honey' grows to 12 in. with variegated foliage. *P. caudatum* and its cultivars have whiter seedheads while *P. seatceum* and its selections are known for pinker flowers.

Did You Know?

The Greek name pennisetum *translates to "feathery bristles," which perfectly describes the beautiful flower plumes.*

Inland Wild Oats

Chasmanthium latifolium

Other Names: Northern Sea Oats;
  Spangle Grass; Wild Oats
Height: 2 to 4 ft.
Spread: 2 to 3 ft.
Flowers: Green to bronze drooping spikes
Bloom Period: Late summer through fall
  (warm-season grass)
Zones: 6a, 6b, 7a, 7b

Color photograph on page 233.

Light Requirements:

Beneficial Characteristics:

Inland wild oats are readily found in the shaded woods of Oklahoma. There is still debate about their origination: Are they native or naturalized? Whatever the answer, this ornamental grass is a good choice for the shade garden. The bamboolike foliage is dark green, especially in shade. When it receives more sunlight, the foliage takes on a light-green, almost yellowish appearance. The plants range in size from 2 to 4 ft. and come back each spring from root crowns or occasionally from seeds. The plants spread in a very weak, almost rhizomatous growth; they are not aggressive. In late summer the fanfare continues with flower spikes shooting up from the tropical-like foliage and turning into showy seeds that droop as they mature. The seed display becomes even more prominent in the fall and winter as seeds turn an almost coppery color. Because the seeds will last through most of the winter, the plant has winter appeal.

WHEN TO PLANT

Plant inland wild oats seeds in the late fall or early spring, preferably in a container. Planting the seeds in the fall after they ripen will eventually mean placing the containers in a greenhouse or sunroom to keep the plants from freezing. Spring planting can be done directly in the ground. Container-grown plants can be set out in late spring or summer.

WHERE TO PLANT

Use these upright plants as background or feature plants, grown in clusters of three or more, or plant them to give a hedgelike appearance to shade gardens. Choose inland wild oats for an edging plant near water or bog gardens. Inland wild oats prefer sandy-type soils but tolerate heavier sites. The plants are fairly tough; their only special requirement is somewhat moist soil.

How to Plant

Plant seeds 3/4 to 1 in. deep. Loosen potbound roots of container-grown plants by cutting off the winding base and severing the sides before planting. Place container-grown plants in holes the same depth that they were grown in their containers and two times wider than the rootballs. Space plants on 2-ft. centers for the best display. Mulch the plantings to minimize weed growth and retain soil moisture. Water after planting and on a regular basis.

Care and Maintenance

Pruning should consist of removing the winter-damaged growth in early spring as the new, green foliage peeks through the soil. Any seedlings that emerge can be transplanted if they arise in areas other than their designated sites. This typically occurs in looser, sandier soils. Fertilize only in poorer soils and in late spring or early summer as new growth begins to elongate. Pests are highly unlikely.

Additional Information

The dormant bamboolike beige foliage and bronze seedheads make a wonderful winter display. Leaving the plants intact will offer beauty throughout the winter and an alternative food supply for a number of birds. The seed stalks are nice touches in fresh cut and dried arrangements. The plants can be divided in the spring. Seed germination is not always very high because many of the flowers are sterile.

Additional Species, Cultivars, or Varieties

Improved cultivars are few and far between in the nursery trade. Inland sea oats are sometimes sold as *Uniola latifolia*.

 Did You Know?

The true sea oats are Uniola paniculata, *which are found along beaches and coastal areas to minimize beach erosion. In some states and coastal areas it is illegal to collect the seeds from plants on the beach.*

Japanese Blood Grass

Imperata cylindrica

Other Name: Red Baron Grass
Height: 15 to 18 in.
Spread: 12 to 15 in.
Flowers: No known flowers
(warm-season grass)
Zones: 6a, 6b, 7a, 7b

Color photograph on page 233.

Light Requirements:

Beneficial Characteristics:

Japanese blood grass is a popular ornamental grass because of its blood-red color and manageable size. Seldom reaching more than 15 in. tall, it spreads by noninvasive rhizomes, forming a small colony of brilliant color. It is one of the few ornamental grasses not offering additional season appeal with its flower and seed plumes. Once you see the magnificent color of the foliage, you will not care that it does not do anything else, however. The new spring growth emerges green with hints of red. The red color progresses with age and in somewhat more light, although not full, hot sun. Its growth habit is predominantly upright, adding texture to the garden and landscape. It achieves the best show of color and vigor in moist soils with partial sun, preferably in the morning. Japanese blood grass also makes a dramatic impact when used as a companion plant in container or patio displays.

WHEN TO PLANT

This plant is often propagated by tissue culture and later sold as a container plant. These specimens can be planted in spring or early summer.

WHERE TO PLANT

Use this exciting grass as a mass planting near borders or edges of water gardens. Combine it with bolder, broader-foliaged plants and even variegated or yellow-leafed shrubs or perennials. Probably the best show and display of color occur when plants are backlit with filtered morning sunlight. Japanese blood grass prefers afternoon or lightly dappled shade. Overall, the plant is fairly slow growing, depending on its soil type and moisture level. It prefers moist, humus-rich, organic soils, but it tolerates sandy loam soils. It accepts heavy clay sites as long as they drain well. Poor, unimpressive growth is assured in poorly drained soils or hot, dry areas.

HOW TO PLANT

Attend to potbound plants before placing them in the soil. Remove the very base of the winding roots, and sever the sides to allow for more horizontal growth and water penetration. Space the plants 10 to 12 in. apart for a quicker fill. Set the plants at the same depth that they were grown, and dig holes somewhat wider than the rootballs. Mulch them for weed control and moisture retention.

CARE AND MAINTENANCE

Japanese blood grass will go dormant in the winter. Each spring trim the old foliage back to the ground before any new, green growth emerges. Occasionally, the foliage will remain semievergreen throughout the winter under mild conditions. Supplemental feeding is generally not needed unless the soils are nonfertile from the start. Apply fertilizer when the growth begins to emerge and is 4 to 6 in. tall in the spring and again in midsummer. This plant has no serious pest problems. Drought conditions will stunt this plant and scorch the foliage quite readily; supplemental irrigation will be needed.

ADDITIONAL INFORMATION

Imperata originated in Japan and has been used quite extensively in the United States for some time. It is gaining in popularity as the perennial ornamental grass craze continues. Again, it makes a nice container companion plant, and the bright, colorful foliage can be cut and used as filler in cutflower arrangements. Occasionally, the plants will try to revert to a green color. Dig out any of these spots to keep the vibrant red and purple colors.

ADDITIONAL SPECIES, CULTIVARS, OR VARIETIES

The most widely sold cultivar is 'Red Baron', which has an even showier reddish foliage color. The color intensifies in the fall.

Did You Know?

Imperata cylindrica *is a green-leafed African native that is very aggressive in coastal areas and is listed as a noxious weed.*

249

Lily Turf

Liriope muscari

Other Names: Monkey Grass;
  Blue Lily Turf; Liriope
Height: 6 to 24 in.
Spread: 12 to 18 in.
Flowers: Purple or white
Bloom Period: Summer (warm season)
Zones: 6a, 6b, 7a, 7b

Color photograph on page 233.

Light Requirements:

Beneficial Characteristics:

Lily turf, more commonly called monkey grass, is probably the most well-known ornamental grass. The lush, thick foliage is heat and humidity tolerant, making it a perfect plant for Oklahoma landscapes. The plant foliage is the primary asset of lily turf and comes in a wide variety of colors from deep, dark green to various shades of yellow or silver variegation. Many selections can be evergreen, displaying the green foliage all winter. An added bonus in some selections is the emergence of the flower spikes in May or June. The predominantly lilac-colored blooms are quite showy and seem to be more prolific when grown in sun. Harder to find are the white-flowering selections. Both can produce small, dark-fruited berries late in the season. Lily turf is truly a dependable plant with a lot to offer any landscape.

WHEN TO PLANT

Liriope can be started in the landscape from container-grown or bare-root plants in the spring, summer, or early fall.

WHERE TO PLANT

The most popular use is as a mass planting for borders or fill. Its low-growing nature makes it compatible with sidewalk or edging locations. Liriope can divide landscape sections where low-growing, contrasting plants are needed. Of course, it is perfect as an upright textured ground cover. Liriope prefers moist, organic soils, but this tough grass will grow in almost any ordinary soil.

HOW TO PLANT

Pull apart potbound roots before planting. In some cases the very base of the roots will need to be cut or severed. Plant them in holes dug the same depth as the plant root system and somewhat wider. Space plants 8 to 15 in. apart, depending on the desired quickness of fill. Mulch them to minimize weed growth and retain soil moisture.

CARE AND MAINTENANCE

Even though lily turf is often evergreen, it frequently succumbs to winter burn of the foliage. Each spring before new growth emerges, shear damaged foliage to the ground. In larger beds it is a common practice to use a lawn mower as long as the plant crown is not scalped. Fertilize when the new growth begins to emerge. Water after fertilizing to prevent spotting of the foliage. Mealybugs and spider mites are occasional pests. Grasshoppers can become pests in more rural areas. Fungal leaf spots and crown rot can occur in wet, poorly drained sites. Plants respond better to supplemental irrigation in severe droughts, although they somewhat accept dry conditions.

ADDITIONAL INFORMATION

L. muscari is typically more clumping in nature with minimal spreading. *L. spicata*, on the other hand, is more spreading by underground rhizomes or stems and somewhat narrower foliage. *L. spicata* is commonly called creeping lily turf and is more conducive for spreading ground cover needs. It has flowers, but they are not nearly as showy as the ones in the *muscari* species. Either species can be readily divided or transplanted anytime throughout the growing season, although spring or autumn is preferable.

ADDITIONAL SPECIES, CULTIVARS, OR VARIETIES

L. muscari improved selections are predominantly purple or lilac in flowering and include such cultivars as 'Big Blue', 'Lilac Beauty', and 'Majestic'. 'Monroe White', 'Alba', and 'Traebert White' are white-flowering forms. If variegated foliage strikes your fancy, consider 'Variegata', 'Silvery Sunproof', 'Silvery Midget', 'John Burch', and 'Gold Banded'. Most variegated types do better with part or afternoon shade; 'Silvery Sunproof' is the exception. Giant liriope (*L. gigantea*) has large, thicker, upright leaves but is hardy only to the southeasternmost locales of the state. In addition to the generic green *spicata* species, there is 'Silver Dragon', a variegated spreading cultivar requiring partial shade.

 Did You Know?

Mondo grass, which is similar to liriope and is often confused with it, is in a completely different genus, Ophiopogan japonicus.

Maiden Grass

Miscanthus sinensis

Other Names: Maiden Hair Grass; Chinese
Grass; Eulalia; Japanese Silver Grass
Height: 3 to 7 ft.
Spread: 4 to 6 ft.
Flowers: Yellow, pink, or red
Bloom Period: Late summer, fall
(warm season)
Zones: 6a, 6b, 7a, 7b

Color photograph on page 233.

Light Requirements:

Beneficial Characteristics:

These robust clumping grasses with narrow, linear foliage and whimsical feathery plumes provide year-round excitement.The foliage emerges each spring, later sending up magical plumes. As the flowers are pollinated, the plumes mature into unique colors of caramel, copper, or golden yellow. The foliage holds up most of the winter, making for a lively presentation, especially when the winter winds bring the foliage to life.

WHEN TO PLANT

Plant containerized grasses like *Miscanthus* in the spring or early summer. Plant bare-root plantlets in late spring.

WHERE TO PLANT

Miscanthus cultivars make perfect singular specimen plants and do well in groups of three or more. I use them most as upright, bushy specimens near corners of structures where they soften harsh angles. Their winter display has a lot of eye appeal, but planting them in combination with evergreen plants makes for an even better combination display. Interplant the narrow-leafed, textured grasses as companions to broadleaf, coarse foliage plants. Some of the taller and wider selections work as hedges to block unsightly views— but only later in the season. The graceful plants may tone down perpendicular structures such as light poles, archways, and two-story homes. These grasses like moisture- retentive but well-drained soils. Fertile soils are more rewarding in vigorous growth; however, these elegant grasses tolerate most sites. They prefer full-sun locations.

HOW TO PLANT

Trim a potbound rootbal to better initiate horizontal root growth. Space plants 2 to 5 ft. apart, depending on the selection.

CARE AND MAINTENANCE

Cut dormant foliage off in early spring to at least 6 to 8 in. from the ground before green growth emerges. Fertilizer is optional, but the grassy plants respond to supplemental applications in late spring and early summer. In severe droughts the plants need supplemental irrigation to send up the beautiful flower plumes.

ADDITIONAL INFORMATION

Pests are generally of no concern; however, over the past few years one insect has surfaced, especially in the nursery trade. Miscanthus mealybug has become somewhat of a problem in production areas. The soft-bodied, fuzzy white critter attaches to stems and is often hidden and protected from insecticides. Home owners typically have nothing to worry about unless it is passed on at the point of purchase. Most *Miscanthus* will outgrow the pest with proper watering and fertilization. Then as the foliage becomes dormant in the winter, it can be removed and discarded.

ADDITIONAL SPECIES, CULTIVARS, OR VARIETIES

'Gracillimus' is one of the tallest, maturing around 8 ft. and blooming late in the season. 'Graziella' is very similar to 'Gracillimus' but not quite as tall and blooms earlier. 'Adagio', 'Dixieland', 'Nana', and 'Nippon' are the smallest *Miscanthus*, reaching only 3 to 4 ft. 'Bluetenwunder' ('Flower Wonder') has a blue tinge to the foliage, and 'Purpurascens' ('Autumn Red') is more reddish, especially in the fall. Variegation types include 'Strictus' (porcupine grass) with horizontal gold bars across the leaf blades. 'Zebrinus' also has bold, horizontal yellow stripes, but the foliage tends to arch more. 'Variegatus' has white-striped, arching leaves. 'Cabaret', 'Cosmopolitan', 'Silberfeder' ('Silver Feather'), 'Goldfeder' ('Gold Feather'), and 'Morning Light' are also variegated. Silver-gray selections include 'Rotsilber' ('Red Silver') and 'Sarabande'. An unusual one to include for the ornamental grass hobbyist is *M. floridulus (giganteus)* maturing to 10 ft.. The earliest blooming species is *M. transmorrisonensis*, sending up flower plumes in the middle of the summer.

Did You Know?

Miscanthus *flower plumes are great for fresh cut and dried flowers. Several species of birds enjoy the seeds during the winter as well.*

Mondo Grass

Ophiopogan japonicus

Other Name: Dwarf Lily Turf
Height: 6 to 12 in.
Spread: 4 to 18 in.
Flowers: Light blue
Bloom Period: Summer (warm season)
Zones: 6b, 7a, 7b

Color photograph on page 233.

Light Requirements:

Beneficial Characteristics:

Mondo grass is often confused with liriope, but mondo has narrower foliage and metallic-blue fruit, is not quite as cold hardy, and prefers shade. The narrower and somewhat shorter foliage exhibits an overall different texture and appearance. Mondo grass can also be evergreen in milder winters. Otherwise the foliage has a tendency to burn, especially on the tips of the leaves. Mondo grass establishes more slowly, but when it does, it will spread more like a ground cover, filling in and around shaded perennial and landscape shrub beds. I have even seen it grow into poorly established lawns in moist sites.

WHEN TO PLANT

Plant mondo grass in the spring or summer. Fall plantings are not recommended since there is generally not enough time for the plants to establish before winter sets in.

WHERE TO PLANT

Mondo grass is the ideal plant for edging sidewalks and borders. Because of its spreading nature, it can be ground cover in larger landscape situations where filler is needed. Sites with afternoon shade or dappled light are necessary in most of Oklahoma.

HOW TO PLANT

Attend to potbound plants before planting. Remove or loosen the winding roots for better horizontal establishment. Space plants 6 to 12 in. apart in fertile, moist soils. Plant them at the same depth that they were grown in their containers, but dig the holes somewhat wider than the rootballs. Mulch them with a light organic product, such as shredded leaves or fine pine bark, to keep weeds at bay until the plants are established. The underground stems emerge more readily in the lighter mulch.

CARE AND MAINTENANCE

If the foliage is burned from the winter, trim it close to the ground in early spring before new growth emerges. Side-dress the plants with a fertilizer in spring and again in early summer. Be careful not to burn the foliage. Reapply mulch as needed until the plants thickly fill the area. Watering during drought is essential. Flowers emerge in the middle of the summer and occasionally produce metallic-green berries. Trim the flower spikes and fruit if they are not desirable. In the first year of establishment, remove the flower spikes to permit more energy to reach the leafy green foliage.

ADDITIONAL INFORMATION

Pests are not always problems, but slugs, snails, and grasshoppers can occasionally chew the foliage. Spider mites may accompany the plants home from the point of sale. Leaf spots and crown rot occur in poorly drained soils and aerated sites.

ADDITIONAL SPECIES, CULTIVARS, OR VARIETIES

In addition to the upright green species there is a 'Variegatus' cultivar with white margins. 'Nana' is the dwarf selection, reaching only 2 to 3 in. It has a very manicured appearance and grows in flowing clumps as it spreads. A truly spectacular mondo grass is 'Black Mondo' (*O. planiscapus*) with deep-purple, almost black foliage. The very slow-growing species is available in several cultivars: 'Ebony Knight' ('Ebknizam'), 'Nigrescens', and 'Nigra'.

Did You Know?

All selections of mondo grass can be used as a filler and textured plant in patio container displays. Mondo is sometimes incorrectly referred to as monkey grass, which is actually Liriope muscari.

Plume Grass

Erianthus ravennae

Other Name: Ravenna Grass
Height: 8 to 12 ft.
Spread: 4 to 5 ft.
Flowers: Silver plume
Bloom Period: Late summer (warm
 season)
Zones: 6a, 6b, 7a, 7b

Color photograph on page 233.

Light Requirements:

Beneficial Characteristics:

Ravenna grass is another alternative to the coarse, overgrown appearance of pampas grass. Pampas grass has its place in wide, open spaces but rarely fits into most landscape situations. Ravenna, on the other hand, has the towering height without the coarseness, making it a perfect landscape ornamental grass. The typical growing habit of *Erianthus* is a clumping grass with long, straplike, greenish-gray foliage offset with a white stripe down the center of the leaf. The flower plumes emerge in late summer with silvery blooms changing to gray as they pollinate and mature. The flowers are characteristically silky in appearance with hairy pubescence predominant on the lower portion of the flower panicle. A mature clump of this stately grass can send up thirty or more flower plumes towering above the clumping foliage for a spectacular late-summer and fall display. Even more appealing is the added bonus of fall color from the foliage. In many years the massive foliage will turn an orangish color in October.

WHEN TO PLANT
Plant ravenna grass in spring or summer.

WHERE TO PLANT
The sheer magnitude of the plant dictates the need for plenty of space, usually at least 4 to 5 ft. square. It is often used as an accent plant, a specimen, or a screen. The linear effect of the foliage is perfect for softening harsh corners in blocky designs or structures. It prefers full-sun locations. Plume grass is truly an exception to the rule as far as typical soil type goes. Plant it in very fertile soil, and the foliage becomes excessive, sometimes falling over. It is more manageable in sites with poorer soils, but avoid poorly drained, heavy soils. Waterlogged sites usually mean certain doom for this rugged plant.

HOW TO PLANT

For a potbound plant, cut off the lower few inches of roots, and sever the sides of the rootball. Otherwise the container plant will take longer to establish and most likely will continue to be rootbound in its new home. In such cases thorough water penetration is almost impossible. Water the grass after planting and on a regular basis until it is established. Mulch it to keep weeds out and moisture in.

CARE AND MAINTENANCE

The dormant foliage should be cut back in early spring as soon as the new, green growth emerges. Ravenna's flower plumes are not as showy throughout the winter as, say, those of *Miscanthus*. It is often necessary to cut out the flower stalks in early winter before they fall over and mask the still attractive foliage. Fertilizer is usually not needed or the plant can become too overpowering. In such cases the foliage clump tends to open up and fall over. There are no serious pest problems.

ADDITIONAL INFORMATION

Ravenna grass occasionally needs to be divided, usually in the spring. The glistening silver plumes (occasionally with a hint of purple) arise above the foliage starting in August or early September, creating an awesome, towering effect. The flower spikes are good additions to fresh cut and dried arrangements. The fall foliage usually turns color, from orange to beige to purple.

ADDITIONAL SPECIES, CULTIVARS, OR VARIETIES

Ravenna grass is also sold as *Saccharum ravennae*. There are no reported improved cultivars at the time of this printing. There are other species of *Erianthus*, however. They include *E. contortus* (better known as bent-awn plume grass) and *E. strictus* (narrow plume grass).

Did You Know?

Ravenna grass is sometime called hardy pampas grass. The true pampas grass (Cortaderia selloana) *is drastically different in appearance and not as cold hardy.*

Reed Grass

Calamagrostis species

Other Names: Feather Reed Grass; Korean Feather Grass
Height: 4 to 6 ft.
Spread: 2 to 4 ft.
Flowers: Pinkish-green plumes
Bloom Period: Early summer (cool season)
Zones: 6a, 6b, 7a, 7b

Color photograph on page 233.

Light Requirements:

Beneficial Characteristics:

With the common name reed, one would think that this plant has a coarse, almost hollow stem. But feather reed grass is anything but hollow or coarse. The glitzy cool-season grass is one of the earliest to bloom, usually around May. The dull-green foliage is somewhat rough to the touch but formed in a tight clump. The foliage definitely takes a backseat to the elegant flower plumes. These flower spikes are some of the most erect of any ornamental grass. The sure upright nature of the inflorescence makes them an architectural dream. The 3- to 4-ft. spikes emerge green with a touch of red. As they mature, they take on a true golden-wheat intensity and last most of the summer. With the approach of fall, the plumes turn almost a light-straw color. Even though reed grass is considered a cool-season grass because of its early bloom, it will perform throughout the hottest days of the summer.

WHEN TO PLANT
Plant reed grass in spring, summer, or fall.

WHERE TO PLANT
Calamagrostis is considered a medium-growing ornamental grass. It can be used as a specimen or in clusters, especially on harsh corners or blocky designs. The upright, vertical form gives height to smaller structures, even though the plant remains around 6 ft. in height with its plumes. This ornamental grass can also be used as a hedge or background plant with proper spacing of 3 to 4 ft. apart. It prefers full-sun locations; however, it accepts some shade, no more than four or five hours. Reed grass does well in fertile or average soils. It tolerates dry or moist sites as long as the soils are not excessively waterlogged.

HOW TO PLANT
Attend to potbound plants before planting. Trim off the roots at the base, and sever them on the sides to allow for more horizontal growth. Mulch

plants for weed control and moisture retention of the soil. Water deeply after planting to encourage good root formation and on a regular basis until plants are well established.

CARE AND MAINTENANCE

Occasionally, this cool-season grass will overwinter as an evergreen in milder winters. The foliage can be damaged in extremely cold periods. Remove damaged or dormant foliage in very early spring. Do supplemental feedings in spring and again in early summer if needed. Reapply mulch as needed. Water plants during extremely dry periods, especially the first year of establishment. Pests are typically nondestructive. Rust diseases may occasionally affect stressed plants.

ADDITIONAL INFORMATION

Planting reed grass in too much shade can decrease flowering and cause the foliage to be more weeping and open. Rust is also more likely in heavily shaded locations. As with most ornamental grasses, the seed plumes make nice flower arrangements.

ADDITIONAL SPECIES, CULTIVARS, OR VARIETIES

'Stricta' and 'Karl Foerster' are the two predominant cultivars, both results of hybrid crosses. In many cases telling them apart is difficult. Supposedly, 'Karl Foerster' is slightly smaller and blooms a couple of weeks earlier than 'Stricta'. Another selection on the market, which is considered a warm-season grass, is *C. arundinacea* var. *brachytricha* with smoky-purple flowers appearing later in the summer and looking almost like bottle brushes. A common name for this somewhat broader species is giant foxtail grass. The foliage does not last as long in the winter as the aforementioned hybrid crosses. *C. aruninacea* var. *oredam* has long, thin leaves with white variegation. The flower plumes emerge a pinkish color that turns golden as the summer progresses.

 Did You Know?

Tony Avent of Plant Delights Nursery in North Carolina calls C. brachytricha *the achy breaky heart grass because of the way it is pronounced. It definitely will still your heart when it is planted, and it is more heat tolerant than the hybrid crosses.*

Sedge

Carex species

Other Names: Japanese Sedge; Leatherleaf Sedge; Black Sedge; Drooping Sedge
Height: 12 to 24 in.
Spread: 12 to 24 in.
Flowers: Tan to brown
Bloom Period: Spring (cool season)
Zones: 6a, 6b, 7a, 7b

Color photograph on page 233.

Light Requirements:
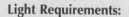

Sedges are the Rodney Dangerfield of ornamental grasses because they do not get any respect. This lack of interest is partly due to the sedge name, which often reminds gardeners of the so-called water grasses wreaking havoc in landscape beds and lawns. Although related to this weedy pest, the ornamental cascading versions are perfect for the woodland garden. Japanese sedge is one of the few grasses to actually thrive in shade. This bushy-tufted grass makes a nice border plant along shade-garden pathways. When the plants are massed, they offer texture and color. Most *Carex* species are semievergreen to evergreen with potentially attractive foliage year-round. Ornamental sedge is quite versatile and will tolerate moist sites near the edge of bog or water gardens. The early-spring flower spikes are not considered showy. *Carex* is definitely grown and known for its colorful and versatile foliage, which will enhance any landscape and garden.

WHEN TO PLANT
Plant *Carex* in spring, summer, or early fall.

WHERE TO PLANT
Use the small mounding plants along shaded garden paths or as a border with sidewalks. Mass plantings in groups of three or five to make eye-catching scenes. The grasslike texture blends with almost any plant. Sedges as a whole are used as shade rock garden plants or as cascading plants over walls. Some species are spreading in nature as a ground cover in moist sites but noninvasive. The plants like rich, humus soils typical of many woodland gardens or moisture-retentive, well-drained soils. If such planting sites are not available, prepare them well in advance of planting time. Be careful not to damage existing tree roots by tilling the soil. Add no more than 6 in. of organic material on top of the ground, without mixing it into the original soil.

How to Plant

Space the smaller clumping plants 15 to 18 in. apart. Plant them directly into the top few inches of soil, and mulch them. Water them after planting and on a regular basis.

Care and Maintenance

In mild winters the plants will eagerly remain green, providing winter interest. In harsh winters the foliage will occasionally burn and can be removed in early spring. Heat-damaged foliage can be cut back in the fall. Trim it close to the ground without damaging the plant crown. Do supplemental feedings as soon as new growth reaches 3 or 4 in. Water as soon as it is applied to wash off fertilizer trapped in or on the foliage. Reapply mulch as needed to keep the soil moist and weed free. Drought conditions will warrant supplemental irrigation. I lost many of my prized *Carex* plantings in the drought of 1998.

Additional Information

Other than an occasional leaf fungus or rust spot, pests are of no concern. In severe cases the foliage can be trimmed back and the new growth sprayed with a labeled foliar disease product.

Additional Species, Cultivars, or Varieties

There are numerous species and cultivars with just about any color foliage. 'Bowles Golden', 'Frosted Curls', and 'Aurea Variegata' are probably the most popular with appealing variegated foliage colors. More unusual colors and somewhat harder to find are 'Fox Red Curly' (reddish bronze), 'Hime Kansugi' (variegated white), 'Nigra' (black), 'Blue Gray', 'Orange Colored Sedge' (orangy bronze), and 'Evergold' (lemon yellow). If you are looking for more unusually shaped foliage, consider *C. muskingumensis* or *C. phyllocephala* (known as palm sedge grass), *C. buchananii* (leather leaf sedge), and *C. ornithodpoda* (bird's foot sedge). 'Wachtposten' is supposedly somewhat more tolerant of dry soils and is in the species *muckingumensis*.

 Did You Know?

Ground cover-spreading sedges are sold as C. speciosa *(mop head sedge),* C. pendula *(drooping sedge), and* C. plantaginea *(plantain-leafed sedge).*

Sweet Flag

Acorus gramineus

Other Names: Japanese Sweet Flag; Acorus; Grassy Sweet Flag
Height: 10 to 15 in.
Spread: 12 to 15 in.
Flowers: Green
Bloom Period: Fall (warm-season grass)
Zones: 6a, 6b, 7a, 7b

Color photograph on page 233.

Light Requirements:

If you have a waterlogged or a poorly drained site in the landscape, consider using sweet flag there. Sweet flag is best known as a water garden container plant but does well in the landscape, especially in moisture-retentive soils. It is cold hardy and can quickly fill such specific sites with colorful foliage. Sweet flag somewhat resembles *Carex* with colorful, variegated foliage. The biggest difference is the thick, clumping, upright growth of sweet flag; most *Carex* ornamental grasses have a tendency to weep or cascade.

WHEN TO PLANT
Plant sweet flag in the spring or summer.

WHERE TO PLANT
The primary environmental condition to provide is wet or moist soil. Sweet flag prefers afternoon shade but tolerates heavier, more dappled shade. Full-sun locations pose the risk of leaf scorching. Acorus is useful as a container-grown water garden plant, bog plant, or landscape plant in moist sites. I have seen it accept six hours of full sun in rich, constantly moist soils. It also works in smaller patio-pot water gardens. The unusual foliage is a contrasting texture plant suitable for windowboxes and patio containers with access to routine watering.

HOW TO PLANT
The plants are sometimes sold bare root when they are carried as water garden plants. They are commonly grown as container plants. Space plants on 15- to 24-in. centers. Set the plants at the same level that they were grown in their containers, in holes slightly wider than the rootballs. Mulch plants to retain soil moisture. Water them after planting and routinely if moist conditions are not prevalent.

CARE AND MAINTENANCE

Sweet flag is also a semievergreen plant under mild winter conditions. When the foliage is burned back during the dormant season, cut it to ground level in the spring before new growth emerges. The flowers have little appeal as part of the plant's decorative value. Many times selections seldom bloom. The plants grow quickly into multiclumped mounds resembling an iris but with finer foliage. They can be divided when needed in the spring. Some species, such as *A. calamus*, are more spreading with rhizomes and can be somewhat invasive, which is an acceptable characteristic in certain bog settings. Otherwise these species should be restricted to a container as a water garden plant. Fertilizing is seldom necessary in bog settings. If supplemental feedings are needed, apply them in the spring when the new growth is 4 to 6 in.

ADDITIONAL INFORMATION

Crushed acorus leaves and rhizomes have an almost cinnamon-like, spicy aroma. Some species of acorus are used medicinally.

ADDITIONAL SPECIES, CULTIVARS, OR VARIETIES

Japanese sweet flag (*A. gramineus*) cultivars include 'Pusillus', a smaller version of the standard green species; 'Masamune' with white-striped leaves; and 'Yodonoyuki' with green-and-light-green variegation. 'Ogon', 'Oborozuki', and 'Variegatus' have various degrees of golden-yellow variegation. 'Minimus Aureus' is a dwarf, variegated golden form. The common, more spreading sweet flag (*A. calamus*) also has a 'Variegata' cultivar with white-striped leaves forming a pale-pink blush in the spring. Both are cold hardy for the entire state.

 Did You Know?

Legend has it that the foliage of sweet flag was thrown on the floors of ancient castles and manor houses. Walking on the foliage and crushing it filled the homes with the spicy aroma.

Switch Grass

Panicum virgatum

Height: 4 to 8 ft. **Spread:** 2 to 4 ft. **Flowers:** Reddish purple to beige **Bloom Period:** Mid- to late summer (warm season) **Zones:** 6a, 6b, 7a, 7b *Color photograph on page 233.*	**Light Requirements:** **Beneficial Characteristics:**

Switch grass is a wonderfully wild-looking ornamental grass. This native prairie grass is found in tallgrass prairies or lowland plains. Switch grass is one of the earliest to bloom with reddish-purple airy flower plumes. The foliage grows in a clumping form with either blue or green foliage, occasionally with a tinge of red. As the plants mature, their landscape appeal improves into late summer with the upright flower plumes and later golden-yellow or bronzy, purplish-red fall color. Switch grass is probably the most drought-tolerant ornamental grass in use. It is a natural companion choice for wildflower or meadow gardens or as a specimen, screen, or backdrop plant in the perennial landscape.

WHEN TO PLANT

Plant switch grass from seed in the fall or early spring, preferably in a container. An even better and more consistent method is to set out pot-grown plants in late spring, summer, or early fall.

WHERE TO PLANT

Panicum is a deeply fibrous-rooted grass, perfect for erosion control in problematic sites. It accepts poor soils as long as they drain well. Richer, fertile soils generally produce a more vigorous plant, and full-sun locations are the most desirable. Use switch grass as a background plant in the perennial garden, cluster it in groups of three in the landscape, or plant it in double rows for a screen later in the summer. Color, height, and texture make switch grass selections an excellent choice for the landscape.

HOW TO PLANT

Trim the bottom of each potbound rootball, and sever the sides of the roots to open up the rootball before planting. Space plants 2 to 3 ft. apart. Place the plants at the same depth that they were grown in their containers, and dig the holes wider than the rootballs to allow for more horizontal root growth. Mulch the plants to minimize weed growth and retain moisture.

CARE AND MAINTENANCE

Remove the dormant foliage in early spring as the new growth emerges. Do supplemental feedings as the new growth reaches 10 to 12 in. and again in midsummer. The colorful and feathery display of seed plumes occurs in midsummer, around July or August, and persists into early winter. The seedheads are favorites of birds; they will eventually bend from the winter weather and can be removed back to the foliage. The foliage turns a beautiful fall color, however, and holds up well most of the winter until its removal in the spring. Pests are minimal. Once established, the plants are drought tolerant.

ADDITIONAL INFORMATION

Panicum species are good additions to fresh or dried arrangements. Switch grass is also considered a warm-season grass, which can be divided in the spring. Many of the improved selections do not come back "true" from seed; therefore, the clumps should be divided as a means of propagation. Switch grass can be planted in light shade with no more than four or five hours of shade. With too much shade the plants bloom more sporadically on less-than-appealing, open and falling foliage.

ADDITIONAL SPECIES, CULTIVARS, OR VARIETIES

'Rubrum' and 'Rehbraun' have more reddish colors on the foliage and flowers. 'Heavy Metal' has metallic-blue, upright foliage. 'Cloud Nine' and 'Prairie Sky' are predominantly blue-gray foliage beauties. 'Haense Herms', 'Warrior', and 'Rotstrahlbusch' are known for their eye-catching red autumn color. A selection with more pink in the inflorescence is 'Squaw'. 'Northwind' is the newest kid on the block, with very erect foliage, yellow flowers, and golden fall color. 'Strictum' is a more upright grower known for its cold hardiness. 'Trailblazer' is a more spreading, almost sod-forming selection, maturing to 4 to 5 ft.

 Did You Know?

Panicum clandestinum (*deer tongue grass*) *has more bamboolike foliage and prefers partial shade with moist soils.*

ORNAMENTAL GRASSES

Tufted Hair Grass

Deschampsia caespitosa

Height: 1 to 3 ft.
Spread: 2 to 4 ft.
Flowers: Loose flower plumes; silvery,
  green, or purple
Bloom Period: Spring (cool-season grass)
Zones: 6a, 6b, 7a, 7b

Color photograph on page 233.

Light Requirements:

Beneficial Characteristics:

Tufted hair grass is often promoted as a tough grass, thriving in Zones 4 to 8 and preferring full sun. That is not necessarily the case in Oklahoma. This unusual clumping grass is more suited to the northwestern locations of the state. It must be grown in shade (preferably afternoon shade) and moist, loamy soils. In other words, it will not perform acceptably in dry, hot, and humid sites like many of the other ornamental grasses. This popular northern grass typically has rich green foliage, sending up profuse, delicate-looking, almost airy flower inflorescences. Tufted hair grass is also considered a cool-season grass, remaining evergreen or semievergreen throughout the winter. As a result it sends up its bloom spikes in early spring or summer. The foliage will remain showy throughout the summer if it is protected from sun and heat. The most attractive *Deschampsias* are the ones with variegated foliage, which offer an added brightness to the shade garden.

WHEN TO PLANT

Occasionally, cultivars are available as seed, which can be planted in a container in early spring. Bare-root plants can be set out in the spring. Container-grown plants are probably the best investment and can be planted in the fall or early spring.

WHERE TO PLANT

Afternoon shade or dappled shade is a must, especially in southern and eastern parts of the state. It prefers moist, loamy soil. Use the clumping grass as a border plant or with darker evergreen background plants. The best use of *Deschampsia* I have seen was as a cluster planting near a water garden where it received early-afternoon shade.

HOW TO PLANT

Tufted hair grass will most likely be rootbound. Cut off the very base of the winding roots, and sever the sides where the rootballs can be opened up to allow for new horizontal growth. Set them out in well-prepared soils at the same depth that they were previously grown. Plant spacing should be 2 to 2½ ft. from the center of one plant to the center of the next, preferably in a diagonal pattern. Mulch the plants to retain soil moisture. Water them after planting and on a regular basis.

CARE AND MAINTENANCE

Since tufted hair grass is a cool-season grass, it makes its best show in the fall and spring. The flower spikes emerge in late spring or early summer, depending on the cultivar and the severity of the winter. As the seed stalks decline, they can be cut back near the foliage. Generally, the summer-tattered plants can be pruned or sheared to the ground when hot temperatures start to break and soaking rains begin in the fall. Doing this will force new growth for the cool winter months. In some years when winter conditions are severe, the plant foliage may succumb to cold damage and can also be trimmed in February to initiate new growth for the season. Moisture is critical, especially during drought conditions. Reapply mulch as necessary. Pests are of no concern. Feed plants in early spring.

ADDITIONAL INFORMATION

Deschampsia is native to more northern climates and is extremely cold hardy. Some selections of tufted hair grass will reseed in the garden and are easy to move each spring. I have had success with some cultivars of *Deschampsia* as a container or patio plant placed next to the east side of a home or on porches.

ADDITIONAL SPECIES, CULTIVARS, OR VARIETIES

'Northern Lights' is without a doubt my favorite selection. It is highly variegated with pinkish-blue undertones. 'Bronze Veil', 'Gold Pendant', 'Golden Veil', and 'Gold Dust' are alternative cultivar designations of German named selections with various shades of green or bronze foliage and golden flower spikes. 'Tardiflora' is later blooming in early summer and somewhat more heat tolerant although still requiring afternoon shade in Oklahoma. *D. flexuosa*, or hair grass, is lower growing and more spreading, and it will grow in denser shade.

 Did You Know?

The inflorescence is also valuable as a cut or dried flower.

Annuals

WARM-SEASON ANNUALS are not cold hardy or tolerant of freezing temperatures. Gardeners plant them every year after the last frost in the spring or early summer. The first frost or freeze in the fall then puts an end to their temporary but rewarding growing season. Some tender perennials, such as lantana and Mexican bush sage, that are not always cold hardy in our state are often grown as annuals. The annuals highlighted in this chapter provide impressive color throughout the growing season, tolerating the summer heat and requiring minimal care. Gardeners can choose from a wide variety of annuals to suit their individual tastes and draw attention to their landscape beds and containers.

Annuals perform best in fertile, moist, but well-drained soils. Mulch is vital to retain soil moisture and reduce the number of weeds. Most of the annuals featured in this chapter actually thrive in our hot, humid Oklahoma summers. Many of them prefer being planted in May, when the temperatures are warmer, instead of in April. The timing works well for gardeners who like to plant cool-season annuals such as pansies, which grow in the fall, winter, and early spring. Pansies will often be at their peak in March, April, and sometimes early May. After the cool-season annuals decline from the heat, summer-loving annuals can be planted in their places.

Spacing plants is a little tricky to get the best coverage for your investment. Many of the larger plants, such as sun coleus, lantana, and esperanza, need to be spaced about 2 to 3 ft. apart. With this spacing, not many plants will be required to fill a landscape bed. You can use the "Calculating Plant Quantities" guide in the introduction for ground covers (see chapter 3) to figure out the number of annual bedding plants needed for a particular area.

Once the annuals are planted and mulched, they respond favorably to a transplant starter solution of liquid or water-soluble fertilizer. To ensure consistent growth and flowering, you can routinely use water-soluble fertilizer applied during watering throughout the growing season. Most of the annuals discussed here are fairly drought tolerant; however, there can be a lull in the flower production if the plants become too drought stressed. The annuals, especially if they are actively and healthily growing, are somewhat resistant to pests. Yet you should always keep an eye out for aphids and spider mites.

Rotating annual flower plantings every couple of years is a good idea. Periwinkles, for example, are known to get a soil root-rot disease when they are planted too early under cool, moist conditions. The pathogen will build up its population when the host is planted in the same site year after year.

Some annuals require deadheading, pinching, or shearing throughout the season after bloom periods to initiate more blooms. Others are self-cleaning, needing no extra work. Some need to be pruned to keep them within their allotted space. After pruning is a good time for a side-dressing fertilizer application. Follow proper spacing recommendations to keep plants from becoming too overcrowded. I know that the newly placed transplants look lonesome with all the space between them, but in no time they will fill in the extra room. Allow for that growth, and you will not have to buy as many plants.

Annuals are perfect for island beds, display beds, mailbox planters, windowboxes, and containers of any shape and size. You will not find any traditional marigolds and geraniums in this chapter. There are far too many other excellent and underused choices for our crispy Oklahoma summers. All of the entries are warm season except for Swiss chard.

Begonia

Begonia semperflorens-cultorum

Other Names: Wax Begonia;
  Fibrous-Rooted Begonia
Height: 8 to 15 in.
Spread: 6 to 12 in.
Flowers: Red, pink, or white
Bloom Period: Summer

Color photograph on page 234.

Light Requirements:

Beneficial Characteristics:

Begonias are popular summer bedding plants, but most gardeners are still afraid to try them in hot, full sun. These succulent-type plants are truly tough annuals. The plants are known for their bronze, green, or variegated stems and foliage. The flowers are traditionally pink, red, or white in either single or double blooms. Most of the bronze foliage selections seem to do the best in full sun. I have also had success with the green-leaf types in full sun. Most of these plants are started by seed at nurseries and are available as container plants for retail sale. The glossy foliage and steadfast blooms on mounding compact plants make for a versatile bedding plant throughout the summer.

WHEN TO PLANT
Plant transplants in April or May for the best summer display.

WHERE TO PLANT
These compact plants are perfect as potted plants for colorful bowls, containers, or windowboxes. They also make perfect border plants near sidewalks or in front of landscape beds. Plant them in clusters for a more impressive display. Begonias like fertile, moist, sandy loam soils with good drainage, and they prefer full sun or afternoon shade. The plants will thrive in heavier shade but not full shade. They need at least two hours of sun. With too much shade, the plants become leggy. The bronze foliage types will be paler in color when they are grown in heavy shade.

HOW TO PLANT
Plant begonias at the same depth that they were in grown in their containers, but dig the holes wider than the rootballs. Mulch them, and keep them watered but not soggy.

CARE AND MAINTENANCE
Begonias seldom need pruning. The plants will fill in nicely with supplemental feedings. Dry, hard soil can cause varied growth among plants.

Mulch retains soil moisture, which is needed especially later in the season, even though the plants are considered somewhat drought tolerant. Irrigation may be needed in severe drought conditions; otherwise plants fail to bloom consistently. Too much water and cooler soil temperatures early in the spring can cause the plants to rot. Botrytis blight, leaf spots, stem rot, and powdery mildew are potential disease problems in wet sites with too much shade or when begonias are planted too early. Mealybugs and thrips are possible insect threats.

ADDITIONAL INFORMATION

A perennial hardy begonia, *Begonia grandis*, will overwinter in Oklahoma, especially in the southeastern parts of the state. Hardy begonias must have partial or afternoon shade. Tuberous begonias (*B.* × *tuberhybrida*) are not cold hardy in Oklahoma, and they prefer partial shade.

ADDITIONAL SPECIES, CULTIVARS, OR VARIETIES

Annual or bedding plant types are typically F1 hybrids grown from seed. (F1 hybrids are the first-generation results of a hybrid cross.) The selections are numerous. Vodka, Cocktail, Wings, Pizzazz, and Excel are popular series of this annual. The Lotto Series is known for larger flowers on compact plants. 'Frilly Dilly' has more wavy leaf petals. 'Pink Charm', 'Red Charm', and 'Lois Burke' are variegated foliage selections. 'Cherry Blossom', 'Sunbrite Red', 'Lady Frances', 'Lady Carol', and 'Lady Snow' are double-flowering types. The cultivar names can change from year to year, depending on breeding programs. 'Pin-Up Flame' is an award-winning, yellow-and-red-bicolored, tuberous begonia suitable for a bedding plant in afternoon sun or partial shade. Another unusual begonia that is neither a fibrous- nor a tuberous-rooted type is 'Dragon Wing'. This hybrid is the first heat-tolerant angel-wing type to perform as a bedding plant or in hanging baskets.

 Did You Know?

Tuberous begonias have beautiful flowers that are also edible. Use them as a garnish or mixed in fruit salad, yogurt, or sorbet.

Bidens

Bidens ferulifolia

Other Name: Yellow Bidens
Height: 10 to 24 in.
Spread: 12 to 24 in.
Flowers: Yellow
Bloom Period: Throughout the season

Color photograph on page 234.

Light Requirements:

Beneficial Characteristics:

B idens may not be a very exciting common name, but the plant is anything but boring! There is something about a yellow daisylike flower for cheering up a garden and the gardener. Bidens easily brightens up any garden spot for the entire growing season, and it has a mild, sweet fragrance. The golden-yellow flowers float atop almost feathery vigorous foliage in masses from planting time until frost kills them. The plants grow upright to the point that they eventually fall over, giving a cascading effect to the garden. The plants thrive in our hot Oklahoma conditions and are fairly drought tolerant. Use them for bedding, container, or hanging basket plants.

WHEN TO PLANT

Place container-grown plants outside after the danger of frost has passed in the spring. Occasionally, seed is available for direct planting in well-prepared beds or in containers.

WHERE TO PLANT

Full-sun locations are best; however, the plants will tolerate a half day of shade. Some cultivars are more prostrate in growth while others can reach a couple of feet in height. Use bidens in annual beds by themselves or in combination with other annuals. Plant them intermittently among shrub and perennial beds. Allow some selections to cascade over walls or windowboxes or from hanging baskets. Add them to container displays as companion plants. They like garden-rich soil but accept poor soil as long as it is not waterlogged.

HOW TO PLANT

With container-grown plants from the garden center, you can get instant and nonstop color. Space the plants 18 to 24 in. apart. Mulch them to minimize weed growth and to hold in soil moisture for the summer. Water them after planting and on a regular basis for the first three to four weeks. Seeds can be planted directly into the landscape bed in mid- to late April when soil temperatures begin to warm. The biggest risk of seed planting is competition from weeds. You can plant the seeds in containers indoors in bright light starting in late February, but buying container-grown plants may be a better choice.

CARE AND MAINTENANCE

This lovely blooming plant is self-cleaning and requires no dead-heading of spent blooms. Occasionally, gardeners choose to trim overgrown, leggy plants back in mid- to late season, but it is not necessary to maintain flowering. Fertilize a couple of times throughout the growing season and especially after shearing the plants. Once the plants are established, they are somewhat toler-ant of dry soils; however, a severe drought like the one in 1998 will shut down the plants completely. Consistent watering with good drainage usually means more prolonged flowering. Pests are of minimal concern, but you should always be on the lookout for spider mites.

ADDITIONAL INFORMATION

Bidens is fairly new to the bedding plant scene and has not really taken on a popular common name, which is just as well since it resembles many other composite-type flowers. Asking for any plant by the genus species name ensures that you get the appro-priate plant. Keep in mind that more compact-growing plants have a tendency to look leggy and elongated in nursery contain-ers. Once they are placed in the ground, they will become more compact in growth. Bidens comes in different cultivars with vari-ous heights; some are solid yellow, and others have a darker center, or eye.

ADDITIONAL SPECIES, CULTIVARS, OR VARIETIES

'Golden Eye' has a darker greenish-brown center but more pros-trate growth. 'Golden Goddess' is more upright and airy with solid-yellow flowers. 'Golden Falls'™ has almost cosmoslike flowers on taller foliage. 'Goldmarie'™ has smaller flowers on cascading foliage. 'Goldie PPAF' is a Proven Winners selection with tiny, bright-yellow flowers on probably the most compact plant to date. 'Snow Falls'™ is a white selection.

 Did You Know?

Bidens makes an excellent companion plant with the even lower-growing purple or pink verbena.

Copper Plant

Acalypha wilkesiana

Other Name: Acalypha
Height: 24 to 36 in.
Spread: 24 to 36 in.
Flowers: Nonshowy; grown for foliage
Bloom Period: Summer

Color photograph on page 234.

Light Requirements:

Beneficial Characteristics:

Color does not always have to come from a flower. Copper plant is a prime example of a plant that can offer knock-your-socks-off color with its foliage. Just as the name implies, the big, bold leaves are brightly colored with various hues of green, red, and copper. It is truly a tropical plant and loves the hot, humid Oklahoma summers. The majestic plant takes up quite a bit of space as the season progresses, which means you do not need many to fill an area. I have seen it growing in Australia as a perennial shrub almost 8 ft. high. But in Oklahoma it is used as a background bedding plant, maturing to 2 to 3 ft. before the fall frost puts an end to its growth. This carefree charmer offers landscape color without a showy flower from spring until frost.

WHEN TO PLANT

Plant it anytime after the last frost from mid-April through May. It is usually available as a container-grown plant.

WHERE TO PLANT

The height and boldness of the copper plant are used to good advantage as background for other annuals in beds. It also makes an attractive display all by itself in a group or alone. Even beds with assorted combinations of copper plants are appealing. I have used copper plants in containers by themselves or with other plants. As companions, plants with yellow, pink, or red flowers complement the colors of copper plant foliage. Planting copper plants in full sun produces magnificent foliage colors. They prefer well-prepared, rich garden soils. The plants will grow in poorer soils but typically will not be majestic.

HOW TO PLANT

Container-grown, vegetatively propagated plants are sold in assorted sizes up to 1-gal. specimens. Watch for potbound roots, and separate them as needed before planting. Set the plants at the same depth that they were grown in their containers, but dig the holes slightly wider than the rootballs. Mulch after planting.

CARE AND MAINTENANCE

Water copper plants on a regular basis, but avoid waterlogged, heavy soils. Pruning is rarely needed. Pinch the plants shortly after planting to encourage more branching and bushy growth. The flowers are produced as discreet cascading plumes among the foliage. Most of the time they are a dull red, taking second stage to the showy foliage. Copper plants respond well to supplemental feedings throughout the season. Other than an occasional mealybug, pests are rare.

ADDITIONAL INFORMATION

Use copper plants in combination with other foliage color plants such as coleus, dwarf purple fountain grass, and Joseph's coat. Arrange the plants in relation to their height so that one does not hide the other. Many acalyphas are known for their unusual-shaped foliage in addition to the colorfully bright colors. Once you use this plant in the landscape, it will easily become a yearly favorite.

ADDITIONAL SPECIES, CULTIVARS, OR VARIETIES

'Macafeana' is a common selection with creamy, copper-variegated foliage. 'Louisiana Red' is a selection with more glossy foliage and red undertones in its variegation. 'Mardis Gras' is absolutely one of my favorites, maturing around 2 ft. with narrow, straplike leaves resembling confetti. 'Kilauea' also has narrower foliage. 'Haleakala' and 'Marginata' have uniquely curled foliage with finely cut margins. 'Macrophylla' has more heart-shaped leaves. 'Chocolate Thunder' offers more earth-tone colors. 'Java White' is variegated with more green and yellowish-white shades, and it prefers afternoon shade. Unfortunately, many of the cultivar names are used interchangeably, making it difficult to correctly identify certain selections. Do not let that stop you from making them a vital part of a summer annual planting.

 Did You Know?

Acalypha pendula (hispida) *is a cousin known for showier flower plumes, occasionally referred to as "catkins." This species is also commonly called chenille, firetail, or red-hot cattail plant. It is primarily grown from seed as an annual bedding plant, which prefers afternoon or filtered shade.*

Esperanza

Tecoma species

Other Names: Yellow Bells;
  Yellow Trumpet Flower or Bush
Height: 2 to 4 ft.
Spread: 2 to 4 ft.
Flowers: Yellow or orange
Bloom Period: Summer

Color photograph on page 234.

Light Requirements:

Beneficial Characteristics:

Tropical plants such as mandevilla and hibiscus are very popular as container or patio plants. Another plant quickly working its way into the tropical container scene is esperanza. I have grown this trumpet-shaped flowering beauty for years as a patio plant and as an annual landscape bedding plant. I am amazed at its fortitude. It keeps getting bigger and better as the season progresses. Esperanza literally blooms the entire season as long as supplemental moisture is provided. The fragrant, large (2-by-2 1/2-in.), showy flowers are tubular shaped and are formed in large clusters on the ends of glossy green foliage. Esperanza can grow into a tree in the tropics, but for Oklahomans it is a perfect choice for a seasonal container or herbaceous bedding plant. Its lush bushy appearance adds to any container display by itself or in combination with other plants. The tall growth with sunny, bright flowers also makes a perfect background bedding plant.

WHEN TO PLANT
Plant this tender herbaceous annual after the last chance of frost, from April through June.

WHERE TO PLANT
The height dictates using this tropical beauty as a background bedding plant in combination with other bedding plants such as low-spreading lantana, periwinkle, Joseph's coat, and summer snapdragon. In a smaller container it can be a single plant. In a larger container it can be a center or background plant with duckfoot coleus, verbena, and Mexican heather, to name a few possibilities. Esperanza likes full-sun locations, but it accepts a half day of shade. Always match companion plant site preferences with those of esperanza. In other words, do not mix shade-loving plants with sun-loving ones, especially in containers. Soil preferences are fertile, organic sites, but the plants tolerate sandy and limestone conditions.

How to Plant

Most garden centers offer esperanza in 1-gal. containers. Loosen the roots of any potbound plants before planting. Set the plants at the same depth that they were grown in their containers, but dig the holes slightly wider than the rootballs. Mulch esperanza in landscape beds and containers. The mulch is decorative and beneficial in both cases.

Care and Maintenance

Esperanza responds to supplemental feedings throughout the growing season. Pruning will not be needed unless you want to control plant height or direct its growth. Potential pests include mealybugs, spider mites, and aphids. The flowers are produced in clusters that open a few at a time on new growth. Old flowers can be trimmed off or left alone in which case they often produce dangling, legumelike seedpods.

Additional Information

Most named esperanza cultivars are hybrid crosses and propagated by vegetative cuttings. The seeds can be kept from the pods and planted, but there can be variation among the seedlings from the parent plant. The seeds should be planted in sandy, well-drained media about 1/2 in. deep. The tropical plant seedlings need protection during the winter in the form of a greenhouse or bright sunroom.

Additional Species, Cultivars, or Varieties

Tecoma stans var. *stans*, *T. stans* var. *angustata*, and *Tecoma alata* are the three primary species used for breeding these delightful plant introductions. Named cultivars to date include 'Lonesp' (yellow), 'Orange Jubilee' (orange), and 'Burnt Out' (burnt-orange flowers).

 Did You Know?

Esperanza *is a Spanish term for "hope." My hope is that you will include this breathtaking plant in your landscape display for all to enjoy.*

Firebush

Hamelia patens

Other Names: Mexican Firebush; Scarlet Bush
Height: 2 to 3 ft.
Spread: 1 to 2 ft.
Flowers: Scarlet or yellow-orange
Bloom Period: All summer

Color photograph on page 234.

Light Requirements:

Beneficial Characteristics:

This plant is so rugged that I sometimes think it could grow in concrete. Firebush is native to Mexico and grows as an evergreen large shrub or small tree in milder zones. In Oklahoma it is grown as a tender perennial or basically as an annual. It blooms nonstop from May until November in hot, full sun and in dry conditions. The attractive elongated, tubular flowers are favorites for hummingbirds. Even showier is the green foliage offering distinctive hues of red, often demanding a second look. Firebush also works well as a warm-season bedding or container plant. The most frustrating part of promoting this plant is its appearance early in the spring at the nursery or greenhouse. It is without a doubt one of the most uninteresting plants for sale. There is seldom any bloom, and because of the cooler conditions, the foliage is not showy. Give it a chance, plant it when the temperatures begin to warm, and firebush will get better and better as the summer heat progresses when most plants look frazzled. It ranked several years as one of the top three plants by visitors to the *Oklahoma Gardening* studio display gardens.

WHEN TO PLANT

Plant firebush as soil and air temperatures warm up. Use it as a warm-season annual to follow cool-season pansy removal in May or early June. It prefers being planted later in the season—in late April, May, or June.

WHERE TO PLANT

Full-sun locations are the most desirable. It accepts a half day of shade, but with more than four hours of shade the plant foliage loses its red color and the blooms are more sporadic. Even though firebush will tolerate poor soils, it grows more quickly and bigger in organic amended beds. It tolerates alkaline and clay soils as long as they drain well. Plant it as a bedding plant in mass or in combination with other annuals. The manageable growth makes it a good choice for container or patio displays.

How to Plant

You are likely to find this plant sold in 4-in., 6-in., or 1-gal. containers. Dig a planting hole that is wider than the rootball and as deep as the plant was grown in the container. Space plants 12 to 24 in. apart; the bigger the plants, the farther apart they should be planted. Mulch to retain moisture and minimize weed growth. Firebush is fairly slow growing. Verbena, petunia, and *Calibrachoa* are great companion plants, especially in white or pink.

Care and Maintenance

Firebush needs no pruning or deadheading. It responds to supplemental feedings throughout the growing season. Potential pests include spider mites and occasional leaf spots. They are likely to be brought home from the point of purchase, or they may occur when firebush is grown in humid, shady locations. Although the plant is drought tolerant, it offers a better display and show if it receives supplemental irrigation.

Additional Information

Firebush will occasionally overwinter in the southern parts of the state with heavy mulch. *H. patens* is such a tough plant that it is worth buying each year even as an annual bedding plant. Firebush has received little interest in the nursery trade because of its early-season lack of appeal to customers. Nurseries will never begin to carry it unless people start asking for the plant by name, including the botanical name.

Additional Species, Cultivars, or Varieties

The most common plant sold is *Hamelia patens* firebush with no named cultivars to date. This species native to Texas and Mexico has smooth foliage with sterile scarlet flowers producing no fruit or seed. Another subspecies or possible natural selection rarely found in the trade is a wild native from Central America and Mexico with fuzzy leaves and scarlet flowers; it produces black fruit. Available in the nursery trade but hard to find is a yellow-orange flowering, primarily sterile selection known as African firebush, also with glossy foliage.

 Did You Know?

Firebush has been recognized by the nursery industry in Texas and Florida as a tough, outstanding plant to include in the landscape.

Globe Amaranth

Gomphrena globosa

Other Names: Gomphrena;
Clover Amaranth
Height: 6 to 36 in.
Spread: 10 to 24 in.
Flowers: Assorted colors with a
cloverlike shape
Bloom Period: Summer

Color photograph on page 234.

Light Requirements:

Beneficial Characteristics:

Gomphrena is an annual that even the non-green-thumb gardener can successfully grow. This old-fashioned flower is tolerant of hot weather, loaded with color, and virtually pest free. It is a shame that it is not used more in the landscape and garden, especially when we consider its broad range of qualifications. The cloverlike flowers available in colors of white, red, purple, rose, and pink are truly stunning in numbers and appearance. The flowers are produced throughout the summer and make great fresh cut and dried arrangements. The biggest selling point is their ability to hold their color after they are dried; these unique annuals are often referred to as everlasting. The flower heads hold up through heat, wind, and rain and require practically no care through the growing season. If you want a truly low-maintenance plant, gomphrena is the one.

WHEN TO PLANT
The plants can be started indoors from seed six to eight weeks before transplanting outside. Container-grown plants can successfully be planted outdoors after the last chance of frost is past.

WHERE TO PLANT
There is quite a bit of variation in size. Taller plants make better background plants, and shorter ones are suitable for front borders. The plants complement other annuals or do well in complete beds by themselves. They are also frequently found near fencerows, in the vegetable garden, or in containers. Mass plantings make the best display. The plants prefer rich, well-drained garden soil, but tolerate poorer sites.

HOW TO PLANT
The seed should be soaked in water a couple of days prior to planting in a container and at least six weeks before planting outside. Any transplants should be hardened off before their journey to the garden. The seed can be

directly sown in the planting site after frost, but the colorful display will be delayed for more than a month. Seed germination takes anywhere from fourteen to twenty-one days at temperatures around 70 degrees Fahrenheit. Buying transplants is easy and fairly inexpensive. Check the plants for potbound roots, and loosen the roots if necessary. Plant them at the same depth that they were grown in their containers. Space plants 12 to 24 in. apart, with more compact plants spaced on 12-in. centers.

CARE AND MAINTENANCE

Gomphrena seldom needs pruning or deadheading. Once established the plants are fairly drought tolerant. Mulch them to minimize weed growth and retain moisture. Pest outbreaks are rare.

ADDITIONAL INFORMATION

The uniquely shaped flowers are a nice change in texture for the annual garden. Cut the flowers early in the morning for fresh cutflower arrangements. If they are to be dried, pick them in the heat of the day, and select fully opened flowers. Cluster them in a bunch, and hang them upside down to further dry in an area with low humidity. Expect a few seeds to drop as they dry. In a couple of weeks the plants are ready to use in dried arrangements. Gomphrena is one of the best dried flowers to retain its color for months at a time.

ADDITIONAL SPECIES, CULTIVARS, OR VARIETIES

Several species of gomphrena make up the annual bedding plant releases. The Buddy and Gnome Series with assorted colors are the most compact, maturing at 6 to 8 in. Taller series releases include Woodcreek, QIS, and assorted mixes. Specific cultivars include 'Strawberry Fields', 'Bicolor Rose', 'Lavender Lady', and 'Aurea' (orange).

Did You Know?

The flowers of gomphrena have a papery sound when rubbed, making them perfect for drying. Other great drying flowers include paper daisy (Helipterum [Acroclinium] roseum) and strawflower (Helichrysum bracteatum).

Impatiens

Impatiens walleriana

Other Name: Busy Lizzie
Height: 6 to 18 in.
Spread: 8 to 15 in.
Flowers: Assorted colors
Bloom Period: Summer

Color photograph on page 234.

Light Requirements:

Beneficial Characteristics:

Impatiens is a well-known, dependable, shade-tolerant plant. Mounding plants provide massive color throughout the summer if they do not get too much sun or become too dry. These glowing annuals are available in numerous solid, blushed, or swirled colors. In addition to the numerous choices of colors there are many variations among size as well as double- or dwarf-flowering forms.

WHEN TO PLANT

Plant impatiens after the last chance of frost is past until early June.

WHERE TO PLANT

Impatiens are favorites around trees; in planters, hanging baskets, and windowboxes; and as bedding plants in shaded sites. One of the most unique displays of impatiens I have ever seen was in a planter made of a strong burlap-type material sewn together in the shape of a peanut and filled with loose potting soil. The transplants were placed in small precut holes and allowed to grow for a couple of weeks flat on the ground before the "potting bag" was draped over the lower branch crotch angles of a maple tree. As the impatiens filled in the area, they looked as if they were growing out of the tree. The unusual container designed by Mrs. Susan Cox of Stillwater was truly a traffic stopper. Impatiens prefer moisture-retentive, well-drained, humus-rich soils.

HOW TO PLANT

Mulch is essential to keep these beauties from wilting frequently in the hot summer weather. Cottonseed hulls do well as a mulch for impatiens. Do not allow the mulch to be too thick on the plant stems; angle it down toward the base of the stem, but keep it about 2 to 4 in. thick between plants. Space plants 15 to 18 in. apart. Water them after planting and on a regularly scheduled basis.

ANNUALS

CARE AND MAINTENANCE

Although impatiens prefer moist soils, they will quickly die in heavy, waterlogged sites or when they are overwatered. The soft, succulent stems can easily rot in such sites, especially early in the season when they are planted in cool, damp soils. Impatiens are notorious for wilting in the heat of a summer day. Wilting is not always caused by lack of water. Instead it may be caused by scorching air or soil temperatures. At the end of the day when the temperatures begin to break, the plants perk up. Impatiens respond nicely to supplemental feedings with a water-soluble fertilizer applied during watering.

ADDITIONAL INFORMATION

Other than an infrequent aphid, thrip, or whitefly, pests are usually of no concern. In cases where high populations are found, control may be needed. Occasionally, impatiens reseed themselves from year to year.

ADDITIONAL SPECIES, CULTIVARS, OR VARIETIES

Impatiens are usually sold as hybrid series with assorted colors. Dazzler, Accent, Mini, Elfin, Tempo, Mosaic, and Splash are a few popular examples. For a dwarf flower on a somewhat compact plant, consider the tiny, vivid flowers of the Firefly Mini Impatiens Series. African impatiens (*I. oncidioides* hybrids) with the added color choice of yellow are more exotic and definitely require more shade. Also exotic are the Indian impatiens 'Blue Angel' with an appearance somewhere between the traditional impatiens and a New Guinea. Double impatiens do not have the bloom coverage of singles, yet their roselike or camellialike flowers are absolutely beautiful. Of course, New Guinea impatiens (*I. hawkeri*) are somewhat more tolerant of sun, although hot, scorching, full sun is not suggested unless moist and wind-protected sites can be provided.

 Did You Know?

The "old-time" impatiens species are fun plants to grow, especially for a kid's garden, even though the flowers are not produced in mass like the improved hybrids. This cottage-garden plant produces seedpods that pop open when touched. Another species of I. balsamina *commonly called touch-me-not, lady slippers, or garden rose balsam also has bursting seedpods.*

Joseph's Coat

Alternanthera species

Other Names: Garden Alternanthera;
  Calico Plant; Parrot Leaf
Height: 6 to 15 in.
Spread: 8 to 24 in.
Flowers: Nonshowy; grown for foliage
Bloom Period: Summer

Color photograph on page 234.

Light Requirements:

Beneficial Characteristic:

Joseph's coat is often overlooked as a bedding plant. The inconspicuous flowers are formed along the stems and hidden by the lush foliage. Instead this annual is known for its dependable glistening, colorful foliage. The variegated foliage—available in various shades of green, copper, yellow, pink, rose, white, and gray—makes Joseph's coat a wonderful companion plant, especially in combination with other flowering annuals. This plant is truly tough, growing in full sun and fairly tolerant of dry soils. One of its best features is its resilience after shearing. Joseph's coat is often used as a miniature hedge plant or as a massive feature plant for spelling out words or designing emblems in the landscape.

WHEN TO PLANT
This tender annual must be planted in the spring after the last chance of frost is past.

WHERE TO PLANT
Plant Joseph's coat in mass by itself or in combination with other annual flowers in a ground landscape bed. The best bet when trying combination plantings is choosing flower colors that match various shades of the Joseph's coat foliage. For example, I like to use pink tapien verbena or pink *Calibrachoa* as a border plant with the pink variegated Joseph's coat as a mid-level bedding plant. In larger beds purple-blooming princess flower and sun coleus 'Fancy' or 'Eclipse' can be used as taller background plants. The same combinations work well in container plantings. Plant container-grown Joseph's coat in full sun or in sites with no more than three or four hours of shade. Soil type is not critical as long as it drains well.

HOW TO PLANT
Dig planting holes that are wider than the rootballs and as deep as the plants were grown in their containers. Space plants 12 to 24 in. apart, depending on the size of the cultivar or selection. Mulch and water them after planting.

CARE AND MAINTENANCE

Joseph's coat needs occasional shearing throughout the season to keep the plants more compact and bushy. Plants used in hedge designs need frequent shearing. Remember to shear the plants at an angle so that the base is slightly wider than the top, allowing for more exposure to the sun. One pest in particular, the ghost caterpillar, favors Joseph's coat foliage in Oklahoma. Gardeners disagree about the correct identity of this pest. I call it the ghost caterpillar not because it is white but because I seldom see the critter. It is a larva that feeds on the foliage, causing unsightly holes and damage. The best way to scout for the larva is to look for its black droppings on the ground and foliage. It feeds primarily at night and hides near the base of the plants by day. It is easy to control with organic and synthetic insecticides once the feeding frenzy begins. Expect two to three cycles a summer.

ADDITIONAL INFORMATION

One of the nice things about Joseph's coat is its ever-changing display. Often variegated alternanthera plants will become various color shades throughout the summer, thus the name calico plant. For example, some of my variegated yellow-green selections may turn more solid green in the summer while others get more yellow. The same plants often revert to their original colors in the fall as the days become shorter.

ADDITIONAL SPECIES, CULTIVARS, OR VARIETIES

There is little consistency in cultivar names of Joseph's coat in the nursery trade. It is often sold as variegated pink, white, red, gray, or yellow. There are named cultivars such as 'Aurea Nana', with green and yellow variegation, and 'Haantze's Red Sport', known for its pink, yellow, and green colors. My favorite is 'Ruby Amaranth', or giant Joseph's coat, with bushy, 3-ft. growth and brilliant, large purple-wine foliage. Leaf shape is interesting among selections with some having spoonlike shapes, others very narrow and almost straplike, and some shaped like a parrot. Most Joseph's coat selections will be available in the *A. dentata*, *A. ficoidea*, or *A. purpurea* species.

 Did You Know?

The flowers of alternanthera are cloverlike—some small and some large—but nothing compared to the breathtaking foliage. Some selections form flowers only under stress.

Lantana

Lantana camara

Other Name: Mexican Lantana
Height: 2 to 5 ft.
Spread: 3 to 6 ft.
Flowers: Yellow, white, pink, red,
lavender, or orange
Bloom Period: Summer

Color photograph on page 234.

Light Requirements:

Beneficial Characteristics:

Lantana is one of the most durable, heat-tolerant annuals for Oklahoma. The shrubby-looking plant is native to south Texas and Mexico where it grows as a vigorous perennial shrub in the hot, humid conditions. This same plant will perform as a fast-growing annual with showy blooms throughout the summer and until frost in Oklahoma. Occasionally, gardeners in the state can persuade this tough plant to overwinter, but it is best treated as an annual bedding plant. Its cascading nature and rugged growth quickly fill large flower beds with color for all to enjoy. The color spectrum is phenomenal with many vibrant choices. The lower-growing, more prostrate selections do well even in hanging baskets and containers.

WHEN TO PLANT

Plant it after the chance of frost is past. In many cases it is wise to plant lantana in May or early June. For this reason it is a great rotational plant to follow cool-season plants like pansies, which start to decline in the heat.

WHERE TO PLANT

Grow it in mass as a bedding plant or in combination with other plants. Use this tough, brilliantly flowering annual as a specimen plant, especially in patio pots. Plant lantana in almost any soil as long as it drains well. It prefers full-sun sites, although it tolerates two to three hours of shade.

HOW TO PLANT

Loosen the roots of potbound plants prior to planting. Plant them at the same depth that they were grown in their containers, but dig the holes wider than the rootballs. Spacing should be 18 to 36 in. from the center of one plant to another. Mulch to minimize weeds and to retain soil moisture.

CARE AND MAINTENANCE

Plants are less likely to flower and often succumb to powdery mildew leaf when grown in too much shade. Routine feedings can ensure continuous

bloom. Shear larger selections to keep plants under control anytime it is needed. The plants are drought tolerant after established but bloom more consistently with supplemental irrigation. Potential pests include whiteflies, spider mites, and occasionally lacebugs.

ADDITIONAL INFORMATION

Some selections will have a lull in flowering as berries are produced. Trim off any berry set growth, and fertilize the plants to stimulate quicker repeat flowering. The berry set can be left alone, however, and in two to three weeks new growth will emerge and produce more flowers. Mockingbirds, blue jays, and cardinals favor the mature fruit during the winter. Sterile releases on the market today do not set fruit and are often more consistent in flowering. One species, *L. trifolia*, is better known for its colorful purple fruit than its flower. The seeds, changing from green to a brilliant purple, are produced on conelike flowers.

ADDITIONAL SPECIES, CULTIVARS, OR VARIETIES

'Confetti' (yellow and pink), 'Gold Mound' (yellow-orange), 'Irene' (rose, orange, and yellow), 'New Gold' (golden yellow), and 'Radiation' (red-orange) are popular named hybrid cultivars also sold as striking "patio tree" specimens. Trailing ground cover types—*L. sellowiana (montevidensis)*—include 'Trailing Purple', 'Trailing White', and 'Lavender Swirl' (purple and white). The Patriot™ Series includes assorted award-winning compact varieties that are slower to set fruit. Variegated foliage selections include 'Lemon Swirl', 'Lemon Marble', and 'Samantha'.

Did You Know?

Dr. Jack Roberson, former Oklahoman and Oklahoma State University veterinary graduate, is the hybridizer of the Patriot™ Series as well as many daylily and canna introductions. His most recent releases are a tribute to his OSU roots with the introduction of 'Patriot Cowboy' lantana and 'Aggie Orange' daylily.

Licorice Plant

Helichrysum petiolare

Other Names: Velvet Plant; Helichrysum
Height: 6 to 28 in.
Spread: 12 to 24 in.
Flowers: Striking foliage instead of flowers

Color photograph on page 234.

Light Requirements:

Beneficial Characteristic:

Licorice plant sounds good enough to eat, and when you see the striking foliage combined with other plants, you may be tempted—although it would not be recommended. If the genus *Helichrysum* sounds familiar, it is the same genus as strawflower, just a different species. The related licorice plant is strictly grown for its soft, colorful foliage instead of a flower. It is often promoted as a component plant, meaning that it is used in combination with other flowering annuals. Licorice plant is a designer's dream come true, especially when used in container gardening where the various shades of soft colors complement other flowering beauties. A prime example is a combination planting of gray licorice with purple verbena in a hanging basket or lemon licorice with 'Fancy' sun coleus and pink million bells.® The nice blend of colors and textures appears almost like a living bouquet, and *H. petiolare* is the right ingredient for a tasty display of brilliance.

WHEN TO PLANT

Licorice plant is a warm-season annual in Oklahoma and should be planted outside after the last chance of frost has passed.

WHERE TO PLANT

This lively plant can be used as a component in ground beds or containers of all shapes and sizes. Always match plants in containers with similar cultural requirements of sun or shade. The plants actually do best with afternoon shade in Oklahoma. Full-sun locations are acceptable with appropriate soils, moisture, and mulch. Good drainage is important both in the landscape and in containers.

HOW TO PLANT

Licorice plant is sold as a container-grown plant propagated from cuttings. Space plants in landscape beds 15 to 24 in. apart.

CARE AND MAINTENANCE

Little maintenance is required for these interesting plants. Pruning to control size can be done anytime throughout the growing season. Supplemental feedings initiate vigorous growth. Overwatering can cause rotting, especially in poor soils. With too much shade, the plants lose their unique coloration patterns. Overly dry situations can cause the plant foliage to scorch. Be aware of moisture conditions, and try to keep soil consistently moist but not waterlogged. I have found that licorice plants require more frequent amounts of water than most annuals require. Other than occasional whiteflies, pests are rare.

ADDITIONAL INFORMATION

Other popular component plants for foliage enhancement include moneywort, ornamental sweet potato, lamium, plectranthus, sun coleus, and Joseph's coat.

ADDITIONAL SPECIES, CULTIVARS, OR VARIETIES

Cultivars include 'White Licorice' (gray-green foliage with a silvery-white fuzzy lining), 'Petite or Dwarf Licorice' (same as white, just smaller foliage and growth), 'Licorice Splash' (variegated yellow and green), and 'Limelight' and 'Lemon' (chartreuse). The most unique one in my opinion is 'Icicles', with gray, narrow, almost straplike foliage.

 Did You Know?

H. petiolare *means "conspicuous petioles." Grow licorice plant, and you'll see where it got its species name.*

Melampodium

Melampodium paludosum

Other Names: Showstar;
Melampodium Daisy
Height: 8 to 24 in.
Spread: 8 to 24 in.
Flowers: Yellow
Bloom Period: Summer

Color photograph on page 234.

Light Requirements:

Beneficial Characteristics:

Melampodium is receiving rave reviews from test gardens across the humid South. This bright-golden-yellow daisylike flowering plant blooms throughout the summer and loves the heat and humidity, making it a perfect choice for Oklahoma gardens as well. Even better is the fact that melampodium is fairly drought tolerant. The flowers typically have yellow petals with yellow centers, or eyes, emerging from pleasant green foliage. The newer releases are more compact in growth; the original species and named cultivars were more upright. Probably the hardest part of growing melampodium is learning to say the name. Try it, and see if it does not rank as a top performer in your garden and landscape.

WHEN TO PLANT

Seeds can be started indoors six to eight weeks prior to planting. Harden off seedlings before placing them in the garden or landscape. Set out container-grown plants after the last chance of frost has passed.

WHERE TO PLANT

Use this compact plant as a perfect border for the annual flower bed, or plant it in mass among perennials or shrubs. Take advantage of its neat growth in container or patio planters. The vivid yellow color goes well with purple-, pink-, or white-flowering plants. Foliage color plants such as sun coleus, Joseph's coat, and dwarf purple fountain grass are good background companions. Melampodium is not too picky about its soil type. Like most plants, it prefers fertile, well-drained soils but will grow in almost any site as long as it is not waterlogged. The plants prefer full-sun locations; however, they tolerate two to three hours of shade.

HOW TO PLANT

Space plants 12 to 24 in. apart, depending upon the cultivar. Expect seed to germinate in fourteen to twenty-one days when you start your own transplants. Mulching is beneficial with this plant as long as the mulch does not thickly cover the stems. As with any mulch, angle it down toward the base of the plant, but keep it 2- to 4-in. thick between plants.

CARE AND MAINTENANCE

This floriferous plant typically is self-cleaning and will not require deadheading of spent blooms. Occasionally, the plant will bloom its heart out and then rest a little while before starting again, especially on the more upright, older releases. During this time the plants can be sheared, fertilized, and watered to initiate more growth and flowers. Do not overfertilize melampodium; pay special attention to high-nitrogen blends. With high nitrogren, the plants will reward you with more foliage and fewer flowers. Pests most likely to favor melampodium are spider mites. Watch for yellowish speckled foliage near the center of the leaf veins. Try the old, reliable white paper test, and tap the foliage on the paper. If the specks start to crawl, they may be mites. With high populations, control may be necessary.

ADDITIONAL INFORMATION

Melampodium may be fairly drought tolerant, but the plants will not thrive through severe drought. They do prefer drier soils, so be careful not to overwater. Allow the plants to dry between waterings. Melampodium is fairly new to the landscape scene. Many of the initial releases are harder to find because of the improved cultivar characteristics of compact, floriferous growth.

ADDITIONAL SPECIES, CULTIVARS, OR VARIETIES

'Derby' is an earlier compact release. 'Million Gold' is the most recent release and the most compact, growing to an 8-in. mound.

 Did You Know?

Melampodium is in the Compositae *family. There are twelve species of the herbaceous plant, and some are native to the southwestern United States.*

Mexican Bush Sage

Salvia leucantha

Other Names: Mexican Salvia;
   Scarlet Sage
Height: 4 to 6 ft.
Spread: 3 to 5 ft.
Flowers: Purple
Bloom Period: Fall

Color photograph on page 234.

Light Requirements:

Beneficial Characteristics:

Mexican bush sage is without a doubt one of my favorite fall-flowering plants. Graceful is a term often used to describe this fall beauty. The velvety purple-and-white flowers form on elongated stems from tall, bushy plants in late summer/early fall and continue until frost. This Mexican native loves the heat and can occasionally be grown as a perennial in the southern tip of Oklahoma. For most of us, though, it is best grown as an annual; it is well worth the investment each year. The foliage is a velvety grayish green as it emerges in the spring and grows all summer long before exhibiting its spectacular color display. Mexican bush sage is occasionally categorized as a herb, although it is not typically used for culinary purposes like the traditional cooking sage (*S. officinalis*). Instead the flowers are used more for fresh cut and dried arrangements.

WHEN TO PLANT

This herbaceous tender perennial can be planted in the spring after the chance of frost has passed until June.

WHERE TO PLANT

Because of the height of *Salvia leucantha*, use it as a background plant in the perennial garden or annual landscape bed. The delightful fall display makes it a nice specimen plant when used among shrubs in the landscape. I like to use it as a hedge or screen along fencerows or to hide eyesores in the landscape. Although typically small in growth, it can be a single specimen in a container where it can be moved front and center in the fall. The lush-growing plants perform well in rich garden soil with good drainage. They grow in partial shade of no more than three or four hours but thrive in hot, full sun.

HOW TO PLANT

Space plants 3 to 4 ft. apart. Dig planting holes that are wider than the rootballs and as deep as the plants were grown in their containers. Loosen potbound roots before planting. Mulch them for moisture conservation and weed control. Water regularly after planting when supplemental water is needed.

CARE AND MAINTENANCE

The only care needed for these beauties is mulching for winter protection in areas marginal for their cold hardiness. For the best insulation, leave the dead tops in place, and then mulch among the frozen stems with about 6 in. of compost, leaf litter, cottonseed hulls, grass clippings, or wheat straw. In spring around late March, remove the mulch and dead tops to allow for new growth. In Zones 6a, 6b, and sometimes 7a, the plants are hard to overwinter—even with protection. Supplemental feedings are not needed if good soil preparation was done ahead of time. Even though the plants are drought tolerant, they bloom best if supplemental irrigation is provided, especially later in the summer and early fall. Other than an occasional spider mite, pests are rare.

ADDITIONAL INFORMATION

Another fall companion for Mexican bush sage is a tender perennial cousin (not as cold hardy) known as pineapple sage, or *S. elegans*. This late-summer and fall fuschia red-blooming salvia truly invigorates the air with a pineapple scent when the foliage is bruised. The flowers are edible and have a pineapple aroma and taste. Hummingbirds love both of them.

ADDITIONAL SPECIES, CULTIVARS, OR VARIETIES

S. leucantha typically has velvety lavender-and-white flowers. 'Midnight' is a solid purple selection. There are other reports of selections with more violet flowers, but they are seldom found in the nursery.

 Did You Know?

Salvias are available in hardy perennial forms as well as tender annuals. Be careful in clarifying what you want at the time of purchase.

Mexican Heather

Cuphea hyssopifolia

Other Names: False Heather; Hawaiian Heather
Height: 8 to 15 in.
Spread: 10 to 15 in.
Flowers: Purple, pink, or white
Bloom Period: Summer

Color photograph on page 235.

Light Requirements:

Beneficial Characteristics:

Mexican heather is another tough perennial Southern native grown as an annual in Oklahoma. The lacy plant offers a texture equivalent to that of a fern but with tiny purple, pink, or white flowers. Occasionally, the plant will overwinter in southern Oklahoma during mild winters, but it does better as a seasonal bedding plant for the landscape or as a container companion plant. Even though the flowers are fairly small, they provide continuous bloom for a dazzling display of color throughout the summer. This durable plant is not at all picky about its light location. It will grow equally well in full sun or partial shade, especially when grown in the ground.

WHEN TO PLANT

Plant Mexican heather after the temperatures begin to warm in the spring and after the last chance of frost has passed.

WHERE TO PLANT

Cuphea hyssopifolia is a great choice for a uniform border plant in a special annual bed or even for seasonal color in the perennial landscape. The compact growth and fine texture make the plants candidates for container combinations, rock gardens, walkways, windowboxes, mail boxes, and just about anyplace you need a plant. Fertile or poor soils are acceptable as long as they do not hold water. Like most plants, they grow more vigorously in loosely prepared organic sites with a top layer of mulch.

HOW TO PLANT

The proper spacing to get the plants to touch is 12- to 15-in. centers.

CARE AND MAINTENANCE

The dainty flowers are definitely self-cleaning, so no deadheading is needed. Because their natural growth habit is compact and somewhat flat, additional pruning is seldom needed. I have seen Mexican heather spaced closer together and sheared as a hedge. The blooming formal appearance made quite an impact. Remember when trying this method to trim the plants so that the base is slightly wider than the top to allow for better penetration of light for more uniform growth. Side-dressing with a fertilizer is rarely needed unless the plants are a chlorotic yellowish color or planted in very poor sites. Blooms will be more consistent with irrigation during severe drought.

ADDITIONAL INFORMATION

The *Cuphea* genus has interesting selections. In addition to Mexican heather, consider growing *C. ignea* (firecracker plant, also called cigar plant) with orange-red, narrow, firecracker-shaped flowers. The Coan Series has red, pink, rose, and white flowers. Also sold as cigar plant or candy corn plant is *C. micropetala* with orange-yellow flowers, which I think more closely resemble candy corn. 'David Verity' is another orange-red flowering hybrid cross between *C. ignea* × *micropetala*. *C. purpurea* has wonderful cherry-red, fireflylike flowers, thus the cultivar name 'Firefly'; however, some folks think they resemble a rabbit's face. Another species very similar to the one just mentioned resembles more of a rabbit's ear and is sold as 'Bunny Ears' (*C. llavea*). My favorite is 'Batface Cuphea' (*C. cyanea*) with purple, slender flowers and red petals making the bat's ears.

ADDITIONAL SPECIES, CULTIVARS, OR VARIETIES

Mexican heather named cultivars include 'Allison' with rose-purple flowers; 'Alba' and 'Linda Downer' with white blooms; 'Palest Pinkie' with pale pink; and 'Rosea' with a more magenta color. 'Dwarf' or 'Compacta' is a more condensed version of 'Allison'. 'Hanging Basket' has more weeping pendulous growth with lavender flowers. *Cuphea* × *glutinosa* is a University of Georgia hybrid selection thought to be more cold hardy through Zone 7 with some winter protection.

Did You Know?

A Cuphea-*like flowering plant known as the 'Twining Firecracker' plant is not a* Cuphea *at all. Instead, it is in the* Manettia *genus.*

Million Bells®

Calibrachoa hybrid

Other Names: Miniature Petunia;
  Liricashower™
Height: 4 to 6 in.
Spread: 2 to 3 ft.
Flowers: Pink, rose, or white
Bloom Period: Summer

Color photograph on page 235.

Light Requirements:

Beneficial Characteristics:

New to my garden and here to stay is *Calibrachoa* hybrid, better known as million bells, which is a registered trademark of the Proven Winners® plant cooperators. This entirely new species of plant in the landscape trade is named after its hundreds of bell-shaped blooms that appear throughout the season. The small, petunialike flowers in colors of pink, rose, and white with sunny-yellow centers are not petunias at all. I had reservations at first about the promotional campaign touting their tolerance to full sun. I expected them to melt down in the hot, humid Oklahoma summers, but, boy, was I wrong. They thrived in the heat, even the heat of 1998, as long as they received supplemental moisture. They bloomed in full sun all right; as a matter of fact, on cloudy days the flowers closed up. Million bells® are receiving accolades from various state university horticulture trials and are definitely bedding plants for the future, especially in the hot summers of Oklahoma.

WHEN TO PLANT

Plant them in spring after the chance of frost has passed, just about anytime from April to June. The drier it is, the more stress on establishing the plants unless supplemental irrigation is guaranteed.

WHERE TO PLANT

Calibrachoa does well in containers and baskets, but even better as a bedding plant ground cover. Full-sun sites are best as long as irrigation can be provided during dry times. The plants accept partial or afternoon shade, but with too much shade the plants become spindly and bloom sporadically. The plants perform in almost any soil type as long as drainage is satisfactory. Moisture-retentive soils that drain well are ideal.

HOW TO PLANT

Space plants at least 2 ft. apart in nutrient-rich soils.

CARE AND MAINTENANCE

Moisture seems to be the key to growing these delightful plants. Whenever I was unable to provide supplemental irrigation, the plants stopped blooming. Moisture-retentive sites or locations with irrigation proved best with continuous bloom throughout the summer. As soon as it became cold in the fall, the plants stopped blooming but provided evergreen foliage most of the winter. In some locations the plants may overwinter; the survival depends on the severity of the winter, the condition of the plants, and the site.

ADDITIONAL INFORMATION

The plants truly have a ground cover growth habit, not reaching more than 4 to 6 in. high but easily spreading 2 ft. Visitors to my garden complimented my seasonal designs with million bells® as a front border in combination with periwinkles in the middle and sun coleus in the background.

ADDITIONAL SPECIES, CULTIVARS, OR VARIETIES

'Cherry Pink', 'Trailing Blue', 'Trailing Pink', and 'Trailing White' are the current releases from the Proven Winners® label. 'Liricashower Blue' and 'Liricashower Rose' are two similar releases from the Flower Fields® marketing campaign introduced by the Paul Ecke Ranch, which is known for poinsettias.

 Did You Know?

Although not a petunia, Calibrachoa *is closely related to it. The difference between the two species is the number of chromosomes, which makes it virtually impossible to create a* Calibrachoa-*petunia hybrid.*

Ornamental Sweet Potato

Ipomoea batatas

Other Name: Sweet Potato Vine
Height: 10 to 15 in.
Spread: 4 to 6 ft.
Flowers: None; grown for colorful foliage
Bloom Period: Fascinating foliage
all summer

Color photograph on page 235.

Light Requirements:

Beneficial Characteristic:

Vegetable plants are finally starting to make their way into the ornamental landscape, and sweet potato is one of them moving front and center. Ornamental sweet potato is a true sweet potato, just like the traditional baking sweet potato. The biggest difference is the colorful foliage of the ornamental. If you think about it, even the garden-type sweet potatoes have attractive foliage, but just not very colorful. The best part of using ornamental sweet potato in the landscape is that few plants are needed to fill in a large area. If you do not trim the long vines to make them bushier, they will easily grow 6 to 8 ft. long—and longer during the summer.

WHEN TO PLANT

Ornamental sweet potato is a heat-loving plant. Just like the garden type, plant it in May or June when the soil temperatures begin to warm.

WHERE TO PLANT

This somewhat aggressive annual grows perfectly as a ground cover. Its vining and cascading growth is also impressive where it can flow over a wall or planter. Use it as a border plant or among taller annuals. Be careful not to use it around short annuals or the vines will quickly overgrow and consume the smaller plants. Plant ornamental sweet potatoes in patio containers and hanging baskets. Full-sun locations are best; however, they accept partial shade of no more than two to three hours. Rich garden soils usually produce even more aggressive vines. These tough plants will tolerate poorer soils, which sometimes restrict the growth. Like garden-type sweet potatoes, ornamental types will not tolerate wet feet.

HOW TO PLANT

Ornamental sweet potatoes are available as plants rooted vegetatively. Space the plants in ground beds a minimum of 3 ft. apart. In a container one plant will be enough.

Care and Maintenance

Tip pruning from time to time to keep the plants more compact and bushy is the biggest task. Doing this will force more side shoots back along the foliage. Expect some white sap to ooze from the wound, which is characteristic of this genus. As the vines begin to spread, trim them from time to time to keep them in their designated location. Mulching the ornamental sweet potatoes will control weeds and retain soil moisture. Potential insect threats are spider mites and aphids. Any sweet potato may become the prey of the sweet potato weevil, although to date it is not commonly found; quarantine and certified growing programs in the veggie types seem to have been effective in controlling the weevil.

Additional Information

Ornamental sweet potatoes produce underground swollen roots, especially in loose soils. Although they are edible, you will not want to try them once you see the anemic-looking color. They are not a golden color like the garden types and are not very tasty either (take my word for it). Some gardeners try to overwinter the swollen roots for next year's planting but often find it easier to buy new plants. Root the vines in water in a container on the windowsill instead of trying to save the storage root if you want to try to keep some for next season.

Additional Species, Cultivars, or Varieties

'Margarita'—sometimes sold as 'Marguerite'—is a lovely chartreuse color. 'Terrace Lime' is a more recent introduction with a similar lime-yellow color. 'Blackie' is a dark purple, appearing almost black, with finely lobed foliage somewhat resembling a star. 'Black Beauty' or 'Ace of Spades' is a "sport" off 'Blackie' with the same deep purple but with unique, heart-shaped leaves. 'Tricolor'—also sold as 'Pink Frost'—is a selection with gray, pink, and creamy-white variegation. Expect even more cultivars soon.

 Did You Know?

Ornamental sweet potato is related to morning glory. Both are in the Ipomoea *genus and members of the* Convolvulaceae *family.*

Persian Shield

Strobilanthus dyerianus

Other Names: Strobilanthus;
  Metallic Plant
Height: 15 to 36 in.
Spread: 18 to 32 in.
Flowers: Inconspicuous; grown for
  metallic foliage
Bloom Period: Foliage color throughout
  the summer

Color photograph on page 235.

Light Requirements:

Beneficial Characteristic:

Foliage color has always been important; just look at the breeding done with bronze- or variegated-leafed flowering plants. Some folks say that color is color, whether it is in the form of a flower or foliage. Others think color can come only from flowers. Persian shield has knock-your-socks-off color but not from a flower; it comes from its silvery-purple metallic foliage. The bold coarseness of the foliage in combination with the unique color scheme makes for a brilliant display. In most of Oklahoma this foliage beauty is best grown in afternoon or partial shade. In rich, moist soils with mulch, it can tolerate full sun, however. Persian shield is an old-fashioned plant, which has not changed much over the years. It is often sold as a houseplant in the foliage section of the garden center, but thanks to creative and open-minded gardeners, Persian shield is now making its way into the nursery trade as a bold, beautiful seasonal bedding plant.

WHEN TO PLANT
Plant Persian shield as the soil temperatures begin to warm up and the chance of frost is past. Most plants can be successfully set out in late April or May.

WHERE TO PLANT
Persian shield maturing at around 3 ft. can be used as a specimen or background plant. It is also appealing massed in ground beds. The stately growth and foliage make it suitable for a companion plant in container displays. It is most often used as a contrast plant like plectranthus, dusty miller, artemesia, and other brilliantly colored foliage plants. Flower colors of purple, pink, and white are perfect choices to plant in association with the silvery-purple colors of strobilanthus. The foliage intensity is best achieved in organic soils in partial shade.

How to Plant

Space the plants 18 to 24 in. apart in groups. Diagonal planting offers better design and fill. Check for potbound roots before planting, and loosen them if necessary. Plant Persian shield at the same depth that they were grown in their containers, but dig the holes slightly wider than the rootballs. Water them after planting and on a regular basis throughout the growing season. Mulch to retain soil moisture and minimize weeds.

Care and Maintenance

Persian shield will start a little slow in the spring after planting, but once the temperatures begin to heat up, it grows fairly rapidly. The prominent foliage and strong stems require no staking. The plants tolerate heat and humidity. Persian shield responds well to supplemental fertilizer applications, especially when grown in poor soils. There are no particular disease or insect problems other than an occasional whitefly when the plants are grown in a greenhouse. Once the plants are placed outside, it is a good idea to pinch them to initiate more compact, uniform growth.

Additional Information

Some plants to use in combination with strobilanthus are petunia, *Calibrachoa*, Mexican heather, ornamental sweet potato, purple heart, scaevola, and verbena for lower-growing ground cover-type sun companions. Summer snapdragon, plectranthus, coleus, princess flower, purple fountain grass, and lantana are taller sun-loving annuals, which complement the texture and color of Persian shield. Impatiens are perfect shade-loving companions.

Additional Species, Cultivars, or Varieties

Persian shield is becoming more readily available at nurseries and garden centers. I am unaware of any improved or named cultivars, other than the species.

Did You Know?

Persian shield seldom flowers out in the garden. Occasionally, it will flower under duress in the greenhouse with small, purplish-white flowers but nothing as showy as the brilliant foliage.

Pinwheel Zinnia

Zinnia angustifolia

Other Names: Dwarf Zinnia; Creeping Zinnia; Spreading Zinnia
Height: 8 to 12 in.
Spread: 12 to 15 in.
Flowers: Yellow, white, or rose
Bloom Period: All summer

Color photograph on page 235.

Light Requirements:

Beneficial Characteristics:

Mention the name zinnia, and many gardeners run the other way—thanks to a notorious disease called powdery mildew. Pinwheel zinnias, however, are tolerant of this dreaded foliage pathogen. The flowers of pinwheel zinnia are not as large as the standard, upright-growing selections, but the massive season-long bloom will help you to remember that size does not always matter. Even better is the fact that most of the flowers are self-cleaning and require little to no deadheading. The lower, more cascading plant growth does not require staking.

WHEN TO PLANT

Start seed indoors in February or purchase container-grown plants to set out after the last frost.

WHERE TO PLANT

Pinwheel zinnias make nice border plants in the annual flower bed or even accent plants in the perennial or shrub landscape. These colorful beauties may be grown in borders of the vegetable garden for color and for their use as cut flowers. Plant them in an area in full sun for the best display or in no more than a half day of shade. Pinwheel zinnias also do well in containers and windowboxes when sufficient sun is available. They prefer rich, fertile garden soil, but the plants perform in poorer soils. Good drainage and air circulation are essential.

HOW TO PLANT

Seed should be started indoors eight to twelve weeks before the last frost. Direct seeding into the ground is risky because of competition from weeds but can be done in April. The easiest method is to buy container-grown plants to set out after the last frost in April. They can be set out as late as May without complications. Space plants 12 to 15 in. apart.

CARE AND MAINTENANCE

Mulch the plants after planting or when the temperatures warm up. Avoid getting the mulch too thick near the delicate plant stems or rotting can occur. Water on a regular basis throughout the summer. Supplemental feeding is beneficial occasionally during the growing season. Pests are seldom a problem. Powdery mildew is not likely on these tolerant selections unless they are stressed and planted in too much shade.

ADDITIONAL INFORMATION

Pinwheel zinnias or spreading zinnias make great fresh cut or dried flowers, even though the blooms are not big. I especially like to mix them with assorted fresh cut flowers and coleus foliage. *Z. linearis* is also a pinwheel type with more linear narrow foliage, small flowers, and great disease tolerance. Gardeners sometimes refer to *Z. angustifolia* and *Z. linearis* as dwarf zinnias. Be careful, however, because other dwarf types in catalogs are not all resistant to powdery mildew. *Dwarf* is a commonly used term to describe the size of the flower and the plant height.

ADDITIONAL SPECIES, CULTIVARS, OR VARIETIES

Seed companies often sell such selections in a series with a given name and assorted colors. Such series are Pinwheel and Star with flower colors of white, orange, rose, cherry, and salmon. Other individual cultivars include 'Crystal White' and 'Golden Orange'. The newest hybrid series introduction is Profusion with two cultivars, 'Profusion Cherry' and 'Profusion Orange', selected as All-America selection Gold Medal winners in 1999. Another zinnia species, *Elegans*, is touted as having disease tolerance. The selection is known as the Oklahoma Series with taller plants and larger, tightly doubled flowers. I have found them to be less resistant than the pinwheel types but still better than most.

 Did You Know?

The flower commonly called creeping zinnia is not really a zinnia at all. It does have zinnia-like flowers but is actually Sanvitalia procumbens. *It seldom reaches more than 10 in. and is also disease tolerant.*

Princess Flower

Tibouchina grandiflora

Other Names: Tibouchina; Glory Bush; Pleroma; Lasiandra

Height: 2 to 4 ft.

Spread: 2 to 3 ft.

Flowers: Purple

Bloom Period: All summer

Color photograph on page 235.

Light Requirements:

Beneficial Characteristics:

Move over mandevilla, allamanda, and hibiscus! Here comes your next competitor as a tropical patio plant—princess flower. This stunning plant with large purple flowers averaging 2 to 3 in. in diameter really does have a royal presence. The vibrant purple blooms form all season long from a shrubby-type plant with velvety foliage. Quite popular in Florida, California, and Texas, princess flower is beginning to make its way to Oklahoma. I have successfully used it as a container plant and as a bedding plant. There is nothing quite like its dynamite flower color, especially when used in association with yellow- or white-flowering or variegated companions.

WHEN TO PLANT

Because of its tropical background, set this plant outside in late April when temperatures begin to steadily warm. It is quite susceptible to cold, so it must not be subject to frost.

WHERE TO PLANT

Tibouchina is elegant enough to be a specimen plant by itself in a container or in a landscape bed. In larger containers it does well in combination with other colorful and textured plants. Ground bed plantings in masses are absolutely breathtaking.

HOW TO PLANT

This towering specimen is sold as a container-grown plant in 1- to 5-gal. selections. When repotting or planting it in the ground, check for potbound overgrown roots. Loosen the roots by severing the sides and cutting off the bottom couple of inches in worst-case scenarios. Plant princess flowers at the same depth that they were grown in the containers, but dig the holes wider than the rootballs. Mulch is beneficial to keep the plant roots moist in both ground beds and containers. Water princess flowers on a regular basis after planting throughout the growing season.

CARE AND MAINTENANCE

The bushy growth seldom needs staking. Pruning is generally needed only to keep plants in a manageable shape. The flowers are produced in clusters opening a few at a time throughout the summer. Severe drought and wind can scorch the foliage and abort the blooms. Consistently moist but well-drained soils are best for this plant. Tibouchina responds to frequent feedings throughout the growing season with water-applied fertilizers high in phosphorus and potassium and low in nitrogen. Insect pests are ones that typically attack tropical flowering plants, primarily spider mites and aphids. I have encountered a larva of some type, which I have not been able to properly identify, that feeds on the flower buds just before they open. The holes in the buds occasionally cause the buds to drop prematurely. If they do open, there will be holes in the flowers. A common name for this critter is budworm, and it can be fairly easy to control with either organic or synthetic insect sprays. I have had success by using Di-Syston insecticide granules in the container.

ADDITIONAL INFORMATION

Princess flower can sometimes be successfully overwintered in a bright, sunny room indoors. Of course, a greenhouse is the ideal location. If such conditions are not available, this plant is well worth the investment each season as a tropical annual plant. Another pleasing characteristic of this plant is the almost fuschialike color of some of the leaves in the fall before a frost.

ADDITIONAL SPECIES, CULTIVARS, OR VARIETIES

T. urvilleana is the most commonly sold species of princess flower with medium-sized foliage and lavender flowers. *T. grandiflora* is harder to find but has larger, bolder, even fuzzier leaves. *T. granulosa* has darker-purple flowers and narrow, sandpaperlike foliage. Most selections sold on the market at this time are the species, but it will not be long before improved cultivars or hybrids are offered.

 Did You Know?

Princess flower is an evergreen plant easily growing 10 ft. in warmer climates. It is cold hardy only through Zone 10.

Purple Heart

Setcresea pallida

Other Name: Setcresea
Height: 6 to 12 in.
Spread: 15 to 18 in.
Flowers: Inconspicuous pinkish white
Bloom Period: Throughout the summer

Color photograph on page 235.

Light Requirements:

Beneficial Characteristics:

Purple heart will melt your heart with its violet-purple fleshy stems and foliage. This lovely spreading plant is proof that breathtaking color can come from foliage as well as a flower. The flowers of setcresea are not very showy, however. The pinkish-white, sometimes pale-lavender flowers are borne in the branch terminals, or leaf axis. The flowers bloom most of the summer but definitely take a backseat to the vibrant foliage. This tropical plant thrives in the heat and humidity of our Oklahoma summers and will grow in full sun or partial shade. Purple heart does not need companion plants when massed as a ground cover, but works well in combination with other annual flower colors and textures. Setcresea is best described as a non-invasive annual ground cover.

WHEN TO PLANT

Plant purple heart in late spring after the chance of frost has passed and when temperatures begin to warm—later April or early to mid-May.

WHERE TO PLANT

The low-growing nature of this plant makes it a perfect border plant near sidewalks or in front of low signs. It is also great to use as a filler around medium-sized bedding plants. It likes full-sun locations but accepts those that receive a half day of shade. Well-drained soils are a must. The foliage will readily rot in waterlogged or overwatered sites. Soil type is not crucial since the plants will grow in poor or fertile soils.

HOW TO PLANT

Plant spacing should be on 15-in. centers. When mulching purple heart, use finer particle mulch such as small pine bark, cocoa bean, pecan hull, or shredded leaf mold. Heavier mulches often hold in too much moisture near the stems, potentially causing rotting.

CARE AND MAINTENANCE

Even though the plants prefer dry soils, they need an occasional watering during a severe drought. Do not be alarmed if some of the water settles in the cuplike foliage and stems similar to a bromeliad. The waxy coating on the foliage forces the water to run off into the crotch angles until it evaporates. Supplemental feedings are seldom needed unless foliage appears nutrient deficient. Full-sun locations cause the foliage to become an even more intense purple. In more shade, the color intensity fades. The sprawling habit of the plant rarely needs pruning.

ADDITIONAL INFORMATION

The vibrant purple foliage complements plants with yellow, pink, or white colors. I have used the plant as a companion in containers with yellow-flowering esperanza, pink tapien verbena, purple angelonia, yellow bidens, and gray plectranthus. In ground beds, pink or white begonia, vinca, sun coleus, scaevola, melampodium, Mexican heather, and pink *Calibrachoa* complement purple heart.

ADDITIONAL SPECIES, CULTIVARS, OR VARIETIES

The plant is generally grown from propagated cuttings. At the time that I wrote this book, I knew of no known named cultivars.

 Did You Know?

*Purple heart is often incorrectly called wandering Jew. The official so-called wandering Jews—*Tradescantia pallida *and* Zebrina pendula—*are primarily sold as houseplants but can be annuals when planted in partially shaded sites. There is also perennial* Tradescantia, *known as spider wort, with* bracteata *and* andersoniana *the most commonly grown species.*

Scaevola

Scaevola aemula

Other Names: Fan Flower;
  Blue Fan Flower
Height: 4 to 6 in.
Spread: 10 to 15 in.
Flowers: Purple and yellow, pink, or white
Bloom Period: Summer

Color photograph on page 235.

Light Requirements:

Beneficial Characteristics:

It is always exciting to see a popular landscape plant in its native habitat, especially when it is indigenous to another country. Scaevola is native to Australia, and a few years ago I had the opportunity to travel to Australia through a cultural exchange by the Rotary Foundation. I frequently ran across this beautiful plant in its native habit of dry, hot sites. Well, this same tough, heat-loving plant thrives in Oklahoma as an annual bedding plant. When planted in masses in ground beds, it makes a wonderful display. It is also conducive to container and hanging basket uses. The flower is unique—almost flat or fan shaped with purple flowers and a yellow center, or eye. Considering that it is a relatively new introduction to the United States, there has been an overwhelming response as evidenced by all the newly named hybrids and selections.

WHEN TO PLANT
The temperatures need to warm up for this plant. Plant it in May or June.

WHERE TO PLANT
I have found scaevola to be the perfect rotational plant for cool-season annuals. Once pansies start to die out in early summer, plant scaevola in their place. The low growth is perfect for a border or a filler plant. It will cascade over rocks or walls and even in hanging baskets. After the temperatures cool in the fall, scaevola declines. Then plant pansies, ornamental Swiss chard, or another cool-season annual. Poor or average soils are preferable for this seasonal plant. Rich, humus soils are acceptable, but they definitely need to drain well. Waterlogged sites mean sure death for this succulent plant.

HOW TO PLANT
Dig planting holes that are wider than the rootballs and as deep as the plants were grown in their containers. Plant them on 12- to 18-in. centers.

Mulching is a good idea but use finer products, such as small pine bark and shredded leaves.

CARE AND MAINTENANCE

Scaevola is a low-maintenance plant. The flowers are self-cleaning, so no deadheading is needed. Trimming or pruning is seldom required. Occasionally, the plants may become yellowish or chlorotic in really poor soils. Correct the condition by using a fertilizer dissolved in water and applied at the time of watering. Other than an occasional spider mite, pests are rare. The biggest problem is rotting as a result of overwatering or poorly drained sites.

ADDITIONAL INFORMATION

The growth of this plant seems to be in direct correlation to hot temperatures. After they are planted in the spring, the plants will have a tendency to sit there until the soil and air temperatures rise. Do not be surprised if the plants decline in the fall when cooler, wet conditions arrive.

ADDITIONAL SPECIES, CULTIVARS, OR VARIETIES

Several species of scaevola on the market include *S. aemula*, *S. albida*, *S. striata*, and *S. serica* as well as a few hybrids. 'Blue Wonder', 'New Blue Wonder', 'Mauve Cluster', 'Petite Wonder', 'Blue Shamrock', 'Fan Falls', 'Blue Fans', 'New Wonder', 'Blue Angel', 'Fancy', 'Sun Fan', and the Outback Series are recently introduced varieties with either purple or purple-and-yellow flowers. There are differences in the growth habit and flower size of these selections. 'Mini Pink' and 'Pink Fan' are pink introductions. 'Alba' and 'White Fan' are white-flowering types. The purple is the most dramatic in bed displays.

 Did You Know?

Fan flower is brilliantly displayed when planted in masses in front of yellow lantana, bidens, melampodium, pinwheel zinnia, or sun coleus.

Shrimp Plant

Justicia brandegeana

Other Names: Hummingbird Bush; Brazilian Plume; Chuparosa
Height: 2 to 3 ft.
Spread: 18 to 24 in.
Flowers: Red, orange, yellow, or white
Bloom Period: Summer

Color photograph on page 235.

Light Requirements:

Beneficial Characteristics:

If you want to add plants to your hummingbird garden, consider this tropical annual. Shrimp plants, with their tubular flowers, are a favorite of hummingbirds. The unusually shaped flowers are described as resembling shrimp, candles, and lollipops. I first became familiar with these interesting plants when I lived in Florida. There they were used as annuals planted in masses, usually in island beds. The hot, humid summers never seemed to faze these nonstop bloomers. In southern Florida they were occasionally grown as a herbaceous perennial, becoming several feet tall. In Oklahoma they are used as warm-season annuals providing rapid growth and season-long color. The uniquely shaped flowers are composed of colorful bracts from which the true flower emerges, which is typically white. Shrimp plants are considered mid-level plants when used in combination with other annuals.

WHEN TO PLANT

Plant these heat-loving plants from the time that the danger of frost is past through late May and early June.

WHERE TO PLANT

In large ground beds plant them in masses or in smaller groups of four or five. Plant them so that the flower colors complement other blooming plants of yellow, red, pink, or white. Foliage color plants such as sun coleus are good background choices for shrimp plants. Plant them by themselves or in combination with other container patio displays. These high-performing plants will produce abundant flowers in full sun or even partial or filtered shade. Fertile, organic soils are perfect for this tropical beauty; however, shrimp plant will tolerate poor or sandy soils with good drainage.

HOW TO PLANT

Space plants 18 to 24 in. apart. Set the plants at the same depth at which they were grown, in holes slightly wider than the rootballs. Mulch and water them after planting.

CARE AND MAINTENANCE

This tropical plant is a dependable bloomer all summer with whimsical upright flower spikes that later droop with weight. Deadhead unsightly flower spikes throughout the growing season to ensure even more vigorous bloom. Prune the plants early on to encourage branching and a denser appearance, and anytime needed during the summer. Feed them occasionally during the growing season. Although the plants are somewhat drought tolerant, provide supplemental irrigation in a severe drought to keep the foliage and blooms from dropping.

ADDITIONAL INFORMATION

There is another plant species with flowers closely resembling those of shrimp plant but with yellow bracts. Look for *Pachystachys lutea*, also known as the lollipop flower. Lollipop flower and shrimp plant require the same growing conditions.

ADDITIONAL SPECIES, CULTIVARS, OR VARIETIES

In addition to *J. brandegeana* with its golden-bronze flower spikes, there is a variegated foliage version sold as 'Variegata'. Another species sold as a bedding plant is known as Brazilian plume (*J. carnea*) with pink flowers. *J. carnea* 'Alba' has lovely creamy-white flowers. *J. candicans*, known as red justicia or hummingbird bush, has a more compact branching habit with red, more distinct tubular flowers. Mexican honeysuckle, or *J. spicigera*, is the most shade tolerant of all the species and has golden-orange tubular flowers. The last two species are more difficult to find in nurseries.

Did You Know?

A hard-to-find vining form is available as Justicia californica, *or chuparosa, with dark-red tubular flowers, which also make nice dried flowers. The stems and foliage have a more grayish color than most of the species.*

Starflower

Pentas lanceolata

Other Names: Pentas; Egyptian Starflower; Egyptian Star Cluster
Height: 8 to 24 in.
Spread: 12 to 24 in.
Flowers: Pink, red, white, or lavender
Bloom Period: Summer

Color photograph on page 235.

Light Requirements:

Beneficial Characteristics:

Pentas have always been a star in my garden, with dainty-pointed, star-shaped flowers that last right up until frost. The flower blooms are formed in a cluster and make quite a show. Even more exciting are the visits of hummingbirds to these tubular flowers. Pentas have deep-green velvety foliage that shows the colorful blooms to advantage. The plants thrive in the heat and are fairly drought tolerant. They work well in ground beds or in containers. Some of the more compact selections are appropriate choices for hanging basket displays.

WHEN TO PLANT
Plant this warm-season annual after the chance of frost is past, any time throughout April or May.

WHERE TO PLANT
The compact selections are perfect border plants and container plants. For borders, place them diagonally to get a better display and fill. Any of the sizes or selections work well planted in masses. The taller versions are perfect as background in the annual flower bed. For containers, choose to plant them in windowboxes, patio pots, or mailbox planters. Always match the plant to its preferred light requirements in ground beds or containers. Starflower will thrive in full sun or a half day of shade. Partial filtered shade is not suggested. Pentas prefer organic, rich soils. Like most plants, they are tolerant of just about any soil type as long as it drains well.

HOW TO PLANT
Space the plants 8 to 24 in. apart—the bigger they will be, the farther apart they should be planted. Check for potbound roots, and loosen them as needed before planting. Water the pentas after planting and on a regular basis. Mulch keeps soils moist in the summer and minimizes weed growth.

CARE AND MAINTENANCE

Starflower is typically self-cleaning, so pruning or deadheading is seldom needed. The taller selections will probably need to be pinched back next to a leaf node after planting to keep the plants more compact. Trim them as needed throughout the season. More compact or dwarf cultivars require little pruning. Pentas are high-nitrogen feeders. The foliage will occasionally become chlorotic in poor soils; the evidence is a yellowish color and green veins. Supplemental feedings throughout the season will invigorate plants. Slow-release applications at the time of planting are beneficial. Potential pests are spider mites, whiteflies, and aphids.

ADDITIONAL INFORMATION

Pentas can be started from seed, but most home owners purchase container-grown bedding plants. Gardeners with greenhouses can more successfully start transplants from seed. Typically, pellated seed is sold, which makes the very small seed easier to handle. Sometimes it is also treated with a fungicide to prevent seedling disease problems. The seed needs light to germinate and should not be covered with soil; just sprinkle soil on top and water. The seed will germinate within ten to twenty days. It takes ten to twelve weeks before the plants are ready to go outside. Do not forget to harden off transplants prior to planting.

ADDITIONAL SPECIES, CULTIVARS, OR VARIETIES

The New Look Series in assorted colors is one of the most compact varieties, reaching 8 to 10 in. The Starburst Series, considered semidwarf at 12 to 18 in., is a bicolor form with vivid colors. 'Cranberry Punch' is a cranberry red of medium height, near 18 to 24 in. 'Alba' or 'White' matures near 24 in. 'Pink Profusion' is semidwarf, averaging 12 to 15 in. 'Orchid Illusion' is an orchid-lavender shade, also of medium height. 'Pearl White' is semitrailing and good for hanging baskets. 'Ruby Glow' is a brilliant red, and 'Blushing Beauty' is a light pinkish white, maturing near 18 in.

 Did You Know?

Pentas *is a native of Africa and has five distinctive flower petals forming the star shape.*

Summer Snapdragon
Angelonia angustifolia

Other Names: Angel Plant; Angel Flower; Angelonia
Height: 18 to 24 in.
Spread: 10 to 15 in.
Flowers: Purple, white, or pink
Bloom Period: Summer

Color photograph on page 235.

Light Requirements:

Beneficial Characteristics:

If you like the shape and look of snapdragon flowers, you will absolutely love summer snapdragon, which thrives in the heat of the summer. In that regard it is unlike the traditional snapdragon, which is a cool-season plant. I always try several new plants each year, and summer snapdragon is a recent trial plant in my landscape. Summer snapdragon was not even fazed by the record-breaking heat of 1998. It bloomed nonstop from spring until frost with supplemental irrigation. The showy, orchidlike flowers are 1/4 to 1/2 in. in diameter and are produced in elongated spikes, opening from the base to the tip while sending up new blooms for a dependable airy display. The colors complement almost any flower combination in the landscape. I used them in masses by themselves in ground beds, in containers, and even in the garden. I plan to use them on a regular basis. Native to Mexico and the Caribbean, angelonia will easily give your garden a hint of the tropics with interesting and colorful blooms.

WHEN TO PLANT
This tropical plant should be placed outside after the last chance of frost is past, typically anytime from mid-April through the end of May and even in early June.

WHERE TO PLANT
Angelonia is absolutely intriguing as a bedding plant in masses. It is so unusual, it works by itself as a single specimen plant. The lovely upright and slightly cascading appearance complements container combination plantings. I have had success combining it with sun coleus, purple heart, plectranthus, verbena, *Calibrachoa*, dwarf purple fountain grass, and ornamental sweet potato. It performs best in full sun or a half day of shade. Too much shade or filtered continuous shade causes the plant to get leggy with sporadic bloom. It accepts average, well drained soil. Like most plants, the tropical beauty performs even better in rich, fertile soils.

How to Plant

Angelonia is primarily available as vegetatively propagated or pot-grown plants instead of seed-grown plants. Space plants on 15- to 18-in. centers. Mulch them after planting, and water.

Care and Maintenance

The blooms are self-cleaning and need no additional deadheading or pruning. The plants have strong growth but do not require staking. Pinching the plants early on will force bushier growth. Irrigation should be available during drought conditions to keep the blooms coming. Additional fertilizer is generally not needed if fertilizer is applied at the time of planting. Pests are of minimal concern; however, you should watch for aphids and spider mites. Virus problems with distorted yellow foliage are also problematic as a result of heavy thrips and whitefly infestations, especially in a greenhouse environment.

Additional Information

One of my most fascinating discoveries with this lovely plant is that the flowers in a fresh cut arrangement last a long time. Some of them have lasted a couple of weeks. They work great with sun coleus and pinwheel zinnia in cut displays. Cut the flowers early in the morning, especially during the heat of the summer. Summer snapdragon is so durable and dependable that it was named a 1998 Florida Plant of the Year.

Additional Species, Cultivars, or Varieties

'Hilo Princess' and 'Lavender Princess' are purple forms. 'Blue Pacific' and 'Tiger Princess' are bicolored with purple and white. 'Alba' and 'White Princess' are white. 'Pink Princess', 'Pandiana', and 'Pink' are, you guessed it, pink.

Did You Know?

The common name angel flower is used because the flower looks like it has wings when turned upside down.

Sun Coleus

Solenostemon scatellariodes

Other Name: Painted Nettle
Height: 15 to 36 in.
Spread: 24 to 36 in.
Flowers: Nonshowy; foliage color instead
Bloom Period: Summer

Color photograph on page 235.

Light Requirements:

Beneficial Characteristics:

Sun coleus is not your grandma's old-time coleus, which quickly went to seed and needed constant deadheading. Sun coleus selections are vegetatively propagated to ensure consistent foliage color and minimal seed formation. And to top it off, the foliage colors are truly traffic stopping. Sun coleus is another example of bright, eye-catching color from foliage instead of from the flower. Sun coleus is perfect as a specimen, contrast, or texture plant. The magnificent foliage is long lasting as a cut flower, especially when used in combination with other flowers. If you want to keep up with the trends, one that is here to stay, place a colorful foliage plant such as sun coleus in your landscape. You will be amazed at what it has to offer.

WHEN TO PLANT

Plant sun coleus after the last chance of frost is past, anytime throughout June. Plant them in the fall as complementary black-and-orange autumn colors for container displays.

WHERE TO PLANT

Use sun coleus as background plants in combination with other annual bedding plants or in masses by themselves for a brilliant display where it does not take many to fill a large area. Even a single plant will speak for itself as a specimen. They grow in patio displays, in the garden for cut flowers, and as a small hedge when alternately planted for late-season coverage. Rich garden soils provide more vigorous growth, but these tough plants tolerate poor or average sites. Full sun is best to get the most brilliant color display. They accept a half day of shade, but more shade means less color

HOW TO PLANT

Space plants 2 to 3 ft. apart. Loosen the roots of potbound plants before planting them. Place them at the same depth that they were grown in the containers, in holes two times wider than the rootballs. Mulch them to keep the soil moist and weed free.

CARE AND MAINTENANCE

Unlike the seedling types, which require filtered shade, sun coleus is truly tolerant of hot sun. Sun coleus will send up flower spikes but nothing as frequent as the old seed types. The flower spikes are usually formed later in the season or under stress. Trim them out to give the plants a more manicured appearance. Pinch the plants at planting and throughout the season to keep them more compact and neat. Supplemental feedings are generally not needed, or the plants will become too overgrown, unless they are planted in poor soils. The plants also slightly wilt due to heat instead of moisture stress, as impatiens does. Supplemental watering should be provided during prolonged dry times. Other than an occasional mealybug, pests are rare.

ADDITIONAL INFORMATION

I like to use the brilliantly colored foliage of sun coleus as a filler in fresh cutflower arrangements. Many gardeners are in the routine of using solid-green foliage as filler in flower arrangements, but there is not a more unique and vivid display than mixing sun coleus with other assorted flowers. The sun coleus will usually root in the vase and last seemingly forever.

ADDITIONAL SPECIES, CULTIVARS, OR VARIETIES

There are literally hundreds of named selections of sun coleus. 'Plum Parfait' and 'Burgundy Sun' are the most sun and heat tolerant; they were deemed super sun coleus in Texas bedding plant trials. 'Fancy', 'Eclipse', 'Spectrum', and 'Japanese Giant' are some of my favorites. 'Rustic Orange', 'Purple Emperor', and 'Dark Star' are great for Halloween fall container companion displays. Another variety of sun coleus that is always found in my garden is the so-called duckfoot coleus, available in colors of purple and green, green, yellow and purple, and red. These selections have more distinct foliage resembling a duck's foot. They are somewhat more compact and prostrate in growth, making better front or mid-level plants. Many of the duckfoot types are good choices to use in containers and hanging baskets.

Did You Know?

The genus species has recently been changed from Coleus blumei *to* Solenostemon scatellariodes. *Coleus is native to Indonesia and Africa.*

Swedish Ivy

Plectranthus species

Other Names: Plectranthus; Velvet Plant
Height: 4 to 36 in.
Spread: 12 to 24 in.
Flowers: Nonshowy; foliage use instead
Bloom Period: Summer

Color photograph on page 236.

Light Requirements:

Beneficial Characteristics:

Most plectranthus selections are grown more for their foliage than their flowers. This genus has a huge number of species with numerous and often confusing common names. Most gardeners are familiar with the so-called houseplant Swedish ivy (*P. coleoides*) and its trailing, variegated, waxy foliage. Numerous other species have brilliant, upright foliage instead, which is useful as a contrast bedding plant and even more as an impressive container companion plant. Many of the *Plectranthus* species will grow in shade or sun. The color and texture are similar to those of dusty miller and artemesia, providing soothing contrast to any landscape. Experimenting with foliage color plants can be very rewarding and advantageous. *Plectranthus* species are no exceptions.

WHEN TO PLANT

Like most tropicals, plectranthus should be planted in late April, May, or June after the last chance of frost is past.

WHERE TO PLANT

Use many of the *Plectranthus* species as companion contrast plants in patio container displays, or plant them in landscape beds. A big portion of the *Plectranthus* species has aromatic foliage, making the plants good choices in herbal gardens. This foliage charmer prefers average soils. It accepts organic soils but may have overly vigorous foliage.

HOW TO PLANT

Space plants 18 to 24 in. apart. Loosen potbound roots before planting. Plant them at the same depth that they were grown in containers, in holes slightly wider than the rootballs. Mulch them for moisture retention and weed control. Water them after planting and as needed throughout the growing season.

CARE AND MAINTENANCE

Depending on the species, plectranthus can send out unappealing flower spikes. Trim them during the season to keep the plants more presentable.

Also like sun coleus, the plants achieve more uniform and bushy growth when pinched at planting and throughout the growing season. Fertilizer sidedressing is seldom needed. There is no pest of significant harm, although whiteflies can be problems in the greenhouse.

ADDITIONAL INFORMATION

Plectranthus goes with flowers of almost any color. These plants make nice cutflower companions in fresh arrangements, and they are ornamental by themselves.

ADDITIONAL SPECIES, CULTIVARS, OR VARIETIES

P. argnetatus, or silver plectranthus, is a soothing velvety blue gray. 'Quick Silver' is one named selection. *P. mboionicus*, or oregano plectranthus or Cuban oregano, is a variegated green and creamy yellow with a more prostrate growth. 'Athen's Gem' is an improved cultivar, which previously won a Georgia Gold Medal Award as an outstanding landscape bedding plant in 1998. *P. coleoides*, *P. madagascarienses*, and *P. minimus* are trailing prostrate types with assorted variegated foliage colors of green and white or yellow. If you seek a plant with strong aroma, consider *P. purpuratus*, which has a strong menthol scent.

 Did You Know?

The showy flowering types of plectranthus include P. fruticosa, P. hilliardiae, *and* P. andoertendahlii *species. The flower colors and shapes range from tubular lavender to lacy white resembling candles.*

Swiss Chard

Beta vulgaris

Other Names: Ornamental Chard, Leaf Beet, or Swiss Beet
Height: 18 to 24 in.
Spread: 12 to 18 in.
Flowers: Non-showy (grown for foliage and stems)
Bloom Period: Foliage color in fall, spring, or early summer

Color photograph on page 236.

Light Requirements:

Beneficial Characteristics:

If you don't think a vegetable can be used as an ornamental . . . think again. As a matter of fact, 'Bright Light's Swiss chard' was named an All-America Selections Winner in 1998. This lovely textured plant is a cool-season vegetable grown during the same seasons as spinach, lettuce, and broccoli. When used as an ornamental, it is grown during the same time as pansy, dianthus, snapdragon, and calendula—although it is not as frost tolerant. Its upright stemmy growth is available in a mix of colors including pink, red, violet, yellow, gold, and creamy white. As the plant grows, the erect stems support luscious green foliage highlighted with colorful veins.

WHEN TO PLANT
The seed can be planted indoors in containers in late January or early February for transplanting around March—or direct-seed into the ground in early March. Plants can be grown in the fall for a cool-season autumn display as well. Start fall transplants 4 to 5 weeks earlier around mid-August, or direct-seed in September.

WHERE TO PLANT
The brilliant rainbow of colors brightens up any landscape as a border plant or in groups as a focal planting. The plants are nice when used as background in association with pansies, tulips, or other cool-season bedding plants. The towering cluster of color will nicely emerge through pansies when used as a ground cover. Swiss chard is also suitable for containers.

HOW TO PLANT
What appears to be one large seed is actually a cluster of individual seeds characteristic of the beet family. The seed should be planted approximately 1/2 in. deep and 18 to 24 in. apart. Later, as the seedlings emerge, the cluster of plants can be thinned to 4 to 6 in. apart. This allows for larger, showier

stems and foliage. Container-grown bedding plants are becoming more available at local garden centers; they should be planted at the 18- to 24-in. spacing. Full-sun locations are best, although the succulent plants will also tolerate some light or afternoon shade. As is true for any vegetable or bedding-type plant, good, rich, fertile, well-drained soils are best.

CARE AND MAINTENANCE

Soon after germination the spindly seedlings look fragile, but in a matter of weeks the plants become stately erect stems similar to those of rhubarb. Leave the plants alone for brilliant seasonal color and texture—or, if you are tempted, harvest a few of the leaves as they grow for consumption. Cut the outside leaves near the ground. This allows the center of the plant to continue its display of non-stop color. New stems and foliage will also emerge. The plants will grow up until the temperatures begin to get scorching hot in July or August where they can then be removed. Don't worry though, in those showy beds where summer color is needed use lantana, copper plant, scaevola, firebush, and sun coleus. These tough plants can easily be planted in the middle of summer without any problems. In milder summers, Swiss chard may grow all season long. In the fall, Swiss chard will tolerate some light frost once established and can even survive the entire winter during mild years. Potential pests include aphids and an occasional spider mite.

ADDITIONAL INFORMATION

The flavor of the cultivar 'Bright Lights' is especially mild. The leaves are great fresh in salads or on sandwiches. The fleshy stems can be sautéed or steamed. It even makes a nice substitute for rhubarb in some recipes.

ADDITIONAL SPECIES, CULTIVARS, OR VARIETIES

'Bright Lights' is the All-America Selection with a rainbow mix of colors. There are varieties with single colors like 'Bright Yellow', 'Vulcan Red', 'Lucullus' (lime green), and 'Ruby Red'. 'Fordhook' or 'Giant Chard' is the standard green Swiss chard with larger stalks and crinkled green glossy foliage.

 Did You Know?

Okra, pepper, sweet potato, lettuce, strawberry, and peanuts also make nice landscape ornamental edibles.

Twinspur

Diascia hybrids

Other Name: Diascia
Height: 10 to 14 in.
Spread: 10 to 14 in.
Flowers: Shades of pink
Bloom Period: Summer

Color photograph on page 236.

Light Requirements:

Beneficial Characteristics:

Many of our plants have a European influence, and diascia is no exception. It is a fairly new introduction to the United States and one well worth the wait. This dainty, cascading plant has masses of tubular flowers that are borne throughout the summer. The plants are perfect for flower beds, windowboxes, containers, and hanging baskets. My first experience with diascia was as a bedding plant grown at the studio gardens of *Oklahoma Gardening*. We used it in a mailbox planter and as a bedding plant. It definitely performed best in afternoon shade and in moist sites. It is a great selection for the entire state when it has some protection from the hot summer conditions.

WHEN TO PLANT

Plant twinspur in the spring after the last chance of frost is past. Start seed indoors ten to fourteen weeks before planting outside.

WHERE TO PLANT

Twinspur likes a site that receives afternoon sun. Filtered or dappled sun is acceptable, but it does not like full shade or full sun. The plants have a tendency to cascade as they grow without becoming invasive. Plant them in any container setting or in the front of a partially shaded flower bed. Good, rich garden soils are ideal. The soils should be somewhat acidic and moisture retentive but not waterlogged.

HOW TO PLANT

Dig a planting hole that is slightly wider than the rootball and as deep as the plant was grown in the container. Space plants 12 to 14 in. apart. Mulching is essential for twinspur to retain soil moisture, moderate hot summer temperatures, and minimize weed growth.

CARE AND MAINTENANCE

Twinspur seldom requires attention. The flowers are self-cleaning and bloom all season without shearing or trimming. Heat, drought, and full sun will most likely shut the plants down from flowering and occasionally scorch the foliage under severe conditions. Like most annuals, diascia responds well to supplemental feedings throughout the season. Water-soluble fertilizers applied at the time of watering work nicely on a regular basis. Supplemental moisture will be required during a drought. Other than the possibility of aphids and spider mites, pests are not a major concern.

ADDITIONAL INFORMATION

Several species of *Diascia* as well as hybrid crosses are used in the landscape trade. *D. barberae, D. rigescens,* and *D. vigilis* are the most commonly sold seasonal plants. *D. vigilis* selections and crosses are thought to be more tolerant to summer heat but prefer afternoon or dappled shade in the southern part of the state. Some selections may overwinter in southern Zone 7b of Oklahoma.

ADDITIONAL SPECIES, CULTIVARS, OR VARIETIES

'Ruby Field' (pink) was the first introduction into the United States. 'Pink Queen' and 'Elliot's Variety' (peachy pink) soon followed. More recently released are 'Summer's Dance' (salmon) and 'Strawberry Sundae' (strawberry pink).

 Did You Know?

Diascia is native to South Africa.

Vinca

Catharanthus roseus

Other Names: Periwinkle; Annual Vinca
Height: 8 to 18 in.
Spread: 12 to 18 in.
Flowers: Pink, white, or lavender
Bloom Period: Summer

Color photograph on page 236.

Light Requirements:

Beneficial Characteristics:

What would a garden be without the big, bold, nonstop flowers of annual vincas? The soothing colors in various shades of pink, lavender, rose, and white are truly a staple of the bedding plant industry. The popularity of these plants almost always puts them in the top ten-selling bedding plants from year to year. Thanks to their tolerance of heat, vincas are always dependable bloomers from spring to frost. The colors go with almost any other annual display. One of the most commented-on annual beds at our display gardens included annual vinca 'Raspberry Red' as the mid-level plant with *Calibrachoa* 'Trailing Pink' as the low-growing border and 'Ruby Giant' Joseph's coat as the background plant. The various shades of violet and purple made for a truly stunning summer-long display.

WHEN TO PLANT

Vinca does not tolerate cool, wet feet. The bedding plants definitely need to be planted in late April in southern Oklahoma and in May in the rest of the state. Annual periwinkle is also a great rotational plant with pansy plantings. As soon as the pansies are removed in May, the vincas can take their place.

WHERE TO PLANT

Border or mass plantings suit these plants perfectly. Vincas, especially the trailing types, are even adapted to containers and hanging baskets. Fertile organic soils with good drainage are a must. Heavy waterlogged sites mean certain death to these bedding plants. Vincas prefer full-sun locations and can tolerate no more than a half day of shade.

HOW TO PLANT

Space plants on 12- to 15-in. centers. Do not mulch these plants too thickly around the stems, or root rot can occur. Mulch more thickly between plants and with finer products. Water them after planting, but allow the planting sites to dry between waterings.

Care and Maintenance

Annual vinca is notorious for rotting in cool, damp soils early in the season when it is planted too early. The soil temperatures need to warm up considerably before you plant these picky annuals. Another problem with periwinkles is caused when they are planted in the same site year after year. The root rot pathogens can build up in numbers and become problematic if rotational planting does not occur. Like most annuals, vincas need to be rotated from the same planting site at least every couple of years to avoid this misfortune. Overwatering early on after planting can be detrimental. As the soil and air temperatures begin to sizzle, water the plants on a more consistent schedule. Supplemental feedings are not needed unless they are grown in poor soils or they show symptoms of nutrient deficiency.

Additional Information

Most periwinkles are started from seed in the bedding plant industry, but home owners will find it easier to purchase inexpensive container-grown plants. The flowers come in solid colors or with white or yellow centers, or eyes and often reseed themselves in ground beds.

Additional Species, Cultivars, or Varieties

Many of the selections are sold in a series with assorted colors. Heat Wave, Peppermint, Pretty In, Tropicana, Pacifica, and Cooler Series are some of the most popular to date. The Little Series is more compact in growth, averaging about 10 in. in height. 'Passion', 'Blue Peal', and 'Caribbean Lavender' are releases in the race for a bluer flower. 'Santa Fe' and 'Terrace Vermilion' are uniquely salmon colored with large flowers. Low-growing, more prostrate periwinkles to consider for hanging baskets or front border plants are the Mediterranean Series, 'Cascade Appleblossom' and 'Vining Pink Star'.

Did You Know?

Annual periwinkle is often confused with the perennial vincas— Vinca minor *and* Vinca major.

ANNUALS

Waffle Plant

Hemigraphis alternata

Other Names: Red Ivy; Red Flame
Height: 6 to 8 in.
Spread: 8 to 12 in.
Flowers: White; grown more for foliage
Bloom Period: Summer

Color photograph on page 236.

Light Requirements:

Beneficial Characteristics:

Most shade gardens are somewhat limited when it comes to annual flower color. Waffle plant is a nice foliage color plant with small, white, tubular blooms tolerant of most shade garden sites. I first became familiar with this plant as a border in assorted beds at Cypress Gardens in Florida. The colorful plant was grown as a bedding plant in partially shaded sites and occasionally in full sun with mulch and moisture-retentive soils. The burgundy-green foliage was quite striking, especially with white-flowering companions. The foliage itself was showy in part because of its color but also because of its crinkled or twisted appearance, thus the name waffle plant. In Oklahoma the plants prefer afternoon or filtered shade. They make stunning hanging baskets. Waffle plant is often found in the foliage section of garden centers where it is sold as a houseplant.

When to Plant
Plant it in beds outside after the chance of frost is past in late spring.

Where to Plant
The low-growing prostrate growth makes a nice ground cover where it frequently roots along the purple stems as it spreads. It is by no means invasive and works great in borders or as filler. One plant will easily fill a 10-in. hanging basket. Use waffle plants as companion plants in container displays with other shade-loving plants. Humus-rich, moisture-retentive soils are perfect. The plants require quite a bit of moisture, especially during drought periods.

How to Plant
Space plants on 12-in. centers. Mulching is a must with this plant to keep the soil moist.

Care and Maintenance
When planted in more sun, waffle plant frequently wilts in the heat of the day. Because irrigation is often needed, place the plants where there is easy

access to water. The plants are truly striking, and the small flower is self-cleaning. The plants are trouble free; they need hardly any attention. They respond to supplemental feedings, especially in poorer soils. Insect pests include whiteflies primarily in the greenhouse and an occasional aphid.

ADDITIONAL INFORMATION

The purple and dark-green colors are perfect for pink or white color combinations. Shade-loving impatiens are excellent companions for waffle plants as well as Persian shield.

ADDITIONAL SPECIES, CULTIVARS, OR VARIETIES

I am aware of no named cultivars in the bedding plant industry to date. Occasionally, gardeners can find a more straplike selection and a smooth, more metallic variety. The plants are almost always sold as waffle plant, or *H. alternata*. All require the same growing conditions and make exceptional shade-loving bedding or container plants.

Did You Know?

Hemigraphis is actually an Asian herb grown primarily in the United States as a tropical bedding plant.

CHAPTER NINE

Turfgrasses

G ARDENERS OFTEN HAVE A LOVE-HATE RELATIONSHIP with turfgrass. Some spend countless but rewarding hours mowing, fertilizing, weeding, and watering. Others dread the very thought of having to mow weekly, let alone expending more funds or time, no matter how impeccably groomed the neighbor's lawn. Turfgrass plays an important role in our landscape. It helps in erosion control, pollution suppression, and temperature moderation, and it is a barrier for outdoor activities. Use turf wisely. Make landscape beds curve naturally with your mowing pattern so that you do not have to stop and back up. In narrower locations, for example, between the sidewalk and the street, avoid using grass. Such sites are hard to mow and dangerous. Consider instead a ground cover that does not need frequent mowing or an ornamental grass that needs a "haircut" only once a year.

ESTABLISHMENT

Turfgrass is started one of two ways—by seed or vegetatively by sod, plugs, or sprigs. Some improved selections are available only vegetatively because of sterile or same-sex plants. Killing existing vegetation with a nonselective herbicide such as glyphosate or glufosinate-ammonium before starting the lawn is worth the investment. It may take several applications of either of these nonselective herbicides to get a complete kill. Soil preparation is vital. Begin with a soil test so that you can discover exactly the nutritional status of the site. Incorporate soil pH-changing products, such as lime and sulfur, as well as slow-moving nutrients, such as phosphorus and potassium, into the soil ahead of time or at planting. The chart on page 15 can assist with amounts to apply based on an existing soil test.

Gently incorporate seed into the loosely worked ground 1/8 to 1/4 in. deep for Bermuda, zoysia, and fescue, but deeper for buffalo grass at 1/2 in. When seeding, apply half the amount in one direction, and the other half in the opposite direction to get better coverage. Rolling the soil with a sod roller provides better contact with the seed and levels the surface. The soil should be moist, not soggy, with either rainfall or daily irrigation for at least ten to fourteen days. Water more in depth and less frequently after the seedlings emerge.

Place sod on loosely worked soil. Layer the sod in a brickwork arrangement to better secure the edges. Again roll the site, and keep it moist for several weeks until the roots have penetrated the ground. Once pegging is evident, water less frequently but for longer periods of time. Plugs are square or circular pieces cut from sod or existing turf areas and spaced 6 to 18 in. on average. Sprigs are the runners or stolons of the grass containing at least four nodes or leaf/root areas. Sprigs are placed beneath the soil with 1/4 to 1/2 in. exposed in alternating rows, again 6 to 18 in. apart, depending on how quickly a fill is needed. Having well-prepared soil, which is rolled and consistently moist, is the standard lawn-starting tip.

MOWING

Home owners take for granted that they know how to mow grass, but it is often done incorrectly. No more than one-third of the leaf area should be removed at any mowing. In other words, to maintain a turf at 1 in., mow it when it reaches 1 1/2 in. Collecting grass clippings is not needed when mowing by these guidelines unless several days or weeks have passed between mowings. Mulching mowers or blade conversion kits are well worth the investment to further pulverize the leaf blades for natural composting into the lawn. Contrary to popular belief, scalping the grass does not reduce the frequency of mowing, and it severely stresses the plants as well as allows more weed encroachment. Mowing according to this one-third rule will not cause thatch, which is a layer of undecayed grass found between the soil and green leaves. Thatch is primarily caused from excessive growth as a result of improper watering and overfertilizing. Keeping a sharp lawn mower blade is of utmost importance so that leaf blades are not torn, which may cause more stress and invite disease. Changing the mowing direction pattern each time prevents further compaction of the soil. Soil compaction can cause problems and usually requires coring or aeration of the lawn.

FERTILIZING

Feeding the lawn with the appropriate fertilizer ratio should be based on a soil test, which should be done every couple of years. The test takes the guessing out and saves money because nutrients are not overapplied. Fertilizer rates are based on 1 lb. of actual nitrogen per 1000 sq. ft. Consider this example using the complete fertilizer 13-13-13. The rate based on this standard formula would be calculated by dividing 1 by .13 (7.7 lb. per 1000 sq. ft. since there is only 13 percent actual nitrogen). The chart on page 14 provides additional fertilizer rates. This formula works, no matter what the nitrogen, phosphorus, or potassium amount. Slow-release, water-soluble, controlled-release, or organic products are considered more guarded as far as leaching after the application.

There are more scientific ways to apply fertilizer uniformly, but I have found in smaller lawns that a hand-held broadcast applicator or seeder works nicely. I can weigh the applicator before and after it is filled with the granular product, and I know how much I am applying based on my prefigured rate. In larger lawns drop and rotary spreaders are the norm.

Apply half the amount of fertilizer one way and the other half the opposite direction to minimize skips and burns. There can still be overlap and skips, but it is better than applying the rate too strong one way. Water the fertilizer as soon as possible to prevent foliage or root burning. Do not apply fertilizer when lawns are severely stressed from heat and drought.

WATERING

Watering early in the morning is better for the lawn. Early-evening watering is often more convenient but is more likely to invite problems. Grass that is watered in the early evening remains wet for a longer period of time, which can potentially increase disease influence. Watering through the night or early morning allows the grass to dry from the morning sun more quickly. The normal rate to apply is 1 to 2 in. per week, depending on the severity of the heat and drought. The best rule to remember is to water more in depth and less often, a practice that encourages deeper, stronger roots more tolerant of drought, cold, and pests. Short and frequent watering does more harm by encouraging shallower roots more susceptible to the elements.

To calibrate your watering system, whether it is an in-ground irrigation system or an oscillating attachment, place several shallow containers in the watering zone of the system. Leave it on for thirty minutes, and measure the average depth. If the average is 1/2 in., then your system applies 1/2 in. in thirty minutes. Allowing the grass to show early signs of moisture stress is a good way to gauge when to water. These symptoms include a grayish color of the foliage, grass being slow to pop up after being walked on, and leaf blades folding in half vertically.

PESTS

Insect, disease, and weed problems are always potential threats to Oklahoma turfgrasses. Healthy lawns can more easily resist these problems. A thicker lawn will smother out sun-loving weeds. Seeking the proper identification of these pests from your local Extension service or nursery professional will help in the appropriate management and control practices.

VARIETIES

The four most commonly grown and adapted lawn grasses in Oklahoma are Bermuda, buffalo, tall fescue, and zoysia. Other grasses, such as centipede, St. Augustine, and perennial rye, are found in the state but not suitable overall. Always check for localized adaptation research before investing in new cultivars. A great resource is the National Turf Evaluation Program Web site at http://hort.unl.edu/ntep/.

Bermuda

Cynodon dactylon

Height: Maintain at 1¹/₂ in.
(mow when 2¹/₄ in.)
Color: Medium green
Texture: Fine
Seeding Rate: Seed 2 lb./1000 sq. ft.;
sprigs 3 to 10 bu./1000 sq. ft.
Fertilize: Late April, June, and August;
or May and July
Zones: 6a, 6b, 7a, 7b

Light Requirements:

Bermuda grass is native to Africa. It has successfully naturalized in Oklahoma, thanks to early introductions as a pasture grass. The best time to establish Bermuda is in late April, May, or June. July and August are acceptable but more stressful because of heat and drought. Fall planting is not recommended since there is little time to establish the grass before winter. Weed-and-feed products, although convenient, are not always the best management tool in Oklahoma with our warm-season grasses. Preemergence herbicide applications should be done separately from fertilizer applications, which should be applied in April or May when the grass actually starts to grow.

It needs water at the weekly 1- to 2-in. rate throughout the growing season, including rainfall. The average cutting height of Bermuda is typically 1¹/₂ in., but a more balanced maintenance program would be 1 in. as it breaks dormancy, gradually increasing to 2 in. during the summer and to 2¹/₂ in. during the fall. The increase in height helps the grass make the transition from coping with summer heat stress, then drought, then winter harshness. Dwarf hybrids can be maintained at a lower height, but they, too, need a gradual increase as the season progresses. Space sprigs and plugs 6 to 18 in. apart, depending on the quickness of coverage preferred. Bermuda seed is available hulled or unhulled. Hulled is more expensive and generally means a quicker germination but only by a couple of days.

Cold-hardy selections are best for Oklahoma, especially in the northwest parts of the state. Spring dead spot is a common problem directly related to the cultivar and its cold tolerance. It is basically caused by a fungus, which feeds on the roots and does not allow the top to green up in the spring. The large, sometimes overlapping dead spots will eventually fill in or can be replugged for quicker coverage. The best management practice to minimize this problem is to use cold-hardy strains and make the last fertilizer application in August. Feedings later than that will stimulate growth that is susceptible to disease and winter injury.

A common practice of many home owners is overseeding Bermuda with ryegrass for green color in winter. Annual rye is most affordable and applied at a rate of 8 to 10 lb. per 1000 sq. ft. anytime from mid-September to the first of November. Maintain the ryegrass at 2¹/₂ in., or mow when the grass reaches 3¹/₄ in. Reduce the mowing height in the spring, so the Bermuda will not be delayed in breaking dormancy.

The most commonly available seed types are 'Guymon' (excellent cold hardiness), 'Arizona Common' (poor cold hardiness), 'NuMex Sahara' (marginal), and 'Sonesta' (marginal). 'Jackpot' and 'Mirage' are newer seed releases with better spring dead spot tolerance, turf quality, and texture.

Readily available vegetatively propagated types, usually sterile in flower production, include 'U-3', 'Tifway' ('Tifton 419'), and 'Tifgreen'. Relatively new to the turf industry with exceptional cold hardiness are 'Midiron' (hard to find and primarily available as sprigs) and 'Midlawn' (easier to find as sod, sprigs, or plugs). 'Tifsport' and 'Quickstand Common' (not sterile but only available vegetatively) are other cultivars with promising characteristics for the state.

Early introductions of pasture- or forage-type Bermudas were 'Greenfield', 'Midway', and 'Hardie'. These selections are not always favorable to lawn settings because of their quick growth, requiring more frequent mowing.

Buffalo

Buchloe dactyloides

Height: Maintain at 1½ to 2 in. (mow when 2¼ to 3 in.)
Color: Blue green
Texture: Fine
Seeding Rate: 1 to 2 lb. of seed burrs/ 1000 sq. ft.
Fertilize: May
Zones: 6a, 6b, 7a, 7b

Light Requirements:

Buffalo grass is a prairie native found in Oklahoma that performs nicely in most soil types, including neutral and alkaline. It actually performs best in the semiarid central and western regions of the state. Buffalo grass is a relatively slow-growing grass, requiring the least amount of watering, fertilizing, and mowing of the primary grasses used in the state. Once established, this native is very heat, drought, and cold tolerant. A popular benefit of buffalo is that it does not have to be mowed frequently. In some situations it does not have to be mowed at all, creating a soft, wavy, almost tufted appearance, reaching 6 to 8 in. In such cases the grass should be left unfertilized and seldom watered. Avoid overfertilizing and overwatering buffalo grass in any situation. It is especially important not to fertilize during a drought unless supplemental irrigation is available. If buffalo is grown as a typical lawn with routine mowing, it should be watered at 1 in. per week, including rainfall. Even though buffalo is drought tolerant, it should not be allowed to go completely dormant like Bermuda, especially the first season of planting.

Buffalo grass spreads by stolons and occasionally by seed in the landscape. There are separate male and female flowers. The male flowers shoot up quickly after mowing, forming what are known as seedheads, or flags, that are not always favorable for a lawn setting. As a result, new female types are being introduced into the turf trade. Buffalo grass is available by seed or vegetatively propagated. The so-called seed is actually a burr containing several individual seeds. Deburred seed is harder to find and quite expensive. Any such chemically treated process can be identified by a greenish- purple color on the seed. The seed should be planted deeper than most turfgrass, around ½ in. It can take several weeks for the seed to germinate. Sod, plugs, or sprigs can be used to start the grass. Overall, buffalo grass is fairly slow growing but not as slow as zoysia. Bermuda is faster growing, quickly encroaching into buffalo lawns, and may potentially take over. Keep Bermuda out with nonselective herbicide spot treatments.

Because buffalo is such a small part of the lawn industry, chemical labeling often excludes this turfgrass. Very few pest control products are officially labeled for use on buffalo grass.

Seed-propagated types are 'Bison', 'Texoka', 'Sharp's Improved', 'Topgun', 'Plains', and 'Comanche'. The seed types contain both male and female plants, which are not quite as appealing as the all-female types, but are improved over the native selection. 'Cody' and 'Tatanka' are the newest releases with even better turf characteristics.

Newly released vegetative varieties include 'Prairie' and '609'. Both are female selections more suitable for a lawn setting; '609' is a slightly darker green than 'Prairie'. 'Buffalawn' is an improved female strain. These are available through sod or plugs, but not seed.

Tall Fescue

Festuca arundinacea

Height: Maintain at 2¹/₂ to 3 in.
(mow at 3³/₄ to 4¹/₄ in.)
Color: Deep green
Texture: Coarse
Seeding Rate: 7 to 10 lb./1000 sq. ft.
for new lawns; overseed at 3 to
6 lb./1000 sq. ft.
Fertilize: March, May, and September
Zones: 6a, 6b, 7a, 7b

Light Requirements:

Fescue is the only cool-season grass tolerant of the hot summer temperatures of the state—and then only with supplemental irrigation. It is more adapted to the eastern half of the state, which receives more natural rainfall. Fescue puts on its best growth in the fall and early spring. As a result the maintenance schedule is somewhat different. The coarse leaf blade should be mowed higher than the fine-bladed grasses. Fescue is somewhat more shade tolerant than warm-season turfs but will not thrive in dense shade. Instead consider shrubs, ground covers, and perennials in more heavily shaded sites. When it is grown in partial shade, the height should be maintained at 3 to 4 in. to allow for more leaf surface. The mowing height should be raised during times of drought and heat stress in the summer. Fescue is a clumping grass and does not spread like warm-season types. It must be overseeded every one to two years to keep a thick, lawnlike appearance. Seeding should be done in the fall or spring during milder temperatures. Weed-and-feed products are suitable for this cool-season grass since the grass is actively growing during the application time. Match the product with the properly identified weeds to control and one labeled for fescue use. Precaution should be taken with any herbicide product used during the seeding process.

Fescue is the least-drought-tolerant grass in the state. During drought periods, it must receive supplemental irrigation of 1 to 2 in. per week, or it can go dormant and die, unlike Bermuda, which generally revives. Always water deeply and less often to encourage deep, strong roots. Because fescue is somewhat susceptible to a fungus disease known as brown patch, select cultivars more tolerant of this problem, and use blends of three to five cultivars in a mix. Pasture-forage fescues, such as 'Kentucky 31', 'Alta', 'Fawn', and 'Johnstone', typically are not as appealing in the landscape as the turf types.

There are numerous tall fescue cultivars on the market, with many coming and going each year. 'Houndog V', 'Crossfire II', 'Guardian', and the Rebel Series are a few performing consistently well in trials across the state. A recent introduction, 'Tulsa', appeared in preliminary tests to be more tolerant of the Oklahoma summers. Unfortunately, it also seems to be somewhat more susceptible to brown patch disease. Lower-growing tall fescues are often requested but are frequently less vigorous.

Fescue sod is infrequently sold because of its clumping growth habit. The sod readily falls apart, unlike other runner-type grasses.

Zoysia

Zoysia japonica

Height: Maintain at 3/4 to 1 1/2 in.
(mow at 1 1/8 to 2 1/4 in.)
Color: Rich green
Texture: Fine
Seeding Rate: 1 lb./1000 sq. ft.
Fertilize: Late April, June, and August;
or May and July
Zones: 6a, 6b, 7a, 7b

Light Requirements:

Zoysia is another popular warm-season turf in Oklahoma. It is slower in growth than Bermuda but fairly similar in other maintenance practices. Zoysia is a fine-textured grass with good green color, spreading by above-ground runners known as stolons. Establishing a zoysia lawn can take the bigger part of the summer for complete coverage (even with early planting) whereas Bermuda can spread and cover a site in a matter of weeks.

Overall, zoysia is thought of as a higher-maintenance lawn, requiring more water and fertilizer to perform at its peak. Be careful not to overdo it, or there can be problems with thatch. Zoysia is somewhat more shade tolerant than Bermuda but not at all tolerant of dense shade, as it is often portrayed to be. Plugs or sprigs should be placed 4 to 6 in. apart to get a quicker fill. The mowing height of zoysia should be raised as the growing season progresses to prepare for the winter months ahead. As with any turf-grass, water deeply and less often to encourage stronger roots. Fertilizer rates should be based on a soil test. Do not apply fertilizer when grass is stressed. After applying fertilizer, water to keep from burning the foliage. Bermuda can be a problem in zoysia since it is faster growing, especially during the establishment period. Spot-treat with a nonselective herbicide to keep Bermuda under control.

Weed-and-feed products are not always suitable for this warm-season grass. It is oftentimes better to apply a properly matched herbicide with the appropriate weeds as a postemergence or preventative control early in the season. And wait to apply the fertilizer separately when the grass begins to green and grow in late April or May.

'Sunrise' is a seed available in the common Korean type. In the case of zoysia, chemically treated, hulled seed is costly but well worth the investment for a better and somewhat faster germination.

Most zoysia grass is available through vegetative means and includes 'Meyer (Z-52 or S-52)', 'Matrella', and 'Emerald'. 'Belair', 'Midwest', and 'Cashmere' are older types occasionally resurfacing in the trade, which have poor cold tolerance in Oklahoma. 'Meyer' is the most cold-hardy selection, followed by 'Matrella' and 'El Toro' (hard to find). There are many new selections with improved density, vigor, and finer texture in the works, one of which is 'Cavalier'.

CHAPTER TEN

Natives as Ornamentals

GARDENERS HAVE SHOWN AN ACTIVE INTEREST in using native plants in the landscape. Just drive across the state and you will see Oklahoma's beautiful and diverse native or naturalized habitat—everything from pines to blackjacks, wildflowers to prairie grass. Native plants are plants that grow without cultivation and are indigenous to an area without being artificially introduced. Naturalized plants are those that have been introduced but have escaped cultivation and continue to thrive and reproduce.

In either case, the plants grow well on their own without assistance from gardeners. This characteristic is usually interpreted to mean that natives are low-maintenance, tough plants, and they can be, but only if they are matched to the proper growing conditions. Native or naturalized plants flourish in very specific preferred sites. For example, dogwoods are native to the state in moist, loamy sites where they are understory trees in filtered shade. Plant this native in full sun next to a hot concrete driveway in heavy soil, however, and dogwood will not readily survive.

Collection of native plants is often controversial among gardeners. Major concerns are that plants may become extinct or that some plants may become invasive threats when introduced into cultivated locations. It is best to buy propagated plants from reliable nurseries specializing in tried-and-tested native plants. You may be surprised to learn that many plants already in the nursery trade are "Oklahoma originals." Some mail-order companies specialize in native plants, but you need to do your homework in selecting plants adapted to your particular region. On page 341 is a list of native plant organizations and nurseries to assist you in locating particular plants.

The native plants in this chapter are quite diverse and include trees, shrubs, ground covers, vines, perennials, and some of their cultivars. For additional growing tips, refer to the specific introduction in the chapter related to the particular category of plant, such as Perennials or Trees. I have included only a few of my favorite Oklahoma natives that have a lot to offer landscape settings.

Native Plant Nature Trails, Gardens, and Arboretums

**Alabaster Caverns State Park and
Nature Trail**
Rt. 1, Box 32
Freedom, OK 73842
(580) 621-3381

**Chickasaw National Recreation
Area and Park**
P.O. Box 201
Sulphur, OK 73086
(580) 622-3165

Clear Creek Farms and Gardens
P.O. Box 89
Peggs, OK 74452
(918) 598-3782

Martin Park Nature Center
5000 W. Memorial Rd.
Oklahoma City, OK 73142
(405) 755-0676

Oklahoma Native Plant Society
c/o Tulsa Garden Center
2435 South Peoria
Tulsa, OK 74114

**Oklahoma Wildscape Certification
Non-game Wildlife Program**
Oklahoma Department of Wildlife
Conservation
1801 N. Lincoln
Oklahoma City, OK 73105
(405) 521-4616

Oxley Nature Center
6700 E. Mohawk Blvd.
Tulsa, OK 74115
(918) 669-6644

Sunshine Nursery and Arboretum
Rt. 1, Box 4030
Clinton, OK 73601
(580) 323-6259

**Tallgrass Prairie Preserve/Nature
Conservancy**
Box 458
Pawhuska, OK 74056
(918) 287-4803

**Wichita Maintains National
Wildlife Refuge and Nature Trail**
Rt. 1, Box 448
Indiahoma, OK 73552
(580) 429-3222

American Beautyberry

Callicarpa americana

Other Names: Callicarpa; French or Spanish Mulberry; Sour Bush; Sow Berry
Height: 3 to 8 ft.
Spread: 3 to 4 ft.
Flowers: Lavender pink
Bloom Period: Late summer
Zones: 6b, 7a, 7b

Color photograph on page 236.

Light Requirements:

Beneficial Characteristics:

This delightful shrub is native to the southeastern United States, including the southeastern locales of Oklahoma. There is not much to the deciduous plant early in the season, but it makes up for the deficiency in the fall with its beautiful lavender berries. The pale-green foliage is somewhat aromatic and leaves are arranged opposite each other on the long stems. By late June—and sometimes even later, depending on the individual plant—the shrub begins to flower profusely. The bloom period can be prolonged into August and later. Most of the time the blooms are a lavender or rosy pink formed in clusters along the leaf nodes. The showy clusters of fruit emerge in August through November, starting out almost translucent to a creamy greenish brown before they mature into a vibrant purple 1/4 to 1/8 in. in size. They often remain a few weeks after the foliage drops until they are consumed by wildlife friends. Many species of birds and a few mammals, such as raccoons, opossums, and foxes, enjoy the fruit throughout the winter. Use this lovely native as a colorful fall enhancer for the landscape and you will not be disappointed.

WHEN TO PLANT

Plant beautyberry in the spring or early fall. Container-grown plants are often available in 1-, 2-, or 3-gal. specimens. Beautyberry is fairly common within the nursery trade.

WHERE TO PLANT

The natural habitat of beautyberry is in rich, moist woodlands where it receives partial sun as an understory plant. It is often found in thickets of massed plants, which when mirrored in the landscape make a brilliant fall display. Plant it in organic, moisture-retentive soils. It prefers afternoon shade or lightly filtered shade. Be careful not to place beautyberry in too much shade or the plants will become straggly with poorer berry production. It sometimes accepts full-sun sites with wind protection and adequate organic, moist soils.

How to Plant

Dig the planting holes the same depth as and two to three times wider than the rootballs. For a mass planting, space the plants 4 to 5 ft. apart. Water after planting and on a regular basis until the plants are securely established. Mulch is very crucial to simulate a woodsy site, holding moisture, keeping soil temperatures mild during the summer, and providing slow-release nutrients.

Care and Maintenance

Pruning is needed only to train or control the size of the large shrub. Some gardeners prune beautyberries yearly to keep them bushier and more compact, depending on the landscape design. Occasionally, dormant pruning may be done to remove dead, weak, rubbing, or damaged branches. The fruit are produced on new or current-season growth; therefore, the plants are best pruned during the dormant season. Avoid excess fertility with supplemental feedings, or overgrown, leggy growth can occur. The original organic soil is usually sufficient. Supplemental irrigation will be necessary during prolonged drought periods. Pests are of minimal concern.

Additional Information

It may take several years for the plant to mature and produce berries, depending on the genetic makeup of the plant and its planting site. Other *Callicarpa* species include *bodinieri* (bodinier beautyberry) and *dichotoma* (purple beautyberry), which are also found in the nursery trade. Both are introduced from China and come in purple- or white-fruiting varieties. 'Profusion' is a selection of *bodinieri* with more prolific berry set. Japanese beautyberry (*C. japonica*) is another frequently grown species also available in lavender- or white-fruiting forms. 'Virginia' is a hybrid cross of *C. japonica* and *C. tosaensis* with larger, violet berries and clusters.

Additional Species, Cultivars, or Varieties

'Lactea' is a beautiful white-flowering and fruiting cultivar of native *C. americana*. There is also a purple-fruiting *americana* species in the trade.

Did You Know?

The Greek name sums up this native in two words, kallos *(beauty) and* karpos *(fruit).*

Blazing Star

Liatrus spicata

Other Names: Gayfeather;
  Button Snakeroot
Height: 2 to 4 ft.
Spread: 1 to 3 ft.
Flowers: Purple, pink, or white
Bloom Period: Summer
Zones: 6a, 6b, 7a, 7b

Color photograph on page 236.

Light Requirements:

Beneficial Characteristics:

Oklahoma is home to several species of this perpendicular-growing perennial. Some bloom early in the summer, others in midsummer, and a few in the fall. Fortunately, their growing conditions are similar—they prefer well-drained soils. Most of the plants are rhizomatous; that is, they slowly spread into colonies or clumps by underground rhizomes. They should not worry gardeners, though, because they are seldom invasive. The erect and showy flower spikes add a unique appearance to the perennial garden. The flowers start blooming on the top of the spike and make their way down so that they have a fairly long bloom period. This native loves the summer heat and brightens up any perennial display.

WHEN TO PLANT
Blazing star is sold as container-grown plants, bare-root corms, or rhizomes. Plant it in the spring, early summer, or fall. Seed can be used to start this perennial native, but two years from seeding to flowering are required.

WHERE TO PLANT
This plant is usually found in somewhat moist, loamy native soils, primarily in full sun. In the landscape it is not too picky as long as it has good drainage. Blazing star accepts sites in partial shade but no more than three or four hours of shade. It is often used in perennial flower beds or in wildflower meadows.

HOW TO PLANT
Plant container-grown blazing star at the same depth that it was growing and in a hole slightly wider than the rootball. Plant bare-root blazing star at a depth of 4 to 6 in. and 3 ft. apart. Water the plants after planting and on a regular basis until they are well established. Mulch after planting to keep the soil moist and weed free.

CARE AND MAINTENANCE

The dormant growth should be cut back each spring before the new growth emerges. Many times the rhizomatous roots will rot during the winter in sites that hold too much winter moisture. Leaving the tops on will often divert water. These plants can be planted somewhat shallow and mulched to avoid rotting problems, similar to the way in which iris is planted. Supplemental feedings are seldom needed in nutrient-rich soils. Poor soils may occasionally need sidedressing, especially when plants begin to look chlorotic, or yellow.

ADDITIONAL INFORMATION

Bees and butterflies enjoy the notable flower spikes. They make great fresh cutflower arrangements by themselves or in combination with other cut flowers. The flower spikes can be staked or allowed to naturally cascade along the ground during the bloom period.

ADDITIONAL SPECIES, CULTIVARS, OR VARIETIES

Several species are found in the state. *L. aspera* var. *intermedia* is found primarily in eastern Oklahoma; it has pink, late-summer blooms. Dotted snakeroot (*L. punctata*) is found in the western part of the state; it has purple blooms in the fall. Elegant blazing star (*L. elegans*) is found in purple- or white-blooming stands, predominantly in northeastern locales. Central and eastern areas are home to prairie button snakeroot (*L. pycnostachya*), which blooms in late summer with purple flowers. Spike gayfeather is found in more moist, southeastern counties; it is often taller with linear purple or white flowers. *L. spicata* and *L. scariosa* are the most frequently used species in the landscape or garden. Improved or named selections include 'Kobold' (gnome), with mauve-pink, more compact spikes, and 'Silver Tip', which is very tall with lavender flowers. 'Alba' is white', and 'August Glory' blooms earlier with bluish-purple flowers. 'Floristan Violet' has more violet flowers, and 'Floristan Weiss' has cream-white blooms. Although not common in Oklahoma native landscapes, *L. microcephala* is a landscape plant with dwarf growth, around 18 in.

 Did You Know?

Blazing star starts blooming from the top down instead of from the bottom up like most spiked flowers.

Bushy Bluestem

Andropogon glomeratus

Other Names: Bushy Broomsedge; Beardgrass
Height: 2 to 4 ft.
Spread: 2 to 3 ft.
Flowers: Off-white
Bloom Period: Fall
Zones: 6a, 6b, 7a, 7b

Color photograph on page 236.

Light Requirements:

Beneficial Characteristics:

Some people think of bluestem as a prairie native, but bushy bluestem is more commonly found in marshy, damp sites throughout eastern and southern Oklahoma. It is often called bushy broomsedge, but do not let that dampen your enthusiasm for it, especially if you are familiar with the dull-looking common broomsedge bluestem (*A. virginicus*). Common broomsedge is found in nutrient-starved pastures in eastern Oklahoma. Bushy bluestem, on the other hand, is quite attractive when taken out of its roadside or pasture setting and placed in the landscape. It has bushy, upright growth, but the flower spikes sent up in the fall are more compact. When grown in clumps, the grass offers a wonderful alternative texture to any landscape. The fall color is a more coppery gold or cinnamon color, and the dormant foliage holds up most of the winter.

WHEN TO PLANT

Plant bushy bluestem in the spring, summer, or fall. This beauty is hard to find in the nursery trade. You may have luck at nurseries in the state known for native plant material or specialty mail-order companies.

WHERE TO PLANT

Plant this unique native in groups of three or more for the best display in the landscape. Use it among colorful flowering perennial beds to offer eye-appealing texture and outline. The upright growth gives the appearance of height to shorter buildings and structures. Plant this deciduous native grass in combination with evergreen shrubs. Rich, moist garden soils often promote even more vigorous clumps. It prefers full sun but accepts a couple of hours of shade.

HOW TO PLANT

Check container-grown plants for potbound roots, and loosen the roots in severe cases. Place the plants in the ground at the same level that they were grown. Space the plants on 3- to 4-ft. centers. Mulch them to hold in more moisture and minimize weed growth. Water them at planting and on a regular basis.

CARE AND MAINTENANCE

The grass is very attractive during the winter. Leave the foliage on until early spring when it can be cut back 4 to 6 in. from the ground. Supplemental fertilizer is seldom needed. Pests are rare.

ADDITIONAL INFORMATION

The bushy plants are quite diverse, growing in moist or even waterlogged sites, and I have seen it grown in bog gardens. Big bluestem (*A. gerardii*), also known as turkey foot, is a prairie native that makes a great landscape plant, thanks to its blue-green foliage, purplish undertone flowers, and bronze-red fall color. 'Pawnee' is a robust, big bluestem variety selected for its superior fall color. *A. hallii*, or sand bluestem, is a dry-land, upright clumping grass with gray-green summer color and golden autumn color with a slightly red hue. *A. capillipes* is a species more common in the southeastern United States with a recent selection from Georgia named 'Valdosta Blue'. It has chalky-blue foliage reaching almost 4 ft. in height; its fall color is burgundy. Little bluestem (*Schizachyrium scoparium*) is very similar in appearance with delicate blue-green foliage and shorter growth, and it is more drought tolerant. Flowering stalks are topped with fuzzy flowers and seed. A couple of named selections include 'Blaze', with fine foliage and russet-red fall color, and 'The Blues', with more bluish foliage and pinkish flower spikes. Taxonomically speaking, botanists often list big and little bluestem in separate genera due to minute differences in the plants.

ADDITIONAL SPECIES, CULTIVARS, OR VARIETIES

Bushy bluestem or bushy broomsedge is primarily sold as the species.

 Did You Know?

*There is some debate about whether bushy bluestem (*A. glomeratus*) is a true native to our state or naturalized. In either case, it makes a lovely landscape companion.*

Butterfly Weed

Asclepias tuberosa

Other Names: Silkweed; Milkweed; Indian Posy; Orange Root
Height: 2 to 4 ft.
Spread: 2 to 3 ft.
Flowers: Orange, yellow, red, pink, or white
Bloom Period: Late spring to midsummer
Zones: 6a, 6b, 7a, 7b

Color photograph on page 236.

Light Requirements:

Beneficial Characteristics:

Milkweed is a common name used to describe the plant's milky sap, silkweed describes the plant's silky-soft, almost white hairs, and butterfly weed describes its tendency to attract—you guessed it—butterflies. This native is often found along roadsides, in pastures, and now frequently in the landscape. The showy clusters of flowers are very appealing to the home owner for aesthetic purposes and for the wide range of butterflies that frequently visit the blooms. Most have deep, fleshy taproots almost tuberous in appearance, thus the species name. They grow best in full sun and thrive in poor, dry soils. Butterfly weed is a good choice for a butterfly garden and perfect for hot, dry, perennial garden sites.

WHEN TO PLANT

Plant butterfly weed in the spring or early summer.

WHERE TO PLANT

Use this colorful beauty as a component plant in the perennial garden where it can be left undisturbed. The showy, starlike flowers enhance this plant's usefulness by itself or in groups. It prefers full-sun locations. In its native location butterfly weed is most commonly found in dry, poor pasture or prairie soils throughout the state. Organic, humus-rich sites are not favorable to this plant unless they drain extremely well.

HOW TO PLANT

Place the container-grown plants in medium-height garden spots. Start seed-grown plants in a container in late winter or early spring. Place the plant at the same depth that it was grown, in a hole several times wider than the rootball. Space butterfly weed on 3- to 4-ft. centers when planting it in groups. Mulching is beneficial to keep weeds in check.

CARE AND MAINTENANCE

Butterfly weed is late to emerge in the spring. Avoid planting it in sites where there will be frequent disturbance of the roots. In other words, planting it in an annual bed is not a good idea. Waterlogged soils mean sure death to this plant unless it is swamp milkweed (*A. incarnata*). Overzealous care and fertilization are not recommended. This plant is truly low maintenance when it is planted in the right location. Most of the time butterfly weed will produce long, pointy seedpods. These can be removed and the flowers deadheaded to encourage more blooms later in the season. Generally, butterfly weed is pest free, but always watch for aphids and spider mites. Leaf spot and rust disease may pose problems on plants in too much shade.

ADDITIONAL INFORMATION

Butterfly weed is a "natural" addition to wildflower meadow plantings. The flowers are frequently used for fresh cut flowers and the seedpods for dried flower arrangements. The showy flower is a favorite of several species of butterflies. Seed or tip cuttings easily propagate this native beauty.

ADDITIONAL SPECIES, CULTIVARS, OR VARIETIES

'Gay Butterflies Mix' is a selection with orange-red, pink, and yellow flowers. 'Hello Yellow' is a vibrant yellow, blooming a couple of weeks earlier than the original orange, native species. Swamp milkweed (*A. incarnata*) has two cultivar selections: 'Ice Ballet' (white) and 'Soulmate' (rose-pink flowers). Do not include the tropical butterfly weed (*A. curassavica*) in your garden as a perennial since it is not cold hardy this far north. Instead, grow it as a beautiful annual bedding or container plant.

 Did You Know?

The common field or pasture milkweed is A. syriaca *and is a great plant for monarch butterfly adults and larvae, even though the flower is not as aesthetically pleasing to most gardeners. It also produces bigger seedpods that release hundreds of cottony seeds.*

Cardinal Flower

Lobelia cardinalis

Other Names: Red Lobelia; Redbirds; Indian Pink
Height: 3 to 4 ft.
Spread: 2 to 2½ ft.
Flowers: Red, pink, or white
Bloom Period: Early to late summer
Zones: 6a, 6b, 7a, 7b

Color photograph on page 236.

Light Requirements:

Beneficial Characteristics:

If you have ever gone hiking near a woodland stream in the middle of the summer, you may have noticed a brilliant-red-flowering native known as cardinal flower. On our farm cardinal flower is a common sight in and near moist stream or creek beds. The vibrant scarlet-red flowers are quite powerful in these moist, shaded sites and are usually seen throughout the summer, starting in June, in most of the state. The plants are fairly narrow and erect with serrated, elongated, deep-green foliage. If you duplicate this native's habitat in your landscape, you can quickly see that it would be perfect as a shade bog plant or water garden plant or in a shady, moist, perennial bed.

WHEN TO PLANT

Start it from seed in the early spring, preferably in a container or directly in a weed-free bed. Set out container-grown plants anytime in the spring or early summer.

WHERE TO PLANT

Amend soils with humus-rich, organic material, and mulch the plants after planting to further simulate preferred growing conditions. Use cardinal flower as a border or background perennial for moist, woodland sites. It will also thrive as a bog or container water garden plant.

HOW TO PLANT

Seed can be germinated at temperatures around 70 degrees Fahrenheit. These beauties naturally self-sow in the wild. When you plant cardinal flower directly in a bed, you should become familiar with the seedling plant appearance so that you will not confuse it with a weed. The seedling grows in a basal rosette form, which gives rise to the stout foliage and flower stalks. Plant container-grown plants at the same depth as the rootballs. Water and mulch after planting to keep soils moist and cool.

CARE AND MAINTENANCE

The flowers are borne on new growth and can be trimmed or deadheaded after the blooms decline to initiate more flowering throughout the season. Leave the flowers intact if you want to collect seeds or allow the plant to reseed. The plants go dormant in the winter. Leave the winter-killed foliage until the following spring; then remove the foliage as new growth emerges. The plants can come back from the root crown or reseed. Divide plants in the spring or fall. Supplemental feedings are not necessary in moist, nutrient-rich, organic soils. There are no serious insect or disease problems. Reapply mulch in perennial beds as needed; do not mulch or cover seedling rosettes formed in the fall.

ADDITIONAL INFORMATION

Another species with high ornamental value is *L. splendens*. The species name describes this breathtaking beauty also sold as Mexican lobelia. It is distinctly different with reddish foliage and showier flowers but prefers the same growing condition of shade but not quite as much moisture. Unfortunately, Mexican lobelia is cold hardy only through Zone 7—and occasionally Zone 6b with winter protection. 'Bees Flame' and 'Queen Victoria' are two named cultivars. *L. siphilitica* (blue lobelia) is also a perennial native to the eastern parts of the state, which requires shade and moisture. The bright-lavender-blue flowers are larger than the flowers of cardinal flower. 'Purple Zepter' is a named selection. Blue lobelia also comes in white 'Alba'.

ADDITIONAL SPECIES, CULTIVARS, OR VARIETIES

Named selections include 'Summit Snow' and 'Alba' with white flowers, 'Heather Pink' with medium pink, 'Rosea' with pink, 'Twilight Zone' with soft pink, 'Arabella's Vision' with brilliant deep red, and 'Angel Song' with salmon-and-cream flowers. Hybrid crosses include 'Oakes Ames' (scarlet flowers with bronze stems and leaves), 'Robert Landon' (cherry-red flowers), 'Wisley' (pale-red flowers), 'Brightness' (bright, glossy-red flowers), 'Ruby Slippers' (velvety-red flowers), 'Fan Scarlet' (purple stalks, red flowers), and 'Compliment Scarlet (Red)' (rich, wine-red blooms).

Did You Know?

Some gardeners tell me that L. siphilitica *is more tolerant of the sun in Oklahoma landscapes than* L. cardinalis. *I have not experimented with the differences, but it sounds worth a try.*

Carolina Buckthorn

Rhamnus carolina

Other Names: Indian Cherry; Yellow Buckthorn; Alderleaf; Polecat Tree
Height: 15 to 30 ft.
Spread: 10 to 18 ft.
Flowers: Creamy green
Bloom Period: Summer
Zones: 6a, 6b, 7a, 7b

Color photograph on page 236.

Light Requirements:

Beneficial Characteristics:

Do not let the name scare you into thinking that this plant is loaded with thorns because it has no thorns. The real beauty of this plant is the berries that form in late summer or early fall. The fruit ripen in August to a red color that eventually turns black or metallic purple. When you get all colors in September and October, it really puts on a show. The deciduous foliage has a very glossy appearance, which complements the brilliantly colored fruit. The perfect, creamy-green flowers, which are not showy, bloom in May and June. Include Carolina buckthorn in the landscape if you like to feed winter birds.

WHEN TO PLANT

Container-grown plants can be set out in the spring, early summer, or fall. Seed can be collected and started in the fall.

WHERE TO PLANT

Use this beauty as a lawn specimen plant where it can have plenty of room to grow. Avoid planting it near sidewalks or the berries will cause problems. Keep in mind that frequent reseeding is likely. I have seen it best displayed in large island or background landscape beds combined with other bird-loving plants, birdbaths, and bird feeders. In the wild, this large shrub or small tree is often found in slightly acidic, moist, fertile sites. It tolerates slightly alkaline soils as well. It can even be trimmed into a hedge.

HOW TO PLANT

Plant container-grown selections at the same depth they were grown, in holes twice as wide as the rootballs. Water and mulch after planting.

CARE AND MAINTENANCE

The plant is considered fairly fast growing and is somewhat weak wooded but not as weak as a silver maple. The younger twigs have a reddish-brown color, which enhances the winter appearance of the dormant, leafless tree especially since the birds eat the colorful fruit. When planting, do not remove too much of last year's growth, however, since most of the fruit is produced on one- or two-year-old wood. Insect pests are minimal but can occasionally include fall webworms. There are potential canker dieback and wilt disease problems, especially in compacted, poorly drained soils.

ADDITIONAL INFORMATION

Seed collectors should harvest the seeds at mature burgundy red just before they change to black. Wait too late, and the birds will beat you to the fruit. Store the fruit for several days at room temperature so that the pulpy flesh loosens and can be cleaned and removed. The bare seeds should be cold stratified for forty-five to sixty days in a moist paper towel in a plastic bag in the refrigerator or in a container of soil placed outside in the fall. Some species need a sulfuric acid seed treatment for twenty minutes, but the cold treatment usually works for our native Carolina species. Sometimes the birds do the stratification process and scatter the seeds over the landscape and garden.

ADDITIONAL SPECIES, CULTIVARS, OR VARIETIES

There are very few named introductions on the market for this native. *R. frangula* (glossy buckthorn or alder buckthorn) has a few improved selections, however. One is 'Asplenifolia' with straplike, glossy foliage giving a ferny appearance where it grows into a large shrub. 'Columnaris' is a more narrow, upright plant often used as a hedge; it is sometimes called tallhedge glossy buckthorn. *R. frangula* became naturalized in the eastern United States after it was brought from Europe or western Asia. Do not confuse Carolina buckthorn with another native called woolly buckthorn or chittamwood (*Bumelia lanuginosa*), which is truly thorny.

Did You Know?

Some botanists think Carolina buckthorn is not truly native but was introduced to the early 1700s and is now naturalized in our state. Whatever the story, it makes a beautiful landscape plant and thrives in our Oklahoma landscapes.

Carolina Snail Seed

Cocculus carolinus

Other Names: Snail Seed Vine; Moonseed; Carolina Moonseed
Height: 6 to 20 ft.
Spread: 3 to 4 ft.
Flowers: Greenish white
Bloom Period: Late summer
Zones: 6a, 6b, 7a, 7b

Color photograph on page 236.

Light Requirements:

Beneficial Characteristic:

If you want an attractive and most unique native vine for use in the landscape, consider Carolina snail seed. The name is derived from the curled, snail-like seed. As for its ornamental purposes, the foliage is quite attractive but sparse, with a shiny, narrow, heart-shaped appearance. The flowers emerge in grapelike, elongated clusters in July or August but are not showy. Soon afterward the berries begin to form and mature into a brilliant-red display. Favorites of many birds, the berries rarely last longer than November. In addition to the colorful fruit, the vining nature of the plant is unusual. The vines and twigs are twining, easily attaching up a support system. As the vines mature, the bark exfoliates into a brownish-green, smooth trunk, which is worth having in the landscape even if it did not produce fruit.

WHEN TO PLANT

Plant container-grown snail seed in the spring or early summer or seed in the fall.

WHERE TO PLANT

Snail seed is naturally found in low, woodland areas or thickets across eastern Oklahoma in fairly rich, moist soils. It grows most often on shrubs, neighboring trees, or fencerows. It prefers filtered shade or afternoon shade.

HOW TO PLANT

Nurseries specializing in native plants or mail-order native plant companies are the best places to find snail seed. Plant container-grown selections near a strong support or trellis system because of the woody nature of the vining trunks. Seed can be used to start the plants in the fall. Allow the seed to mature and go through a cold stratification process before it will germinate in the spring. Refrigerate the cleaned seed or plant it in a container outside for this cold-inducing process. Space them 3 to 4 ft. apart when massing the plants.

CARE AND MAINTENANCE

Like most vines, the plant will grow to the size of its support system. Prune it to train and keep the vining growth under control. Tipping the growing points early on will help the vine to bush out more, or it can be allowed to grow as a singular vine. Mulch should be applied as needed to keep weeds from competing and soils moist. Supplemental fertilizer is rarely needed in organic, prepared sites. Water snail seed during drought periods. Pests are rare on this native.

ADDITIONAL INFORMATION

Unfortunately, some folks confuse this vine with the pesky *Smilax* vine. Both have heart-shaped foliage, but *Smilax* has more leathery foliage, thorny stems, and round seed. Snail seed vine has no thorns and gets woodier as it matures. The best time to see the distinctive appearance of the seed is in the fall after the seed is mature. Clean off the pulpy seed flesh or break the seed in half, and you can begin to see the curled, snail shape.

ADDITIONAL SPECIES, CULTIVARS, OR VARIETIES

There are no named cultivars to my knowledge. There are other species that make attractive landscape plants, however. Diverse leaf snail seed (*C. diversifolius*) is a native with very similar growth and appearance but with narrower, sometimes semievergreen foliage. The fruit also matures to a bluish black. Common moonseed vine (*Menispermum canadense*) is native to the state but has more star-shaped foliage and black-maturing fruit. It is more of a herbaceous than woody vine.

 Did You Know?

All of these species are in the same family of moonseed (Menispermaceae) *and have the distinctive curled, snail- or moon-shaped seed.*

Elderberry

Sambucus canadensis

Other Names: American Elder; Sweet Elder; Pie Elder
Height: 8 to 12 ft.
Spread: 6 to 8 ft.
Flowers: Yellowish white
Bloom Period: Summer
Zones: 6a, 6b, 7a, 7b

Color photograph on page 237.

Light Requirements:

Beneficial Characteristics:

This native is a common sight in the state, especially along low, moist stream beds, fencerows, or rights-of-way. Many gardeners are familiar with its medicinal and culinary uses. In the landscape it can be used as an ornamental or a small fruit. Ornamental types have various foliage colors and fruit displays. Small fruit types are selected more for their production capabilities. And we cannot forget that elderberries are a favorite food source for an assortment of wildlife, particularly birds.

WHEN TO PLANT
Plant elderberries in spring or early summer.

WHERE TO PLANT
Elderberries' versatile growth makes them excellent candidates for summer screens or background walls. In the garden they can be grown like blackberries in a row for production purposes. Their growing habit is stoloniferous, forming multistemmed plants. This native plant prefers rich, slightly acid, moist soils. It tolerates heavy, compact, or poor sites but with some variation in vigor. It also accepts slightly alkaline soils. It is faster growing in more humus-rich sites. Some species and cultivars perform in full sun and others in more filtered shade.

HOW TO PLANT
Attend to potbound roots before planting. Space plants for ornamental purposes 6 to 8 ft. apart. Mulch the plants to conserve soil moisture.

CARE AND MAINTENANCE
Elderberries are very shallow rooted and do not like root disturbance. Depending on the site and cultivar, they have a tendency to send up suckers. The fruit are borne on the previous season's growth, so be careful when pruning. Some selections fruit on current-season lateral growth on one-

year-old wood. Dormant or an early-spring pruning will reduce fruit production unless you take care to select older canes or trunks. Plants grown for ornamental purposes can be pruned as needed. Dormant pruning might mean removing older, thick, woody canes and congested or conflicting branches. Some folks like the plants for their lacy foliage and prune them back to 3 ft. each spring to keep plants more uniform and compact. Potential pests include aphids and spider mites.

ADDITIONAL INFORMATION

For fruit production purposes, plant elderberries 5 to 6 ft. apart and 10 ft. between rows. In good soil one plant has the potential to produce 15 lb. of fruit. Most plants will not set fruit the first year of planting. Because elderberries are considered poor self-pollinators, plant more than one cultivar for increased fruit production. Harvest the entire ripe fruit cluster in August or September, depending on the cultivar. 'Adams' is one of the most publicized fruit-production cultivars.

ADDITIONAL SPECIES, CULTIVARS, OR VARIETIES

Canadensis selections include 'Aurea' (golden-yellow foliage), 'Maxima' (large flowers), and 'Rubra' (red fruit). *S. nigra* is the most widely used species for ornamental purposes and not as much of a problem in sending out suckers. The most popular selections include the dark-foliage types such as 'Guincho Purple' (chocolate purple) and 'Purpurea' (purple). 'Marginata', 'Aureomarginata', and 'Madonna' are variegated cultivars. 'Plumosa Aurea' and 'Sutherland Gold' are chartreuse foliage types, which do best in afternoon or filtered shade. 'Laciniate' and 'Lace' are known for their feathery foliage. *S. pubens* (scarlet elder), *S. mexicana* (Mexican elder), *S. caerulea* (blueberry elder), and *S. racemosa* (European red elder) are also used in the landscape trade. 'Dissecta', 'Redman', Tenuifolia', 'Golden Locks', and 'Plumosa Aurea' are selections from these species.

 Did You Know?

Some folks question whether elderberry is native or naturalized. Because it is well adapted to our state and has many ornamental and culinary uses, I for one am not going to worry about this issue. It is also favored by some forty-five species of birds, deer, and even cattle. The hollow stems make great whistles and popguns for the kids.

False Indigo

Baptisia australis

Other Names: Indigo Lupine;
  Blue Indigo; Wild Indigo
Height: 3 to 4 ft.
Spread: 3 to 4 ft.
Flowers: Purple, yellow, or white
Bloom Period: Spring or summer
Zones: 6a, 6b, 7a, 7b

Color photograph on page 237.

Light Requirements:

Beneficial Characteristics:

B lue indigo is another prairie native commonly seen across the state between May and July. The showy, pealike flowers are characteristic of this coarse-foliaged plant. The flowers are formed in upright spikes above the grayish-green, almost eucalyptuslike foliage. Black, pendulous seedpods, which are often used in dried arrangements, usually follow the flowers. The winter color is unique to these plants and is a dark brown or grayish black. In the landscape *Baptisia* is a delightful perennial offering a distinctive coarse texture, which complements finer-textured plants such as ornamental grasses, coreopsis, daylilies, and *Artemesia*. *Baptisia* is often touted as a low- to no-maintenance plant.

WHEN TO PLANT

Plant seed in the fall, preferably in a container. Set out container-grown plants in late spring or early summer. Plant bare-root plants in the spring or fall.

WHERE TO PLANT

This perennial garden plant can be used as a specimen or background border plant. In its native state *Baptisia* grows in dry, poor soils, typically in full sun. In the landscape or garden be careful not to grow *Baptisia* in extremely nutrient-rich soils. In too much shade and rich soils, the plants tend to become more sprawling. Good drainage is a necessity.

HOW TO PLANT

The planting hole should be the same depth as and slightly wider than the rootball. Space the plants about 3 ft. apart when growing *Baptisia* in groups. Mulch the plants but do not get it overly thick, especially on the stems.

CARE AND MAINTENANCE

The plants may need to be staked when they are grown in too much shade and rich soils. The plants are very hardy and quite drought tolerant once they are established. Water them after planting to establish them, but then reduce the amount of water as the plants mature. The unique flowers start to emerge in early summer and last for a couple of weeks. Some gardeners choose to cut back the flowers to encourage more blooms later in the summer. Others allow the seedpods to form for use in dried arrangements. The flowers are nice in fresh cut arrangements as well. I usually wait to trim this dormant plant back in late spring to see where the new growth of the season will emerge. Occasionally during a mild winter, the plants will send out new growth along the stems. In severe winters the plants come back from the root crown. In some meadow garden settings the plants can reseed.

ADDITIONAL INFORMATION

The seed coats are very hard and often have erratic germination. Acid, physical, or cold treatment is customarily required for improved germination. The roots can be divided as another method of propagation. Stem cuttings are occasionally used. *Baptisia* is a legume plant forming nitrogen-fixing bacteria along the fibrous roots, so supplemental feedings are often not needed. Pests are of little concern.

ADDITIONAL SPECIES, CULTIVARS, OR VARIETIES

B. australis is the blue-flowering species and the variety 'Minor' is a more compact version of the species. Nuttall's baptisia (*B. nuttalliana*) and golden wild indigo (*B. sphaerocarpa*) are yellow-flowering natives to the state. Other yellow types found in the nursery trade are *B. perfoliata* and *B. tinctoria*. White-flowering species include *B. alba*, *B. leucantha (lactea)*, and *B. pendula*. There are very few named selections to date. 'Purple Smoke' is a North Carolina hybrid known for its dusty-smoke-purple flowers arising from charcoal-green foliage.

Did You Know?

The generic name comes from the Greek word bapto, *meaning "to dye." That fittingly describes one of Baptisia's uses as a dye extract.*

Gaura

Gaura lindhermeri

Other Names: Whirling Butterflies;
Wand Flower
Height: 3 to 5 ft.
Spread: 3 to 4 ft.
Flowers: White or pink
Bloom Period: All summer
Zones: 6a, 6b, 7a, 7b

Color photograph on page 237.

Light Requirements:

Beneficial Characteristics:

This native roadside, pasture, and prairie wasteland plant is not always showy in its native setting combined with other vegetation. But place it in the landscape, and you will be amazed at its whimsical growth habit. The plant has nondistinct foliage, somewhat dull in appearance. In early summer the bushy growth sends up erect flower spikes full of white, butterflylike flowers. At times there are so many that the flower stems begin to weep. Combine this with our Oklahoma winds and the plant literally comes to life with movement of dangling and fluttering flowers, thus the common name of whirling butterflies. Most of the native species have white, creamy-white, or pale-pink flowers that bloom throughout the season. Gaura is a perennial with a long season bloom perfect for any perennial garden.

WHEN TO PLANT

Plant container-grown selections in the spring or summer. Start seed indoors in a container during the winter.

WHERE TO PLANT

This tall, mounding plant is often used as a background border in the perennial garden. It is delightful in association with evergreen shrubs as well. Its unique growth habit and flowers make it a good choice for a singular specimen plant. It prefers full sun. It tolerates partial shade but no more than four or five hours of dense shade. In its native setting gaura is often found in loamy, moist sites. In the landscape these conditions should be duplicated with good drainage, which is essential. Poor planting soils are acceptable but require additional feedings and care.

HOW TO PLANT

Loosen potbound roots before planting. Dig the hole the same depth as and two times wider than the rootball. Space plants 3 to 4 ft. apart. Mulch plants to control weeds and retain soil moisture.

CARE AND MAINTENANCE

The plants bloom most of the summer and require little pruning. Occasionally, there will be a lull in flowering, and the plants can be sheared back to the leafy foliage then to encourage more growth and blooms. Do not overfertilize them or the plants will become more open and sprawling. Supplemental irrigation is recommended during extreme dry periods. Potential pests include spider mites and leaf spots. Planting sites with good air movement minimize pest problems and allow for more movement of the flowering spikes. Heavily shaded sites are more likely to be subject to leaf spots.

ADDITIONAL INFORMATION

In a patio or container display, the weeping, whirling appearance of gaura makes for quite a conversation piece. The plants can be grown separately or planted in combination with other textured plants.

ADDITIONAL SPECIES, CULTIVARS, OR VARIETIES

There have been several recently named selections in addition to the common species. 'Franz Valley' is a fragrant, white-flowering selection with more compact growth. 'Corrie's Gold' has variegated foliage with pink-and-white blooms. One of my favorites is 'Siskiyou Pink', with deep-pink flowers, burgundy tints to the foliage, and more compact growth. Another named selection, 'Whirling Butterflies', is reported to be more floriferous, with sterile white blooms, than the species.

 Did You Know?

The generic name gaura comes from the Greek word gauros, meaning "superb." This appropriately named plant is a superb choice for the perennial garden.

Goldenrod

Solidago canadensis

Other Name: Solidago
Height: 1 to 6 ft.
Spread: 2 to 4 ft.
Flowers: Yellow
Bloom Period: Late summer, fall
Zones: 6a, 6b, 7a, 7b

Color photograph on page 237.

Light Requirements:

Beneficial Characteristics:

Contrary to popular belief, this native is not the source of your fall allergy problems. Goldenrod is often blamed for this allergy outburst because of its showy flowers that coincide with sneezing, sniffling, and headaches. The culprit is ragweed, with not-so-showy flowers and light pollen easily distributed by the wind. Goldenrod pollen, on the other hand, is heavy and insect carried and seldom found in allergy pollen counts. So, relax. This native beauty has a lot to offer. The color yellow is said to soothe or invigorate people. Well, this fragrant, eye-catching bloomer will do just that when given a chance in the landscape. The blooms last for several weeks in the late summer and fall with truly vivid-yellow or orange-yellow color.

WHEN TO PLANT

Plant container-grown selections in the spring or early summer.

WHERE TO PLANT

Plant the taller selections at the back of the perennial bed or they will quickly outgrow other plants. Use dwarf selections as border plants or in masses as a mid-level choice. The fall blooms of goldenrod will extend the blooming season of any perennial flower garden. The native American species grows 4 to 6 ft. tall and is most often found in well-drained soils with average fertility in partial or full sun. Heavy or waterlogged soils mean sure death for goldenrod, and abundant fertility will promote leggy, vigorous growth.

HOW TO PLANT

Plant the container-grown herbaceous perennials in holes the same depth as and two times wider than their rootballs to allow for their shallow root growth. Space plants on 3-ft. centers when you cluster them. Mulch and water to establish plants. Avoid overwatering during this time, especially during a time of spring rains.

CARE AND MAINTENANCE

The plants bloom starting in late July, August, or September and continue to bloom until frost. They rarely need deadheading. The only pruning should occur in the spring to remove dormant foliage before the new growth emerges. Supplemental feedings are not encouraged. Once plants are established, water them from time to time only during extremely prolonged dry spells. Larger, upright-growing selections may need to be staked. As with any perennial, goldenrod gets better the second and third years after planting. Potential pests are spider mites, thrips, and leaf miners, and occasional diseases include leaf rust and powdery mildew. Properly spaced plants with good air circulation between them and with afternoon shade are less likely to succumb to these problems.

ADDITIONAL INFORMATION

Goldenrod is a great fresh cut flower as well as a nice dried flower. Many people use it for potpourri. It is finding its way into culinary and medicinal applications. The plants are interesting displayed in association with ornamental grasses, fall asters, and mums. Overgrown plants can be divided every three to four years as needed. Many plants on the market today are hybrids grown from cuttings. Look for the appropriate plant height to match your particular planting site.

ADDITIONAL SPECIES, CULTIVARS, OR VARIETIES

The most compact varieties are 'Golden Thumb' and 'Sweety', averaging about 12 in. in height. 'Golden Baby', 'Golden Fleece', 'Cloth of Gold', 'Toto', and 'Crown of Rays' are more compact selections, maturing around 18 to 24 in. Taller, golden-yellow selections that reach 3 to 5 ft. and more include 'Yellow Submarine', 'Tara', 'Goldenmosa', 'Golden Shower', 'Golden Wings', 'Fireworks', and 'Peter Pan'. 'Lemore' has large, creamy-lemon flowers on fairly tall plants. A hybrid cross between aster and goldenrod is sold as solidaster or asterago, which is fall blooming and useful as a cut flower.

Did You Know?

There are at least seven species of goldenrod found in the state of Oklahoma: S. speciosa, rigida, nitida, missouriensis, nemoralis, radula, *and* canadensis. *All are fall blooming.*

Indian Blanket

Gaillardia pulchella

Other Names: Gaillardia; Blanket Flower
Height: 1 to 2 1/2 ft.
Spread: 1 to 2 ft.
Flowers: Yellow and red, red, or yellow
Bloom Period: Summer and fall
Zones: 6a, 6b, 7a, 7b

Color photograph on page 237.

Light Requirements:

Beneficial Characteristics:

Proud "Okies" must include the state wildflower in their landscape or garden. The legend of the Indian blanket revolves around a talented Indian blanket maker who was on his deathbed. He wove a blanket with his favorite colors of brown, red, and yellow for his burial. The following spring the old man's grave was covered with this beautiful flower in the same colors of his blanket, thus the name Indian blanket flower. It is thought to be a gift from the Great Spirit as a constant reminder of the old man's work. Once you include gaillardia in your landscape, you will be amazed by the intricate colors of the beautiful flower, truly a fine piece of work from our Creator. The large, showy flowers (sometimes 2 to 3 in. in diameter) begin to bloom in the summer around May and usually continue until September.

WHEN TO PLANT

Gaillardia is becoming more widely available at garden centers. Plant container-grown selections in the landscape in spring or early summer. Plant seed very shallow in the fall or early spring. Some growers of the crop scatter it on the surface of the soil in a container where it will better germinate under light in about 2 to 3 weeks at warmer temperatures of 65 to 70 degrees F.

WHERE TO PLANT

Dwarf types may be used for border plants. Gaillardia do well as filler plants for mid-level areas of the perennial bed. They are often used as wildflower or meadow garden plants. This durable native performs in containers and windowbox displays. In their native sites gaillardia are most often found in dry, average soils in full sun. Well-drained soils are the first priority. More organic soils usually produce vigorous plant growth, but flower production is evident in either soil type. The plants tolerate a pH range of 6.5 to 7.5.

HOW TO PLANT

Plant Indian blanket on 12-to 15-in. centers when planting in masses. Moisture is crucial during the establishment period the first year, but allow the plants to dry out between waterings.

CARE AND MAINTENANCE

Gaillardia has a tendency to grow in small clusters of plants. Most of the time deadheading the spent flowers will keep the plants tidier and encourage more rebloom but may also limit plant perpetuation. In wildflower gardens and meadows the flower seedheads should be left in place and allowed to completely dry, especially at the end of the season to encourage seed distribution. In the maintained perennial bed the flowers come back from the root crown or seed, and deadheading is often encouraged. Deadheading too much, however, causes the perennial to be somewhat short-lived, lasting only three or four years in the landscape. Replant it, or allow more flowers to reseed. Dormant growth can be removed early in the spring before new growth appears. This also allows most of the seed to fall and be redistributed. Insect threats may be the common spider mite and leafhopper. Potential diseases are powdery mildew, leaf spot, and sometimes aster yellows virus. Too much shade will increase the chance of disease.

ADDITIONAL INFORMATION

Gaillardia × *grandiflora* is a hybrid cross between *G. aristata* and *G. pulchella* noted for larger flowers. The plants are available in single- or double-flower types. Look for powdery-mildew-tolerant selections as new ones are introduced each season. Some of the popular named selections include 'Baby Cole' (dwarf plant, bicolor), 'Bremen' (scarlet), 'Dazzler' (yellow flower petals, maroon center), 'Goblin' (dwarf plant, red flowers with yellow margins), 'Sun God' (yellow flowers with brown center), 'The Sun' (golden yellow), 'Tokajer' (rusty orange), 'Mandarin' (tricolor), and 'Yellow Queen' (solid yellow).

ADDITIONAL SPECIES, CULTIVARS, OR VARIETIES

The native species, *G. pulchella*, has named cultivars and selections, such as 'Butterscotch Bronze' (tricolor), 'Lollipops' (tricolor), 'Raspberry Red' (dwarf plant, scarlet flowers), and 'Red Plume' (double).

 Did You Know?

The "Indian Blanket" was approved as Oklahoma's official state wildflower in 1986.

Indian Grass

Sorghastrum nutans

Other Name: Wild Sorghum Grass
Height: 5 to 8 ft.
Spread: 2 to 4 ft.
Flowers: Golden yellow
Bloom Period: Late summer
Zones: 6a, 6b, 7a, 7b

Color photograph on page 237.

Light Requirements:

Beneficial Characteristics:

My first impression of this native, warm-season prairie grass wasn't that illuminating. But a second introduction to Indian grass a few years later in a different display bed really caught my attention. The bluish-gray-green foliage was very stately and robust. The single specimen plant had the most delightful golden-yellow flower spikes that contrasted nicely with the foliage color. I guess the plant was much more robust in its cultivated organic garden spot whereas my first sighting was in a dry, average soil, prairie display with other similar native grasses. It just goes to show that using the plant in the right place in combination with other plants can make all the difference in the world. As a result, this lovely native grass now has a place in my landscape, and I could not be more pleased. The show really starts with reddish-pink plumes shooting up in mid- to late summer. As the flower spikes are pollinated and mature, they turn yellowish, then a golden-brown color by fall. The flower and seed spikes hold up well into the winter when they are even showier in combination with the fall color of the foliage.

WHEN TO PLANT

The plant can be divided in spring or fall. Plant container-grown selections in late spring or early summer. Start seed in the spring.

WHERE TO PLANT

Use this handsome prairie grass as a background border plant in perennial displays or as a summer hedge planted in alternating rows. I have seen it used in combination with other perennials along fencerows. This popular native is commonly used in prairie restoration plantings or as part of meadow or wildflower plantings. Its lovely display of color changes makes it perfect as a single specimen plant. Indian grass is most often found in the wild in masses scattered along with stands of bluestem in moderately dry, average soils. Indian grass can tolerate moist sites as long as they are not waterlogged, and it really puts on a show in fertile, deep, moist soils. It prefers full sun.

How to Plant

Loosen potbound roots before planting. Dig a planting hole the same depth as and slightly wider than the rootball. Mulching is beneficial with ornamental grasses to keep weed competition down and soil moisture in, especially during the first couple of years of establishment.

Care and Maintenance

Remove dormant foliage from this late-blooming grass in early spring before the new growth emerges. Doing this allows the plant to show off its winter display and feed the birds with its sorghum-related seed. Cut the plant back to about 6 in. from the ground. Supplemental feedings are occasionally beneficial in poor soils, but usually one application per growing season is plenty. Occasionally, the grass will spread by reseeding in the fall. It is usually easy to pull unwanted seedlings in late spring and relocate them or give them to gardening friends. In extreme drought situations the plants will reward you with seed plumes and fall color when you provide supplemental irrigation. Garden pest problems are rare.

Additional Information

When the erect clumps become too big, they can be divided every three or four years in early spring or fall. The seed plumes are often used in fresh cutflower displays as well as in dried arrangements. Most nurseries specializing in native plants have access to this native plant.

Additional Species, Cultivars, or Varieties

There are two named selections in the nursery trade in addition to the species *nutans*. 'Sioux Blue' is an upright-growing selection from Longwood Gardens in Pennsylvania with even bluer, almost metallic-blue foliage. 'Bluebird' is touted as having a nice blue summer color as well as a showy fall display.

 Did You Know?

In addition to Indian grass (S. nutans), big bluestem (Andropogon gerardi), switchgrass (Panicum virgatum), and prairie cordgrass (Spartina pectinata) are the dominating components of a tall-grass prairie.

Indian Paintbrush

Castilleja indivisa

Other Names: Texas Paintbrush;
  Scarlet Paintbrush
Height: 8 to 24 in.
Spread: 4 to 6 in.
Flowers: Red-orange
Bloom Period: Early summer
Zones: 6a, 6b, 7a, 7b

Color photograph on page 237.

Light Requirements:

Beneficial Characteristics:

This lovely, unbranched plant appears more frequently in sandy soils of the western and southwestern parts of the state. It is becoming a more common sight along Oklahoma roadsides, thanks to the Oklahoma Highway Beautification Program. Unfortunately, this herbaceous plant is somewhat tough to grow in cultivated landscape sites. It is perfect for the meadow or wildflower garden. The erect flower spikes produce an intriguing bright-red-orange show from April until June. The species typically found in Oklahoma is *C. indivisa* with its characteristic neon color and compact height. More western species can grow to almost 3 ft. and come in assorted colors

WHEN TO PLANT
Plant seed in the spring or fall.

WHERE TO PLANT
This somewhat complex plant should be used in wildflower or meadow gardens where it can easily reseed itself. In landscape perennial beds it is more of a challenge but worth the effort, thanks to new research. It must be planted in close association with other host plants and allowed to grow in colonies. Space plants about 1 ft. from other companion plants. In the wild, Indian paintbrush is often found in sandy or sandy loam soils on elevated sites in full sun.

HOW TO PLANT
Broadcast the seed on the surface, and roll it with a sod roller to level the site and get contact with the seed. Do not cover the seed, however. Water it, and keep the soil moist but not soggy until the seedlings emerge. I highly recommend learning wildflower seedling identification so that you do not mistake seedlings for weeds. The seed is very small and takes only about 1/4 lb. per acre.

CARE AND MAINTENANCE

This wildflower native requires little care, other than remembering to allow the plants to mature and dry for reseeding themselves each year. Hummingbirds, hummingbird moths, assorted butterflies, and moths are known to pollinate the dainty flowers. Indian paintbrush responds favorably to supplemental feedings throughout the growing season. Pest problems are seldom a concern. Good site drainage is the most crucial factor. The plants take several years to establish a large and showy colony, but once they are established, they are very drought tolerant.

ADDITIONAL INFORMATION

Indian paintbrush is seldom sold as a container plant. Most often it is available by seed. Research has shown that *Castilleja* is hard to grow in containers because it is somewhat parasitic (hemiparasitic) or dependent on other companion plants in the wild for nutrition. Grown by itself in a container, the plant almost always weakens and dies. One way to overcome this problem is to routinely apply 100 to 200 parts per million (PPM) of nitrogen from a water-soluble fertilizer supplementing the plants. To figure PPM, follow this simple example: 1 oz. per 100 gal. equals 75 PPM. If you are using a 10-20-10 water-soluble fertilizer, how much should you use to obtain a 200 PPM nitrogen solution? Here is the math: 200 divided by 75 divided by .20 nitrogen equals 13.3 oz. per 100 gal. of water or approximately 4 tsp. per 5 gal. of water. Researchers also found that it was necessary to wait until the plants have at least three sets of leaves before transplanting them into the garden. In a perennial bed setting I suggest routinely fertilizing the transplants for the first several months until they have successfully attached their roots to other companion-type plants. Some good companion plants are bluebonnets, dwarf ornamental grasses such as 'Little Bunny' pennisetum, or mondo grass.

ADDITIONAL SPECIES, CULTIVARS, OR VARIETIES

There are no known hybrids or improved selections at the time of this printing other than the native species *C. indivisa*.

Did You Know?

The showy red orange is not really the flower. It is actually colored leaves known as bracts. The actual flower is a creamy white to yellow found inside the colorful bracts.

Joe-Pye Weed

Eupatorium fistulosum

Other Names: Eupatorium;
 Hardy Ageratum; Mist Flower;
 Snakeroot; Boneset
Height: 3 to 8 ft.
Spread: 2 to 3 ft.
Flowers: Purple, white, or pink
Bloom Period: Late summer
Zones: 6a, 6b, 7a, 7b

Color photograph on page 237.

Light Requirements:

Beneficial Characteristics:

If you are familiar with the annual ageratum bedding plant, then think of that type of showy flower on a taller plant and you have joe-pye weed. It dots the countryside from July through October with purple flowers atop elongated stems in pastures and on roadsides and forest edges. I have seen some species in my pastures in shady, moist locations reach almost 8 ft. tall, but other species in full sun seem to stay around 4 to 5 ft. The flower heads are large clusters, offering a nice finale of color at the end of the season when so many other flowers have already bitten the dust. Eupatorium is in the *Compositae* family like so many lovely flowering plants such as goldenrod, aster, and chrysanthemum. Do not let the weedy common name fool you. This native can be a great accent for any perennial garden.

WHEN TO PLANT

Plant eupatorium from container-grown selections in the spring, summer, or fall. Root crown divisions in the spring. Start seed in the fall or early spring.

WHERE TO PLANT

Match the size of the particular selection with your growing location. Some are good background plants, others make late-summer hedges, and some of the more compact releases will work as mid-level plants. This plant performs best in average, moist, well-drained soils. It accepts full sun or a half day of shade.

HOW TO PLANT

Give the plants plenty of space to grow. Space them on 3- to 4-ft. centers. Water and mulch them to keep the soil moist during the establishment period. Reduce frequency of watering to about four to six weeks after planting.

CARE AND MAINTENANCE

The plants can sometimes become leggy in rich soils. As the plants emerge in the spring, cut back the stems above a leaf node a couple of times to encourage more compact growth. Some selections may require staking. The dormant plant foliage can be removed anytime in the winter or early spring. The plants are late to emerge from the ground—sometimes not until April or even early May. Supplemental feedings are rarely needed unless the plants appear nutrient deficient. Pest problems seem to occur in crowded sites with too much shade and include diseases such as powdery mildew, leaf spot, and occasionally rust. Potential insect threats are aphids, leaf miners, and spider mites.

ADDITIONAL INFORMATION

The plants have a tendency to spread by clumps, so division may be needed every three years or so. Most named plants are sold by vegetatively propagated cuttings. Seed collection will not guarantee uniformity among plants. Seed usually needs to be cold stratified to encourage better germination. As with most perennials, eupatorium gets better with age.

ADDITIONAL SPECIES, CULTIVARS, OR VARIETIES

In Oklahoma *E. fistulosum*, *E. coelestinum*, and *E. purpureum* are commonly found. *E. fistulosum* is often the most common species with named selections in the landscape trade. *E. coelestinum* is found more in the state near moist sites such as margins of lakes, streams, and ponds, and it works well as a bog garden plant. *E. purpureum* is more often found in heavier shaded sites with pinkish-lavender blooms. Named cultivars include 'Alba' and 'Bartered Bride' (white), 'Atropurpurem' (purple), 'Gateway' (mauve), 'Cori' (pale blue), 'Flore Plenum' (double pink), and my favorite 'Chocolate' (beautiful white flowers and chocolaty-purple foliage and stems).

Did You Know?

E. fistulosum *is the tallest species with purple flowers, reaching up to 12 ft.; it is sold as giant joe-pye weed. The most tolerant of dry soils is* E. havanense *with white flowers. It is not as cold hardy and is best suited for Zone 7b.*

Passion Flower

Passiflora incarnata

Other Names: Maypop; Passion Vine; Apricot Vine
Height: Up to 25 ft.
Spread: 2 to 2½ ft.
Flowers: Purple, white, or pink
Bloom Period: Summer
Zones: 6b, 7a, 7b

Color photograph on page 237.

Light Requirements:

Beneficial Characteristics:

This native looks almost too exotic to grow in our state. The large, astounding flowers, sometimes 2 to 4 in. in diameter, are colorful with unusual leaf petals appearing somewhat stringy or frilly. The flowers are complete with showy male and female parts; they make it easy for you to study up on your botanical sex identification and terminology. The vines with lobed leaves emerge late in the spring and vine up neighboring support trellises or plants. In May the lovely display of color and character begins and lasts throughout July. Later in the season egg-shaped fruit emerge (reported to be edible) and loaded with seed. I have not tried them, but I know the cows enjoy them at our farm by quickly stripping the leaves and the fruit to the ground each summer. In no time flat the plants have put out a new flush of growth and start all over with their lovely blooms and fruit. That tells me passion flower is a pretty tough vine for most landscape settings.

WHEN TO PLANT

Pot-grown plants can be set out in the spring or early summer. Seed can be started in containers in the late winter or early spring or planted in the ground in the fall.

WHERE TO PLANT

Allow this vining beauty to scurry up a trellis, arbor, tree, or fence, or along the ground as a ground cover. In many cases it can grow as tall as its support system. It has tendrils that easily attach to just about any object. The plants are typically herbaceous vines, not as heavy as other woody vines. They prefer full-sun locations; however, they tolerate minimal shade. In a natural setting maypops are often found growing up fencerows, shrubs, or trees in average, moist soils in primarily eastern parts of the state. Soils either amended with organic matter or average will host this lovely plant.

How to Plant

Place the plants at the same depth that they were grown, in holes two to three times the diameter of the rootballs. Space them 3 to 4 ft. apart. Plant seed 1/4 to 1/2 in. deep. Add mulch to retain soil moisture and minimize weed growth. Water on a regular basis.

Care and Maintenance

The vines will almost always be killed back to the ground during the winter. Remove the vines and foliage in early spring. The new growth emerges in late April and quickly grows as a source of shade. Some of the flowers open in the morning and close at night while others remain open for several days. A few are lightly fragrant, but all are awesomely beautiful. Rich, fertile sites rarely need extra care. Reapply mulch as needed, and water during extremely severe droughts to keep bloom consistent. Other than an occasional aphid, pests are not a concern.

Additional Information

Maypop does well as a container plant when it is allowed to grow up a neighboring support system. The tropical-looking flower can be enjoyed on patios and decks for all to see. The flowers can be used in fresh cutflower arrangements, even though the shelf life is three or four days. They are frequently used in culinary and medicinal applications. Warning: there are reports of potential toxicity if they are not used appropriately. It is imperative when using any plant part for purposes other than ornamental to research the use and ask experts and physicians about any health hazards.

Additional Species, Cultivars, or Varieties

When you select a passion flower for a perennial vine, always check its cold-hardiness guidelines. Some are more tropical and will not overwinter in the state.

Did You Know?

There are many symbolic interpretations of this plant's association with Jesus' crucifixion—all dealing with the various parts of the flower.

PawPaw

Asimina triloba

Other Names: Custard Apple; Custard Banana; Fetid Shrub
Height: 15 to 25 ft.
Spread: 15 to 25 ft.
Flowers: Maroon
Bloom Period: Early spring
Zones: 6a, 6b, 7a, 7b

Color photograph on page 237.

Light Requirements:

Beneficial Characteristics:

This native received national exposure a few years ago when it was voted one of the six most delicious fruit by restaurant connoisseurs. The fruit emerges from a very ornamental small tree or large multistemmed shrub found growing in partially shaded, moist valleys of the eastern part of the state. In early spring it blooms with maroon blossoms about 1 in. in diameter before or as the leaves emerge. The flowers, though not showy, are fascinating. The elongated, soft-green foliage itself is an ornamental treat and turns a glistening yellow fall color. The fruit begin to form after pollination into little clusters, maturing up to 4 in. long by the end of the summer. The green fruit turns a yellowish color with brown splotches, later to a brown, almost black, when fully ripe.

WHEN TO PLANT

Plant container-grown stock in the spring, early summer, or fall.

WHERE TO PLANT

The small tree is used as an ornamental in the lawn or landscape or as a fruit tree in the garden. It prefers afternoon shade or light-filtered shade in moist sites. It is often found in its native locations along stream banks in rich, moist soils as an understory tree similar to dogwood. Site selection is crucial. Well-drained, fertile, slightly acidic soils high in organic matter will pay off in the long run.

HOW TO PLANT

Transplanting pawpaws from the wild is often difficult. Nursery-grown plants transplant better. Place the plant in a hole the same depth as and two to three times wider than the rootball. Mulch for moisture retention and water on a regular basis during the establishment period of about two years. Clean off the fleshy pulp and separate the seeds prior to planting. Plant seeds in the fall about 3/4 in. deep. Cold stratification is needed for the seeds to germinate.

CARE AND MAINTENANCE

The trees usually produce fruit five or six years after planting. Commercial growers of the fruit proclaim better fruit set with an additional different cultivar. Flies and certain beetles carry out the pollination process. There is a short window of opportunity for pollination and fertilization to occur. Because the female ripens before the male pollen, the plant is not effective as a self-pollinator. The 3- to 6-in-long fruit typically ripen in August or September in Oklahoma. The tree has somewhat pungent-scented leaves and twigs when bruised. It is quite cold hardy and tolerant of most typical disease and insect pests. Supplemental fertilizer is not needed unless plants are nonvigorous or show foliar nutrient-deficiency symptoms.

ADDITIONAL INFORMATION

The ripened fruit has received much publicity for its health benefits. It is high in vitamins A and C, potassium, iron, phosphorous, magnesium, and sulfur. It is often compared to a banana in texture and in nutrition. The pulp has custard color and texture, although it is not stringy or fibrous. I think it tastes more like a mango than a banana and not nearly as sweet. Most folks either love the unique taste or hate it.

ADDITIONAL SPECIES, CULTIVARS, OR VARIETIES

Most nursery plants are native selections discovered from seedlings in the wild. Believe it or not, there are more than fifty named selections (more for fruit production), primarily found on the Eastern Seaboard. Popular named fruiting cultivars include 'Sunflower', 'Davis', 'Sweet Alice', and 'Overleese'. A couple of improved hybrid crosses include 'IKL' and 'Kirsten'. Selections known for their large fruit, up to 1 lb. each, are 'Jack's Jumbo', 'Lynn's Favorite', and 'Convis'. Dwarf pawpaw (*A. parviflora*) is a smaller tree with smaller fruit, more indigenous to the southeastern United States; it makes a unique native garden or landscape plant in moist, shaded sites. For diehard pawpaw folks there is a PawPaw Foundation. For more information write to the founder at P.O. Box 23467, Washington, D.C. 20026.

  Did You Know?

Pawpaw is being studied as a potential cancer-fighting plant. Researchers have isolated a powerful chemical found in the twigs and branches.

Sassafrass

Sassafras albidum

Other Names: Cinnamon Wood; Smelling Stick
Height: 25 to 40 ft.
Spread: 15 to 30 ft.
Flowers: Yellow
Bloom Period: Early spring
Zones: 6a, 6b, 7a, 7b

Color photograph on page 237.

Light Requirements:

Beneficial Characteristics:

Mention the name sassafrass to people and many childhood memories arise. I have heard stories of the distinct sassafras fragrance, sassafras tea, and sassafras switches. And who hasn't had their breath taken away by the vivid fall color? So why aren't more of these beauties found in the landscape? Unfortunately, they are hard to transplant and often have a tendency to form underground suckers from the roots. Sassafrass is most often found in thickets in moist, somewhat acidic conditions, especially in eastern Oklahoma. In addition to the unique sassafras aroma, there are the very exclusive shiny, mitten-shaped leaves. Rarely do people get to enjoy the flowers, which are quite showy and are born dioecious (male and female on separate plants). The yellow flowers emerge from terminal buds in March and April. The female trees later produce a greenish fruit, which changes to a metallic dark blue in the fall. The birds quickly consume the fruit, leaving the fruit stem and pedicel, which sometimes is confused with the actual fruit. The vibrant kaleidoscope of fall colors ranges from orange to red to purple. The pros definitely outweigh the cons, and with careful placement this native can offer the same unique characteristics in your landscape.

WHEN TO PLANT
Some native nurseries are beginning to offer this picky tree, which can be transplanted from container-grown stock in the spring or fall.

WHERE TO PLANT
Folks with large acreage and lots are more likely to find a home for this colorful native. Possible sites include the edge of woodland settings, naturalized locations, rough areas that are hard to mow, and an island bed in large lawn areas. It is not a good idea to try to incorporate sassafrass into the formal landscape because of the plant's suckering nature. This plant prefers full-sun or partially shaded sites with moist, somewhat acidic, but well-drained soil. Avoid planting it in full shade.

How to Plant

The elaborate taproot and tangled root system make this an especially hard tree to transplant. Container-grown seedlings are more likely to be successful. Make the planting hole the same depth as and two to three times wider than the rootball. Mulch after planting, and water as needed. It is especially helpful to devise a planting ring with excess soil around the rootball after planting to hold water for better penetration into the root zone.

Care and Maintenance

Once the trees are established, avoid planting or root disturbance, which promotes even more root suckering. The trees have a tendency to grow in a pyramidal form and seldom need pruning other than to remove older damaged, weak, or conflicting branches. In higher pH soils, iron chlorosis, resulting in yellow foliage with green veins, can sometimes be a problem. Mulching under the drip line, watering more uniformly and deeply, applying soil sulfur, and fertilizing with ammonium sulfate according to directions can manage this problem. Few insect and disease problems affect this plant in Oklahoma.

Additional Information

Compared to oaks and other majestic, long-lived natives, sassafras is a fairly short-lived tree, particularly in improper planting sites. After twenty-five or thirty years the trees start to fall apart, losing branches and thinning. That is about the same longevity for a very popular landscape tree, the ornamental pear, and it has not stopped people from planting that species. Look for interesting developments in this beautiful tree in the future when it will eventually become more of a common landscape addition.

Additional Species, Cultivars, or Varieties

Most of the nursery-sold selections are native species seedlings. Occasionally, a variety of *S. albidum*, known as *molle*, is available in the South with slightly pubescent or hairy twigs, buds, and foliage. This selection is often sold as silky sassafras.

 Did You Know?

Sassafras fruit is consumed by at least twenty-eight species of birds, woodchucks, quails, deer, rabbits, and black bears.

Sunflower

Helianthus species

Other Names: Prairie Sunflower;
Hairy Sunflower; Common Sunflower;
Maximillian's Sunflower;
Rough Leaf Sunflower
Height: 2 to 12 ft.
Spread: 2 to 4 ft.
Flowers: Yellow
Bloom Period: Summer and fall
Zones: 6a, 6b, 7a, 7b

Color photograph on page 237.

Light Requirements:

Beneficial Characteristics:

Sunflowers are popular cut flowers, trendy decorations, and a favorite seed crop. More than six species are commonly found in the state along roadsides and in meadows, prairies, and wastelands blooming their hearts out from June through October. Most of these natives do not have the large, droopy flower of the culinary annual seed types, but their massive and continuous show of color is equally impressive.

WHEN TO PLANT

Most nurseries carry some species of perennial sunflower, usually as container-grown plants. These tough beauties can be planted in spring or early summer or even in the fall. Plants can be started from seed, usually in the spring in containers or directly into the ground.

WHERE TO PLANT

Taller varieties do best in the back of perennial beds. Many are used along fencerows or massed front and center near mailboxes and other hardscape items. Smaller versions make great mid-level perennials, and a few can be used as border plants. They are popular meadow or wildflower plants. Most sunflowers are found growing in their native sites in sandy, average soils. They are not picky about soil type as long as it drains well.

HOW TO PLANT

Plant seeds in soil-prepared sites 1/4 to 1/2 in. deep. Spacing should be based on the height and width of the plant, usually 3 to 6 ft. apart.

CARE AND MAINTENANCE

Prune the dormant growth in early spring just before or as new growth emerges. Doing this will allow the birds to scavenge the flower seeds in the winter. Like most perennials, they get better the second and third years after planting, so allow the appropriate space for the plants to mature. Some selections are self-cleaning while others benefit from deadheading the old, faded blooms. Taller varieties often need staking. Do not overfertilize them or the plants will become even more vigorous and floppy.

ADDITIONAL INFORMATION

The most commonly found sunflower in Oklahoma is rough sunflower (*H. hirsutus*) with dense, hairy branches and solid-yellow blooms. Oblong-leafed sunflower (*H. laetiflorus*) thrives in sandier sites, also with numerous solid-yellow flowers and more elongated foliage. Maximillian's sunflower (*H. Maximiliani*) inhabits dry prairie lands across the state with more lemon-yellow flowers and a smaller yellow eye on tall plants anywhere from 4 to 12 ft. *H. mollis* (hairy sunflower) has large, light-green foliage supporting a few solitary, solid-yellow blooms often arranged in double rows. The common sunflower (*H. annuus*) is also found in the state as well as prairie sunflower (*H. petiolaris*). Both are found in the southwestern counties of the state; the other species are found more often in the eastern and northeastern counties.

ADDITIONAL SPECIES, CULTIVARS, OR VARIETIES

Look for improved hybrids like 'Capenoch Star' (lemon yellow), 'Multiflorus' and 'Flore Pleno' (double yellow), 'Morning Sun' (brown eye, yellow petals), and 'Meteor' (semidouble, golden yellow). Another sunflower, Jerusalem artichoke (*H. tuberosus*), is grown more for its roots than flowers, although the flowers are also attractive. It should be grown in contained areas, or it can easily take over unless the tubers are harvested each year.

 Did You Know?

Another popular native is the false sunflower, Heliopsis helianthoides. *It is somewhat smaller in growth and has predominantly semidouble flowers.*

Sumac

Rhus glabra

Other Names: Smooth Sumac;
   Scarlet Sumac; Shoe-make
Height: 6 to 15 ft.
Spread: 3 to 4 ft.
Flowers: Greenish
Bloom Period: Summer
Zones: 6a, 6b, 7a, 7b

Color photograph on page 238.

Light Requirements:

Beneficial Characteristics:

Sumac often gets a bad rap with gardeners because of its relatives poison sumac, poison oak, and poison ivy. The most common native in the state is smooth sumac, which is colonized along roadsides throughout the state. Most people never even notice it until the fall when it is one of the first plants to change colors, bursting into brilliant scarlet tints. Smooth sumac is similar to sassafrass in that it forms colonies or thickets of neighboring plants as a result of suckering roots.

WHEN TO PLANT

Seeds are generally scarified in nursery propagation by sulfuric acid methods and later planted in containers. Occasionally, the plants are started by cuttings to ensure uniformity among named selections. Home owners will do better starting sumac by purchasing container-grown specimens and planting them in the spring, early summer, or fall.

WHERE TO PLANT

Sumac is a fast-covering plant for banks or disturbed sloping sites where the erosion control benefits are invaluable. The low-growing spreaders make great ground cover and filler plants for borders or fencerows, or for connecting tree specimens into island beds in partially shaded sites. Avoid planting them in foundation or landscape beds unless you are willing to manage the formation of additional suckers.

HOW TO PLANT

Space plants 3 to 5 ft. apart. Mulch and water them as needed.

CARE AND MAINTENANCE

The plants are dioecious (separate male and female plants). Both have showy, greenish-yellow flowers, especially when they are used in a landscape setting for better viewing. The flowers emerge in April through July, depending on the species. The male, clustering flowers are typically bigger than the female. The berries begin to take shape in August or September, turning from a grayish green to an almost deep blood red in the fall and persisting into the winter. There have been reports of occasional aphids, mites, scale, and fungal leaf spots.

ADDITIONAL INFORMATION

Poison sumac, formerly *R. vernix* and now listed as *Toxicodendron vernix*, is most often found growing as a woodier plant near swamps and bogs. It is best identified by its oppositely arranged pairs of compound, glossy, velvetlike, smooth-edged leaflets numbering seven to thirteen, with a single leaflet on the end. The drooping fruit of poison sumac matures to a greenish ivory white at the sides of the small branches. Nonpoisonous sumacs have red berries formed on branch ends as well as winged or toothed leaflets. Poison ivy, formerly *R. radicans* and now *T. radicans*, has compound leaves with three leaflets on a vine. Another relative is poison oak, formerly *R. quercifolium* and changed to *T. quercifolium*, which is a low-branching, almost shrubby plant with three leaflets in the shape of an oak leaf.

ADDITIONAL SPECIES, CULTIVARS, OR VARIETIES

An ornamental species is *R. aromatica* (fragrant sumac) with lovely spreading growth and compound foliage, generally with three leaflets. Named selections include 'Gro-Low', which has more of a ground cover-type growth, and 'Green Globe', which is more upright and spreading. Staghorn fern sumac (*R. typhina*) has unique, lacy foliage on large shrub-type growth. 'Laciniata' and 'Dissecta' are deeply cut-leafed cultivars. 'September Beauty' is a named cultivar of Chinese sumac (*R. chinensis*) with more of a loose-spreading form and winged, lustrous foliage. Flameleaf, winged, or shining sumac (*R. copallina*) has shiny, brilliant foliage and spectacular fall color. The leaves have winged leaflet midribs but not as serrated as smooth sumac (*R. glabra*), which has no wings. Chinese sumac also has occasional winged foliage but also with more serrated margins.

Did You Know?

Skunkbush sumac (R. trilobata) obviously gets a bad rap from its common name but is not that odiferous. 'Autumn Amber' is a low-growing, prostrate shrub form.

Winged Elm

Ulmus alata

Other Names: Cork Elm; Wahoo Elm
Height: 30 to 60 ft.
Spread: 25 to 30 ft.
Flowers: Reddish yellow
Bloom Period: Early spring
Zones: 6a, 6b, 7a, 7b

Color photograph on page 238.

Light Requirements:

Beneficial Characteristics:

Winged elm is considered a medium-sized tree, usually maturing around 40 ft. The light-grayish-green leaves are a typical elm shape but more leathery than those of American elm. Distinguishing characteristics are the grayish-brown twigs and stems with slender, opposite, corky wings, which are most pronounced on young, vigorous shoots. The unique stems are attractive during the dormant season, adding winter interest. The overall growth of the tree is upright and spreading at an early age, maturing into a more rounded specimen with age. Winged elm is thought to be more tolerant of the dreaded Dutch elm disease, which is prone to attack American elm (*U. americana*) and slippery elm (*U. rubra*). Winged elm is found across the state, particularly in the eastern part, and is often considered native. Some reports proclaim that this tree was an introduced species around the early 1800s; thus, it would be a naturalized tree. Whatever the case, the tree performs well and should be used more as a shade tree in the landscape.

WHEN TO PLANT
Plant winged elm in the spring, early summer, or fall.

WHERE TO PLANT
This resilient tree is a great choice for a shade tree in full-sun locations with good drainage. It is quite tolerant of average, poor soils and even a heavy clay site as long as it is not waterlogged. In their naturalized locations winged elms are most often found in a range of soils in upland areas of central and eastern Oklahoma and less often in damp, lowland locations.

HOW TO PLANT
Dig the planting holes two to three times wider than and the same depth as the rootballs. It is a good idea to build a little barrier around the planting surface with excess soil, especially on sloped areas, to hold water long enough for it to soak down to the root zone. Otherwise the water runs off the surface and does not sufficiently penetrate the roots to encourage estab-

lishment and deeper roots. Mulch plants to keep weeds at bay and retain soil moisture.

CARE AND MAINTENANCE

Prune it each dormant season to train and direct branch growth. Leave the lower branches on for the first two to three years after planting to help size up the trunk. Staking the trees is not generally needed unless they are extremely top heavy. Supplemental fertilizer should be applied the following spring or fall after planting to allow time for the roots to be well penetrated. Keep weed whackers and lawn mowers away from the tree trunk. The small foliage on elms is especially nice in the fall with minimal fall cleanup.

ADDITIONAL INFORMATION

Pest problems are usually not significant for most of the state; however, in some of the eastern counties there is a critter of concern. The hopping elm flea beetle is black and emerges in the spring just as the new growth does. It skeletonizes the foliage as it matures. In severe cases the leaves will drop prematurely, followed by another flush of growth. The pest is usually gone in a few weeks but can do quite a bit of damage on elms, even ones with thick foliage like winged elm. Controls are insecticides labeled for beetles on trees and applied as a contact spray. Winged elm occasionally gets powdery mildew in shaded sites with poor air circulation.

ADDITIONAL SPECIES, CULTIVARS, OR VARIETIES

I am not aware of any named cultivars to date sold locally. Most of the time the tree is found at nurseries specializing in native plants. Another native is cedar elm (*U. crassifolia*), which is also an underutilized tree in the landscape. It makes a great shade tree with minimal problems. Cedar elm is often confused with winged elm but does not quite have the corky, winged growth of the winged selections. Cedar elm is somewhat more tolerant of Dutch elm disease, but there are reports of infestation in stressed conditions.

 Did You Know?

Winged elm blooms and produces seeds in the spring, and cedar elm flowers and fruits in the fall.

CHAPTER ELEVEN

Western Oklahoma Plants

*L*ANDSCAPING IN OKLAHOMA'S INFAMOUS NO-MAN'S-LAND can be quite a challenge and oftentimes very isolating. Just ask any gardener living in northwest Oklahoma and the Panhandle, better known as "red carpet" country. This area of the state is rich with history and plant material, but the gardening conditions are somewhat confining. The growing season is shorter and drier, the winters are often colder, and the elevation is higher. The soils range from heavy clay to pure sand and often are very alkaline. Add consistent gusty winds and you have a whole new growing climate with distinct differences from the rest of the state. The growing climate definitely fits the Great Plains environmental grouping depicted in the USDA Forest Service map found on page 7.

Oklahoma has been described as the ecological crossroads between eastern and western species of plants, and the evidence to support this description is found in the northwest region. Landscaping success starts with plants tolerant of a particular growing climate or region. Many of the plants highlighted in other chapters will thrive in the far northwestern locales of the state and are appropriately noted. The plants covered in this chapter, however, are truly adapted for this region and often do not perform well in the rest of the state. The general planting and maintenance guidelines are covered in more detail in other chapter introductions, depending on the plant category. The challenging part will be finding some of these plants in the nursery trade. They are more likely to be available from wholesale growers in southwestern or Great Plains states and distributors to your retailer. Many can be found through mail-order nurseries. If there is no interest in a particular plant, the nurseries are not likely to carry it. The key to getting a plant in your particular area is requesting it from the nursery and telling your friends to ask for it.

Oklahoma

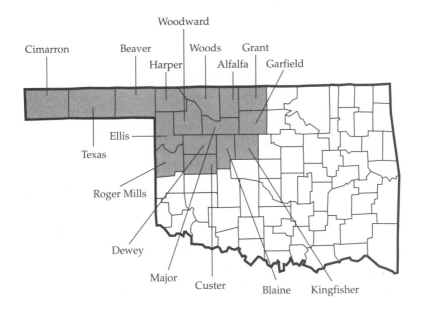

Woodward

Cimarron   Beaver   Woods   Grant

Harper   Alfalfa   Garfield

Ellis

Texas

Roger Mills

Dewey

Major   Custer   Blaine   Kingfisher

Alaska Cypress
Chamaecyparis nootkatensis

Other Names: False Cypress; Alaska Cedar; Nootka Cypress

Height: 20 to 40 ft.

Spread: 15 to 20 ft.

Flowers: Nonshowy

Zones: 6a, 6b

Color photograph on page 238.

Light Requirements:

Beneficial Characteristic:

*C*hamaecyparis is often considered a Pacific Northwest plant, thriving in cool, moist climates, which is true. But do not let that discourage you gardeners in the Panhandle and northwestern areas of the state. This evergreen tolerates warmer and more humid sites as well. The biggest concern with it is the effect of the frequent scorching winds. With careful placement next to a home or adjacent to other trees and shrubs, this medium-sized tree can be a gorgeous plant for this part of the state. The foliage is a dark bluish or grayish green with long, weeping, flat sprays of color. The relatively slow overall growth is somewhat pyramidal or conical, especially early on. I used this plant as a single specimen on the north side of my home in Stillwater, and it was the focal point of the landscape.

WHEN TO PLANT
Chamaecyparis is most often available as a balled-and-burlapped plant. Set it out in spring or early summer. Fall planting is riskier because of the dehydration of the foliage during the winter if roots have not established well.

WHERE TO PLANT
Alaska cypress has multiple uses as a windbreak (in association with other background plants), screen, foundation, or border plant. The downwardly weeping or cascading foliage is ideal as a single specimen or accent planting next to multiple-story homes. It does well in large island beds with other trees, which can give some protection from wind in open lawn settings. Partial shade on the east or northeast side of structures provides protection from the hot, scorching, summer winds. This plant demands well-drained soils.

HOW TO PLANT
Dig the hole the same depth as and two to three times wider than the rootball. In heavy soils set the rootball slightly above grade to allow for better drainage and aeration. Remove string and excess burlap down to the base

of the rootball after it is placed in the hole. If the rootball is firm enough, remove all of the burlap. Apply mulch at least 4 in. thick to hold soil moisture in and keep weeds out. Water on a regular basis during the establishment period, especially the first year after planting.

CARE AND MAINTENANCE

Pruning is seldom needed but is best done in early spring. Small, directional pruning can be done anytime throughout the year. Leave the lower branches on to keep the plant more natural looking. It encourages a bigger, stronger trunk and provides more protection from wind desiccation. Supplemental feedings may be needed in nutrient-poor soils and should be done in early spring. Potential pest problems include disease fungal blights, root rot in waterlogged sites, bagworms, and spider mites. Supplemental irrigation will be needed during dry summers since the plants prefer well-drained, moisture-rich soils.

ADDITIONAL INFORMATION

This coniferous evergreen has monoecious male and female flowers on the same plant. The female flowers later form small, green cones, which ripen to a reddish brown the second season after formation.

ADDITIONAL SPECIES, CULTIVARS, OR VARIETIES

'Pendula' is a wonderful selection with a central leader and even more of a cascading or weeping form. 'Glenmore' and 'Compacta' are more shrub forms, typically growing in a rounded habit up to 6 ft. Retail nurseries will most likely find this plant from wholesale growers in western or northwestern states.

 Did You Know?

There are literally hundreds of species, varieties, and cultivars of this genus. It is native to the Pacific Coast all the way up to Alaska, but does better in our prairie conditions than most folks would expect.

Arizona Cypress

Cypressus arizonica

Other Names: Arizona Smooth;
Pinte Cypress
Height: 30 to 40 ft.
Spread: 20 to 25 ft.
Flowers: Inconspicuous
Bloom Period: Spring
Zone: 6b

Color photograph on page 238.

Light Requirements:

Beneficial Characteristic:

If you like the shape of the resilient eastern red cedar but want a change in color, consider Arizona cypress. There are mixed reports about its cold hardiness, but it is found growing and thriving in northwestern areas of the state—and that speaks for itself. Planting it in the Panhandle may be pushing it as far as its cold hardiness goes, but it is worth trying, especially in the northwestern quadrants. The growth habit is somewhat pyramidal, like red cedar, but with a silver-gray cast to the green needle foliage. The branching is also more open and loose than its *Juniperus* comparison. Once it is established, the tree is very durable and somewhat drought tolerant. It is a common sight in the Southwest where it prefers drier conditions. Humidity is probably the biggest adversary because it promotes disease. It is not an appropriate tree for the eastern parts of the state.

WHEN TO PLANT
Plant this evergreen in early spring to allow plenty of time for it to get established before winter. It is available as a container or balled-and-burlapped specimen. It is not a very common retail nursery plant in Oklahoma unless the nurseries' wholesale sources are from western or southwestern state suppliers.

WHERE TO PLANT
Plant Arizona cypress in full sun in well-drained sites. Heavy, waterlogged soils spell sure death for it. Use it as a single specimen, or plant it in groups for a windbreak or barrier. In the Southwest it is used for erosion control. It is considered fairly fast growing.

HOW TO PLANT
Place the plant in a hole the same depth as and two to three times wider than the rootball. Plant Arizona cypress slightly above grade to achieve better drainage in heavier soils. Always mulch to protect shallow roots in such

instances. Water on a regular basis, but allow the soil to dry between applications of water. Deep, infrequent watering encourages deeper roots, which in return promotes the plant's cold tolerance.

CARE AND MAINTENANCE

The plants are fairly low maintenance. In some instances they may become chlorotic (yellowish) in extremely high-alkaline soils, but the condition is corrected with sulfur and mulch applications. Fertilizing in such cases with ammonium sulfate at a very low rate is beneficial. Never fertilize past June, or growth can be more cold susceptible. Reapply mulch as needed. Water during severe droughts. Pests are not serious threats, but watch for bagworms, spider mites, and leaf blights (especially in more humid areas).

ADDITIONAL INFORMATION

Like Alaska cypress, Arizona cypress is monoecious, with male and female flowers on the same plant. Scalelike cones later emerge from the female flowers and mature to a reddish brown. As the plants mature, the wood takes on a reddish brown to grayish hue, which complements the silvery-grayish-blue foliage.

ADDITIONAL SPECIES, CULTIVARS, OR VARIETIES

Cold-hardier selections are best if they can be found. There are several distinct varieties of Arizona cypress, including blue, compact, dwarf, and pyramidal. Named selections are 'Blue Pyramid', 'Gareei', 'Pyramidalis', 'Greenwood', and 'Glabra'. Check the differences before you buy your plant to make sure you are getting the correct growth form for your site.

Did You Know?

Cypressus arizonica *is named after its native state; it is most commonly found in Arizona.*

Cockspur Hawthorn

Crataegus crusgalli

Other Names: Cock's Spur;
Crus-galli Hawthorn
Height: 15 to 30 ft.
Spread: 15 to 25 ft.
Flowers: White to pinkish white
Bloom Period: Summer
Zones: 6a, 6b

Color photograph on page 238.

Light Requirements:

Beneficial Characteristics:

Hawthorn is known for its showy flowers and brilliant-red fruit in the fall, similar to crabapple. Unfortunately, it often has thorns that can be very dangerous in the landscape. Thanks to some exciting introductions, this lovely and resilient plant is now available with thornless selections so that it can be moved into the landscape for all to enjoy without fear of injury. The overall growth habit is very dense, broad, and somewhat rounded. The deciduous foliage color is a lustrous dark green, which later changes to a brilliant-bronze-red or purple fall color. Around May the showy, perfect flowers emerge with a hint of fragrance. In just a short few weeks the blooms give rise to pomelike fruit, ripening to a vivid red sometime in September or October. The fruit persist into late fall/early winter and are enjoyed by several species of wildlife. The thick, branching stems provide protection and nesting support for birds.

WHEN TO PLANT

The tough plant is available in container or balled-and-burlapped forms. Plant it in early spring, summer, or fall.

WHERE TO PLANT

The thorny types should not be used in the landscape where children might play, but they are perfect for windbreaks, screens, or barriers when planted in groups. I have seen them used as a hedge where they were routinely pruned. The thornless selections are nice in the landscape, especially in lawn settings where they are allowed to grow in their natural from. Cockspur hawthorn does not demand a particular soil type as long as it drains well. It thrives in poor, average, or rich, garden soils, and it tolerates high pH soils. Plants do well in full sun, with good air circulation between them.

How to Plant

Place the plants in holes at least two to three times the width and same depth of the existing rootballs. Space plants on 15- to 20-ft. centers when growing in a group. Mulch and water as needed.

Care and Maintenance

The plants are quite prone to pest problems, and stressed situations make them more susceptible. Selecting disease-resistant strains is the first step in managing these problems. Watch for potential diseases, such as bacterial fireblight, fungal leaf blight and spots, rusts, and powdery mildew. The eastern red cedar (*Juniperus virginiana*) is one of the alternate hosts of cedar apple rust. Insect problems may include aphids, webworms, tent caterpillars, scale, and mites.

Additional Information

The plants should be mulched as needed and watered during severe droughts, even though they are tolerant of dry soils. Pruning is seldom needed. The plant may be allowed to grow in its natural bushy form—leave the lower branches on for an even more brilliant bloom and fruit show. Mulching under these branches early on will keep weeds out and reduce the need to mow or use a weed trimmer under the branches. Hawthorn also tolerates heat and heavy, clay soils.

Additional Species, Cultivars, or Varieties

Hawthorn has literally hundreds of species and varieties, including small shrubs to large trees. *C. crusgalli* variety *inermis* is the thornless selection. It is often sold under the cultivar name 'Crusader'. Many more thornless named releases are in the works. Additionally, glossy hawthorn (*C. nitida*), English hawthorn (*C. laevigata*; cultivar 'Crimson Cloud', leaf blight resistant), and green hawthorn (*C. viridis* 'Winter King') are tough, cold-hardy, attractive landscape specimens for the northwestern locales of the state. A thornless green hawthorn (*C. viridis* var. *micracantha*) is found native in Arkansas. The columnar Washington hawthorn (*C. phaenopyrum* 'Fastigiata') is another upright selection considered fairly disease resistant.

 Did You Know?

Cockspur hawthorn is native in Canada to the north and southeast into Oklahoma.

Colorado Spruce

Picea pungens

Other Names: Blue Spruce; Silver Spruce
Height: 30 to 40 ft.
Spread: 10 to 20 ft.
Flowers: Nonshowy
Bloom Period: Late spring
Zones: 6a, 6b

Color photograph on page 238.

Light Requirements:

Beneficial Characteristics:

This lovely evergreen is often associated with the beautiful Rocky Mountain region. Gardeners are notorious for wanting to bring some of the trees ·back after a visit to the area. Gardeners in the Panhandle and northwestern counties of the state are in luck, but those in the rest of the state would be undertaking a risky venture to plant Colorado spruce. The evergreen thrives in upper elevations with milder summers, which are more typical of the growing regions highlighted in this chapter. The plants are known for their blue-gray foliage and pyramidal growth. They flower in late April or May and form oblong cones, which ripen with a scaly, yellow-brown appearance in August.

WHEN TO PLANT

Plant blue spruce in the spring or early summer. Fall planting of evergreens in the northwestern parts of the state poses a risk for winter burn from desiccation and poorly established roots. The plants are sold in container or balled-and-burlapped forms.

WHERE TO PLANT

The uniquely colored plant is most often used as a single specimen to enhance a landscape design or structural feature. It is hard to blend with other plants and textures. It can be used in groupings for a screen, windbreak, or wildlife cover. Probably the best use is in association with other forested plants and conifers where it can be part of a naturalized setting. It likes full-sun locations in the northwestern areas and afternoon shade in the rest of the state. The plant prefers rich, moist, well-drained soils. Colorado spruce is more tolerant of dry sites and drought than most other spruces.

HOW TO PLANT

Place the plants in holes the same depth as and two to three times wider than the rootballs. Plant this coniferous evergreen slightly above grade in heavy, poorly drained sites to help in aeration and drainage. Mulch is especially needed in this case, but mulching is very beneficial with this plant in any Oklahoma location. Water deeply to thoroughly soak the entire root system and on a frequent basis until the plants are established. Be careful not to overwater. Allow the soil to dry slightly between applications of water.

CARE AND MAINTENANCE
The worst thing a home owner can do is to trim the lower branches. This tree should be left alone so that the natural pyramidal shape can be enjoyed. Mulch past the branches and underneath to keep the weeds and grass out. Then you will not have to worry about trimming weeds and mowing under the tree. Supplemental fertilization is seldom needed unless the tree is planted in a poor site. In that case apply fertilizer in the spring. Provide supplemental irrigation during prolonged droughts, even though the plants are somewhat tolerant after they are established. Insects pests are the typical mites, aphids, and bagworms, and diseases include needle cast or rust.

ADDITIONAL INFORMATION
In the right planting site and environment the trees are somewhat slow to moderate growing but fairly long-lived. Numerous species of birds eat the seeds. The thick branches make nice homes for certain nesting birds as well. The diverse plants hold up well to snow and wind. Heat and humidity are their downfall.

ADDITIONAL SPECIES, CULTIVARS, OR VARIETIES
There are numerous varieties of Colorado spruce—anything from pyramidal, flat, and round, to gray, blue, and yellow. Some of my favorite cultivars include 'Fat Albert' (blue, wide, upright, and pyramidal), 'Argentea' (silvery white), 'Iseli Foxtail' (more heat tolerant with twisted new growth), 'Glauca Globosa' (round), and 'Glauca Pendula' (prostrate growth).

  Did You Know?
The Black Hills spruce (P. glauca variety densata), although hard to find, is another tough plant for the northwestern parts of the state.

European Mountain Ash

Sorbus aucuparia

Other Name: Berry Ash
Height: 20 to 30 ft.
Spread: 15 to 20 ft.
Flowers: Showy white
Bloom Period: Summer
Zone: 6a

Color photograph on page 238.

Light Requirements:

Beneficial Characteristics:

This fast-growing tree is suited for northern climates, including the Panhandle and northernmost parts of Zone 6b. It is a rare sight in most of Oklahoma because it has problems with heat. But for gardeners in the right zone, it is worthy of any landscape setting. The compound, deciduous foliage is a dull, dark green on top and a lighter color, almost fuzzy gray, underneath. The growth early on is erect and towering but later matures to a graceful, open specimen. The real show comes in the summer when the white-flowering clusters open, later forming small, orange-red berries in the fall. The fruit in combination with the foliage makes for a great display. The birds love them, so they do not usually last much longer than October or early November.

WHEN TO PLANT
Mountain ash is available as a balled-and-burlapped or container-grown plant. Plant it in the spring, early summer, or fall.

WHERE TO PLANT
Use mountain ash as a single-tree specimen in lawns or in adjacent woodland borders. It is not a good choice for a sidewalk or street tree because of its fruit. Moist, well-drained, fertile soils provide the best growth, especially when prepared before planting time. The European mountain ash prefers somewhat acidic soils.

HOW TO PLANT
In high pH or alkaline sites, till and amend the soil with soil sulfur and organic material before planting time. Do not backfill the planting hole; instead mix it into the soil of the planting site. Plant the trees in holes the same depth as and two to three times wider than the rootballs. Mulch and water on a regular basis.

Care and Maintenance

This underused tree is fairly strong-wooded, considering its fast-growing nature. The aging tree trunks take on a unique, smooth, grayish appearance, also very appealing during the winter. Any major pruning should be done early in the dormant season, around December or January. Keeping the soils moist during extreme drought is imperative and is best achieved with mulch in addition to supplemental watering. Potential pest threats include fireblight and canker disease or aphid and borer insects. The pests are more prevalent in poor sites with improper planting techniques.

Additional Information

Many of the named selections are grafted or budded instead of seedling plants. The seed can be started after a cold, moist stratification period of three to four months by planting directly in a container outside or by storing them in a refrigerator before planting.

Additional Species, Cultivars, or Varieties

S. aucuparia (European mountain ash) is the most readily available with numerous named selections. It is also probably more prone to pest problems and is definitely picky about its acidic soil type. Korean mountain ash is more pH adaptable and less likely to have pest problems, but the leaves are simple, not compound. Arizona mountain ash (*S. dumosa*) is shrubby in appearance and more tolerant of the heat and sandy soils. All prefer moist sites and good drainage. 'Coral Fire' (*S. hupehensis*) is a unique selection with red stems and bark, white flowers, and coral-red berries.

 Did You Know?

Most of the mountain ash species are native to Europe. They were introduced and naturalized into the United States in the 1800s.

Korean Evodia

Evodia daniellii

Other Name: Evodia
Height: 20 to 30 ft.
Spread: 20 to 25 ft.
Flowers: White
Bloom Period: Late summer
Zones: 6a, 6b, 7a, 7b

Color photograph on page 238.

Light Requirements:

Beneficial Characteristics:

If you like trees with showy flowers and fruit like those of European mountain ash but a little easier to grow, consider Korean evodia. This Asian native is much more tolerant of heavy soils and higher pH. It has showy, white flowers forming on new season's growth late in the summer, around July or August. The flowers are somewhat scented and borne in masses, making for quite a display. Soon following are capsulelike fruit turning an almost reddish-black color when they mature in the fall. The lustrous, green foliage is compound and occasionally semievergreen. The tree is fairly fast growing, especially as a seedling. As the trunk matures, it takes on an attractive smooth texture and color. The delightful plant is hard to find in the nursery industry but well worth the search. It is the chicken-and-egg dilemma of which comes first. If you do not ask for new plants, many nurseries will never carry them.

WHEN TO PLANT

Plant Korean evodia in the spring. Young seedling plants are somewhat more cold sensitive and at risk of winter injury with later-season plantings. It is most often found as a container plant.

WHERE TO PLANT

Use this small tree as a specimen plant in the lawn, or plant it in combination with other decorative small trees such as redbud and ornamental pear when designed in their own island bed. The bed display will then have a long season of bloom, fruit presentation, and fall color. Like most plants, this unique plant performs best in well-drained, moist, fertile soils. It tolerates average or poor soils but has less growth. Plant it in full-sun locations.

HOW TO PLANT

Dig the planting holes the same depth as and two to three times wider than the rootballs. Soil amendments and root stimulators are not recommended in the planting holes. Mulch the plants, and water them as needed.

CARE AND MAINTENANCE

There are conflicting reports about the strength of the wood. Some say it is fairly weak, causing the tree to be short-lived, like an ornamental pear. Others refute such claims. Prune it during the dormant season to encourage stronger branches. Supplemental feedings are not usually needed in fertile soils. Supplemental irrigation will be needed during drought periods.

ADDITIONAL INFORMATION

Because this underused tree is quite tolerant of heavy clay and alkaline soils, it is a perfect choice for western Oklahoma. Its tolerance of a wide range of conditions makes it suitable for the entire state, however.

ADDITIONAL SPECIES, CULTIVARS, OR VARIETIES

The tree is primarily sold as the species. It is also sold as *Tetradium daniellii*. Named selections are rare at this time.

 Did You Know?

The seeds of Korean evodia are about the size of buckshot and are fairly easy to germinate. Some gardeners tell me that birds occasionally help in the process.

Osage Orange

Maclura pomifera

Other Names: Horse Apple;
Hedge Apple; Bois d'Arc; Yellow Wood
Height: 20 to 40 ft.
Spread: 20 to 30 ft.
Flowers: Inconspicuous
Bloom Period: Summer
Zones: 6a, 6b, 7a, 7b

Color photograph on page 238.

Light Requirements:

Beneficial Characteristic:

Osage orange is one of the most drought-, wind-, heat-, and cold-tolerant trees in the state. It has a rich, fascinating history with numerous uses. Members of the Osage tribe used the hard, durable wood to make bows. As a result, early French explorers gave the tree the common name bois d'arc. My favorite story concerns its use for natural fences along the prairie states. It was said that a fence had to meet certain requirements of being horse high, bull strong, and pig tight, and Osage orange easily met those qualifications. The plant has never caught on in the landscape because of its thorns and messy fruit. But thanks to selective propagation, the plant is now available with male thornless cultivars perfect for the landscape. Aesthetically, the Osage orange offers a distinct yellow-colored bark, shiny, thick, green, deciduous foliage, and yellow fall color. The yellow-tinted wood of this long-lasting tree is very hard.

WHEN TO PLANT
Set out the plants in the spring, early summer, or fall.

WHERE TO PLANT
The new and improved selections work as single-specimen, medium-sized trees in lawn settings. They are effective as windbreaks because of the weeping nature of the branches. They can be planted in groups in alternating rows or in combination with other rows of trees. The resilient plant is very pollution tolerant and is being considered as an urban street tree. The soil type is inconsequential and, in many cases, the poorer, the better as long as it is not waterlogged.

HOW TO PLANT
Most often the new selections are budded varieties grown in containers. Dig the planting hole the same depth as the rootball and two to three times wider. Mulch to keep weed competition down and soil moisture in during

the establishment period. Water at planting and on a regular basis for at least a year until the plants are well established.

CARE AND MAINTENANCE

The fairly fast-growing trees remain strong wooded. They respond well to light applications of supplemental feedings. Pruning may be required in landscape settings to train and direct branch growth; it should be done during the dormant season. When these trees are used for barriers or windbreaks, pruning is rarely needed. Pest problems are not serious, although a few fungal leaf spots have been reported with certain selections. Remember to provide supplemental irrigation during drought periods for the first year or so. Once the plants are established, they are quite drought tolerant.

ADDITIONAL INFORMATION

The fruit are formed on female trees; in other words, the plants are dioecious, with male and female plants. The large, round, yellow-green fruit have a brainlike rind appearance. They are an aggregate of many small fruit with the seed buried in the thick flesh of the ball. The balls contain a sticky milky juice and usually fall on the ground when they are ripe. Once the fruit begin to rot, they can become a smelly mess.

ADDITIONAL SPECIES, CULTIVARS, OR VARIETIES

Many of the thornless types are from the variety *inermis*. Even some of the so-called thornless types may have smaller thorns on juvenile growth but later outgrow them. 'Whiteshield' seems to be the most-favored, male, thornless introduction to date by growers. 'Wichita' is another popular selection thought to be the most thornless overall, and 'Double O' is a male form with more upright growth. More cultivars are in the works.

Did You Know?

Osage orange has been used to make dyes, bows, wagons, furniture, hedges, fences, and cockroach repellent.

Pinyon Pine

Pinus cembroides

Other Names: Mexican Nut Pine;
 Mexican Pinyon
Height: 15 to 20 ft.
Spread: 10 to 15 ft.
Flowers: Nonshowy
Zones: 6a, 6b

Color photograph on page 238.

Light Requirements:

Beneficial Characteristics:

This western native is relatively bushy and rarely reaches 20 ft., although there are reports of its maturing to 60 ft. in moist, rich sites. Pinyon pine has a lovely dark-gray-green color with a rather stiff, upright appearance similar to scotch pine. It is often found growing naturally in sandy loam sites in higher elevations in the western parts of the state. The pine cones are distinctly different as well, maturing in late summer with large, edible seed. The plants make great landscape and lawn choices for most of northwestern Oklahoma, including the Panhandle.

WHEN TO PLANT

Most evergreens should be planted in early spring or summer. Fall planting is riskier since the roots are not well established and the foliage becomes more susceptible to winter dehydration.

WHERE TO PLANT

This lovely plant can be used as a single specimen or grouped in the lawn. It is frequently used in windbreak plantings as a background or mid-level plant. Foundation plantings are not as common but occur occasionally in combination with evergreen and deciduous plants. It prefers full-sun sites with well-drained, sandy loam soils.

HOW TO PLANT

Amend heavy, waterlogged soils before planting time with a sandy organic mix, and till it into the ground. Do not apply these products in the planting hole as fill, or root growth can be restricted. Dig the planting hole the same depth as and two to three times wider than the existing roots. Place the plants slightly above soil grade in heavy soils. Good drainage is key to growing any pine or conifer. Mulch to keep weeds out. Water on a regular basis, but allow plants to slightly dry between applications.

Care and Maintenance

This particular plant is more attractive when the lower branches are left alone. Sporadically, dead branches occur with age and can be removed at any time. Excess pruning or stress to the tree is discouraged. Mulch under the drip line, and it will be easier to maintain. Avoid excess fertilizer, tilling or planting around the roots, weed-trimmer or lawn mower damage to the trunk, and any other stress-related actions. Such activity can increase the risk of borer insects. Other potential pest problems are fungal needle diseases, sawflies, pine moths, and pinewood nematodes.

Additional Information

Do not be alarmed by brown needle drop in the late summer or fall, especially if it occurs from older needles toward the center of the trunk. This is a normal drop of two- or three-year-old needles, a common practice even on evergreen conifer plants. The branches can have a somewhat natural orange sheen to the wood and bark in certain species.

Additional Species, Cultivars, or Varieties

P. embroides (pinyon or Mexican nut pine) is a rather bushy, small tree with needles primarily in clusters of three per bundle (rarely two). Another small-growing pine often related and sometimes confused with Mexican nut pine is *P. edulis* (Colorado pinyon pine). This pine has thicker needles usually in bundles of two (rarely three). Otherwise both are similar in growth, care, and use, and both thrive in drier, elevated sites. Some botanists believe the two occasionally hybridize in nature, with Mexican nut pine being the stronger species.

WESTERN OKLAHOMA PLANTS

 Did You Know?

The seeds are a human delicacy and are eaten raw or roasted. They are also favorites of squirrels, chipmunks, porcupines, black bears, quails, and turkeys.

Rocky Mountain Juniper

Juniperus scopulorum

Other Name: Colorado Red Cedar
Height: 20 to 40 ft.
Spread: 5 to 15 ft.
Flowers: Inconspicuous
Bloom Period: Spring
Zones: 6a, 6b

Color photograph on page 238.

Light Requirements:

Beneficial Characteristics:

Just look around the state and you can easily see that junipers do pretty well here, especially in the west-central and northwestern counties. Most people forget that the almost pesky eastern red cedar (*J. virginiana*) is actually a juniper. There are additional species, and *J. scopulorum* (Rocky Mountain juniper) is one of the best. It does better the farther west you go. In some literature Rocky Mountain juniper is listed as *J. virginiana* variety *scopulorum*. In either case the tough trees are similar in growing requirements. They provide evergreen color, shade, wind barriers, and wildlife habitats. Both are pyramidal in growth early on but mature to a more rounded top. The trees are fairly slow growing and long-lived. The foliage color for Rocky Mountain juniper ranges from dark green to blue or yellow green, depending on the selection. Rocky Mountain juniper will grow through Zone 7 of the state, but it prefers the areas covered in this chapter because of less summer humidity. It is more naturalized in higher elevations and thrives in sandy, rocky, or heavy soils. Eastern red cedar is a consistent dark green and thrives statewide.

WHEN TO PLANT

Rocky Mountain juniper is often available as container or balled-and-burlapped specimens, which can be planted in the spring or summer. Fall planting is somewhat risky since the roots are not well established and the plants may dessicate.

WHERE TO PLANT

The trees are valued for their background color benefits as well as for barriers, screens, and hedges. They work nicely for foundation landscape plantings and can be used in masses or alone. There are numerous cultivar variations, one to fit almost any landscape need. The trees like poor to average soils. They accept rich, fertile soils, but all soils need to be well drained.

HOW TO PLANT

Place the plants in the planting holes the same depth as and two to three times wider than the rootballs. Avoid organic backfill, and use only the natural soil. Mulch to conserve moisture and keep weeds at a minimum. Water on a regular basis for the first several months to establish the roots. Allow for drying times between applications instead of keeping the soil consistently moist.

CARE AND MAINTENANCE
The strong-wooded trees need pruning only to make an occasional directional cut or to remove damaged branches. The species are more beautiful if the lower branches are left intact to form a natural growth habit. Once established, the species is quite drought tolerant, but responds to supplemental irrigation during prolonged dry periods, especially the first couple of years after planting. Potential pests are spider mites and phomopsis fungal blight. Both are alternative hosts to cedar apple rust. Most of the pest problems, especially for Rocky Mountain juniper, are more prevalent the farther east the plants are grown because of the presence of moisture and humidity.

ADDITIONAL INFORMATION
Like many junipers, the plants have separate male and female flowers. They can occasionally be on both plants, especially Rocky Mountain juniper (monoecious), but are more likely to be separate (dioecious). The female miniature cones or seed ripen the second year from pollination.

ADDITIONAL SPECIES, CULTIVARS, OR VARIETIES
Many of the popular named selections or cultivars of Rocky Mountain juniper have a blue hue to the evergreen foliage. There are pyramidal, low-spreading, and rounded forms representing more than thirty named types. 'Skyrocket' is a popular columnar selection. 'Wichita Blue', 'Blue Haven', and 'Sutherland' are standard favorites. 'Fariview' is touted as more resistant to cedar apple rust. 'Blue Creeper' and 'Silver King' are more ground cover types, and 'Lakewood Globe' and 'Table Top' are more compact, maturing at 6 to 8 ft.

Did You Know?

The variety or species scopulorum *refers to its rocky cliff habitat. The fruit is eaten by several species of birds and even bighorn sheep (you probably will not have to worry about them too much in Oklahoma).*

Western Soapberry

Sapindus drummondii

Other Names: Indian Soap Plant;
  Soap Tree
Height: 25 to 50 ft.
Spread: 25 to 30 ft.
Flowers: Creamy white
Bloom Period: Late spring
Zones: 6a, 6b

Color photograph on page 238.

Light Requirements:

Beneficial Characteristics:

Western soapberry is often touted as the tree for all seasons, offering beautiful spring flowers, attractive summer fruit, colorful fall foliage, and picturesque winter bark. That list is enough to encourage gardeners to use them more in the landscape, but do not forget about their resiliency in heat, drought, cold, alkaline soils, and wind. It is close to being the perfect tree, especially for western areas of the state. It is native to the arid Southwest and thrives in limestone or sandstone soils. Soapberry grows in a shape similar to an umbrella with a large canopy. It is generally considered a medium-sized shade tree, around 35 ft., but has been reported up to 50 ft. in moister locations. The trees offer great shade because of their alternately compound, deciduous leaves, which are considered a medium-green color. You cannot go wrong with this tree that grows at a moderate pace and is long-lived.

WHEN TO PLANT
Soapberry can be planted in the spring, early summer, or fall as a container-grown or balled-and-burlapped specimen or bare-root tree seedling.

WHERE TO PLANT
The tree is often found in the wild but is not as popular in the nursery trade as it should be. At one time it was a favorite for shelter belt plantings in the West. In the landscape it works nicely as a singular-shade tree in the lawn. Soapberries function in groups for barriers, windbreaks, or groves. They like full-sun locations. Avoid planting them near sidewalks or driveways because of the potentially messy fruit. Trees planted in lawn areas are more likely to minimize feral seedling emergence than those planted in mulched landscape beds. Soil type is not as crucial as good drainage. The trees naturally thrive in dry, poor soils and grow even bigger in moist, humus-rich sites.

How to Plant

Dig the planting hole the same depth as the rootball and two to three times wider. Mulch to keep moisture in and weeds out. Water on a regular basis for a couple of years until the plants are readily established.

Care and Maintenance

The trees are fairly carefree. An occasional pruning may be needed to direct growth or to help in branch development. It is a good idea to leave the lower branches on the first two to three growing seasons to encourage a bigger, stronger tree trunk. Supplemental feedings are beneficial—but on a limited basis. Water during prolonged drought periods, especially the first couple of seasons after planting. Reapply mulch as needed. Pests are minimal, other than occasional box elder or soapberry bugs.

Additional Information

Most often the trees are thought to be separate male- and female-flowering plants. Others claim the plants have both perfect and imperfect flowers on the same tree, a trait of polygamous plants. In either case the fruit form as clusters of translucent berries in the summer, ripening to a more golden yellow in the fall. The fruit remain on the tree for most of the winter where they eventually turn a blackish color. The black, round seed germinates by cold stratification or acid scarification methods.

Additional Species, Cultivars, or Varieties

The species is the primary tree available in the nursery. Named cultivars are unknown at this time. Soapberry is often found at garden centers specializing in western or native plants.

 Did You Know?

Native Americans and Mexicans used the crushed berries to develop lather used for soap, thus the name soapberry. The fruit are not considered edible.

GLOSSARY

Alkaline soil: soil with a pH greater than 7.0. It lacks acidity, often because it has limestone in it.

All-purpose fertilizer: powdered, liquid, or granular fertilizer with a balanced proportion of the three key nutrients—nitrogen (N), potassium (P), and phosphorus (K). It is suitable for maintenance nutrition for most plants.

Annual: a plant that lives its entire life in one season. It is genetically determined to germinate, grow, flower, set seed, and die the same year.

Balled and burlapped: describes a tree or shrub grown in the field whose soilball has been wrapped with protective burlap and twine when the plant is dug up to be sold or transplanted.

Bare root: describes plants that have been packaged without any soil around their roots. (Often young shrubs and trees purchased through the mail arrive with their exposed roots covered with moist peat or sphagnum moss, sawdust, or similar material, and wrapped in plastic.)

Barrier plant: a plant that has intimidating thorns or spines and is sited purposely to block foot traffic or other access to the home or yard.

Beneficial insects: insects or their larvae that prey on pest organisms and their eggs. They may be flying insects, such as ladybugs, parasitic wasps, praying mantids, and soldier bugs, or soil dwellers such as predatory nematodes, spiders, and ants.

Bract: a modified leaf structure on a plant stem near its flower that resembles a petal. Often it is more colorful and visible than the actual flower, such as in dogwood.

Canopy: the overhead branching area of a tree, usually referring to its extent including foliage.

Cold hardiness: the ability of a perennial plant to survive the winter cold in a particular area.

Composite: a flower that is actually composed of many tiny flowers. Typically, they are flat clusters of tiny, tight florets, sometimes surrounded by wider-petaled florets. Composite flowers are highly attractive to bees and beneficial insects.

Compost: organic matter that has undergone progressive decomposition by microbial and macrobial activity until it is reduced to a spongy, fluffy texture. Added to soil of any type, it improves the soil's ability to hold air and water and to drain well.

Corm: the swollen energy-storing structure, analogous to a bulb, under the soil at the base of the stem of plants such as crocus and gladiolus.

Crown: the base of a plant at, or just beneath, the surface of the soil where the roots meet the stems.

Glossary

Cultivar: a naturally occurring form of a plant that has been identified as special or superior and is purposely selected for propagation and production.

Deadheading: a pruning technique that removes faded flower heads from plants to improve their appearance, abort seed production, and stimulate further flowering.

Deciduous plants: unlike evergreens, these trees and shrubs lose their leaves in the fall.

Desiccation: drying out of foliage tissues, usually due to drought or wind.

Division: the practice of splitting apart perennial plants to create several smaller-rooted segments. The practice is useful for controlling the plant's size and for acquiring more plants; it is also essential to the health and continued flowering of certain plants.

Dormancy: the period, usually the winter, when perennial plants temporarily cease active growth and rest. Some plants, such as spring-blooming bulbs, go dormant in the summer.

Established: the point at which a newly planted tree, shrub, or flower begins to produce new growth, either foliage or stems. This is an indication that the roots have recovered from transplant shock and have begun to grow and spread.

Evergreen: perennial plants that do not lose their foliage annually with the onset of winter. The term refers to needled or broadleaf foliage that persists and continues to function on a plant through one or more winters, aging and dropping unobtrusively in cycles of three or four years or more.

F1 hybrid: the first-generation result of a hybrid cross.

Foliar: of or about foliage. It usually refers to the practice of spraying foliage, as in fertilizing or treating with insecticide; leaf tissues absorb liquid directly for much faster results, and the soil is not affected.

Floret: a tiny flower, usually one of many forming a cluster that comprises a single blossom such as a lilac or spider flower.

Germinate: to sprout. Germination is a fertile seed's first stage of development.

Graft (union): the point on the stem of a woody plant with sturdier roots where a stem from a highly ornamental plant is inserted so that it will join with it. Roses are commonly grafted.

Hardscape: the permanent, structural, nonplant part of a landscape, such as walls, sheds, pools, patios, arbors, and walkways.

Glossary

Herbaceous: plants having fleshy or soft stems that die back with frost; the opposite of woody.

Hybrid: a plant that is the result of intentional or natural cross-pollination between two or more plants of the same species or genus.

Low-water-demand: describes plants that tolerate dry soil for varying periods of time. Typically, they have succulent, hairy, or silvery-gray foliage and tuberous roots or taproots.

Mulch: a layer of material over bare soil to protect it from erosion and compaction by rain, and to discourage weeds. It may be inorganic (gravel, fabric) or organic (wood chips, bark, pine needles, chopped leaves).

Naturalize: (*a*) to plant seeds, bulbs, or plants in a random, informal pattern as they would appear in their natural habitat; (*b*) to adapt to and spread throughout adopted habitats (a tendency of some plants that are not native).

Nectar: the sweet fluid produced by glands on flowers that attract pollinators such as hummingbirds and honeybees for whom it is a source of energy.

Organic material, organic matter: any material or debris that is derived from plants. It is carbon-based material capable of undergoing decomposition and decay.

Peat moss: organic matter from peat sedges (United States) or sphagnum mosses (Canada) often used to improve soil texture. The acidity of sphagnum peat moss makes it ideal for boosting or maintaining soil acidity while also improving its drainage.

Perennial: a flowering plant that lives over two or more seasons. Many die back with frost, but their roots survive the winter and generate new shoots in spring.

pH: a measurement of the relative acidity (low pH) or alkalinity (high pH) of soil or water based on a scale of 1 to 14, 7 being neutral. Individual plants require soil to be within a certain range so that nutrients can dissolve in moisture and be available to them. Philadelphia-area soil is typically slightly acidic, measuring about 6.3.

Pinch: to remove tender stems and/or leaves by pressing them between thumb and forefinger. This pruning technique encourages branching, compactness, and flowering in plants, or it removes aphids clustered at growing tips.

Pollen: the yellow, powdery grains in the center of a flower. A plant's male sex cells, they are transferred to the female plant parts by means of wind or animal pollinators to fertilize them and create seeds.

Pond liner: a molded fiberglass form or a flexible butyl or poly fabric that creates an artificial pond for the purpose of water gardening.

Glossary

Rhizome: a swollen energy-storing stem structure, similar to a bulb, that lies horizontally in the soil, with roots emerging from its lower surface and growth shoots from a growing point at or near its tip, as in bearded iris.

Rootbound (or potbound): the condition of a plant that has been confined to a container too long, its roots having been forced to wrap around themselves and even swell out of the container. Successful transplanting or repotting requires untangling and trimming away of some of the matted roots.

Root flare: the transition at the base of a tree trunk where the bark tissue begins to differentiate and roots begin to form just prior to entering the soil. This area should not be covered with soil when planting a tree.

Self-seeding: the tendency of some plants to sow their seeds freely around the yard. It creates many seedlings the following season that may or may not be welcome.

Semi-evergreen: having functional and persistent foliage during part of the winter or dry season.

Shearing: the pruning technique whereby plant stems and branches are cut uniformly with long-bladed pruning shears (hedge shears) or powered hedge trimmers. It is used in creating and maintaining hedges and topiary.

Slow-acting fertilizer: fertilizer that is water insoluble and therefore releases its nutrients gradually as a function of soil temperature, moisture, and related microbial activity. Typically granular, it may be either organic or synthetic.

Sucker: a new growing shoot. Underground plant roots produce suckers to form new stems and spread by means of these suckering roots to form large plantings, or colonies. Some plants produce root suckers or branch suckers as a result of pruning or wounding.

Tuber: a type of underground storage structure in a plant stem, analogous to a bulb. It generates roots below and stems above ground (example: dahlia).

Variegated: having various colors or color patterns. The term usually refers to plant foliage that is streaked, edged, blotched, or mottled with a contrasting color, often green with yellow, cream, or white.

White grubs: fat, off-white, wormlike larvae of Japanese beetles. They reside in the soil and feed on plant (especially grass) roots until summer when they emerge as beetles to feed on plant foliage.

Wings: (*a*) the corky tissue that forms edges along the twigs of some woody plants such as winged euonymus; (*b*) the flat, dried extension of tissue on some seeds, such as maple, that catch the wind and help them disseminate.

PUBLIC GARDENS

Honor Heights Park
641 Park Drive
Muskogee, OK 74403
(405) 369-3224

John E. Kirkpatrick Horticulture Center and Gardens
900 N. Portland Avenue
Oklahoma City, OK 73107
(405) 945.3358

Lendonwood Gardens
1310 W. 13th Street
Grove, OK 74344
(918) 786-2938

Myriad Botanical Gardens and Crystal Bridge
100 Myriad Gardens
Oklahoma City, OK 73102
(405) 297-3995

Oklahoma Botanical Garden and Arboretum and Affiliate Gardens
360 Ag Hall
Stillwater, OK 74078-5027
(405) 744-6460

Omniplex Gardens and Greenhouse
2100 N.E. 52nd Street
Oklahoma City, OK 73111
(405) 602-6664

Will Rogers Horticulture Gardens and Arboretum
3500 N.W. 36th
Oklahoma City, OK 73112
(405) 297-2356

Woodward Park, Rose Gardens, and Arboretum
Tulsa Garden Center
2435 S. Peoria
Tulsa, OK 74114
(918) 746-5125

BIBLIOGRAPHY

Ajilvsgi, Geyata. *Butterfly Gardening for the South*. Dallas, TX: Taylor Publishing Co., 1991.

Bender, Steve and Felder Rushing. *Passalong Plants*. Chapel Hill, NC: The University of North Carolina Press, 1993.

Dirr, Michael. *Manual of Woody Landscape Plants*. Champaign, IL: Stipes Publishing Co., 1983.

Masters, Ron, John M. Dole, Steven H. Dobbs, and Stephanie Smith. *Landscaping and Gardening for Birds*. Stillwater, OK: OSU Extension Fact Sheet 6435. 1996.

McCoy, Doyle. *Roadside Trees and Shrubs of Oklahoma*. Norman, OK: University of Oklahoma Press, 1981.

McCoy, Doyle. *Roadside Wild Fruits of Oklahoma*. Norman, OK: University of Oklahoma Press, 1980.

McCoy, Doyle. *Wildflowers of Oklahoma*. Lindsay, OK: Doyle McCoy Publisher, 1987.

Schopmeyer, C.S., *Seeds of Woody Plants in the United States*. Washington DC: USDA Forest Service, Ag Handbook 450, 1974.

Still, Steven. *Manual of Herbaceous Ornamental Plants*. Champaign, IL: Stipes Publishing Co., 1994.

Smith, Stephanie, Ron Masters, Paul Mitchell, Ken Pinkston, Don Arnold, and John M. Dole. *Landscaping to Attract Butterflies, Moths, and Skippers* Stillwater, OK: OSU Extension Fact Sheet 6430. 1996.

Vines, Robert. *Trees, Shrubs, and Woody Vines of the Southwest*. Austin, TX: University of Texas Press, 1990.

Welch, William, C., *Perennial Garden Color*. Dallas, TX: Taylor Publishing Co., 1989

Welch, William, C., and Greg Grant. *The Southern Heirloom Garden*. Dallas TX: Taylor Publishing Co., 1995.

Whitcomb, Carl E., Ph.D. *Know It and Grow It, II*. Stillwater, OK: Lacebark Publications, 1983.

Woods, Christopher. *Encyclopedia of Perennials*. New York, NY: Facts on File, 1992.

Young, James A., and Cheryl G. Young. *Seeds of Wildland Plants*. Portland, OR: Timber Press, 1986.

CATALOGS

Bluebird Nursery Wholesale Catalog. Clarkson, NE, 1998,1999.

Bluemel, Kurt, Inc., Wholesale Nursery Catalogue. Baldwin, MD, 1998,1999.

Glasshouse Works. Mail Order Catalog. Stewart, OH, 1998.

Greenleaf Nursery Wholesale Catalog. Park Hill, OK, 1999.

Green Leaf Ent., Inc., Wholesale Starter Plants Catalog. Leola, PA, 1998-99.

Logee's Greenhouses. Mail Order Catalog. Danielson, CT, 1998.

Monrovia Wholesale Catalog. Azusa, CA, 1998.

Plant Delights Nursery, Inc. Raleigh, NC, 1998, 1999.

Siskiyou Rare Plant Nursery. Mail Order Catalog. Medford, OR, 1998.

Wayside Gardens, The Complete Garden Mail Order Catalog. Hodges, SC, 1999.

White Flower Farm, The Garden Book. Mail Order Catalog. Litchfield, CT, 1998, 1999.

INDEX

Index

Index

Index

Index

Index

Index

Index

Index

Index

ABOUT THE AUTHOR

STEVE DOBBS is an award-winning horticulturist, garden writer, and lecturer. He was host and producer of the popular television show *Oklahoma Gardening* from 1990 to 1995, which was selected as the Best TV Gardening Program in the Nation by the Garden Writers Association of America in 1992. Since his graduation from Oklahoma State University and the University of Arkansas in horticulture, he has worked in the retail and wholesale trade, and in landscape design, installation, and maintenance, as well as in education as an Extension Horticulturist in both Oklahoma and Florida. For fourteen years he worked with volunteers through the Cooperative Extension Service equipping gardeners to better solve horticulture problems and answer questions. This vast array of experience has uniquely qualified him as one of the leading horticulturists in the state.

Dobbs wrote the *Oklahoma Gardener's Guide* to fill the need for a localized ornamental guide with detailed information on some of the top plants adapted to the state.

Dobbs and his wife Jo Alice own and operate Morning Star Farms near Vian in eastern Oklahoma. They specialize in seasonal greenhouse plant sales and production of uncommon bedding plants and perennials, as well as raising Tiger-stripe cattle.

GARDENING TITLES
FROM COOL SPRINGS PRESS

The What, Where, When, How & Why
of Gardening in Your State

Alabama Gardener's Guide	ISBN 1-888608-28-5
Arizona Gardener's Guide	ISBN 1-888608-42-0
California Gardener's Guide	ISBN 1-888608-43-9
Colorado Gardener's Guide	ISBN 1-888608-48-X
Florida Gardener's Guide	ISBN 1-888608-31-5
The Garden Book for Wisconsin	ISBN 1-888608-53-6
Georgia Gardener's Guide	ISBN 1-888608-08-0
Illinois Gardener's Guide	ISBN 1-888608-41-2
Indiana Gardener's Guide	ISBN 1-888608-40-4
Kentucky Gardener's Guide	ISBN 1-888608-17-X
Louisiana Gardener's Guide	ISBN 1-888608-33-1
Michigan Gardener's Guide	ISBN 1-888608-29-3
Mississippi Gardener's Guide	ISBN 1-888608-44-7
Missouri Gardener's Guide	ISBN 1-888608-50-1
New Jersey Gardener's Guide	ISBN 1-888608-47-1
New Mexico Gardener's Guide	ISBN 1-888608-55-2
New York Gardener's Guide	ISBN 1-888608-45-5
North Carolina Gardener's Guide	ISBN 1-888608-09-9
Ohio Gardener's Guide	ISBN 1-888608-39-0
Oklahoma Gardener's Guide	ISBN 1-888608-56-0
Philadelphia Gardener's Guide	ISBN 1-888608-46-3
South Carolina Gardener's Guide	ISBN 1-888608-10-2
Tennessee Gardener's Guide	ISBN 1-888608-38-2
Texas Gardener's Guide	ISBN 1-888608-30-7
Virginia Gardener's Guide	ISBN 1-888608-11-0